Mystic Medusa's

sun signs
& soul mating

Mystic Medusa's

sun signs

&

soul mating

What your friends won't tell you, your sun sign will

THUNDER BAY
P · R · E · S · S

San Diego, California

Contents

sun signs

soul mating

sun
signs

Astro clichés

The question most commonly asked of astrologers is, does astrology work? It's always a noble thing to argue your beliefs, but these days, I simply ask, how can astrology not work?

That person playing tennis while bellowing intimate gossip across the court is bound to be a Sagittarius. The person who constantly brings the most pedestrian conversations around to sex is obviously a Scorpio. People who use guilting as a communication tool? They're Virgos. Anyone with more than 20 mirrors in their house? A Leo.

And the folks who relentlessly and almost scientifically work their way upward through an organization without ever having an identity crisis? They have to be Capricorns, just as the corporate misfits who seem to create socio-psychic disturbance simply by walking into the meeting room are so often Pisceans.

In my columns and books I have come to think of Sun-sign traits as astro clichés. I know an astro cliché is real when after years of recognizing it, and guessing it correctly, it still holds true.

For instance, when I see a beautiful set of moon eyes on a person prone to mawkishness, I'm pretty sure I'm dealing with a Cancerian. If someone at a table is sharing a painful memory, and another person butts in with "that reminds me of what happened to me today," then I would put money on that person being an Aries.

If astro clichés are not true, and Leos don't have a thing about their hair, and Librans aren't very good looking, and Geminis actually tell the truth because their conscience tells them to, then you could start to dismantle astrology piece by piece.

But followers of astrology who may have been separated by language, geography, and the centuries, have noticed the same traits attributable to certain Sun signs: Taureans are stubborn and given to absolutism, Aquarians are totally beholden to logic and seem passionless, Leos are glamorous, and Virgos are tidy...

The astro clichés aren't always a question of character: Arians have loud, carrying voices, even when they're whispering; Scorpios have the ability to hiss while they're talking just as Pisceans so often have sibilance as their signature sound. Leos don't talk, as such, they deliver lines. Librans purr, Sagittarians interject, and Virgos articulate.

Like many who are interested in astrology, I like its system and the fact that we can approach it either very seriously or for a bit of a stir. We are humans—we can deal with the stars according to our moods, our wants, and our questions.

Unlike total-truth religions and imposed political systems—which make demands of how we should be—astrology allows us to make our demands of the oldest system we know, that is, the movement of the planets through the cosmos. At the same time, we can have a giggle at the expense of friends, families, and lovers.

I hope you enjoy reading my *Sun signs* as much as I enjoyed writing it.

Mystic Medusa

Aries

march 21–april 20

Ramzilla the greatest

"If you ask me what I came to do in this world, I, an artist, will answer you: I am here to live out loud."

Emile Zola (1840-1902), French novelist and critic with a social conscience

Q: How many Arians does it take to change a light bulb?
A: None. Arians are not afraid of the dark.

Arians aren't afraid of anything...except being made to look a twit by someone not showing them enough respect. They love being the first sign of the zodiac. Insanely competitive, Arians need to be first in everything. They're first of their peers to have sex; first to adopt the latest fashions; first to do Pilates, then first to give it up because their abs are so great naturally; and first to vote for the new-breed politician yet first to denounce them. In fact, they are first in whatever, so long as it's first.

This being-first fetish of theirs translates into eloquent action. For example, the first female associate justice of the U.S. Supreme Court, Sandra Day O'Connor, is an Aries. Think also, black singers Aretha Franklin, Sarah Vaughan, Billie Holiday, Diana Ross, and Bessie Smith—all Arians. Maybe it takes Aries' oomph power to combat the twin evils of racism and sexism—Aries are against "isms" on principle.

Like Sagittarius and Leo, Aries is a Fire sign. Give them enough oxygen and they're off. They throw themselves into everything they do and they don't like wet blankets. Essentially it means, as any one of them would elaborate, that they are *so* hot.

Their self-esteem is suitably sizzling. Asked to explain the source of his confidence, an Aries confided: "We Arians are too smart not to cause offense and too beautiful to care either way." They also like things to be named after them—the U.S. Pulitzer Prize for arts and the Bunsen burner are both named after their Arian creators, Joseph Pulitzer and Robert Wilhelm Bunsen.

Aries is as optimistically dynamic as cousin Leo, but less pompous and less obsessive. Their vanity is deed-oriented. They are idealistic like cousin Sagittarius, but are more tactful and certainly more ambitious.

Aries is symbolized by the Ram, hence the name Ramzilla, because this sign is more than just a male sheep. The word "sheepish" has become a synonym for being meek and easily led but, in reality, isn't that most likely a reaction to centuries of sheepdogs, shearing, and slaughter?

Rams are idiosyncratic, headstrong, and pushy. They are prone to engaging their hard heads and charging against whatever irks, regardless of direction. All Arians have at some pivotal point in their lives vowed no more "yes sir, no sir, three bags full sir." This is a key tenet of the Aries fraternity.

As with all the signs of the zodiac, Aries has an astro motto; theirs is "I am." An Aries genius, French philosopher René Descartes, coined the expression, "I think, therefore I am." But most Ramzillas don't go so much for the thinking bit. They just are. Just being an Aries is marketable enough.

In ancient astrology Arians are ruled by action-planet Mars but they prefer the term "sponsor planet," because nothing rules over Ramzilla. In the pantheon of Roman gods, Mars is mostly in charge of combat, heated lust, and city states that rise in a night. Planet Mars is said to be stricken with blistering hot winds that could strip skin off in mere milliseconds. On a social level, this description can sometimes befit a conversation with an Aries!

"There are only two races on this planet—the intelligent and the stupid."

John Fowles (1926-), British novelist. His best-known works, *The Collector*, *The Magus*, and *The French Lieutenant's Woman*, have been made into films.

Aries on form is...

"Do not dwell in the past, do not dream of the future, concentrate the mind on the present moment."

Buddha (6th century B.C.), jolly Indian religious leader who founded Buddhism

SELF-ACTUALIZING Long before it was fashionable, like even in the Dark Ages, Arians wake up far too early and, while looking at a reflection of themselves in a lake, pond, or mirror, they screech: "Every day, in every way, I get better and better!" This lot are real doers. They believe in show, not tell.

SIMPLE The archetypal Aries is proud to be shallow. They think being profound is a defense mechanism for the slow-brained or less attractive of the human species. Basically, Arian life principles go like this: They believe only boring people get bored and that people won't want to know you if you're gloomy. Also, you should not tell tales. And, you can cheer yourself up by doing something for someone else. Pitching in for charity, they believe, will cure any case of boredom, depression, or, as Arians call it, grizzling. They are also meritocratic—the Ramzilla ethos is to admire achievement, without envy or concern of the achiever's race, gender, religion, or social background.

HONEST Arians are direct and gallant and they get upset by caddish conduct. They think all lies are black. If your Aries doesn't promise to call for a date, they say, "I won't call unless I get this drunk again..." or "Have a great life." Even a simple piece of social bull such as "I'd love you to stay for dinner but..." does not trip lightly off the Aries tongue. They feel sinister and treacherous for telling even the teensiest fib and so they don't! But, beware, Aries is adept at spotting a liar. There is but one exception to the Arian automatic truth-detecting mechanism: They will accept the most outrageous falsehood if it is flattering enough—to them!

COMPETENT Results are Ramzilla's raison d'être. Aries is as Aries does. While even the most functional Arians are up themselves to an awesome degree, they are given to belittling their genuine accomplishments. An Aries will storm out in a huff if you are not garrulous enough about their new haircut or latest victory over a hangnail. Then they'll turn around and be too embarrassed to talk about a neighborhood social-justice coup or winning a Nobel peace prize. "It was nothing," they shrug as they wander back into the house, having climbed Mt. Everest backward or whatever. As the famous German composer Johann Sebastian Bach said, "All one has to do is hit the right keys at the right time and the instrument plays itself."

POSITIVE Ramzilla rocks. Even people who literally can't bear to be in the same room as an Aries will testify to their inspirational optimism. Their glass is always half-full and they want yours to be too. Arians like their gossip to be life-enhancing. They do not partake in what the Germans call *Schadenfreude*—malicious glee in another's misfortune. It's partly because they are superstitious and don't want to "catch" the ill wind, a bit because they're bored by news that is not about themselves, but, mostly, it's due to chirpy goodwill toward humankind.

BRAVE Arians are rugged idealists. Stress doesn't stress them. They will not accept any form of inertia, be it corruption, poor service, or a non-adoring spouse. Ramzilla revels in the fact that they employ the government, that marriage is an adventure, and life is too good to be subtle. Aries is the person who, having not exercised for a year, suddenly enters a triathlon. When Arians get fed up with their jobs or a client, they sack themselves before any form of disrespect can take place.

Aries off form is...

"I have been uncompromising, peppery, intractable,
monomaniacal, tactless, volatile, and, at times, disagreeable."

Bette Davis (1908-1989), First Lady of the American screen

ARGUMENTATIVE When Arians argue, they fantasize about being
in a courtroom where the audience is gasping in awe at the power
of their oratory. You may think the issue is a simple dispute but in
the megalomaniacal mind of Aries they are performing in front of
an invisible jury made up of reasonable men and women quite
unlike you. An Aries would cheerfully take on "the earth is flat"
side of a debate and win. Entering into an argument with an Aries
is ill-advised because they enjoy the sound of their own rant—it is
music to their little ears.

EGOMANIACAL Self-realization? Arians realized themselves at
birth; it's everyone else who has to realize them. They live in flux
between a sense of grandiose brilliance and a fear of never
achieving their total potential. You say self-help, they think
"learning to accept my superiority." You say something along the
lines of bloated ego. Ramzilla says, "So what!" Let's say you are
discussing your tennis-elbow problem with an Aries. They'll snap, "I
don't get tennis elbow. I don't get that sort of thing. Never have—
even though I am a fantastic player..."

HYPER-COMPETITIVE Arians hotly deny this because, in their
mind, there is no competition. But a Ramzilla is competitive in the
same way that a fish takes up swimming. All of them are perfectly
capable of standing in front of sculptor Michelangelo's statue of
David and announcing that their physique is better. Actually, a trip
to any art gallery with an Aries can be challenging as they have
very clear confidence in their innate artistic talents. So, while

everyone else is meandering around commenting in quiet murmurs, the Aries boom suddenly resounds throughout the room: "Good grief! Are they mad? I could knock up something better than that with house paint and a roller!"

CRAZY Aries are crazy at work, crazy in the sack, and ego-crazed to boot. It's so lucky that sanity is relative. It's not the Scorpio conspiracy-theory madness, nor even the Piscean stream of consciousness "I am an artiste so don't question my sexuality" rave. People forced to spend more than 20 minutes with Ramzilla start wondering whether shooting a tranquilizer dart into the thigh would stop the rant. Aries doesn't get this. In conversation they look over and see someone clenching their jaw and think the person is battling a gigantic crush on them. They think subtlety is for suckers; over-reaction is not a concept recognized by Ramzilla. Any Aries reaction is always appropriate, you understand.

"Negotiation means getting the best of your opponent."

Marvin Gaye (1939-1984), American *Sexual Healing* soul singer

Motivating and manipulating an Aries

"Every really new idea looks crazy at first."

Abraham Maslow (1908-1970), self-actualizing U.S. psychologist

1 Aries people think the secret to their modesty is that they wear their greatness so lightly. Flattery works big time. Just bring it. No compliment is too outrageous for Aries to accept without question.

2 Make your whim sound mission-oriented. That way, when eager Aries heads off to source a special biodynamic lime juice for your gin and tonic, they feel fabulous.

3 Gifting the Aries? Always give a gift card. Or even just cash in a snazzy envelope! Ramzillas trust their own taste above that of all others and will appreciate you recognizing this.

4 If you want Aries to fall in love with you, offer a challenge. Dare them to seduce you. Or tell them that you would never commit to someone like them—the Aries ego will do the rest.

5 Lack of respect is an Aries grudge flashpoint. If you want them to see less of a certain someone, tell them that the said person exhibits disrespect toward the Aries greatness.

6 Quote them to them even if they didn't actually utter the genius. An Aries can hear a brilliant quote from, say, Albert Einstein and be convinced it was, in fact, they who said it.

7 Aries like to-do lists. If you put "improve interpersonal intimacy skills" onto a list, they get cracking on it as soon as possible.

8 Understand that Arians don't dislike anyone. They may note that someone is threatened by the Aries beauty, dignity, and genius but they rarely harbor personal enmity, so don't try to evoke it.

9 There is no point in trying to coax Aries into being a corporate game-player type. Even if their best friend were made head of the universe, Aries would refuse on principle to accept a gig from them.

"People who give me advice are often wrong."

Warren Beatty (1937-), Hollywood actor and retired playboy

Ramzilla role models

"Always entertain great hopes."

Robert Frost (1874-1963), U.S. poet and four-time winner of the Pulitzer Prize

- Reba McEntire—the queen of country music in the U.S. This award-winning singer and actress "sings songs about ordinary women and the extraordinary demands life places on them."

- David Suzuki—Canadian environmentalist and "gladiatorial geneticist" with a positive vision for a sustainable future. "He's passionate, driven, irreverent, brilliant, charismatic, and controversial, usually in the same sentence."

- Diana Vreeland—fashion editor of *Harper's Bazaar* in the 30s, 40s, and 50s and editor-in-chief of U.S. *Vogue* from 1963-71. She was renowned for her sense of style, elegance, wit, and charm. "People who eat white bread have no dreams."

Sun signs

- Hans Christian Andersen—Danish actor who became a fairytale writer. Some of his more popular stories include *The Ugly Duckling*, *The Brave Tin Soldier*, and *The Emperor's New Suit*. The little boy in the last one is the archetypal Aries. Hans Christian Andersen always took a coil of rope with him when staying in hotels, in case of fire.

- Maya Angelou—African-American poet and civil-rights activist. She wrote "Love is that condition in the human spirit so profound that it allows me to survive and, better than that, to thrive with passion, compassion, and style."

- Abraham Maslow—innovative U.S. psychologist who founded "humanistic" psychology where he focused on the positive aspects of human behavior. He also coined the term "self-actualizing" and created a comprehensive list of what constituted a self-actualizer. Show it to any Aries and watch as they gasp in recognition.

"Every obstacle yields to stern resolve."

Leonardo da Vinci (1452-1519, multiskilled Italian genius—painter, sculptor, architect, engineer, musician, mathematician, and scientist

Aries in vogue

"I don't wish to be told what to do."

Bette Davis (1908-1989), First Lady of the American screen

Unable to be influenced and fancying themselves as natural beauties, Arians are immune to the vagaries of what is or is not in vogue. They're not victims of anything, least of all fashion.

Distinguishing characteristics: a mark on their face, often a scar from some ludicrously daring childhood exploit—you'll get to hear all about it, at length; the trait of poking their head about 12 in. forward from their body, as if they are leaning into an opposing gale, and a booming voice.

Male Ramzillas like to get around looking non-suave and relying upon swaggering machismo to carry the moment. They believe in the magical potency of their body-odor pheromones. The Aries guy is excellent at the projection of raw manliness—an excellent example of the ultimate Aries style is Warren Beatty in the 70s movie *Shampoo*.

Naturally, there is no way that the Aries man wears the name of another man anywhere on his clothing—not even a Calvin Klein, Pierre Cardin, or Yves St Laurent. The idea of bossing around a tailor is a far more appealing pursuit for Ramzilla.

Aries female beauty is pert, jaunty, and often comes complete with a defiant little thrusting chin for taking on the world.

No matter what the current "in" fad, the female Ramzilla will remind you that she did the Capri pants, burgundy blusher, and corkscrew perm, etc. when she was just 12 years old. That's right, she did it first.

Arians prefer body-conscious garb of whatever brand. They don't bother looking for flattering clothes because they are flattering the gear by wearing it, you understand.

ARIES SPUNKS Alec Baldwin, Warren Beatty, Marlon Brando, Jackie Chan, Joan Crawford, Russell Crowe, Bette Davis, Céline Dion, Shannen Doherty, Sarah Michelle Gellar, Ashley Judd, Lucy Lawless, Heath Ledger, Elle Macpherson, Ewan McGregor, Steve McQueen, Eddie Murphy, Sarah Jessica Parker, Julia Stiles, Emma Thompson, Reese Witherspoon

"If you want to see the girl next door, go next door."

Joan Crawford (1904-1977), screen legend and *Mommy Dearest*

Brilliant career

"Follow your bliss."

Joseph Campbell (1904-1987), U.S. academic who popularized ancient legends

"Make something happen before lunch."

Swifty Lazar (1907-1993), legendary American literary agent

Anyone who has been with an irascible Aries standing in a bank queue knows they hate to wait. They don't even go on hold on the phone. People should also be aware that they only have one chance to return the calls or respond to an email of an Aries. Do it too late and Ramzilla will bark: Who? Why are you calling me?

So, how does our Aries function in the workplace? Ideally, as a free agent. Also, their brilliant attributes can't be unleashed in an environment that they feel is beneath them. They are rabidly anti-authoritarian unless they are the authority in question. And, anyone who does not slavishly adore them is a real idiot. Weirdly, Arians cherish a delusion of themselves as skilled players in the world of workplace politics.

The process of following one's vocational bliss can be particularly hard on younger Arians. After all, it's not as if they're going to listen to anyone's suggestions. They are also convinced that as the most interesting person in any room, they have no vocational limitations. Why shouldn't *they* be the first astronaut who drinks and smokes? Why can't *they* become a big movie star and skip the stupid acting-lesson bit? Why does the Pope have to be Catholic, and a man?

Seething with lava-like resentment, it can be irksome for young Ramzilla to realize that they may not receive recognition on the garish global scale of their fantasies.

Action Aries works best under a deadline. An Aries with an impossible challenge is a happy Aries. Not that this stops them from bitching and grumbling but, secretly, they're gloating with bliss. The high energy level of Aries makes them excellent at mission-oriented work, sales, troubleshooting, business start-ups, inspiring underlings, and being famous.

They are less suited to anything requiring face time, a dress code, or protocol. They will be unable to stop themselves from subverting the dominant paradigm. Their secret fear is that naturalist Charles Darwin's survival-of-the-fittest theory was wrong—after all, it's not like Charles was an Aries or anything—and that survival of the fittest is not the case. What if it is the most mediocre who thrives? What if a process of *unnatural* selection culls the clear genius of Ramzilla, leaving sucky Earth signs in charge of everything? Stopping such an event from ever occurring is the key force behind an Arian's ambition.

Fiscal reality

"It is good to collect things but it is better to go on walks."

Anatole France (1844-1924), French writer, critic, and Nobel Prize winner

Arians don't owe anybody anything—except money. In their earlier years, Arians often succumb to a peer-pressure-inspired spate of op-shopping or checking out church fairs for second-hand bargains. Thankfully, so far as our Aries is concerned, this phase is short-lived. Arians may respect old folk but they hate old things. An Aries is not the sort of person who meanders into a thrift shop and emerges with an amazing vintage-designer buy. They haven't the knack and, anyway, someone could have died in it.

So what if it is cheap? They hate the smell and they hate the vibe. They hate the shocking service one tends to get in such places. "I had to wait two minutes." If the CD player skips a beat, it's in the trash and Ramzilla is halfway to the mall exhilarated at the prospect of retail conquest.

New clothes, new cars, new gadgets—the Aries has to be the first person to have it. They loathe the euphemism "preloved." They point out, quite logically, that the object in question can't have been loved that much.

An Aries is a feng shui consultant's dream client. They go along with the Asian philosophy that one's house must only have new furniture. If someone gave Aries an exquisite, rare, and valuable antique, the piece would have a high chance of being thrown out with the trash quick smart. "Who knows who could have touched it?" they bellow.

Even when it comes to shiny new things, Arians don't bother to bargain-hunt. Hello? Who has the time? So what if the toilet paper is 10 cents cheaper at the other supermarket? It's only toilet paper. Arians save that sort of emotion for when they feel they have been ripped off. It has to be a matter of consumer injustice exhibiting a deep lack of respect for them to engage emotionally.

The Aries idea of comparison shopping is when they mentally compare the elegant fountain pen in the display case to their ballpoint at home before buying it.

Fiscal conservatism does not come naturally to Ramzilla. An Aries in stingy mode is, in fact, an Aries on the verge of losing it.

"The sound of laughter is the most civilized sound in the universe."
Sir Peter Ustinov (1921-2004), British actor, director, novelist, and playwright

Chez Ramzilla

"Exaggeration is the only reality."
Diana Vreeland (1906-1986), style diva and editor-in-chief, U.S. *Vogue*

Heart? Ha! Ha! Home is where the ego is. The Aries home merely reflects the glory of its number-one citizen. No trivial conversation pieces detract from the brilliance of the owner. An authentic minimalist, Aries abhors clutter, shabbiness, and anything remotely second-hand. This bunch would rather have one absolutely spectacular sofa than an array of cheaper furniture. They become inspired gazing at ads depicting a room that's bare but for an awesome stereo.

Despite their disdain for "hippie" culture, Aries goes right along with feng shui's insistence upon new furnishings. They think that antiques are a high-falutin' con game. "New, new, new" is their mantra and with no time to stuff around bargain-hunting, they zoom toward designer brands. Just don't mention the money. The Arian burn rate is legendary.

As befits the most "me" sign of the zodiac, no matter how happily Aries lives with their soul mate, their fantasy abode resembles an affluent bachelor pad: primary Lego-style colors, remote-controlled dimmers, a coffee table hewn from granite, and sprawling shaggy rugs. Scarily, they fancy themselves as natural-born architects.

"I guess I'm too self-obsessed to think of anything that isn't personal."

Quentin Tarantino (1963-), U.S. film director—*Reservoir Dogs, Pulp Fiction*

An Aries in love

"Ever tried? Ever failed? Try again. Fail again. Fail better."

Samuel Beckett (1906-1989), Irish playwright—*Waiting for Godot*

Arians don't have relationships as such. They impose an Aries-archy. Your whim is their "attack on personal dignity." As they are so inordinately proud of their oratory skills, they like to practice them with the occasional state-of-the-relationship rant: If you forget to put the trash out, you're not merely forgetting to put the trash out. It is a symptom of a deeper malaise. Something is rotten in the Aries-archy. Their biggest turn-on? Obedience.

If your partner is an Aries you should ideally be: independently wealthy yet financially naïve; amazingly intelligent yet awed at the Arian intellect; excitingly domineering but still thrillingly compliant, and superbly skilled sexually yet giving off virginal vibes.

Yes, it can take a while for our Aries to find a suitable life partner but they do become less obnoxious with time.

In their minds love doesn't conquer all, conquest conquers all. The good news is that, once captured, Arians go over the top in establishing a thrilling and fulfilling ongoing love affair. They are closet true romantics.

Everyone who has ever lived under an Aries-archy knows that Ramzilla has ways of being understood and that anyone not totally simpatico with the Ramzilla reality is either disloyal or mentally defective.

Arians are so proud of their debating skills that they'll stay up on an all-night rant, if that's what it takes to win. But this doesn't do much for their relationships. They tend to pick partners who hate logic, let alone arguments, then try to convert them into the ultimate sparring contestant.

Don't try to make your Aries lover read a self-help book or see a shrink. As every Arian knows, sitting around analyzing things is a total waste of precious time. They are perfectly adept at holding the floor with their self as topic without having to pay anyone a cent. They already feel the fear and do things anyway. Arians prefer to use their own data to pick their way through life. If they're wrong, they'll just ram their way through and worry about the repercussions later.

Aries-Aries

Forget about Yin and Yang. This duo is Yang and Yang. Together they have a high burn rate: money, dull people, careers that fail to thrill, second chances, and the carpet (from all that frenzied pacing). Both are comfortable with a high-energy style of life. Aries finds Aries utterly stimulating and diverting. They understand each other only too well, able to grasp the other's genius yet empathize with their lover's suddenly-not-so-secret insecurity. Each is capable of revving the other up to new heights of positivity, achievement, and/or stupidity. Neither is utterly comfortable with overt vulnerability from the other. With Aries folk likely to freak out at what they see as weakness, an Aries-Aries relationship can become a show of strength and hype, as Ramzilla One vies with Ramzilla Two for top place. Love lingers longer when both parties silence the super egos and act in tandem. A nonstop flow of unctuous flattery lubricates the liaison, making it less likely to wilt under the glare of each Aries' spotlight. Each takes turns playing rowdy cheer squad for the other.

Hot duos: Matthew Broderick & Sarah Jessica Parker, Steve McQueen & Ali McGraw, Ric Ocasek & Paulina Porizkova, Berry Berenson & Anthony Perkins

Aries-Taurus Taurus loves Aries' mega-high energy levels and radiant charisma. The Taurean aura of sexy stability sucks our Aries in quick smart. Taurus and Aries agree on what constitutes gracious living and fulfillment, even though Aries does not care to have stupid old common sense choking off the flow of genius. Aries says, "I have writers' block, let's fly to a great beach so I can think straight." In this relationship, Taurus acts as the "bridle of sobriety on the horse of enthusiasm." Taurus says "wait"; Aries says "right now." Sometimes Aries hits the roof waiting while Taurus takes half an hour to explain one boring concept. Taurus then gets angry with Ramzilla, and becomes bug-eyed, tight-lipped, and throbbing as a result of having to shut up. Aries thinks that Taurus should learn to communicate more succinctly, like Aries does. Taurus cannot believe the unmitigated gall of Arians. Bedwork brings these two together once Taurus accepts that Arians like things fast but frequent. The sheer mega-adequacy of Taurus helps to soothe secret Arian insecurities while the Cow Person is uplifted by frequent blasts of Ramzilla enthusiasm and exuberant lust for life.

Hot duos: David E. Kelley & Michelle Pfeiffer, Ashley Judd & Dario Franchitti, Karen Blixen (Isak Dinesen) & Denys Finch Hatton, Spencer Tracy & Katharine Hepburn

Aries-Gemini Gorgeous, funny, and able to grasp the Ramzilla genius, Gemini is a stimulating trophy partner for our Aries. Aries thinks, "Wow, finally! Someone nearly as amazing as me!" The Gemini elusiveness fires up the Arian lust for conquest and Gemini loves the sky-high vitality levels of Aries and all is well. Sort of. Each eggs the other on and they attract tons of friends though secretly preferring

one another's company. Aries doesn't mind the Gemini penchant for sibling-combative love affairs. Gemini loves exploring the wild ideas spewing out of Ramzilla on a half-hour basis. But Aries is also a super control freak, believing that possession is nine-tenths of a relationship. Gemini, to put it mildly, has a freedom fetish. One little fib from Gemini, just because they can, sends Aries into a towering spiral of "I have been betrayed" angst. Gemini wants their space and ego-run Aries says "fine, go ahead and leave me." But once these issues are resolved, it's a cute coupling, blissfully free of what each fears most: boredom.

Hot duos: Warren Beatty & Annette Bening, Mary Pickford & Douglas Fairbanks Sr., Charlie Chaplin & Paulette Goddard, Chris Henchy & Brooke Shields

Aries-Cancer Aries is a bona fide live-in-the-now character.
Crabs deeply revere tradition, background, and the past. Aries abhors nostalgia and sees Crab sentiment as mawkish. Crab cries. Or worse, power-sulks. Aries culls friends when the link no longer fulfills. Crab cherishes ye olde friends and all forms of memorabilia. Aries rants and Crab guilts. Ick? Maybe not. Secretly, Aries envies Crabby emotional intelligence and ability to bond with others. Crab loves the way Ramzilla bolshiness remedies their tendency toward defeatism. If Crab agrees to get rid of some moldy old heirloom bed, a lot of issues can be worked through in the sack. Aries has to honor Crab sensitivities. For example, Aries must accept that their lover might need counseling just to throw out an old bus ticket—and let Crab run the photo album. Crab ideally moderates the mood-swinging and learns to just love the demonstrative Aries nature, which is fully capable of annihilating any Crab doubts.

Hot duos: Ewan McGregor & Eve Mavrakis, Mary Walsh Hemingway & Ernest Hemingway, Jackie Chan & Feng-Jiao Lin

Aries-Leo

Friends line up for tickets to the clash of the giant super-egos. Aries and Leo are instantly drawn by one another's brilliance, beauty, and success potential. But neither can believe the vanity of the other. The egos take over and have their own hot mini-relationship within the love affair at large. "Now, can we talk about me?" can become the dominant motif of conversation. Fun, work, business, pleasure, and bedwork mesh into power-coupling once the egos are in amicable agreement. Aries understands that, okay, the Leo is a more pompous creature than Ramzilla and declines to point out occasions when the "emperor is naked." Or balding. Or dressing in an unbecoming too-youthful fashion. Leo lets Aries win arguments, chess, tennis. The duo decides either to be aroused by bouts of competitive flirting with others to prove which one is more popular or to ditch the game altogether. Each agrees on basic lifestyle tenets. The motto that keeps them together: "More is more."

Hot duos: Al & Tipper Gore, Debbie Reynolds & Eddie Fisher, Robin Wright Penn & Sean Penn, Brenda & Norman Schwarzkopf

Aries-Virgo

Aries worships the holistic coolness of Virgo. And Virgo adds a whole new dimension to Arian thought power. Virgo loves how Aries waves away doubts and objections, making Virgo's life feel so much more open and imbued with possibilities. Yet Aries makes things happen. Virgo explains exactly why they can't happen yet. Aries does and Virgo complains. Love thrives when Virgo learns that Aries' brilliance is not meant to be analyzed into less than zero. And then Aries has to tackle the martyrdom of St. Virgo. Aries' temper is like a summer storm and if Virgo tries to put the guilt trip on Aries, it won't work. Each person's genius is so enhanced by the other's, it can be worth indulging in role-switching. Let Virgo rave about their impossible dream while Aries balances the books and compares mobile-phone plans. This relationship requires constant adjustments and fine tuning to ensure it remains on course, tracking toward true compatibility.

Hot duos: Reese Witherspoon & Ryan Phillippe, Claire Danes & Ben Lee, Jill Goodacre & Harry Connick Jr., Billie Piper & Chris Evans

Aries-Libra Aries loves Libra and Libra loves Aries, often at first sight and sometimes forever. Each sees in the other something they want. Libra longs for Ramzilla's self-assuredness and confidence. Aries would like to be as suave, charming, and socially desirable as Libra. Each also has a unique capacity to irk the other. Aries think they are the official template of perfection, with everything else being a bizarre deviation. Aries are precious about their tastes. Librans actually have taste. Libra has an astute awareness of other people's points of view—Aries thinks "so what?" Libra plays devil's advocate; Aries gets angry at the lack of loyalty. Libra is passive-aggressive. Aries is aggressive-aggressive. In Aries-Libra Utopia, Aries learns to adore Libran fairness, letting it enhance Ramzilla's life. Libra agrees to honor the gargantuan Aries ego so long as Libra can throw out Aries' substandard T-shirts, furniture, friends, and ambitions. Then it turns into *The Bold and The Beautiful* without the soapy psychodramas.

Hot duos: Russell Crowe & Danielle Spencer, Bonnie & Clyde, Heath Ledger & Naomi Watts, Kofi & Nane Annan

Aries-Scorpio Sex brings them together and sex can keep them apart. Scorpio says "nuh" to Aries' "ram-bam" style of sexuality. Aries doesn't quite trust the Scorpio interest in lengthy sensual "explorations." Aries finds Scorpio very fascinating, like a character in a cult movie only without helpful subtitles. Scorpio's strange hobbies, conspiracy theories, and never-ending lists are an interesting contrast to Ramzilla simplicity. But Aries is incapable of bearing a grudge. Aries forgets before they've even had a chance to think about forgiveness. Scorpio compiles a dossier detailing slights and hurts. Aries can't stand that Scorpio wants to have

secrets—Scorpio could at least pretend to have told all. And then there's the Scorpio innuendo: Aries sits at the lunch, drumming fingers impatiently on the table, snarling "get to the point." Scorpio spins out the moment, like a spider playing with a fly, until Aries gets fed up and storms off. Love stays longest when each truly admires the other's genius.

Hot duos: Catherine Keener & Dermot Mulroney, Rhea Perlman & Danny DeVito, Mili Avital & David Schwimmer

Aries-Sagittarius So happy together? You bet. Except that Ramzilla could seriously do without Sagg's candor. Sagg is supposed to be your lover, not someone who deigns to notice non-issues like cellulite (not that Aries has it). But Sagg is not freaked out by revved-up Ramzilla energy levels, positivity, and genius. Sagg kind of likes it. Each inspires the other into ever-better degrees of accomplishment, fitness, creativity—whatever area each is competing in that week. Other star signs are intimidated by Aries' competitiveness—they want a relationship they can settle into like a daggy old dressing gown. Sporty Sagg is made to compete and is happy to sit up all night debating until dawn. Sagg is prone to escapism, thinking everything will be just fine if they can cash in some Frequent Flyer points and whiz off to a beautiful beach. It has to be unafraid-of-confrontation Aries who points out that Sagg taking up yoga isn't going to make the bills disappear. Each thinks the other is like a good-luck talisman.

Hot duos: Elton John & David Furnish, Lady Clementine & Sir Winston Churchill, Peter O'Brien & Miranda Otto, Talisa Soto & Benjamin Pratt

Aries-Capricorn Aries says "show me the love" and Capricorn snaps "show me the money." Aries gets soppier as true romance goes on. Capricorn can be cold and undemonstrative. Aries is a risk-taker, the official wild card within any organization or—even better—a free

agent. Capricorn, a more corporate beast, thinks that's literal insanity. Capricorn is a trophy partner gifted with the eerie ability to look younger as they get older. Vain Ramzilla is not exactly thrilled with the idea of looking decrepit by contrast. Sex zings—neither wants to mess around with any tantric rot or long preludes though Aries may be too simple for the goatish lusts of Cap. Aries hero-worships ambition and competence which are key traits of our Capricorn. Ramzilla rants, Capricorn is more circumspect. If Aries is a wayward genius in need of firm management from Cap, this relationship rocks. Aries gets aroused seeing Capricorn in suit mode marching out to seal deals. Cap gets off on being the CEO of the relationship.

Hot duos: Céline Dion & René Angelil, Kate Hudson & Chris Robinson

Aries-Aquarius Aries has an ultra-low boredom threshold—few have ever been bored, as such, by Aquarius. Infuriated, yes. Aquarius loves Aries' energy, verve, and originality. Aries gets off on Aquarian detachment—a constant challenge for Ramzilla's conquest-oriented romantic nature—and the Aquarian intellect. Each loathes nostalgia; Aries lives in the now and Aquarius outdoes by living in the future. Each is exhilarated by the other. Aquarius absolutely relishes the Aries love of debate—each likes it when the other disagrees. Aries may tire of the Aquarius lack of sentiment, requiring grandiose shows of affection in order to fuel the insatiable Aries ego. Aquarius gets sick of having to say, "Yes, your biceps really do look particularly awesome today, you are such an incredible being." Aries suspects that Aquarius sneakily considers themself the genius of the couple. This rankles Aries. Both are idealists, longing to create a brighter, shinier world. If Utopia can start at home and Aquarius can learn to gush more, these two are a neo-duo.

Sun signs

Aries-Pisces Aries is Yang and Pisces is Yin. Aries thinks Pisces is happy to get whooshed up in the jet stream of Aries genius. But Pisces only plays at being weak. Pisces' vulnerabilities are overt, evoking Aries' protective urges. Pisces refines the often too-broad sensibilities of Ramzilla. The Fish heals the hurt, satisfies Aries' bedwork urges, and will never ever trash Aries' dreams. It can be a knight-in-shining-armor-with-pretty-princess kind of relationship so long as it is understood that Aries is in charge. At least, that's how it must appear. Nobody must suspect that Pisces is, in many ways, directing Aries. But Pisces vies with Gemini for being the most sneaky and cunning sign of the zodiac, two traits Ramzilla deplores. Pisces tells a lie for the sake of it, just to embellish something into a far more interesting tale—Aries gets angry and launches into a two-hour rant. Pisces shifts into "there, but not there" mode—they think Aries raving about respect is so dull. Ideally, Aries should learn to harness harsh carping. Once Pisces learns that Aries thinks truth is literally beauty, these two can end up bonding beautifully.

Hot duos: Henry Luce & Claire Booth Luce, Sarah Michelle Gellar & Freddie Prinze Jr., Queen Isabella & King Ferdinand

Are you really an Aries?

1 Your company requires you to attend a wilderness retreat involving a five-day horse trek across mountains. You have barely ever ridden a horse. You...

(a) Decline. Your corporate performance is beyond reproach. You don't need to take part in an endeavor so irrelevant to the job at hand.

(b) Agree, but book ahead to ensure that you are given a "safe mount" and schedule a series of horse-riding lessons as soon as possible.

(c) Agree, and opt for a stallion called Sauron (for experienced equestrians only) because you are not a wimp.

2 Your partner appears to be openly admiring a model in a magazine in front of you. You...

(a) Feel naturally insecure and ratty. This brings up issues relating to your own body image and sexuality.

(b) Point out to your partner that this photograph is not only a result of air-brushing and genetic freakery but evidence of a culture that is in decline, valuing aesthetic attributes over achievement.

(c) Strip down to your undies and then bellow, "Hey, baby, here is the real thing!"

3 At an art gallery you are invited to view an exhibition involving electric toasters, neon lights, and naked apes. Asked to comment about it, you...

(a) Feel out of your depth, admit as such, but reaffirm your feeling that true art has many avenues of expression.

(b) Rant on for a while about performative architecture and the-everyday-objects-school-of-installation art, without knowing anything about it but sounding fantastic.

(c) Honk, "What a load of crap. I could do this—what's the money like?"

4 At a social event, you hear that a former lover is telling blatantly vile fibs about you and the relationship. You...

(a) Instantly retaliate with a series of even more explosive revelations, true, false—whatever—to maximum effect.

(b) Explain that you've evolved to be in a really good space where you don't play the blame game but that you're sorry to hear that your ex harbors such bitterness.

(c) Say, "Who's that?" You have actually forgotten all about what's-his-name.

5 You are about to pitch a huge deal to important clients. At the last minute, the printer breaks down, your key point is suddenly unviable and your associate is busted for sleaze. You...

(a) Cancel the meeting for an inner-sanctum huddle because nothing can be done until the core rot is resolved.

(b) Fix your hair, pour yourself a very large screwdriver, and suggest to the clients that they get to know you and the company ethos better over lunch.

(c) Say, "Just bring it on." This is a very big gig and you're not paid to panic or opt out. You are about to (somehow) turn it into a personal coup.

6 Your favorite celebrities are the ones who...

(a) Use their profile and wealth to help create a better world.

(b) Inspire you by having struggled to overcome adversity.

(c) Remind you of you.

Answers: If you checked mainly (c) answers, then you are an official Aries—a raving Ramzilla and, yes, a towering genius in your field. If you checked (a) or (b) answers, you have other astro influences competing with your Arian Sun.

Taurus

april 21-may 21

The tao of Taurus

"I'm more tough than sweet."

Penélope Cruz (1974-), Spanish actress who's cruising with Tom

Q: How many Taureans does it take to change a light bulb?
A: None. Taureans don't like to change anything.

Taurus is a "Fixed" Earth sign: stubborn, sensual, and conservative. They like to think of themselves as the rock *and* the hard place. Their comfort zone is so defined as to make the Taurus practically agoraphobic within it.

The astrological symbol for Taurus is the Bull. Or, if you prefer, the Cow. Anyone who has ever seen a cow or bull go berserk will know that bovine is not merely a synonym for placid. Slow to anger, they are implacable once their ire has been aroused.

Taureans are one of the most beautiful Sun signs of all. Along with cousin Libra, they swell the ranks of the world's most celebrated beauties. Both signs are ruled by Venus, aka Aphrodite, the goddess of love, beauty, and easy money. Cow People are endowed with an authentic aesthetic appreciation of things, good looks, and sybarite sensibilities. In short, they're real spunks, who know how to have a good time. They work hard at both business and pleasure.

The typical Taurean has a flair for music, design, and the decorative arts. Unlike some of the other signs, who seek endless expert advice as to what colors the walls should be painted, or keep moldy stacks of "stuff to be framed," Cow People create a harmonious and pleasing interior seemingly without effort.

Each sign has an astrological motto, basically a summary or mission statement of that sign's ethos. For our Cow, it is "I have" (as in having it all). Material reality is very important to Taurus. They obsess over financial security, drool over objects of desire, and let much of their conversation dwell on what they have, what they intend to have, and their values. It can be hard for some of the signs to get that a Taurus going on about hedge funds, their clock collection, or taxation bracket is actually being profound, Taurean style.

Keen advocates of correct procedure, Taureans can freak out other signs. An Aries, for instance, borrowing a book from our Cow, is amazed to find a 10-page follow-up fax the next morning. A Pisces helpfully confiding the salacious details of someone's vastly inappropriate affair can't believe Taurus is trying to bring the subject back to how much the dysfunctional duo paid for their house.

In youth, Taurus people often appear a lot more grown-up than their peers. While everyone else is racing around scavenging planks to create a bookshelf, Taurus is chortling over fully fledged furniture. Some of them definitely risk early "shredded" status by knocking themselves out and taking uncool jobs in order to buy property or the accoutrements of a grown-up lifestyle. But guess who laughs heartily when others finally get around to settling down and Taurus has already set up a snazzy little nest? Suddenly stability doesn't seem so unsexy.

Another perfectly appropriate astro motto for Taurus, with their lewd sense of humor and lusty libido, is "I have it off."

"Without discipline there's no life at all."
Katharine Hepburn (1907-2003), Hollywood legend—*The African Queen, The Philadelphia Story, Guess Who's Coming to Dinner?, On Golden Pond*

Taurus on form is...

"That which is excellent endures."

Aristotle (384-322 BC), Greek philosopher and tutor of Alexander the Great

SENSUAL Whether slipping between freshly sun-dried, lavender-scented linen with the highest thread count they can afford, flexing just-pedicured feet, or trying out a new bedwork move, Cow People are genuinely in their bodies. Think glam piano man Liberace luxuriating in his bubble bath. Musically inclined, Taureans are blessed with beautiful singing voices.

DEPENDABLE Taureans are there for you, not necessarily to hash through the situation, but in a practical way: They will bake you a high-carb comfort dinner, pay the bail, or babysit your kids. They sometimes feel trapped by this trait. No-one else can calm down Aunt Thing after her third gin and they know it. The Bulls and Cows are dignified folk. They'd all be pillars of society if only they could find a society decent enough. Meanwhile, they make do with any organization that lets them be treasurer. Blessed with a sense of adequacy, our Cow feels at home in the world and welcomes you as well.

SERENE Taureans are the relaxation gurus of the zodiac. Left to their own devices, they like hanging out with their offspring, cooking, gardening, and/or taking to the couch with a bottle of plonk, a hunk of bread, and a cuddly companion. The Taurean couch exerts a gravity pull akin to Jupiter on his moons. The only difference is that our Taurus resists the gravitational force of the couch for as long as it takes to get to the fridge and back. They know that so-called mindless entertainment fulfills all the requirements of Zen—that is, pure enlightenment. Taurus has no need of the umpteen books released every year instructing one in the art of doing nothing, letting go, kicking back, just being...they're already there.

EARTH-ANGELIC Unlike Fire signs, who can wilt even a bamboo plant with one bitchy gaze, Taurus is green-fingered. Their fantasy house is a luxury shack in the woods where Taurus romps around lush grassy fields like something out of a Scandinavian shampoo ad. They are also natural-born healers, but not as in the Virgoan School of Healing, where St. Virgo advises the sinners on what vitamins to take. Taurus emits a calming vibe capable of soothing the most hysterical person and can even effect so-called miracle cures. Thus, a disproportionate amount of brilliant body-workers, medics and healers are Cow People.

CIVILIZED Taureans know how to relish life's pleasures without being sleazy or devious. Sensational socializers, they are fabulous company, "mostest" hosts and officially "good" guests. As neurosis is alien to their nature, they don't pull any of the nervy tricks known to other signs. A socially adequate persona enables them to put everyone at ease and they can be relied upon to behave. They never, for instance, try the "You're a gynecologist? Great! I've had this itchy discharge..." type of stunt. They adore recommending top accountants, nail artistes, and all of their myriad tips for better living.

STABLE They may not know what status quo means, but they know they like it. Regardless of trends, Taureans are grounded in the realm of their own tastes. Happy to confess that they dislike most music released after they turned a certain age, they don't care that the certain age was 25. Being around Taurus puts one in touch with one's own inner straight person. There is nothing wrong with choosing comfort, the good life, and nice furnishings over nerves and insanity. Straight may be the new avant-garde.

Taurus off form is...

"Trying not to be a dick takes work."

George Clooney (1961-), hunky Hollywood actor and modern-day matinee idol

GREEDY Taureans think greed is good, only they've made it New Age and called it "manifesting abundance." They lust after Things and, like devotees of an ancient cargo cult, they think objects have souls with which they commune. In his will, William Shakespeare left Mrs. Shakespeare his "second-best bed." Taurus returns from an exotic holiday with the high point having been the vicious haggling of some hapless street merchant. Even wealthy Cows can often not resist referring to the cost or alleged elite nature of their latest Thing. They are especially irksome when ensuring that the correct charges are extracted for a group dinner. After all, why should Taurus pay for a barely-nibbled-at bruschetta?

TYRANNICAL Taureans think right equals might and, naturally, they are right. They may not be the guilt-inducing champions like cousin Virgo, but they try some fairly hefty moral judgment calls. They can't help seeing themselves as respectable standard-bearers of common decency. Sundry irritants of life such as a surly sales assistant become markers of social decline. Demonstrating the flip side to their loyalty, they can also turn into social stalkers: Some friends are for life...or else. Another reason they are so good at hanging onto old acquaintances is that they see them as visible proof that nothing has, in fact, changed. One needs a lawyer to insult Taureans, as that is practically the only insult they notice.

CONTROL-FREAKY Heaven help the person who doesn't want to do what the Taurus wants them to do, like eating the food they think you should like, attending an art exhibition they know you will benefit from, or dating them because you need proper structure in your life. The Taurean "no" means "piss off" but your "no" is a mere formality, a bleat of stupidity because you are too weak-minded to properly grasp that the Taurus has made up their so-called mind. Resisting the Taurus is not exactly futile but it does leave you open to a long-winded, pompous lecture full of ponderous moralizing drivel. Taurus knows that you will eventually be bored into submission.

OBSTINATE Taurus is akin to a big boat that takes ages to respond to the wheel but then charges off full steam ahead, almost unstoppable. Their so-precious respectability cloaks inertia. Some are so old school that they still want to write their control-freaking memos with a quill dipped in ink, to be delivered by personal carrier pigeon. A room of their own? They crave a rut of their own. Even if the Taurus is completely wrong, they will bulldoze through, oblivious to everything but their own power of will. This is obviously wonderful for when they're giving up smoking or single-handedly building a new garage in a day, but vile when they're fanging down the freeway in the wrong direction, oblivious to any advice because they know best.

"Truth is always concrete."

Vladimir Ilyich Lenin (1870-1924), Russian revolutionary leader and writer

Motivating and manipulating a Taurus

"Sometimes the road less traveled is less traveled for a reason."

Jerry Seinfeld (1954-), American funny man who starred in his own TV show

1 Remember that Taureans feel taken advantage of by flittier folk. Flatter them as being secretly something quite wild.

2 Find something to grumble about which isn't the same any more. For example, the golden days of luxury train travel or how fantastic it was when one got to know the local bank manager.

3 Don't bug the Bull on anything to do with core values—they alter their minds every decade or so, if that.

4 Gifting a Cow? Think sensuality. Even the bitchiest Bull is tamed via fluffy towels, the purest cotton pillowcases.

5 Fake compliance. Taurean policy is that, as soon as you accept their point of view, they shall be in complete agreement with you.

6 Remember that Taureans are highly sensitive to having their things moved. Never move even their toothbrush from its usual spot.

7 Appreciate that they enjoy corny trappings of seduction. They like time-honored techniques such as dimmers, martinis, mood music, and burgundy velveteen headboards.

8 Reassert your admiration of their ethics. Thrill them by telling a story about some flake and how difficult they were—unlike Taurus.

9 Taureans respond well to and breathe new life into clichés. Don't be afraid to make statements such as "No point in crying over spilt milk," or "Pull your socks up!"

"I passionately hate the idea of being with it."

Orson Welles (1915-1985), larger-than-life Hollywood actor and director

Sacred Cows

"The beginning is always today."

Mary Wollstonecraft (1759-1797), British radical thinker and early feminist

- Burt Bacharach—Timeless Taurean songwriter and composer, embodying Cow Person mellifluence and sensuality. He is an exponent of the favorite Taurus musical genre Lounge. He wrote *Raindrops Keep Falling on My Head, Close to You,* and *I Say a Little Prayer.*

- Joanna Lumley—Gorgeous, witty, and adored actress, comedienne, writer, and vegetarian bon vivant. Best known for her role as Patsy Stone on *Absolutely Fabulous.* "When you get home, on go the rugger socks and holey jersey and out comes the tin tray with baked beans on toast in front of *Blind Date.*"

- Dwayne Johnson aka The Rock—Nicknamed the Brahma Bull, he is a singer, dancer, wrestling champion, and the next big action movie star. The Rock radiates Taurus machismo. Some of his favorite quotes include "You will go one on one with the great one" and "Just bring it."

- Tamara de Lempicka—Sensual Polish aristocrat who, after fleeing to Paris, became a famous Art Deco artist. "Tamara had a strength of self-knowledge and sense of who she was in the world that no-one else conveyed."

- David O. Selznick—Film producer of such greats as *Gone with the Wind*, *Rebecca*, and *The Thin Man*. He discovered the master of suspense, director Alfred Hitchcock. Famous for his memos, Selznick issued instructions to his writers such as "write whatever you want so long as there is a love scene and the girl jumps into the volcano at the end."

- Donatella Versace—Diamond-dripping, perma-tanned, and chain-smoking international fashionista. She has full-on Taurus tastes like vines and flowers growing in her ballroom-sized bedroom and bovine key traits of being brilliant in business yet loving the louche life.

"When you arise in the morning, think of what a precious privilege it is to be alive, to breathe, to think, to enjoy, to love."

Marcus Aurelius (AD 121-180), philosophizing Roman emperor

Chic Cow

"I never thought I was attractive to boys."

Michelle Pfeiffer (1958-), checkout operator who became a superstar

How now, comely Cow? Venus-ruled Cow People are absolutely stunning. They are blessed with natural glowing good looks, mellifluous voices and harmonious facial features. The men are often clichéd hunks who carry off traditional-style clothing with unique flair. People take one look and just yearn to lean on them.

Like cousin Libra, Taurus favors sensually textured clothing. Watch their hands reach out to reassuringly stroke whatever fabric—silk, cashmere, velvet—comforts the most.

Their deep sense of what is and is not appropriate will often see even youthful Taureans opt for a below-the-knees twinset, tweed jacket, or whatever they feel is most correct for their advancing years.

But the joke is that maturity becomes our Cow. The investment dressing strategy pays off and their true beauty begins to shine over those with less enduring appeal. Comfort is a huge priority for bovine folk. If they see someone out in the street dressed haphazardly for the weather, they react with grim relish: "That girl's legs must be frozen. I wouldn't be at all surprised if she ended up with chilblains." Queen Elizabeth appears edgy in a chintzy get-up yet so much happier tramping around in gumboots and a warm scarf wrapped around her head.

Taureans are total fiends for what they call "proper" jewelry. They don't care about the design, they dislike modern jewelry almost as much as they despise abstract art—they just care about the rock. Via their voodoo ability to commune with the souls of material objects, they can intuit designer copies and, yes, they disapprove...unless, of course, it is the Taurus exhibiting uncommon sense in having saved a few thousand dollars. Nobody will ever know because Taureans look so-o-o-o expensive.

BOVINE BEAUTIES Anouk Aimée, Candice Bergen, Cate Blanchett, Pierce Brosnan, George Clooney, Penélope Cruz, Daniel Day-Lewis, Kirsten Dunst, Linda Evangelista, Chow-Yun Fat, Dame Margot Fonteyn, Audrey Hepburn, Katharine Hepburn, Enrique Iglesias, Grace Jones, Jessica Lange, Jay Leno, Joanna Lumley, Andie MacDowell, Michelle Pfeiffer, Uma Thurman, Renée Zellweger

Brilliant career

"If you can stand the heat and do go into the kitchen, be prepared for napalm in the frying pan."

Joanna Lumley (1946-), *Absolutely Fabulous* British actress

Gutsy and mentally robust, Taureans don't go looking for trouble. They also know that there is no point attributing to malice something which can be adequately explained by stupidity. They're comfortable with a hardcore slog regime so long as it scores them a desirable outcome. As a result, they are successful at whatever career they choose to grace with their awesomely steady presence. The Taurus work ethic, along with their controlling nature and ability to project stability, makes them particularly desirable in the corporate and political worlds.

Even in a disliked job, Taureans never pretend to be busy—they *are* busy. Not that they're martyrs. If they haven't got the time, they hire someone who has. They delegate without guilt. Though avaricious, hardworking, and ambitious, Taurus is not normally a careerist. They value their homes...and their couch.

They tend not to bother with cant—"Why is that woman going on about a glass ceiling? It's bloody plasterboard!"—and are definitely not hyper-stressed Type A personalities. The only occupational misguidance in our Cow's career comes if the security fetish keeps them stuck in a boring gig. At worst, Taurus turns into a bureaucratic dictator, putting people on infinite hold and making the most out of being the "no" person, nipping budding projects on the grounds of unfeasibility. This type of Cow Person must remember that sometimes the next pasture really is a lot greener.

Ethics are their key competency. The Taurean lawyer won't try to bribe the judge. The Taurus taxi driver will return whatever you left in the back seat. Showbiz Taurus won't use the couch for casting, they will whisk you off to a swank hotel and be very frank about your sleeping-your-way-to-the-top prospects.

If a Taurean resumé says they commanded an elite military corps, were afforded an honorary degree, or they were the cover subject in a magazine about business excellence, then it's true.

"Power without principle is barren but principle without power is futile."

Tony Blair (1954-), British prime minister. At 43, in 1997, he became the youngest prime
minister since Lord Liverpool in 1812.

Fiscal reality

"I can't stand to see red in my profit-and-loss column.
I'm Taurus the bull so I react to red."

Barbra Streisand (1942-), singer, director, and actress—*Funny Girl, Yentl*

Taureans often end up in two minds with fiscal reality. Mind One is frugal. It says: Save pieces of string; clip out those coupons even if you do have to cross town to redeem them, it saves you $4.50; borrow books from the library and forget to return them; use No Frills-brand petroleum jelly as a moisturizer; grow your own mung beans in recycled tap water; use disinfectant as an aftershave; amass wealth via thrift; and think scarcity.

Mind Two is prosperity conscious. It loves the idea of being a sugar daddy or mommy. It says: Spend it to make it; blow the electricity money on coffee-table books for inspiration; one must always have fresh flowers; a personal Pilates coach is a necessity if one is going to think straight; the universe is abundant and so are credit providers; life is too good to be subtle; and luxury comes from the Greek word for light. You can see that this is a dilemma.

Sun signs

Learning how to distinguish between what they truly need and what they think they want is a cosmic, deeply spiritual issue for Taureans. Yes, having beautiful possessions can cultivate inner beauty and harmony. No, waking up at 2 a.m. and freaking out about a credit-card bill does not induce serenity.

What the bovine ones are after is security but the highly evolved Taureans realize that Thing Lust won't do it. It's great that Taurus is good at hanging onto and utilizing stuff. Geminis, on the other hand, will give away a Gameboy because it "attacked" them; Pisces are capable of chucking out a clock that emitted "bad vibes"; and Librans can ditch suddenly unfashionable furniture to "start afresh."

But true Taurean stability must arise from the harboring of inner resources. The Taurus attitude toward lucre is so important, for it determines their feelings toward everything else in life.

"I don't wake up for less than $10,000 a day."

Linda Evangelista (1965-), Canadian supermodel with staying power

Chez Cow

"Everywhere I go, I find a poet has been there before me."

Sigmund Freud (1856-1939), founder of modern psychoanalysis and dream interpretation

and inventor of the Freudian slip

Just like Ferdinand the friendly bull who didn't want to take part in bullfighting, Taureans often find no place so sweet as home pastures. The typical Taurean residence oozes peace and abundance. Even the most serenity-challenged visitor feels a zap of Zen-type tranquility. The Cow's home is a reminder that Taureans are the tactile fabric freaks of the zodiac. They thrill to the sensation of crushed velvet, cool Egyptian cotton, and wool-blend sisal on their pedicured feet.

Cow People redefine sensuality. Their homeware of choice includes bright-colored cashmere throws, big plush cushions, and tubs of French lavender hand cream beside every tap. (This lot thinks that dry skin is a disease.) Fittingly for these relaxation gurus, the couch is the gravitational center of the Taurean universe. It's always strong, supportive, and forgiving. Other furniture is preferably traditional-looking. Taureans sometimes fantasize about medieval décor, complete with a banquet table and a stool on which the lyre-playing pageboy would sit.

Rustic at heart, they're inordinately fond of paintings depicting pastoral scenes and green fields to muse upon at leisure. Every Taurean possesses an inner flower child and their gorgeous gardens tend to steal into the interior of their homes—a trailing wisp of wisteria here, tulips there, and perhaps one perfect November lily in the toilet.

"There is only one difference between a madman and me.
I am not mad."

Salvador Dali (1904-1989), Spanish surrealist painter who loved to shock

A Taurus in love

"Insane people are always sure that they are fine. It is only sane people who are willing to admit that they are crazy."

Nora Ephron (1941-), witty screenwriter of the film *Sleepless in Seattle*

Taureans have fantastic long-term lover potential—age doesn't weary them and familiarity turns them on. Taurus represents a robust libido and a kind heart, looking toward an enduring romance of equals.

So why, when their key requirements include someone who is socially acceptable and sane, do they so often attract such idiots? How can someone who values the serene life keep getting it on with sexy hysterical types?

Is it that they subconsciously need someone to act out their repressed inner chaos? Remember, Taureans truly believe that chaos is only a theory.

Ideally, they grow out of dependence on dysfunctional relationships and wind up in something beautiful. There is enough angst in the relationship to stoke the bovine libido but it is sufficiently peaceful for quality time with a lover on the couch.

The nightmare scenario is a nonstop dynamic involving Taurus as the straight, parental figure mopping up smashed absinthe bottles, ministering to a damaged diva ego, and cringing at yet another scene in a suburban car park.

Stubborn to the nth degree and hearing selectively, Cow People can pursue the most incompatible partner, hoping to lure devious Libra via business credentials or trying to jinx the heart of jittery Gemini with a home-cooked dinner spell.

They can even patronize their lover's foibles, smothering their dreams until they reach breaking point. Then Taurus Cow bitches about how there are no real men left and Taurus Bull complains there are no proper women who can handle the heat. This situation must not be allowed to happen. Deep down, Taureans see themselves as the last great lovers, deliberately evoking a legendary standard of purity and devotion.

"Cry now—laugh later."

Grace Jones (1952-), flamboyant entertainer, songwriter, and icon

Taurus-Aries

Cow People instantly realize that their secret fear of being boring is not going to materialize if they can just stick with this character. The Ramzilla vision and daring intoxicates the more practical character of Taurus. Aries loves Taurean directness and stoicism, sensing perhaps that it lends dignity and solidity to their own streakiness. Taurus cheers Ramzilla's victory over mediocrity, the quarter-written screenplay, a dogged hangnail or whatever the Aries Thing de Jour. There is nothing wrong with the Taurean energy levels once they are activated. But Taurus also fears that Aries embodies the triumph of hype over reality. Aries can appear brash and naïve to the worldly Cow Person. The Ram is defined by a go-get approach to missions large and small, but sensual Taurus wonders why Ramzilla has to do *everything* so fast. Aries thinks "get on with it." Having consulted the wild Ramzilla, Taurus sets a steady course, calculated to accomplish the duo's long-term plans with ease and grace. Then Aries barges in to announce that "everything has changed" after some five-minute encounter with a stranger. In Taurus-Aries Utopia, the Cow gets more crazy and optimistic. Aries learns to let Taurus keep the books and provide—lengthy, detailed (yawn)—sanity checks.

Hot duos: Michelle Pfeiffer & David E. Kelley, Dario Franchitti & Ashley Judd, Denys Finch Hutton & Karen Blixen (Isak Dinesen), Katharine Hepburn & Spencer Tracy

Taurus-Taurus

Ladies and gentlemen, the libidos have landed. Taurus is the most tactile sign of all and when these two bond, they can barely keep their sensual little paws off one another. Taurus-Taurus is the sort of ultra-physically demonstrative couple who nauseate less touchy types. Not that either Cow cares about that. Together, they're a mutual esteem-boosting machine, built for success and longevity. What blights the bliss? Taurus is obstinate, determined that their view will win out and so is the other Taurus. Taurus vs. Taurus won't speak for a year, yet stay together, each willing the other to succumb. Neither buckles and romance heaven turns into hell. Ideally, this pair uses their love of protocol to establish early agreements about what will and will not be tolerated. The dream remains real only so long as both Cows are prepared to put aside their pushy dictatorial whims and honor the other's reality. Once that occurs, peace, prosperity, and ongoing satisfaction are assured.

Hot duos: Posh Spice (Victoria) & David Beckham, Lord Waldorf & Lady Nancy Astor

Taurus-Gemini Taurus spots Gemini and thinks "whoa!"

Taurus thinks twice and then again before entering the Gemini zone. Gemini, though lust-stricken, thinks bugging the Bull could be good fun. Decent, dependable good loving doesn't always cut it with thrill-craving Gemini. There has to be a "hook" and it often comes when Taurus has planets in nearby Gemini or vice versa. Gemini wants a lover who's there but not there all of a sudden when Gemini feels the solo urge. Gemini likes variety—Taurus thinks the need for nonstop novelty signifies neurosis but Gemini says "So I'm neurotic, now what?" Gemini is highly strung with a musical, sometimes staccato, speaking style. Taurus swings low as in a hammock or sofa, and seems unhurried, even when panicked. Taurus has an official libido, Geminis like a lot of their lust life to remain pure theory. Gemini flirts for a hobby and without follow through. Taurus doesn't bother unless they are going to "close the deal." Gemini loves how serene Taurus makes them feel but then gets anxious. It feels *too* relaxed. The Cow Person is easily bored by Gemini jumpiness. There is actually a lot of goodwill in this relationship. Gemini has to put their famed flexibility to good use. Taurus must tolerate.

Hot duos: Andre Agassi & Steffi Graf, Queen Elizabeth II and Prince Philip, Enrique Iglesias & Anna Kournikova, Natasha Richardson & Liam Neeson, Steve Berra & Juliette Lewis

Taurus-Cancer

To have and to hold—neither of them cares who does what, the attraction is awesome and potentially enduring. Values tend to be shared and domesticity blissful. This is a deeply canny couple, each happy to do whatever it takes. Crab raves about tradition, family and doing things properly—Taurus says fine. Crab angst is annihilated by full-on, steady Taurean loving. Each admires the other, totally empowered by the love. Irksome issues arise when Crab wants more than just a Taurean assurance of everything being "in hand." Crab wants to emote. Taurus says "get a grip." Crab goes wandering off to phone an ex, just for validation. Crabby libido crumples without simpatico communion. The Taurean sex drive can survive direct blows to the ego. It can operate in an intellectual vacuum. Crab shrieks, "How could you?" For this beautiful bond to go on and on, Taurus must get with the confessional Crab reality and Cancer must fake some sanity. Together, these two get healthy, wealthy, and annoyingly wise.

Hot duos: Barbra Streisand & James Brolin, Homer & Marge Simpson, Royston Langdon & Liv Tyler, Joanna Lumley & Stephen Barlow, Jessica Alba & Michael Weatherly

Taurus-Leo

Leo is jealous of Taurus. Cow People are natural beauties. Leo works at it. Leo sees image as show time, requiring spartan regimes of hair insanity, grooming, and gargantuan makeovers. Taurus slips out the door, able to seduce with a dab of lip gloss and the hint of a comb. Leo starts bitching about split ends, standards, and things the cat may or may not drag in. Ugliness ensues. The Leo libido is as high as our Cow's but the leonine thirst for admiration may leave Taurus languishing among a field of fresh devotees. Nobody loves Leo like Leo so the good heart of Taurus is unsure. Leo feels like an invisible audience is always watching, frustrating the free expression of Taurus lust. Leo settles in for the night in designer trackpants, with lifestyle-media sanctioned wine to accompany the à la carte meal. The Cow is not happy, longing for a stir-fry instead. But along with admiration, Taurus amasses money with a steady strategy. This is great because Leo always appreciates a sky-high discretionary budget. There are many things that hold this duo together: They are both *so* sexy and interested in bedwork. While Leo comes at this from the glam end of the attraction spectrum—and Taurus is more sexual—neither sign has time for the bait-and-switch sexual games that other signs get up to. When it's on, it's on.

Hot duos: Bianca & Mick Jagger, Siân Phillips & Peter O'Toole

Taurus-Virgo Sleeping Bull is awoken by Prince/Princess
Virgo and everyone profits. Once the Cow Person gets over the energy of action-oriented Virgo, Taurus falls hard in love. Virgo was smitten from the first. Corrective nagging from Virgo annoys Taurus less than it does from anyone else. Taurus knows that Virgo is right and Virgo loves that Taurus sees their innate beauty and brilliance. Values, sexuality, and gracious living ideals are usually entwined in love and productivity. Tension may arise via the Taurus Thing Lust and the Virgoan hobby of throwing things out. Taurus makes Virgo feel safe and assured. Virgo honors Taurus reality because it is reality. The bond is nigh psychic, in that each gets the other's emotions and thoughts as they are being felt. Taurus doesn't care about Virgoan guilting and Virgo loves Taurean moral-judgment plays. The Taurean adequacy totally calms Virgoan nerves, their fetish for details, and their hypochondria. Love blooms amid nonstop cool conversation and ever-renewing attraction.

Hot duos: Audrey Hepburn & Mel Ferrer, Roberto Rossellini & Ingrid Bergman, Tim McGraw & Faith Hill, Don Bacardy & Christopher Isherwood, Tony Blair & Cherie Booth Blair

Taurus-Libra
The beauty and the beauty: People can scarcely believe this bonding because it seems so right. But is it? Both are ruled by Venus, goddess of love. Sensual compatibility and ongoing allure are not remotely an issue. But compared to Libra, even a wayward Taurus is the most straightforward character on Earth. Libra goes Yin and then Yang before deciding on something seen by Taurus as cowardly compromise. This dynamic can be played on the most petty level, beneath either party but seemingly unable to be avoided. Libra pretends to go along with the more exact whims of Taurus. One night it all comes out and Libra admits that sometimes "maybe" just means "maybe"—the Libran mind is never fully made up in any direction. Taurus can literally not believe anyone could live their life in this fashion. But Taurus had better believe it for the love of a Libra is not won by willpower. Libra likes to be tantalized and seduced anew every few hours. All else resolved, these two create a charmed oasis of bliss and style.

Hot duos: Lady Emma Hamilton & Lord (Horatio) Nelson, Eva (Evita) & Juan Peron, Pierce Brosnan & Keely Shaye Smith, Janet Jackson & Jermaine Dupri

Taurus-Scorpio
This is *never* a brief encounter. Taurus and Scorpio either pass one another without giving a damn or get it on for (more or less) ever. Each yearns for a purposeful love affair, something more than the sum of its parts, and this relationship delivers. Once bonded, this duo goes into shutdown mode. No indiscreet confidence or over-familiar ex-lover shall be allowed into fortress Taurus-Scorpio. Each has huge issues with loyalty. Friends who are not absolute fans of the liaison get culled quick smart. Ditto, any fancy idea that doesn't

suit the other. Sex is insanely satisfying along with shared values and boundary awareness. Scorpio just *knows* when not to bug the Bull and Taurus reciprocates by truly understanding Scorpio's privacy legislation. Technically, these are opposite signs of the zodiac; Scorpio conspiracy theories stretch Cow-Person credibility—Taurus likes to go out and enjoy a meal with a few drinks, not spend all evening listening to stuff about moon landings and fluoridation secrets. Likewise, Taurus annoys Scorpio by going with "consensus reality." Careful Bulls realize early on that Scorpio takes individualism very seriously—to Taurus, it's just a small logo on a shirt but to Scorpio this is evidence of selling out and pandering to multinational thought control. But once they are soul mates, neither cares.

Hot duos: Uma Thurman & Ethan Hawke, Jessica Lange & Sam Shepard, Pierre & Marie Curie, Candice Bergen & Louis Malle

Taurus-Sagittarius Taurus is a brute realist and Sagg hates any variety of what they call "negativity." Taurus is into Thing Lust and stability. Saggo values the experience and, given the chance, would swap the sofa in two seconds for a plane ticket to a big party somewhere really cool. The Taurus mind is initially boggled by Sagg. The attraction between these two is clear, the way ahead to an enduring partnership not so obvious. Candor brings them together as Taurus loves the Sagittarian ability to speak their mind. Sagittarius gets off on Taurean stability but when Taurus says "that money is earmarked for the tax insurance," Sagg tunes out. Taurus tunes in and thinks "where did I drop myself off?" Like it or not, the way this pair handle shared money, ambition, and values determines where they wind up. Sex is an antidote but not forever. In Taurus-Sagittarius Utopia, Sagg is grounded by Cow's worldly grace and Taurus is unbelievably inspired by Sagittarius.

Hot duos: Graham Payn & Noël Coward, Bing & Kathryn Crosby, Francesca Annis & Ralph Fiennes, Kirsten Dunst & Jake Gyllenhaal

Taurus-Capricorn Upon first meeting, each senses that the other is going to be good for them. Then, because both are perverse, they try their best to screw it up. Taurus and Capricorn have an understanding, impossible to get from the outside but so fulfilling for either party. Sensual rapport builds into an unbeatable best-friend-and-best-ever-bedwork combo and neither can believe they ever bothered with anyone else. Each wants fun and success in equal measure. Taurus gets fed up with Capricorn's negativity but recognizes that cheering up Capricorn is like a life mission. Capricorn goes all out to impress the Cow Person in every regard, vowing not to complain about crumbs in the bed, less-than-desirable dress standards or any of the usual Capricorn complaints. Or maybe Capricorn does decide to complain? In that case, this duo is doomed. The struggle is dear to the Capricorn heart. Taurus needs to feel mega-accepted but understands that Cap needs a few points for effort. Only then can the love and largesse flow fully.

Hot duos: Carl Dean & Dolly Parton, Coretta Scott King & Dr Martin Luther King

Taurus-Aquarius Taurus sees Aquarius and thinks "this person needs structure in their life, this person needs...me." Aquarius twigs, thinking finally someone is onto them. And someone is. The Taurus-Aquarius relationship defies reason as both worship reason. Both are "fixed" signs, stubborn, distinct, and utterly definite in who they are. A deep admiration of the other's previous achievements always helps this pair. Aquarius is used to being seen as "the flake"—Taurus sees straight through that and recognizes true Aquarian stability. Aquarius tends to evoke some secret aspect of Taurus that our Cow feels can be poorly—if at all—expressed elsewhere. Taurus is weird about things the Aquarius takes for granted, such as societal change and evolution. The Aquarian goes gaga at the idea of attending a pre-ordained function, abhorring anything official and organized. Each helps the other deal with deep personal issues. If the effort is not too

exhausting, this duo can be soul mates, forever sensitive and loving of one another's differences.

Hot duos: Cate Blanchett & Andrew Upton, Alice B. Toklas & Gertrude Stein, Daniel Johns & Natalie Imbruglia

Taurus-Pisces
Pisces enchants and annoys Taurus in equal measure. Taurean emotion from this onslaught fluctuates to the point that Cow sanity could be threatened. Pisces oscillates between loving bovine stability and loathing the encroachment on space. Taurus will not give up control and Pisces will not be controlled. Taurus thinks Pisces could be the Muse. Pisces wonders whether Taurus is going to bankroll their genius. The whole time this weird encounter is playing out, each struggles with a sensual attraction. Taurus meets Pisces and vows immediately not to be drawn into Pisces' madness. Pisces spots Taurus, fancies the creature, and becomes determined not to be conquered. Bedwork is bucolic and brilliant by turns. Neither has any complaint although Taurus may not wish to join the lush fantasy life of the Fish. On the plus side, Taurean strength helps cure Piscean drama-queen tendencies. There is nothing like the Bull's groundedness to put an end to the Fish's habit of self-embezzlement and lunch-time drinking. The Piscean intuition, while a source of much pain for the Cow, is a useful back-up to Taurean sense and decency. Taurus may say that the joint venture contract is done; Pisces only sees the new partner's shifty eyes and liar's vibe. This is a duo that can agree to agree about getting on. Pisces gets real. Taurus goes surreal.

Hot duos: Robert Browning & Elizabeth Barrett Browning, Eugen Boissevain & Edna St. Vincent Millay, Ken & Barbie Doll, Benoît Magimel & Juliette Binoche

Are you really a Taurus?

1 A visitor to your home is rude about your living-room couch. You...

(a) Explain to the philistine exactly how it is an embodiment of style and current interior chic.

(b) Don't care—it is just something to sit on.

(c) Sit out the evening but vow never to have this person at your place again.

2 Employed in an office position, it becomes apparent that someone has stolen your favorite stapler. You...

(a) Don't really care—you can always get another stapler.

(b) See it as an indicator that this job is not really you.

(c) Bring the entire floor to a halt until the culprit is found and forced to return the stapler.

3 At an otherwise brilliant party you are trapped with an amazingly dull and yet creepy person in the kitchen. They are alarmingly attracted to you. You...

(a) Escape as soon as possible on whatever pretext is possible.

(b) Evoke dormant social-worker skills. This poor person needs your help!

(c) Flirt your head off—it is your duty. Beauty has obligations.

4 You think people who are embroiled in public sex scandals should...

(a) Be felt sorry for. Nobody deserves such scrutiny of their private lives, least of all paparazzi staking out their home.

(b) Whatever. Who cares, you're above such sleaze.

(c) Consider what YOU would do in such a situation.

5 Shopping in a busy city street, you suddenly have a massive anxiety attack, complete with hyperventilation. You...

(a) Utterly freak out and book in with the first counselor or psych-person you can organize. Mental health is so-o-o precious to you.

(b) Blame the cheap scent of the shirty shop assistant you just encountered and arrange an aromatherapy massage from your mobile phone.

(c) Get a good grip and carry on completely as if nothing has actually happened.

6 In a relationship with a much-loved but low-lust person, it becomes apparent that this duo is simply not going to deliver the bedwork you require. You...

(a) Go on a massive workout regime so they will be unable to resist your sheer personal hotness and read up on sex tips.

(b) Take them out for a romantic dinner and gently explain your needs, etc.

(c) Deliver an ultimatum. They either put out or get out. And by the way, it's not as if you're exactly without offers. Hello?

Answers: If you checked mainly (c) answers, then you are an official Taurus—a courageous Cow Person and, yes, a symbol of strength and solidity. If you checked (a) or (b) answers, you have other astro influences competing with your Taurean Sun.

Gemini

may 22-june 21

Gemini of ages

"Everything has been figured out except how to live."

Jean-Paul Sartre (1905-1980), French philosopher who turned down a Nobel Prize for

literature in 1964

Q: How many Geminis does it take to change a light bulb?
A: Two, plus a mobile phone, an Internet link, and a copy of *The Bluffer's Guide to Changing Lightbulbs.*

Gemini folk are ruled by Mercury, messenger of dreams and the fastest-moving planet of all. In mythology, Mercury was known as the trickster of the Gods, due to his amorality, gossiping, and scandal mongering.

In one legend he steals his half-brother Apollo's oxen and when asked about their whereabouts calmly responds, "What are oxen? I'd never even heard of the word until today."

Hello? Does any of this strike a chord? U.S. poet Walt Whitman, originally a journalist, kickstarted his career by self-publishing a volume of verse and then writing glowing reviews of it under various pseudonyms. Mercury, then, is why Gemini can best be described as "mercurial."

Each sign has an astrological motto, a mini-summary of that sign's basic ethos. Gemini's is "I think" and they certainly do. Geminis have no problems separating mind from emotion because they have no emotions, at least not as normal people know them. In their own weird way, they are quite self-actualized. If the tiniest hint of an undesirable emotion creeps into their psyche, Geminis think "boring" and swat it away.

They are huge believers in their own thought power. As Hollywood hunk Clint Eastwood once said, "If you think it is going to rain, it will rain." Or as U.S. billionaire Donald Trump said: "So long as you're going to be thinking anything, think big." Geminis are living proof that the unexamined life is worth living. If they have a short attention span it's your fault for being so boring. Communicators and observers, they are compelled to analyze and broadcast human foible.

The astro symbol for Gemini is the Twins. They're often bi-everything, into double standards, and hovering between left and right brain activity. They're simultaneously heaven and hell, Jekyll and Hyde, Yin and Yang. And they fancy themselves as "street angels and home devils."

Like cousins Libra and Aquarius, Gemini is also an Air sign: sanguine in temperament and breezy by nature. Air signs are mind-based, intellectual, adaptive, and communicative. Never dull, a Gemini will at least not wind up talking about "the weather." But this is partly because they have their own very strange internal weather system, complete with atmospheric lows and sudden cold fronts.

One moment a Gemini can be acting as if they have just fallen so in love with you, hanging upon your every word and gazing at your beauty in rapt adoration. Then Twin Two enters and it is as if Gemini has iced over. Their demeanor switches to "Do I know you?" If it is any consolation, they truly can't help it. As well as being an Air sign, they are what is called "Mutable." This means that along with Sagittarians, Virgos, and Pisceans, they are fickle little *merdes*.

"It's easy for me to live in denial. I forget my problems. I'm a putterer. I can keep busy. I can get the worst news in the world and not even think about it."

Courteney Cox (1964-), clean-freak Monica in the U.S. hit TV series *Friends*

Twin One is...

"Scatter joy."

Ralph Waldo Emerson (1803-1882), one of America's favorite poets

ALLURING Charming, witty, and sexy, Gemini is attractive to all comers. Buzzing around in honey-bee mode, a Gemini flatters, flirts, and plays with advanced innuendo. They are the sign most likely to leave a swathe of bemused hearts in their wake.

UPLIFTING Their cheery amorality is soothing to those more prone to turgid emotion. Guilt is an unknown emotion to Geminis. Confide it and Gemini's reaction will be a stupefied, "So what? You did what you had to do. Don't worry about it. I wouldn't..." They also specialize in distraction tactics. A Gemini who is being audited by the tax office, sued by an ex-lover, and about to be fired from that dream job is a Gemini busy planning a group theater excursion. A friend in need is, to the Gemini mind, a friend who needs to be taken to a cat show, cocktail bar, yoga class, and film premiere all in one day.

"It is so lovely to wake up and know that One is lovely One..."

Diana Mitford (1910-2003), dazzling beauty whose husbands included the heir to the Guinness fortune and the British fascist politician Sir Oswald Mosley

ADAPTABLE Able to process anything in two seconds flat, Gemini is ultra-flexible. Their hyper-fast mind keeps them from being stuck in any form of rut and they are able to relate to absolutely anyone. This lot can get along anywhere and be taken any place. Just when one thinks one knows Gemini, they go and add a new facet to their already multifaceted persona. This can be hard for slower acquaintances to keep up with—they'll go and book tribal dancing lessons to be more attuned to the Gemini they love. Then Geminis will say they're over all that now and they have developed an interest in the Dark Ages.

BLITHE Some call it shallow, but those who know better recognize Gemini's light heart as a gift. Always inspirational, vibing much like a traveling minstrel of old, the Gemini is perpetual poetry in motion.

AMUSING Able to lighten even the darkest situation by their mere presence and a few quips, Geminis are an asset to any social scenario. They know how to "sing for their supper" and may be safely relied upon never to bore for a moment. Nobody fears being stuck with a Gemini in the kitchen at a party, just in a bedroom.

INFORMED Focus groups could profitably consist entirely of Geminis. They are what advertising shrinks call "key influencers." Gadget, jargon, attitude, genre, word of the day...Gemini is a walking Zeitgeist of what's hot and what's not. They have the latest news, info, gossip, and jokes. Geminis can talk about anything. Whatever the subject, Gemini will know something about it—even if they make it up. Gemini hates clichés unless they are advising you on your romantic life. If it is to do with emotions, all Gemini can often summon up is a string of "water under the bridge" isms.

"Been there, done that..."

Brian Eno (1948-), whiz music producer of Irish group U2 and other bands

"Don't let them tame you."

Isadora Duncan (1878-1927), charismatic dancer who pioneered modern dance as an artform. She took her inspiration from classical Greek art to produce free barefoot expression.

Twin Two is...

"Imperious, choleric, extreme in everything, with a dissolute imagination the like of which has never been seen, atheistic to the point of fanaticism, there you have me in a nutshell, and kill me again or take me as I am, for I shall not change."

Marquis de Sade (1740-1814), notorious author of exotic stories whose topics include sex and cruelty. The word "sadism" is derived from his name.

AMORAL Geminis rarely feel remorse. They are living proof that you can run *and* you can hide. Eco-marine guru Jacques Cousteau apparently provoked octopus fights by tipping black ink into the ocean. Geminis are excellent at appearing attentive to what one is saying yet without actually listening. If required, they feed it back at you parrot fashion, without having understood anything. They rely upon the power of glib. A good description of this sign is in Françoise Sagan's novel *Those Without Shadows*: "twin themes of attraction and disentanglement...the characters all move without shadows, uncertain of what they want from life, portraying the paradox of aimlessness and apparent longing for stability."

DISHONEST "Don't expect confessions, revelations...not even the truth," writes actress Isabella Rossellini in her autobiography *Some of Me*. "It is a habit of mine to embellish and color events until I lose sight of what really happened...I lie, I always did." It's as if fibbing were part of the Gemini respiratory process. They tell white lies, whopper lies, and the whole gamut in between. Even if Gemini did have a genuine ability to feel guilt, lying would not be the issue to evoke it. A large proportion of the thespian population is Gemini. This could have something to do with the Gemini dual nature or maybe it is because they are such fake people anyway, as acting—being paid to lie—comes naturally to them.

"Nobody's interested in sweetness and light."

Hedda Hopper (1890-1966), Hollywood gossip columnist who loved hats

A FLAKE Fearing that mediocrity is some kind of airborne affliction, Geminis seek to inoculate themselves against it by being gaga. A Gemini in freewheeling-flake mode is fearsome. No idea is too stupid to be entertained and no relationship so over the top or improper that Gemini won't launch it with gusto. Taboo turns them on—as sociopaths they're immune to guilt. They think insomnia is constructive extra time and being mood-disordered is quite normal. They can come across as an aging baby. You seek closure, they seek the door. Asked to get in touch with their feelings, they switch into "life is a laboratory" mode, starring Gemini as the mad doctor and you as the lab rat. In the Gemini mind is a drop-down menu of what they imagine to be reasonable excuses.

HEARTLESS This lot are cruel to perfectly nice people who just happened to bore Gemini. They say something vicious as a fast way out of the conversation. Unless they have a psycho-sexual motive to be nice to you, they are almost utterly lacking in empathy. Be warned that they can make an amusing anecdote out of anything. While you're getting over your hideous affair with one, Gemini is busy turning the fiasco into a sitcom. Gemini spouses can be observed at dinner parties, quietly freaking out as a chortling Gemini regales the crowd with funny stories about your vasectomy, diet, or strange parents. Geminis have no sympathy for naïvety in anyone over the age of about 12. Their fave comment in conversation is "Let's move on." They don't take anything personally—even when it is personal.

"Laugh at yourself first before anyone else can."

Elsa Maxwell (1883-1963), hostess with the mostest and confidante to the stars

Motivating and manipulating a Gemini

"Mediocrity knows nothing higher than itself but talent instantly recognises genius."

Sir Arthur Conan Doyle (1859-1930), novelist, playwright, and poet. He is best known for his detective novels starring super-sleuth Sherlock Holmes.

1 Change the subject before they can—it makes them think they're in the presence of a higher life form.

2 If a heavy "us" subject comes up, just give a tinkly little laugh and change the subject.

3 Give up trying to guilt them. They don't like you preoccupying their finely tuned mind with the recommended daily allowance of chablis or chocolate.

4 To make a Gemini fall in love with you, be unavailable. They like love that is requited but without responsibilities or toxic familiarity. Also, keep the vibe going in "sibling-combative" mode—they love that sibling nitpicking and rivalry stuff.

5 Accept that Geminis are analytical but only about your foibles. Ask them to examine their own and they short-circuit.

6 If you have information you want broadcast to society at large in the minimum of time, tell a Gemini.

7 Muck-rake as much as you like with a Gemini. The Twins like to be teased. But don't try to moralize or preach. They don't even know where the high moral ground is.

8 Gifting a Gemini? Make it something gimmicky such as a gadget or the latest computerized toy. But, really, all they want is a new and interesting tidbit of information at least twice a day.

9 Let them dabble in temporary fads without nagging.

"To be really great in little things, to be truly noble and heroic in the insipid details of everyday life, is a virtue so rare as to be worthy of canonization."

Harriet Beecher Stowe(1811-1896), author of *Uncle Tom's Cabin (1852)*. This book caused controversy as it focused public interest on the issue of slavery.

Gemini role models

"Less is only more when more is no good."

Frank Lloyd Wright (1867-1959), rebel American architect who showed his peers new ways to build their homes and see the world around them

- Donald Duck—enduring star of television and comic books with the dual personality: He is a cantankerous uncle but a bashful beau; and the duck who can't keep a job and is disastrous at entrepreneurial pursuits. The Gemini clue? Those high-speed vocals and low-boredom threshold.

- Rupert Everett—Debonair actor, singer, model, and writer. He once sent samples of his pubic hair to dissatisfied theater-goers who had complained about his performance in the Noël Coward play *The Vortex*. He could have been a concert pianist, but gave up at age 13 because "it was very boring."

Sun signs

- Rachel Carson—ecologist, biologist, science writer who campaigned against the use of pesticides, and founder of the environmental movement in the U.S. Her cult book *Silent Spring* (1962) made president John F. Kennedy a fan. "The more clearly we can focus our attention on the wonders and realities of the universe about us, the less taste we shall have for destruction."

- Marilyn Monroe—beautiful movie star who defined "mass allure." She was smarter than she acted and swung between romance extremes: from baseball player Joe DiMaggio to aging playwright Arthur Miller. A Gemini believer in white lies: "All little girls should be told they're pretty, even if they aren't."

- Christo—the artist famous for wrapping things like small islands and large buildings in mile-long bolts of fabric or plastic. A real stirrer who refers to his works as "gentle disturbances" of the public's thought patterns. He once created an "Iron Curtain" of oil barrels in the middle of Paris.

- Confucius—wise-cracking Chinese philosopher and teacher who spent his life traveling so as to keep ahead of the annoyed bureaucrats, politicians, and nobles that he had riled with his wit. His influence lives on in his Gemini anthems: "Goody-goodies are the thieves of virtue."

"Any reaction will do so long as it is an over-reaction."

Kylie Minogue (1968-), Australian pop diva and actress

Gemini in vogue

"Do you really call that a coat?"

Beau Brummell (1778-1840), British dandy, wit, and key influencer of men's fashion in Regency England. He was known as Buck Brummell at school.

Gemini chic is sophisticated but cute and youthful. Okay, so maybe sometimes it's a little bit too youthful. Along with Leo, Gemini is the sign most bonded to their inner adolescent and can sometimes cling too long to the style of yesteryear. Menopause and mini-skirts are not problems for Gemini in denial mode.

Fidgety, Geminis like things they can fiddle with in place of chewing their fingernails to the quick. Gemini men are often watch guys, specializing in retro rarities or timepieces capable of calculating the wind speed on Mercury. The women favor dangly earrings and gimmicky jewelry. Unafraid of noise and color, Geminis like it if they can shine, rattle, and jingle as they move through the world.

Fashion and fad-loving, as well as being way ahead of the crowd, these "key influencers" don't care if they are temporarily the object of ridicule from more staid characters. Cheap chic is also a Gemini speciality. They tend toward a knack of making anything look cool. Note how their appeal is worldly, urbane, and "with it". What some may lack in classic good looks is easily made up for in naughty verve, energy, and wit.

Gemini chic is symbolized through Josephine Baker, the performer whose barely-there dresses, no-holds-barred dance routines, and exotic beauty caused a sensation in the U.S. and France. Known as Black Venus, she received at least 1500 marriage proposals and adopted 12 children deliberately of all different skin colors, so as to form a "human rainbow." Awarded a medal for her work for the French Resistance movement during World War II, she adorned herself with beautiful clothes, jewelry, and wild-animal pets. Her most famous outfit is *très* Gemini: 16 bananas strung into a skirt.

GORGEOUS GEMINIS Naomi Campbell, Joan Collins, Johnny Depp, Melissa Etheridge, Rupert Everett, Joseph Fiennes, Michael J. Fox, Lauryn Hill, Elizabeth Hurley, Angelina Jolie, Nicole Kidman, Anna Kournikova, Marilyn Monroe, Liam Neeson, Stevie Nicks, Michelle Phillips, Natalie Portman, Priscilla Presley, Prince, Jane Russell, Brooke Shields, Leelee Sobieski, Mark Wahlberg, Venus Williams

"The secret to the fountain of youth is to think youthful thoughts."

Josephine Baker (1906-1975), Afro-American dancer who performed risqué routines

mostly in Paris in the 20s and 30s

Brilliant career

"Claim your own at every hazard."

Walt Whitman (1906-1975), perennially popular American poet

Geminis don't believe in the propaganda of *Aesop's Fables*. They know that the hare always beats the tortoise. They're full of brilliant but hare-brained ideas, information that they seem to absorb practically by osmosis, and stuff that they can speed-read.

Sometimes just being a Gemini can be a career-limiting maneuver; the power of glib is not always as appreciated as Gemini would like and so many jobs attempt to slow down the fast flow of Gemini wit. Even at school, Geminis were the ones bouncing up to exams, confident that their quick perusal of the study notes would suffice. They get the giggles with anything resembling an authority figure or sit in meetings with one foot throbbing like a locust. Geminis don't like getting sucked into co-signing someone else's crap.

Classic business assessment tools such as Key Performance Indicators don't work too well on our Gemini. The only KPI you can apply to one of this lot is whether they're still in the building or not. A Gemini worker won't bother with all the usual rubbish of trying to improve or negotiate better job conditions. They'll start using the office as a fantastic base to maximize their potential: a spot of free-agenting, liberal use of cab charges, or mass mail-outs. Then they'll sleep late one gorgeous morning, wake up feeling liberated, and get someone to ring in with a figment of untruth. Though gifted and creative, Gemini is not necessarily an entrepreneurial sign. They like some other entity to take on the "back office" responsibilities. They excel in acting, sales, marketing, journalism, PR, advertising, and any gig requiring communication skills. A field where competence at lying is an advantage would clearly be ideal.

Geminis don't mind being establishment whores—they just don't want to be low-rent ones. Their concern is more buying in than selling out. They become super-successful once they learn to follow through on the brilliant ideas and to fake some stability of personality.

"Only the wisest and the stupidest never change."

Confucius (551-479 BC), Chinese philosopher and teacher of the principles of conduct

Fiscal reality

"Don't knock over the honey pot if you want honey."

Norman Vincent Peale (1898-1993), U.S. author of *The Power of Positive Thinking*

Price on application? Geminis will take it. Gemini folk do not like to put limits upon themselves. Because they are such accomplished bullshit artistes, a Gemini without money is not necessarily broke. Instead, they may be rejecting capitalist values, embracing a buy-nothing policy, or simply becoming part of the voluntary simplicity movement.

Their idea of money management can be to promise anyone anything and then get out of it later. Gemini can wake up in an absolute fiscal mess, formulate a fresh plan, and be shouting magnums of Champagne by dusk. It may or may not be in another city they've just flown to but it will certainly be a deductible business expense.

Natural-born cheaters, Geminis can be inclined to cut corners. But, ideally, they learn to access their inner straight when it comes to money, as the Gemini desire for freedom and choice can really only be quenched with full on cash flow.

A creature of impulse, they dislike having to delay gratification. If they do, maybe they'll forget what it is they thought they wanted.

Deeply non-snobby, Geminis have no interest in so-called status symbols. They like objects that facilitate their preferred feeling of being carried along in the river of life, with everything a learning experience.

Security is not a high priority for these characters. Let other signs go paranoid about insurance cover or about getting proper advice before investing in mail-order schemes; the Gem is most comfortable when money is in play and there's a chance of winning. Even when Geminis mature and stop chasing every pyramid opportunity, they are still interested in talking about who is making money and how. They want the facts, not the moral judgment. The one thing about Geminis is that they always live within their income, even if they have to go into debt to do so.

"Style is when they're running you out of town and you make it look like a parade."

William Battie (1704-1776), U.S. author of one of the first books on psychiatry

Chez Gemini

"When nothing is sure, everything is possible."

Margaret Drabble (1939-), multi-award winning British novelist

A Gemini abode can resemble the *Mary Celeste*, the mystery ship that was found adrift without any crew in 1872. Where did the crew go? Out to buy yet more gadgets? There's ample evidence of fads taken up, then ruthlessly abandoned—$500 worth of organic Indian cooking ingredients, stacks of DIY Pilates videos, a one-tenth-written bodice-ripper novel. Nobody has a lower boredom threshold than Gemini, and their base camp reflects this.

As the multitasking sign of the zodiac, Gemini's tastes tend toward ergonomic chairs for posture enhancement while they relax; mind machines to stimulate Gemini's brainwaves; and MP3 players so they can download a rant from a favorite author, then listen to it while applying an emergency face mask and surfing cable television. And what would be the Twins' fantasy home improvement? Why, a fridge with double glass doors, of course, so they wouldn't have to waste time with door-opening to see what's inside. Geminis like to be in the know, so don't be surprised to find a rare television news service from outer Mongolia blaring from the huge German TV screen that dominates the living area—that would explain the enormous satellite dish on the garage.

Time is never quite on Gemini's side, so they appreciate state-of-the-art clocks with multiple time zones and alien ray-gun alarm tones. Aesthetically, they're partial to a light, spindly, hi-tech style of furniture and they're also capable of buying it sight unseen—ordering it over their satellite phone, of course.

"If you have to be in a soap opera, try not to get the worst role."

Boy George (1961-), louche, flamboyant British pop icon, and 80s gaylord

A Gemini in love

"But I am always true to you, darling, in my fashion. Yes, I'm always true to you, darling, in my way."

Cole Porter (1891-1964), one of America's greatest tunesmiths who penned such classics as *Anything Goes, I Get a Kick out of You,* and *Begin the Beguine*

Maddening and elusive, Geminis are much in demand among those who relish a challenge. Shrieking on about space they oscillate between ratty and clingy. They phone ex-lovers on some pretext or their osteopath who has a crush on them, whispering breathily into the phone like Marilyn Monroe late to the set again.

They want someone who lets them be themselves—at last, although they have no idea who that self is, how to recognize it, or whether they'd like it. Secretly, they prefer lots of hot chit-chat without the pressure to even put out, let alone commit. They can enjoy intrigue, secret crushes, and/or an impossible love affair—so impossible that it never happens.

Although not the steadiest lovers in the world, Geminis don't carry baggage about whether or not someone is loyal to them. They make a cynical Gemini gesture to placate the needy control freak and move on.

Because Geminis are so good at masking what they think of as their "real emotions" with smart quips, they assume everyone else is more or less the same. This is why Geminis often go out and purchase guides to stuff such as body language. They think there must be some tricky technique that they should swot up on.

A Gemini can look at an emotionally tormented partner with an expression that suggests they're watching a really bad television show but are too tired to get up and go to bed.

Once a Gemini has decided that a certain person bores them they are casually ruthless. People often think they are being deliberately cruel and creepy but they simply can't help it. Some of them have spectacularly bad methods of breaking up: via fax, email, or by getting their PA to phone through the news.

The world is full of half-bitter, half-still-besotted former lovers of Gemini; the irony is that Gemini, sign of the Twins, so flourishes once they've found their soul mate.

"There are two types of people; drains and heaters. Some people drain you and some warm you up. If people become too much of a drain, I say that's it—time to say goodbye."

Joan Collins (1933-), British actress, best-selling author, and producer who became famous for her role as Alexis Carrington in the hit TV series *Dynasty*

Gemini-Aries
Few lovers relish Gemini genius, wit, and speed as much as Aries. Each magnifies the other's core traits, making for fun in both business and pleasure. Aries and Gemini each get off on life. Neither is bored. Okay, so Gemini is more sensually inventive than the hardcore and energetic but unimaginative Ramzilla. Aries won't take kindly to Gemini suggesting any "funny stuff." And Gemini's idea of a decent love affair is when Gemini gets to zoom off for the weekend, with maybe a little bit of flirtation, some kinky innuendo or maybe not, and return to a rapt reception from Ramzilla. Well, ha ha. Aries likes their partner to abide by the laws of the Aries-archy and that does not include much of a need for space. Who on earth would want to be away from the shining light that is Ramzilla? Gemini might after a few blasting rants from Ramzilla. A teaser at heart, Gemini may not be willing to put in the full-on ego-maintenance work that Aries requires. Once these issues are resolved, Aries and Gemini bond in bliss for ever.

Hot duos: Annette Bening & Warren Beatty, Douglas Fairbanks Sr. & Mary Pickford, Paulette Goddard & Charlie Chaplin, Brooke Shields & Chris Henchy

Gemini-Taurus
What wisdom for a Gemini hoping to fend off a Taurus? Just be yourself, dear. Gemini perversity sends Taurus into a towering spin—Gemini shrugs. Taurus says, "values" and Gemini says, "pass the remote." There is a screwball-comedy aspect to this romance of being equal but different. Taurus turns mega-straight to protect their Qi energy from Gemini flippancy. Gemini provokes Taurus. Gemini flirts insanely. Taurus sanely sets up a loving and stable relationship. However, these two can come together: Taureans let themselves be mentally stimulated while Gemini finds peace in the gentle pastures of the Bull. Gemini feels earthed and able to better appreciate life's slower, more sensual pleasures. Each provides something the other lacks and each can be most intrigued by the other. Ground rules should probably be established early. For example, Gemini should not move any Taurean

possessions around the place. Taurus should not begrudge our Gemini the mental, emotional, and physical space that they seem to need continually.

Hot duos: Steffi Graf & Andre Agassi, Prince Philip & Queen Elizabeth II, Anna Kournikova & Enrique Iglesias, Liam Neeson & Natasha Richardson, Juliette Lewis & Steve Berra

Gemini-Gemini A Gemini in love is a Gemini in denial. Each

Gemini is so accustomed to avoiding anything resembling a real feeling that it is a miracle if this relationship even launches. Each would rather skid around the fact, pretending that nothing is going on. "Just good friends" is Gemini vs. Gemini, refusing to honor the romance. But once bonded, this is a liaison of lust, stimulation, and nonfstop amusement. Only another Gemini can truly understand a Gemini. Neither is bored by the other although acquaintances could become jangled by the full-on Gemini vibe created by these two in motion. Each can hurt the other via the Gemini penchant for game-playing, flirting, and varying space requirements. Neither is going to show a shred of emotion at the other's carry-on. A Gem-Gem combo at a loose end could be disastrous—one Mercury child is trouble enough, but a duo of them sounds like an opportunity for hurtful mind games to erupt. A Gemini-Gemini team in exciting creative collaboration is often the best form of this duo. Ditto a scenario in which each agrees on how to maintain personal freedom and close loving.

Hot duos: Dashiell Hammett & Lillian Hellman, Donald & Daisy Duck, The Notorious BIG & Faith Evans, Waylon Jennings & Jessie Colter, Barbara Bush & George Bush Sr., Christo & Jeanne-Claude

Gemini-Cancer Crab People value tradition, comfort, and

security. Gemini values change, excitement, and romantic challenge.

Gemini likes life in hyper-flux. Gemini doesn't mind the idea of feelings but sees no need to spell everything out or make huge emotional statements. Gemini is detached. Crab is attached. If there is a chance of lightening up a turgid scenario via the funny comment, Gemini makes it. If Crab can escalate an emotional situation, Crab will. The crabby penchant for emotive scenes bores Gemini senseless, and once bored, Gemini is gone, no matter what kind of guilting the other party turns on. Crab thinks Gemini is out of touch with emotion. This duo works best when one party has a personal planet in the other's sign so the Gemini has, for instance, Venus in Cancer, giving them an "in" to the other. And Crab has Mercury in Gemini, tuning them into the Gemini reality and need for excitement. This accomplished, each is a constant light in the life of the other.

Hot duos: Tony Curtis & Janet Leigh, Wallis Simpson & the Duke of Windsor, Michael J. Fox & Tracy Pollan, Jessica Tandy & Hume Cronyn

Gemini-Leo

There are four people in this relationship: two Geminis because their astro symbol is the Twins, the Leo, and the Leo's ego. Gemini must learn to get along with the Leo ego as well, and the only thing it respects is nonstop drooling, flattery, and respect. Awkward? You bet, but it can also be amazingly convenient. During a spat with Leo, Gemini need only appeal to the ego via a compliment about Leo's hair looking beautiful tonight, and the ego instructs the Leo to shut up and make love. It's pretty cool. Leo loves Gemini trendiness (who are we kidding? Leo will copy Gemini trendiness) and social genius. Gemini and the Lion make a good couple. Each finds endless amusement in the other's presence, particularly if Gemini gives Leo the worship they crave and Leo learns to let Gemini have their precious space. The Leonine ego may not like it when Gemini glides out without Leo on some slender pretext but it is the only way to make this sizzling scenario pan out.

Hot duos: John F. & Jacqueline Kennedy, King George VI & the Queen Mother, Irving Thalberg & Norma Shearer, Emmanuelle Seigner & Roman Polanski

Gemini-Virgo
Gemini wonders if Virgo has been sent to them as a karmic trial. Virgo suspects something similar. Virgo feels guilty—Gemini doesn't give. Virgo nags and Gemini ramps up the offensive behavior in question. The intellectual compatibility is immense—each adores the other's rapid and analytical mind. Each is comfortable with the other's level of neurosis. Virgo loves helping Gemini through those 3 a.m. flip-out sessions but won't be so thrilled when Gemini refuses to get up so they can wash the sheets post-sex. Each is kinky, fluid, and flexible. Worldliness and low-boredom thresholds can keep them together in romantic bliss. Virgo learns to be more spontaneous like a Gemini. Gemini gets off on the Virgoan obsession with developing a workable system for living. Each, thankfully, loves a debate without too much bitching up of the feeling factor. But if the dynamic goes off the rails, and these two start showering one another with their worst excesses, they risk triggering Gemini's desire to provoke and Virgo's instinct to call the police. Virgo will rarely embarrass the Gemini, in public at least. Virgo understands that corrective nagging is unlikely to win the Gemini heart, and so love blossoms.

Hot duos: Queen Victoria & Prince Albert, Sarah O'Hare & Lachlan Murdoch, Liz Hurley & Hugh Grant, Lady Sheila & Sir Richard Attenborough, Courteney Cox & David Arquette

Gemini-Libra
This is traditionally one of the happiest couples of the zodiac. Sensing a challenge, Libra falls instantly in love with Gemini's speedy wit and glacial heart. Libra and Gemini are mentally and physically so compatible that, as long as everything else in the relationship is vaguely functional, one another's company is sufficient.

Each stimulates the other's genius and inspires all those around them. If issues do arise they have to do with jealousy. Gemini is used to being the most interesting person in any room and could wind up resenting the seemingly effortless Libran charisma. Heaven help the relationship should Gemini start trying to undermine it by pointing out that behind every Libran butterfly is a messy and chaotic chrysalis. Libra will retaliate by being even more charming and accomplished, making Gemini freak out. Each must accept that this is a liaison of official heartbreakers, of two flirtatious people. Libra simply worships Gemini genius, good looks, and even the mysterious Gemini soul.

Hot duos: Paul & Linda McCartney, Marilyn Monroe & Arthur Miller, Ethel & P. G. Wodehouse

Gemini-Scorpio
Once established, these guys become super-bonded. Sex and work bring them together. Addicted to one another in the sack, they pull together outside of it to score their strange version of the good life. Gemini glib charm and Mercurial mind are complemented by Scorpio's deeper awareness of power-gaming. Gemini absolutely adores Scorpio's strength, willpower, and ability to inspire fear in others. Scorpio loves Gemini's laconic cool, good looks, and knack of lightening up the darker Scorpio moods. Both are kind of self-reliant. Gemini is more spontaneous than Scorp, but once Gemini charms Scorpio into a scheme, Scorp stays loyal and supportive. This is an alluring couple who, deep down, don't really need anyone else. Gemini could tire of Scorp possessiveness and rebel, making Scorpio withdraw into glacial disapproval. Scorp could become annoyed with a few too many quasi-legit money schemes and constant faxes from the Gemini's accountant. Scorp thinks there are some things you stay straight about. But once the "rules" are established, this relationship can go on for ages. What really binds these two together? Neither of them gives a genuine damn about what anyone else thinks.

Hot duos: Sir Laurence Olivier & Vivien Leigh, Lady Diana & Sir Oswald Mosley, Ann Druyan & Carl Sagan, Prince Rainier & Grace Kelly (Princess Grace)

Gemini-Sagittarius

Gemini and Sagittarius are both bright, attractive, in-demand sort of people. They share an adventurous spirit and a joie de vivre. The difference? Sagg is mentally more boring than Gemini. Each thinks a lot. But Sagg can simply rant on and on about a particular issue. They don't even mind if no-one is listening to them. Geminis, on the other hand, will always "sing for their supper." Happily, Gemini has enough anecdotes and wit for the pair of them. Saggo dirges on about how they would run the world. Gemini inserts the humor. In private life, these two are gloriously compatible, feeling a more or less constant and almost magnetic attraction. Sagg is one of the few signs capable of giving Gemini the mental (and physical) space they require in a relationship. Sagg doesn't bark, "Where were you?" when Gemini walks in two hours late from the gym. Why? Because Saggo has flown off to some fantastic beach they heard about. Gemini loves Sagg's joy and spontaneity. When not freaked out, Sagg is forever drawn to Gemini charisma.

Hot duos: Marilyn Monroe & Joe DiMaggio, Charles & Ray Eames, Gena Rowlands & John Cassavetes, Margaret Bourke-White & Erskine Caldwell, Paul Bettany & Jennifer Connelly

Gemini-Capricorn

Go-go Gemini meets apparently cold-hearted Capricorn and decides it's a cool challenge. Gemini loves that Capricorn doesn't care if they've been flouncing about town all night, just so long as standards are kept up. Capricorn doesn't care about Gemini amorality. Capricorn loves Gemini's wit and charm. They agree on a laissez-faire policy about certain aspects of intimacy. But Capricorn deplores sloth and slackers. Capricorns admire those who can function within a corporate environment, create correct goal-setting mechanisms, and get their life together. Gemini thinks Capricorn should just get a life. So Gemini is spared clingy, needy emotional scenes but forced to shape up fast, to satisfy the Capricorn needs for security and status. Capricorn likes structure. Gemini likes to question structure, at length, and in a long gossipy dialogue. Capricorn says, "What are you on about?" Gemini sneaks out to find kindred spirits. But no matter—for ambitious Geminis (perhaps with planets in Taurus) who don't mind Capricorn's goose-gander philosophy, this is it.

Hot duos: Sadie Frost & Jude Law, Jean-Paul Sartre & Simone de Beauvoir, Charles Saatchi & Nigella Lawson, Jefferson Hack & Kate Moss, Johnny Depp & Vanessa Paradis, Priscilla & Elvis Presley

Gemini-Aquarius Talking is the motif of this relationship.

These two are seekers, philosophers, and critics. They bond over shared opinions and insights. Gemini is used to having to dull down—Aquarius lifts their game quick smart. Gemini is used to being dismissed as wayward or wicked. Aquarius wonders whether Gemini is not too straight for their tastes. Gemini likes hard-to-get lovers and Aquarius is almost impossible. Each is soon hooked on the other. Gemini—a genuine person of the people—may be irked by the secret Aquarian snobbery. Aquarius is annoyed by the Gemini trait of changing their mind about everything and playing "devil's advocate," just because they can. But bedwork, socializing, brilliant career, and values generally all come together in glorious synergy with these two. Each likes to bait the other. Gemini should know that loyal Aquarius is easily hurt by flirtation, no matter how casual, and despite the official Aquarian approval of "free love." Given trust, Aquarius gives Gemini the necessary space and true liberation of the mind.

Hot duos: Gia Carides & Anthony LaPaglia, Isabella Rossellini & David Lynch, Kim Novak & Prince Aly Khan

Gemini–Pisces

Gemini and Pisces are instantly drawn to each other. The air between them seems to scintillate. Gemini loves that Pisces doesn't give a damn, just like them. Pisces appreciates that Gemini shares a fishy dual nature. Each feels they may have met their match in the madness and brilliance stakes. They know how to give one another a good time in every respect. But Pisces needs nonstop romantic synergy and this relationship has the potential to degenerate into daytime soapie-style psychodrama. Gemini will stalk the room ranting and raving. Pisces will writhe around grizzling about emotional responsibility. Each is capable of lying their head off to protect their respective personal space. Each is charismatic and amorally inclined. The garden of love turns into a tangled web of intrigue. But both are so similar that, particularly given mental bonding and shared interests, this can be a beautiful and enduring partnership. In Gemini-Pisces Utopia, Gemini gives Pisces the reassurance they crave. Pisces stays a tad mysterious, not letting fishy insecurity cloy the Gemini soul.

Hot duos: Violet Trefusis & Vita Sackville-West, Phil Bronstein & Sharon Stone, Laurie Anderson & Lou Reed, Fabrizio Moretti & Drew Barrymore

Are you really a Gemini?

1 Social circumstances require that you tell a white lie to someone whom you admire. You feel...

    (a) Guilty—lying for whatever reason goes against your grain.

    (b) Concerned that you could somehow be found out.

    (c) Fine.

2 On a hot third date, your new interest reveals a dream in which you and this person were blissfully married. You are...

    (a) Touched and thrilled by this sentiment. Maybe it was psychic?

    (b) Excited but cautious. You play it safe with love.

    (c) Out of there. In a hurry to get home and have your phone numbers changed. What an idiot.

3 The project you're in charge of at work has gone way over budget and your boss is looking for someone to blame. You feel...

    (a) Completely freaked; this is officially all your responsibility.

    (b) Sanguine. These things happen and you have been diligent.

    (c) Whatever—like you care about someone else's budget.

4 People who need people...

    (a) Are the luckiest people in the world.

    (b) Is a cliché.

    (c) Need help. They probably have a codependency problem.

5 One of your closest friends, a woman who is married, reveals that she has an intense crush on her personal trainer. You feel...

(a) Incredibly sorry for her. She must not be happy at home.

(b) Outraged at such sleazy conduct; why doesn't she change trainers?

(c) That it will make excellent news to take to your party that night.

6 Innocence and/or naïvety tends to...

(a) Attract you. You love the chance to enlighten another.

(b) Make you feel nostalgic for your own early days.

(c) Bore you senseless.

Answers: If you checked mainly (c) answers, then you are an official Gemini—a gorgeous genius and, yes, so sought after and admired. If you checked (a) or (b) answers, you have other astro influences competing with your Gemini Sun.

Cancer

june 22-july 23

Crab People

"If I can't dance then it's not my revolution."

Emma Goldman (1869-1940), Russian-born anarchist who fought for better working conditions in the U.S., Russia, and Europe

Q: How many Cancerians does it take to change a light bulb?
A: One, plus a therapist to help them process the emotions.

Why are Cancerians so crabby? Because Cancer is Latin for crab!

Like the Crab in nature, they are prone to nipping if they feel their security is threatened. Once they've latched onto something they never let go. Crab People conceal their emotions beneath a tough carapace, only their bedroom eyes reveal the sensitivity within. Fun-loving and cutely capricious, they can make anyone feel cherished and at home.

Crab People are "ruled" by the Moon. Note that the word "lunatic" comes from the Latin word "luna," aka Moon. Though most people are affected by the Full Moon—just ask a fireman or nurse—Crabs are immunized by being moon-ruled and batty most of the time. The moon changes sign every two-and-a-half days but this is nothing compared to the Cancerian hyper-flux of feeling. This person is a mood-swinger extraordinaire.

Each sign has an astro motto that is a summary of the sign's core ethos. The Crab motto is "I feel" and they certainly do. Nobody needs to tell a Cancerian how to emote. They talk about their feelings, not in an artificial therapy style but with sincerity that is secretly the envy of the more glib.

Cancerians can come right out in ordinary conversation and say something along the lines of "I am so bitter." Or even quiver as they simper "Hold me." Cancerian people feel your pain. They feel their pain. They feel all pain. They can still sense the pain from running over a slug when they were five years old. They could take you back and show you the exact spot on the pavement where they crushed the poor creature under their tricycle. They have their own personal woes collection to wallow in when vulnerability strikes.

But in a society where logic has been placed high on a pedestal, we all need Cancerians. They should not allow less sensitive souls to ridicule their superior emotional nature.

Cancerians are a so-called Water sign, along with Pisces and Scorpio. They automatically value feelings over thought, art over science, music over facts, and love over all else. But they are also a "Cardinal" sign, like Aries, Capricorn, and Libra. They start stuff, they're innately entrepreneurial, and into being the boss.

Because so many Crab People wear their psyches on their sleeve, others make the mistake of thinking they're total drips. It is true that when you see a Cancer working themselves into an absolute frenzy over a dead bird in the garden or cracking up over some discrepancy on their credit-card statement, they can seem to lack a certain control.

But it is a dreadful mistake to underestimate our Crab. They're stingy yet deeply compassionate when it counts. A trivial irk can cause a near nervous breakdown—in a crisis, they exude gracious strength and comfort to the needy. They are the ultimate emotional strategists, brilliant in business, and once they have mastered mood management, they are the most together sign of all.

A Crab on form is...

"As we let our own light shine, we unconsciously give other
people permission to do the same."

Nelson Mandela (1918-), South African leader, freedom fighter, visionary, and 1993
Nobel Prize winner for his work toward ending apartheid

EMPATHETIC Cancerians ooze simpatico emotion in the same
way other people perspire. They can relate to anyone: the celebrity
going through a nasty divorce, the junkie who stole the Crab's
stereo. Just confiding to one of these folk is soothing. They are
excellent at assuring one that "everything is going to be all right,"
issuing very profound advice, and putting issues into perspective. It
is as if they can actually absorb other people's foul moods and
transform them into joy for existence.

ARTY Cancer is the sign most likely of all to be a known artist. For
example, Modigliani, Gustav Klimt, Rembrandt, Frida Kahlo, Marc
Chagall, David Hockney. Their artistic nature is never a toss, merely
part of their being. Gifted with the soul of a poet, they are able to
see and transmit the world's beauty, peek into the hearts of us all,
and honor what has been forgotten. All Crab People, no matter
how worldly and pragmatic, should find a way to evoke this
blessed creativity.

SEDUCTIVE Crab People are dangerously alluring and literally
enchanting. Their usual mode of operating is to appear mega-
compliant. Later, when the lover is hooked, they unleash the
madness of their moody side. Eligible suitors stalk the Crab Person,
longing to hear every detail of their latest hair issues, unresolved
adolescent angst, or creative blocks. The sane friends of our Crab
are furious: How can anyone be so seemingly deranged and yet
utterly in demand? The Crab shrugs, busy re-reading a deep and

meaningful Hermann Hesse novel for insight into their fascinatingly complex persona.

NURTURING Kind, sweet, and generous, Crabs are the gift that keeps on giving. At any one time, they tend to be mentoring a variety of folk. They are deeply understanding of the foibles of children, old people, the disadvantaged, and the lovelorn. The Crab's home is often a center of comfort and love, home for the homeless, a haven for the psychically displaced. They give shelter and love and withdraw into their cave with their chosen loved ones.

PSYCHIC Without much fanfare, Cancerians pick up on a lot of signals. Their perceptions are eerily apt and they are especially gifted in the realms of psychometry: picking up vibes from objects and places. They do well to take up home-witchery arts such as feng shui, geomancy (harmony with the environment), or space-clearing. But their spooky powers are just as useful in whatever brilliant career they choose for themselves.

TRADITION-HONORING Cancerians make sure they do events like weddings or Christmas correctly. They will have the biggest tree, the best banquet, the "goodest" goodwill. They are absolute geniuses at maintaining photo albums and keeping up with every single niece and nephew. They make fabulous family historians; so do Capricorns but it's an attempt to find ancestors of status. Geminis don't bother because they can just fib about it. Pisceans look into the family background to find an excuse for their own conduct. Crabs do it because they truly revere their family story.

"To live means to be awake, joyously, drunkenly, serenely, divinely aware."

Henry Miller (1891-1980), American novelist. His highly emotional sexual candor shocked readers but his books nonetheless became literary classics.

A Crab off form is...

"Guilt is never to be doubted."

Franz Kafka (1883-1924), angst-ridden Jewish Czech author who wrote about modern
man's alienation in a hostile and indifferent world

SULKY Okay, so Crab People are really into feelings but, guess what? Sometimes it's just *their* feelings. They invented the Power Sulk, capable of petrifying anyone against the crabby whim of the moment. Huffing out an inky black fog of disappointment, they use their psychic powers to beam a "you screwed up badly" message. Ask what's wrong and they'll say, "nothing," before zooming off to call an ex-lover in secret. They never forgive but will pretend to forget just so they can bring out their hurt as an unexpected shock tactic. They think nobody understands them and, actually, nobody does.

SUBJECTIVE Crab People are capable of boring everyone else to tears with subjective accounts of their feelings. They believe urban myths but get hurt and pouty when someone scoffs. Why should any conversation be interesting or amusing if the Crab is in the mood for a good wallow? They genuinely think that other people are acting cheerful because they lack Cancerian genius enough to figure that the world is going to hell. It's as if because nobody else is dwelling on crap, that they haven't grasped the situation. So the Crab Person feels they should simply go on and on. "Wouldn't it be horrible to drown? No, really, it would be." It has to be all about how the Crab feels they would feel. They move from grizzling about their neighbor who apparently doesn't feed the cat enough into a rant about share-market rip-offs without losing a beat. If, say, the TV breaks down, Aries or Scorpio will be in combat mode. Pisces or Libra would see it as a sign from the universe that they should go and take a bubble bath or drink gin in the garden. Crab People see it as a chance to evoke some ancient angst: "Oh, no! This is bringing up my body image issues!" It was said of novelist George Orwell (*Animal Farm*) that he could not blow his nose without moralizing on conditions in the handkerchief factory.

"Gloom we have always with us, a rank and sturdy weed, but joy requires tending."

Barbara Holland (1925-1988), witty American writer and poet who riveted U.S.

audiences with her readings

OVER-NOSTALGIC This is the only sign who seems to think things were always better in history. Never mind plagues, witch-burnings, or lack of sanitation, weren't the frocks lovely? Didn't they make wonderful furniture in those days? Think French writer Marcel Proust (*Remembrance of Things Past*) yearning over the taste of a cookie from yonks ago. Crabs are perfectly capable of bugging someone over an apparent whim of memory: "Surely you remember?" They can become haunted by a snatch of song and stalk around for weeks trying to make everyone else recognize the thing: "You must remember this, it goes 'dum de dum de dah'. It's at the back of my mind." But a lot of things lurk at the back of Crab's mind and not all of them need daily dredging up for reappraisal.

GUILTING Which Sun sign is the greatest guilter of all? It always comes down to a play-off between Virgo and our Crab. Virgo is definitely better at verbalizing. If you want pithy words to drill straight down into your own guilt complex, just let a Virgo down one day. But the Crab method of guilting is more diffuse. They can just glance at the culprit and leave them in a heap of remorse. They like to guilt the light fantastic, to make it Shame Week at Crab Central. Virgo does it for a hobby but Cancer is the guru of guilt. Cancerians plan blame-storming expeditions. They answer the phone in a voice rich with recrimination. They drunk-dial a former lover not to say "Come around right now" but to make them feel guilty for wrecking Crab's life. They can deliver dinner party "victim impact" statements years after you lost a book they lent you. But their fave technic is to link a mini domestic mishap with their worst emotional pain ever. Then they bring it up again later in bed. They also favor the "Why do you always...?" approach.

"We flatter those we scarcely know
We please the fleeting guest.
And deal many a thoughtless blow
To those who love us best."

Ella Wheeler Wilcox (1850-1919),

prolific American writer of 40 volumes of verse

Motivating and manipulating a Crab

"Embrace decision."

Julius Caesar (100-44 BC), Roman emperor—"the noblest Roman of them all"

1 Don't trust that smirk; this lot specializes in radiating dulcet compliancy, then going ahead and doing whatever they like anyway.

2 Try not to abuse their capacity to empathize. Crabs need to reset boundaries by, for example, telling a whiny friend to see a shrink.

3 Accept that grumbling is vital for the health of the Crab psyche. Keeping quiet about injustice, even if it is just their being on hold for too long waiting to speak to their supposed "personal banker," sends them crazy.

4 Don't bother trying to make them update their tastes. If the Crab gets off on listening to ye olde golden hits, let them.

5 Your telling them to "get a grip" won't help. Showering them with inspirational ancient quotes will, such as this old Chinese saying "It's better to light a candle than to curse the darkness."

6 Never throw anything of theirs out—even a chip wrapper or bus ticket—without working through the issue with the Crab first.

7 Understand that while the Crab Person is not a total bullshit artiste such as Gemini or Pisces, they are prone to embellishment. Their excuse? That they are speaking an emotional truth. The mere fact that something actually didn't happen doesn't mean it wasn't real for the Crab.

8 Telling them to get out more will only turn them into a major agoraphobe, huddling in the Crab home, and freaking out about the savage streets.

9 Never bag out anyone in the Crab clan, even if they are estranged from the said person, and even if it's just you mentioning that the family dog looks a bit mangy.

"Every exit is an entry somewhere else."

Tom Stoppard (1937-), English playwright (*Jumpers*) who won an Oscar for Best Screenplay for the film *Shakespeare in Love*

Crabby role models

"It is only with the heart that one can see rightly; what is essential is invisible to the eye."

Antoine de Saint-Exupéry (1900-1944), French writer. His most famous work, *The Little Prince*, has been translated into 50 different languages.

- Princess Diana—iconic royal who could have lived a shallow life of privilege if she wasn't so empathetic. Whether hugging AIDS patients, confessing to being hurt by a cad, or campaigning against land mines, her big, loving eyes became a weapon for good: "I adored him," she confessed to millions of live TV viewers worldwide, referring to her former lover James Hewitt.

- Pamela Anderson—buxom, blonde beach bunny from the TV series *Baywatch* with a penchant for heavy rockers. The Canadian actress has developed from playmate to mother to a feminist-magazine columnist. She is also an animal-rights activist. "The worst thing you can do is tell me *not* to do something."

- Dalai Lama—smiling leader of the Tibetan Buddhists and advocate for an independent Tibet. The Nobel Peace Prize winner, who was born into a peasant family, was identified as a spiritual leader as a two-year-old and became the 14th Dalai Lama at age five. He projects the classic Crab good-heartedness: "Love and compassion are necessities, not luxuries."

- Buckminster Fuller—brilliant American architect and engineer with no formal training. He invented many things, including the geodesic dome, and was awarded 25 U.S. patents. He had a strong streak of idealism and concern for the world: "Either war is obsolete or men are."

- Jean-Jacques Rousseau—paranoid show-off and philosopher. His early attempts at writing operettas and art criticism gave way eventually to earnest pamphlets such as *The Social Contract*, in which he declared all people to be equal—it's still a mainstay idea of left-wing politics.

- Meryl Streep—gorgeous leading lady of Hollywood who still maintains theater cred. Her roles in *Sophie's Choice*, *The French Lieutenant's Woman*, and *Out of Africa* saw her blend strength and vulnerability in the one character. Like most Crabs, her "eye-acting" is devastating.

"When the going gets weird the weird turn pro."

Hunter S. Thompson (1937-), author of *Fear and Loathing in Las Vegas*

Chic Crab

"My hair has always been weird colors—I change it a lot. A color only works if I feel the color."

Vitamin C (1972-), high-energy American pop star

Crab People tend to express the most extreme traits of their gender. Crab guys are the cutest: hunky but sensitive-looking with those great big goggle-like eyes. Female Crabs often evoke glamour-puss icons of the past—all liquid eyes, power pout, and heaving womanly bosom.

Not into power-dressing, they favor comfort clothes and even monied Crabs aim for the stealth-wealth look. They don't judge others by their garb and they don't tend to expect such scrutiny in return. Adoring vintage clothes if they can get away with it, they like to create a mystique. They have the knack of disappearing into some ratty charity shop and emerging with a never-worn antique ball gown. Cancerians form very emotional attachments to clothing, can even give items names, and find it nigh impossible to throw out anything of sentimental value. To them, it's all of sentimental value.

As a result, they can develop fashion fetishes. "I didn't have 3000 pairs of shoes," explained spendthrift former First Lady of the Philippines, Imelda Marcos. "I had only 1060 pairs."

They can hoard clothes for years under the delusion that it will be just fine for when the fashion comes back again.

Crabs are more affected than others by revivals. They see a pink fishnet singlet top with a Madonna-circa-1983 crucifix and head off on a yearning, snivelling nostalgia trip.

They sometimes disappear into their closet to croon over clothes and the memories they hold. They genuinely love it when someone bequeaths them an item of note such as a wedding dress.

COME-HITHER CRABS Isabelle Adjani, Pamela Anderson, Selma Blair, John Cusack, Vin Diesel, Corey Feldman, Travis Fimmell, Jerry Hall, Tom Hanks, Josh Hartnett, Anjelica Huston, Cheryl Ladd, Cyndi Lauper, Juliette Lewis, Gina Lollobrigida, Courtney Love, Tobey Maguire, George Michael, Chris O'Donnell, Sylvester Stallone, Liv Tyler, Meryl Streep, Prince William

"Fashion is dead."
Giorgio Armani (1934-), fashion designer renowned for minimalist, understated, and "deconstructed" look. He created the influential image of 80s hit television series *Miami Vice*.

Brilliant career

"Patience is bitter but its fruit sweet."

Jean-Jacques Rousseau (1712-1778), 18th century French philosopher and writer. His

most famous work is the essay *The Social Contract.*

John and Nelson Rockefeller, John Astor, Conrad Hilton, Estée Lauder, E. I. DuPont, Stavros Niarchos, and the Sultan of Brunei...So many official (and rich) moguls are Crabs, how can this be?

Yes, Crab People are capable of citing ennui as their reason for not turning up to work one day. But this is often our Crab before they've got it together. Searching for an environment that suits, they float around in agony before finding their niche. Beneath those goobly eyes and ability to empathize lurks the business shark. Once engaged, they are motivated to swim toward the most profitable prey in business, career, and investment.

Comfortable with ambiguity, Crab People can be successful in the arts, law, business, and politics. They can easily sniff out the truth, the slightest whiff of instability, and the quickest way up.

They use their other-worldly air to best advantage, happily letting themselves be underestimated if it scores them the desired outcome. Their security fetish comes in handy when hustling up the bucks, their intuition inspires them to win any form of negotiation. They're clever, canny, and entrepreneurial too.

Without realizing it, Crabs can create a "family" atmosphere in the workplace. This is fantastic for when the Crab is mentoring or sucking up to a boss, not so good when the dynamic turns toxic.

"If I create from the heart, nearly everything works. If from the head, almost nothing."

Marc Chagall (1887-1985), Russian-born French painter and stained-glass artist whose

works are distinguished by their surreal inventiveness

Fiscal reality

"My mother gave me a hundred bucks to take drama instead of home economics in seventh grade."

Tobey Maguire (1975-), liquid-eyed, sentimental-vibing Hollywood heart-throb

Although they like saving for the security it offers and can make sage-like investment decisions, Crab People are too sensual to amass wealth via total stinginess. But they are canny. They're not just canny in the coupon-clipping sense although some certainly are. They're canny in that they can go to a garage sale and walk away with actor Richard Burton's original etchings or a pristine Art Deco tea set from the bottom of an old suitcase.

Like cousin Taurus, the Crab likes things but more for sentimental value than their actual worth. They love to hoard: heirlooms, tickets to a concert they saw in 1994, string, whatever. She-Crabs are worse in this respect. Do they really think someone they know is going to want to start a lipstick museum?

Trying to get a Crab to throw anything out is very difficult. They think everything comes in handy some day and they are often right. Their version of a "cull" is to get rid of a rotten celery stick, sadly because they intended it to "die" gladly as part of some salad scheme. They mourn the wasted chance.

Stressed-out Crabs can sometimes "act out" in an orgy of financial insecurity and paranoia, avenging slights—imagined or not—in a toxic spending binge where the credit card and retail credibility get stretched in equal measure.

"Distrust any enterprise that requires new clothes."

Henry Thoreau (1817-1862), French essayist, humorist, and social commentator

Chez Crab

"Any artist should be grateful for a naïve grace which puts him beyond the need to reason elaborately."

Saul Bellow (1915-), U.S. novelist. He won the Nobel and Pulitzer Prizes in 1976.

Cancerians are blessed with a natural nesting instinct. By some mysterious alchemy, they can turn even the lowliest dive into a cozy haven. The Crab's home is a nurturing sanctuary, a stress-free zone without the performance anxiety of the outside world.

In winter, a clothes dryer fluffs up the dressing-gown while a crockpot bubbles away with immune-system-enhancing onion soup. Summer sees the hammock hanging enticingly over the veranda. To say that Cancerians are nostalgic is to understate their deep reverence for the past. Shocking hoarders, they're unable to let go of anything with emotional significance. Memorabilia is their main decorative motif like chintzy, Neo-Victoriana antique themes. Yet the classic Crab pulls it all together. Visitors leave Chez Crab determined to make their own abode reflect heart, family, and love so eloquently. No other Sun sign can turn a jumble of old sports trophies, family photos, and precious antique lace into a spiritually sustaining yet stylish statement.

"I'm not a Stanislavski kind of actor. I just want to communicate with people on the street."

Tom Cruise (1962-), Hollywood superstar—*The Last Samurai*

"All good fortune is a gift from the Gods and you don't win the favor of the ancient gods by being good but being bold."

Anita Brookner (1928-), British novelist specializing in ultra-emotional subjects

A Crab in love

"One shouldn't force sex to do the work of love or love to do the work of sex..."

Mary McCarthy (1912-1989), American theater critic and novelist, whose tools of trade were wit and satire. Her best-known novel is *The Group*.

Once they learn not to bring up childhood, parenting, or fear of poverty issues before the third date—or after that third Margarita—Crab People think they will do just fine at relationships.

They do find it very tricky to separate mind from body. Often they can't stand to be touched unless they feel loved and valued...sex opens their third eye and they need someone willing to sit and listen to their crabby spiel.

Even when they are simply indulging lusty appetites they attempt to justify the scenario by pretending that they are in deep love. This can obviously be troublesome.

These are deeply romantic creatures. The Duke of Windsor—briefly King Edward VIII—abdicated his throne for the love of Wallis Simpson, an American divorcée (and Gemini!) whom he could not have married as a king.

Plenty of them are so sentimental that they wind up in "I gave my life savings to a pole dancer" type of tabloid stories. The women excel at convincing themselves that the strong silent hunk they're unrequitedly in love with resembles a bodice-ripper hero more than the inarticulate control freak he is in real life. Worst-case scenario: Crabs get themselves into a hideous relationship because their spouse needs them.

She-Crabs also have an "I'm everywoman" thing going on. He-Crabs like to feel that they're not like the others. He demonstrates this through a willingness to perform decades of oral sex or a nonstop analysis of your former lover's foibles...whatever it takes. They like to feel that they can really relate to women. Once they meet their soul mate, Crab People are ever-doting, forever fascinating partners, and are highly in demand among unhappily married friends.

"Happiness is as a butterfly which, when pursued, is always beyond our grasp but which, if you sit down quietly, may alight upon you."

Nathaniel Hawthorne (1804-1864), American writer, most renowned for his novel *The Scarlet Letter*—a sensational exposé of a Puritan society and its struggle with sin, guilt, and pride

Cancer-Aries

Crab is over-sensitive. Ramzilla is under-sensitive. But neither side cares...at first. This coupling often starts with a "racing off at the party" dynamic. Nobody can believe the overt longing and groping that these two perform. The sensual bond is present and correct. The *merde* hits the fan as soon as the Crab demands that their emotions be more honored. Aries is the original one-minute navel-gazer. "I'm with you, aren't I? What's your problem?" Crab has many problems with this approach. Ramzilla's ranting about possibly mad career policies infuriates slow and steady Crab. Crab has a holistic view of requirements for the good life such as comfort, understated luxury, and reverence for the past. Aries loathes any form of nostalgia and fantasizes about one perfect Ferrari, even if it does have to be parked outside their post-office box. What to do? Crab agrees to help boost Ramzilla's ego, ideally on an every half-hour basis. Ramzilla really gets that the Crab should be allowed to take most of the lead on anything requiring emotional intelligence.

Hot duos: Eva Mavrakis & Ewan McGregor, Ernest Hemingway & Mary Walsh Hemingway, Feng-Jiao Lin & Jackie Chan, Kermit the Frog & Miss Piggy

Cancer-Taurus
Crab meets Cow and instantly relaxes. Cow falls wildly in love with the Crab at more or less first sight. This romance receives a AAA-ranked compatibility rating. You agree on practically everything and delight in one another's company. Bedwork is bliss, values are so shared, and together these two create a cozy little cashmere comfort world apart. Yes, Taurus can get irritated with Crab grizzling. Taurus is a doer and has no time to waste sitting around whining about whatever they read in the paper that morning. Crab wonders how Taurus can let so many subtle clues to character and people's emotions not even register. Taurus frets at Crab's allure and penchant for attempting to mesmerize people, even though Crab is safely with Taurus. Taurus will definitely resent being made to play straight control freak with Crab as wild-at-heart *enfant terrible*. These are but small obstacles, easily surmountable by this enduring duo. While they quietly succeed in life, each comes to admire, fancy, and dote upon the other.

Hot duos: James Brolin & Barbra Streisand, Marge & Homer Simpson, Liv Tyler & Royston Langdon, Stephen Barlow & Joanna Lumley, Michael Weatherly & Jessica Alba

Cancer-Gemini
Crab wants Gemini to ring in. Gemini throws their phone away. There are people married to Geminis who don't know their mobile number. Crab says "time to talk about us." Gemini says "let's move on." Crab values solidity and an environment in which emotions can be safely processed. Gemini processes emotions about anything in a few seconds. But in other ways, these two are so similar. Both are changeable and easily misperceived by outsiders. Each is eccentric, intuitive, and wildly drawn to the other. Whether it lasts depends on how much Crab can fake being independent and Gemini can get in touch with a few emotions. Gemini needs to honor the Crab by not changing the subject in the middle of a lengthy Crab rant and Crab could get to the point more quickly. Gemini romance needs to be nonstop captivating. Crabs need to feel secure and to learn how to manipulate Gemini without counter-productive

quilting. You two bond well in that you are both very good at figuring out other people. This can be such a special love affair but it flows so much more easily when each party has planets in the other's sign.

Hot duos: Janet Leigh & Tony Curtis, the Duke of Windsor (Edward VIII) and Wallis Simpson, Tracey Pollan & Michael J. Fox, Hume Cronyn & Jessica Tandy

Cancer-Cancer
Lucky these two are both so emotionally articulate and in touch with their feelings for this relationship brings up a lot of them. Crab and Crab are ultra-compatible in that they are obviously similar and have no issues with understanding what each other is on about. Each feels the other's pain and bliss. Each is well equipped to go there and deal with it. Both are nostalgic and into cocooning at Crab's home. However, problems arise if both want to play a parenting role in the relationship, or when one of them starts guilting. Crab One is found gazing wistfully into the mirror, a little tear tracking down that radiant complexion. "No, nothing is wrong," simpers Crab One tremulously. "Nothing at all...really." This kind of carry-on can work wonders with a Scorpio or even the doting Ramzilla. But try it with Crab Two and those invisible guilting rays get beamed right back. This duo is so dynamic: sensually compatible and highly charismatic, caring, and compassionate. Guilting and blame-storming should not be allowed to undermine the attraction in this relationship.

Hot duos: Gerald & Betty Ford, Selma Blair & Jason Schwartzman, Lionel & Diana Trilling

Cancer-Leo
Welcome to the land of moonlight and poses. With Crab People ruled by the Moon and Leos by the Sun, this has the potential to be a glorious coupling. Crab is one of the most romantic signs of all, and Leo loves clichés of romance: flowers, chocolates,

scent, and outlandish declarations of everlasting true love. Crab's nurturing heart is elated by great big gorgeous leonine expressions of adoration. Crabby intuitive perceptions inform and exhilarate the not-always-so-attuned Lion. As Leo is a sign which projects glowingly outward, Leo may not always be aware of nuance. In fact, they may not be especially aware of anything outside of themselves. Crab gets jaded if forced to do all the socio-emotional work of the relationship. If Crab senses a cowardly or inadequate Lion beneath the flamboyant bluster, they're cruel in condemnation. Nobody gets disappointed like a Crab and nobody is more sensitive to criticism than Leo. Crab must be understanding and Lion must live up to neo-Leo potential.

Hot duos: Jerry Hall & Mick Jagger, Josephine de Beauharnais & Napoleon Bonaparte, Kevin Bacon & Kyra Sedgwick

Cancer-Virgo
Falling in love? It's natural. Even the most hyper-strung Virgoan grouch can become an object of crabby desire. In many ways these two are made for one another. They fall deeply in love, creating a whole new version of life in the process. Crab loves that Virgo is so smart and funny. Virgo loves Crab's finely tuned emotions. Each desperately fancies the other and together they score sensual fulfillment beyond belief. Crab must learn to keep their sanity in the face of Virgo anxiety. Virgo should get that Crab needs comfort and serenity, not Virgo ranting on about the state of the baseboards or having a 3 a.m. whine session about some minor workplace psycho-drama. Crab ideally understands that Virgo is (a) analytical rather than emotion-based and (b) likes a good laugh. Each has to join forces to combat mutual hypochondria, guilting, and corrective nagging. Crab and Virgo can be a long-haul success machine, each happy to do what it takes for personal Utopia.

Hot duos: Ringo Starr & Barbara Bach, Imelda & Ferdinand Marcos, Isabelle Adjani & Jean-Michel Jarré, Sally Quinn & Ben Bradlee, Thandie Newton & Oliver Parker

Cancer-Libra
Crab needs to be able to express emotions in a receptive and supportive environment. Nobody must mess with the Libran idea of the world as elegant and harmonious. Feelings can be inconvenient, and heaven forbid that someone leave a tear stain on the Libran's soft furnishings! Too harsh? Actually, this relationship can work wonderfully. The slightly different temperaments offer a few exciting challenges but there are also similarities. Both are bossy, entrepreneurial self-starters who tend to do well in life. Once the power-struggling ceases, each hopefully learns how to respect the other's sensitivity. Librans don't like things to be too emotionally soggy—they prefer interactions to be light and punctuated by bubbles of tinkly laughter, as opposed to the Cancerian habit of turning social occasions into episodes of self-shrinkery. Of course, Librans do have feelings, which Crab ought to at least pretend to take seriously. Crab is kind when Libra dithers. And Libra is more patient when Crab is a little tense and not particularly amusing in a social setting. Crab develops a tougher shell so as not to be affected by Libra's auto-flirt mode. Crab accepts that Libra may be unable to be physically affectionate should Crab not be looking their best. When these two accept their Yin/Yang situation, love can triumph.

Hot duos: Richie Sambora & Heather Locklear, Mel Brooks & Anne Bancroft, Babe & William Paley

Cancer-Scorpio
This is one of the most mysterious and enduring couplings of the zodiac. Both are Water signs—deeply at home with thoughts and emotions others care not to even acknowledge. The astro symbols for Crab and Scorpio are both amphibians, at home on dry land and in murkier ocean realms. Both too are used to being misunderstood by less aware lovers. Something clicks the second Crab meets Scorpio. It's as if they must merely figure out a few practicalities. The temptation toward psycho-sexual game-playing is intense. Personal boundaries seem to dissolve. These two have the potential for such profound love but also the capacity to really wound one another. Ideally,

each drama queen is candid about their feelings. Crab calms Scorpio's more extreme conspiracy fears. Scorp lets Crab peek behind their glacial exterior. Physically they are totally compatible. There is something about Crab and Scorpio that is akin to a pair of beautiful sea monsters, pincers clamped together for ever, swimming in synchronicity.

Hot duos: George W. Bush & Laura Bush, Princess Diana & Prince Charles, Camilla Parker Bowles & Prince Charles, Harrison Ford & Calista Flockhart, Leisha Hailey & kd lang, Phoebe Cates & Kevin Kline, Jessica Simpson & Nick Lachey

Cancer-Sagittarius Sagg's brash style of so-called conversation alienates Crab at first sight. Sagg performs in class-clown mode to try and lift Crab's melancholy tendencies. Crab sighs. Sagg likes space and lots of it. Crabs get off on cozy togetherness. To them, it's not really a proper relationship if their lover is not close at hand—in bed, shopping, accompanying Crab to a traumatic dentist trip. Sagg grandstands for attention, sulking as Crab, silent and sexy, secretly lures in more interest. Both agree on being bon vivants, ready to party at the drop of a hat. Each adores the other's sense of humor, utterly different from their own, yet so compatible. Sagg is smitten by Crab's sensual appeal and complexity. Sagg optimism heals Crab Moon moods and if Sagg is receptive to Crab genius—that is, very physically attracted—then Crab finds in Sagg a rapt pupil. And Crab mopes less. Sagg is more inclined toward expressions of tenderness and happiness reigns.

Hot duos: Tom Hanks & Rita Wilson, Frances McDormand & Joel Coen, Frida Kahlo & Diego Rivera, Meryl Streep & Don Gummer, Michael Williams & Dame Judi Dench, Ingmar Bergman & Liv Ullmann

Cancer-Capricorn
Clinging to Capricorn's ankles as they try to walk out the door doesn't do much good. Candor, beseeching, and wistful guilting fail to melt the Capricorn heart. What Capricorn (secretly) wants is nurturing and Crab is an expert at such behavior. Goat People stride competently around the world, conquering corporations, creating new business systems, doing whatever it is that Capricorns do. But really, deep down, they want someone to ask if they're getting enough vitamin C. And really mean it. In this relationship, each has something the other wants. Once the Capricorn "unbends" enough to enter into a reciprocal relationship, Crab benefits from their poise, experience, and maybe even money. Whole areas of life meld into focus, seen through the goaty gaze. Crab gently leads the Goat into an understanding of their feeling nature. Once Capricorn respects the crabby emotions, their bedwork blossoms. If these two can actually bond, they will keep one another forever young and so in love. They are opposites, experiencing a magnetic attraction.

Hot duos: Charlotte Gainsbourg & Yvan Attal, Prince Egon & Diane von Furstenberg, Pamela Anderson & Kid Rock

Cancer-Aquarius
Crab runs on emotion, Aquarius on logic. Compared to Crab, Aquarius is a different sort of life form. But both share strong psychic powers and a belief in alternative realities. Canny Cancerians would do well to harness the Aquarian trend-spotting powers in their business. Aquarius madly needs Crab's emotional intelligence to balance their over-reliance upon "logic." Crab benefits from Aquarian's objectivity. Aquarius is mega-inspired by the Crab's mere presence. Crab's sensuality helps Aquarius appreciate that sex is more than some kind of a political construct. Aquarius can rebel against their often straitlaced approach to life, especially career and celebrations that Crab feels have to be traditional. Aquarius runs away from anything obligatory or involving "manufactured sentiment." Crab is usually organizing it. Any bash that celebrates someone simply existing becomes a massive, teary

extravaganza when put in the hands of the Cancerian. The photo collections of these mawkish events have their own albums. Crab says "I feel." Aquarius says, "I know," as in "belt up." Shared interests—especially political beliefs or creative projects—bind this duo together, healing all differences.

Hot duos: Jennifer Saunders & Adrian Edmondson, Nancy & Ronald Reagan

Cancer-Pisces Crab and Pisces bond instantly. Crab senses that Pisces could widen their horizons and they're right. Pisces loves that Crab really gets their joke. This can be one of the most compatible and enduring couplings of the zodiac. These two are an official item, sharing core values, humor, and a penchant for staying in bed together whenever possible. Pisces sticks up for Crab's brilliance, easily recognizing what less gifted souls can't. Crab heals Piscean insecurities. Each is sensitive, eccentric, and sought after. Each feels this is true love, that the other may be the only person in the world they can ever truly relax with. But Pisces is a wild child at heart and some of their more dysfunctional conduct can send Crab into a spin. No other pairing but this one can specialize in such extremes of saint/sinner carry-on. Hint: It's only when Crab refuses to cling or starts to guilt that Fish falls straight into line; and it's only when Pisceans stop their mind games and recreational fibbing that the Crab is fully lured into this love affair. When this happens, their bewitching and mutual psychic powers can be used to maximum advantage in both business and pleasure.

Hot duos: Courtney Love & Kurt Cobain, Anna Friel & David Thewlis, Cameron Crowe & Nancy Wilson, George Sand & Frédéric Chopin

Are you really a Cancerian?

1 While cleaning out a cupboard you find a cache of steamy love letters from your ex. You think...

(a) Nothing. They go straight in the bin.

(b) That maybe you could sell them?

(c) That you will have them laminated and put in a special presentation folder as a keepsake.

2 A missionary comes to the door, keen not only to preach but to ask you all sorts of dull questions. You do...

(a) Nothing because you haven't even answered the door to this character.

(b) Whatever you can to flip the person out and ensure they will never darken your doorstep again.

(c) Your best to make them feel comfortable and appreciated even though you don't agree with a single word they say.

3 Away for business you are staying alone in a luxurious but impersonal hotel for several days. To feel more at home, you...

(a) Hang out heaps in the bar with a bunch of cool people you befriend.

(b) Take a bath to relax and center yourself. You value the solo quality time.

(c) Unpack your various souvenirs: the room spray, potpourri, teddy bears, embroidered cushions, photographs of family and pets, core self-help books, and special security blanket.

4 After a big night out, you arrive home and, on a whim, telephone your ex-lover. You say...

(a) I will never, ever love anyone the way I loved you.

(b) Why don't you haul your dysfunctional ass over here for some good loving?

(c) I still can't get over how rude and disgusting you were that time my parents came over for dinner...

5 You are about to leave the house, looking fantastic, for an important work pitch when suddenly it begins to rain hard. You...

(a) See it as a wonderful omen—the drought has broken! Rain equals abundance and nourishment.

(b) Order a taxi to the door: Nothing's going to wreck your hot look and composure today.

(c) Sense the rain's echo of tears forming. This reminds you of the day your pet mouse died, of the rhododendrons at your grandmother's house, of a first—horribly unrequited—love.

6 Your moods are...

(a) Something you are above. You control how you react to situations and you are one of life's winners.

(b) Dependent on your nerves, hormones, and current nutritional status.

(c) Nobody's business. How dare anybody even question your right to feel how you feel when, anyway, it isn't your fault when you have to cope with such an unfeeling, hideous...

Answers: If you checked mainly (c) answers, then you are an official Crab Person—charismatically cute yet in touch with your inner weirdness and that of the cosmos. If you checked (a) or (b) answers, you have other astro influences competing with your Cancerian Sun.

Leo

july 24-august 23

The Lion King/Queen

"How many cares one loses when one decides not to be something but to be someone."

Coco Chanel (1883-1971), founder of the French fashion house Chanel, global style-setter, and creator of several eponymous scents

Q: How many Leos does it take to change a light bulb?
A: One, to hold it while the world revolves around him or her.

The astro symbol for Leo is the Lion. But if you want to understand Leo, it is no use watching nature programs on TV featuring motley-looking lions stalking around, letting gazelles get away, and trying to ignore the embarrassing voice-over. Ditto, lions languishing in the zoo, obviously.

No, you have to think of the Metro-Goldwyn Mayer (MGM) version. Leo the Lion appears roaring at the beginning of movies. Around him are the words "Ars Gratia Artis" (art for the sake of art). That, ladies and gentlemen, is our Leo. The astrological motto is basically a sort of mission statement of a Sun sign's ethos. In the case of Leo, it is "I rule." And they do.

Many modern-day Leos seem to be drawn to perhaps the only place that really resembles an old-fashioned court situation—the film set. Heaps act but they are also likely to become film directors. Think: Stanley Kubrick, Roman Polanski, John Huston, Peter Bogdanovich, Blake Edwards, Peter Weir, Bruce Beresford, Leni Riefenstahl, James Cameron, Alfred Hitchcock, Cecil B. DeMille.

Life to a Leo is an epic production. And it may have a cast of thousands, but Leo is always the producer, director, and star. While Aries considers any criticism to be slander and Sagg will see it as vague background noise, our Leo dismisses negative comment as some form of bad review.

To the theatrical mindset, critics don't count. Only the applause matters. Leos don't walk into a room. They make an entrance. Their bathroom is more akin to a dressing room. They are always on stage.

A troubled personal life? Leo yells out "Cut!" Could someone recast them in a different role, perhaps? Or does the whole script need to be rewritten?

Yes, this lot are drama-queens, luvvies at large, and prima divas. But astrology distinguishes between "cowardly" lions and ultra-glam, follow-their-bliss type Leos. There are neo Leos who light up whatever room they grace with their presence and there are hubris-ridden, tatty old tarty Leos who simply assume that they are the most interesting person in any room.

Like Aries and Sagittarius, Leo is a Fire sign. Leos share many traits with their fellow Fire signs, including radiance, courage, and a flair for the dramatic. But to be fair, the other Fire signs lack the leonine fashion sense and pomposity.

As Leo is also a "Fixed" sign, a Lion is easily as stubborn as a Scorpio, Taurus, or Aquarius. But Leo is the only Sun sign to be actually ruled by the Sun.

That's right. Every other sign gets merely the Moon or a boring old planet. Leos get the Sun—big, hot beyond belief, and with everything else revolving around it. Just like a Leo, really.

"Keep the feet warm, the head cool and the heart free and you may defy the world, the flesh, and the devil..."

Lady Caroline Lamb (1785-1828), British writer of poetry and potboiler romances. Her love life provided much of the material for her works.

Leo on form is...

"I was born with sophistication and sex appeal."

Mae West (1893-1980), blonde bombshell, comic, actress, writer, and producer

GLAMOUROUS Legendary for their passion and dazzle, Leo is glamour-puss galore. Think Jacqueline Kennedy Onassis alighting from a private jet in huge sunglasses, Jennifer Lopez and Ben Affleck escaping from the paparazzi, Prince Harry playing polo, Charlize Theron in full regalia, or Antonio Banderas in his dressing-gown. There is something awesome about Leo's practically tantric appreciation of the power of personal hotness.

BRAVE Leos are dashing, courageous, and blessed with an innate sense of chivalry. Larger than life, they simply will not stoop to conquer. Often their show-bizzy philosophies—the show must go on—provide them with the impetus to overcome whatever crap is thrown in their way and emerge as shining superstars. The idea of giving in is a threat to the Leo ego and thus not even entertained.

ARTY Art, drama, and music are an integral part of Leo's life. For some, it is their life. "Creation is a drug I can't do without" said film director Cecil B. DeMille. His 1923 epic film *The Ten Commandments* went so over budget that studio heads sent him telegrams saying "You have lost your mind. Cease filming and return to Hollywood at once." DeMille continued to build his city of the Pharoahs on a Californian beach. It's very Leo to have an arty vision to fulfill. Think poet Omar Khayyam, cartoonist Gary Larson, painter Andy Warhol, and 1940-50s swimming nymph Esther Williams.

BIG-HEARTED Leos get into living well minus the "revenge" clause. Never small minded, they are big headed, big hearted, and big haired. They are unfailingly sweet to older people and children alike. Three of the English-speaking world's most revered children's authors are Leos: J. K. Rowling, Enid Blyton, and Beatrix Potter. When Leo politicians kiss babies, they actually mean it. But Leos are not particularly likely to go into politics. Too grubby and too many stupid meetings where other people's stupid opinions have to be considered.

INSPIRATIONAL Radiantly optimistic and divinely scented, the Leo presence is itself a morale booster. Leo is always a glorious sight. Large as life itself, melodramatic, and lover of fun, Leo whirls past in "never complain, never explain" mode...a blur of beauty, peace, and luxury.

FAMOUS For people who, like every other sign, officially make up only about eight percent of the population, Leos are highly visible. In fact, they are the sign most likely to be famous. Naturally it was a Leo, Neil Armstrong, who managed to be the first man on the moon. But isn't every Leo step a giant step for the rest of us? Once celebrity is achieved, the Leo is unlikely to grouch about fame's burdens. They always give thanks to their mentors, assistants, and the public who love them.

"Life itself is the proper binge."
Julia Child (1912-2004), American bon vivant who revolutionized the cookbook industry
and pioneered television cooking in the U.S.

Leo off form is...

"Nothing is so easy to fake as the inner vision."

Robertson Davies (1913-1995), Canadian novelist, playwright, and essayist who loved to

write about what he called "the world of wonders"

VAIN In a public toilet, without a single word being exchanged, it is possible to tell if someone is a Leo or not. How? Leos wash and dry their hands without taking their eyes off the mirror for a moment. Then they will step back to assess their full and side views. Often they will leave the room, but then duck quickly back to try and catch their reflection unaware or make one final hair adjustment. The person who invented the public toilet hand-dryers that can be tilted upward to whoosh through the hair was probably a Leo. Leonine vanity defies belief. They will believe even the most absurd compliment. Next to applause, awed gasps at their beauty, hair, or wit, and the sound of their own voice, "My God! You are brilliant!" is the noise Leos most like to hear.

ATTENTION-SEEKING Leos suffer dreadfully from Attention Deficit Disorder. They cannot get enough of it. A Leo is capable of getting jealous of an animal if it appears to be scoring the Lion's share of the spotlight. And although it has been noted that Leos are genuinely kind to children, it still wouldn't do for the child to act cuter than Leo. This is not a sign that takes kindly to being upstaged and they can perform some fairly ugly antics to regain any lost limelight. Loved ones who question the Leo right to rule or insist (gasp) on doing their own thing without supervision always infuriate Leos. Like some megalomaniac film director, they demand mastery over every aspect of a production. Leos should learn not to worry when their partner undermines their precious personal dignity. They should worry when they stop. Whenever a Leo does manage to compromise or apologize for something, they expect the canonization certificate in the mail. They are not able to stop themselves bringing up their great moment of clemency again and again. No matter how humiliating or tedious this is for Leo's partner or friend, Leo insists on relating the incident if it makes them look good.

GRANDIOSE Even when Leos are relaxing, they have a self-conscious view of themselves as relaxing. They may call someone just to pass on the news that they are relaxing in their Leo-designer outfit of the day, on their very trendy deck furniture, drinking a bottle of award-winning sauvignon blanc, and reading a book by the latest Booker Prize winner. Heaven help the celebrity or official personage who has even the briefest encounter with our Leo. Decades later, the scenario will still be retold—perhaps embellished to afford Leo more of a starring role—and the superstar quoted nonstop on whatever subject, just to burnish the ever-demanding leonine ego. Italian fascist leader Benito Mussolini, the man who coined the term "benevolent dictator"—in relation to himself, naturally—said that "the history of saints is mainly the history of insane people" (as opposed to the history of dictators, of course). In true Leo style, Mussolini slapped on stacks of make-up when he made his public appearances and quite fancied himself as a novelist.

EGOMANIACAL An amazing number of Leos are hardcore atheists and, while this may seem logical for many reasons, in Leo's case it is hard not to suspect the obvious: Leo has a problem with the concept of a superior being. Their secret belief is that they are some sort of a higher power and, on a good-hair day, quite divine. According to actress Tippi Hedren, Alfred Hitchcock (an ordinary-looking film director) thought of himself as looking like Hollywood pin-up boy Cary Grant. "That's tough, to think of yourself one way and look another." Not for our Leo it's not. Introduced to an official genius, Leo will happily rave on for hours about how they determined their mega-high IQ via an Internet quiz. Leo meeting a celebrity chef insists on sharing Leo's brilliant omelet recipe. A Leo wouldn't hesitate to pass on hamstring-stretching tips (even if only used every few months or so) to an Olympic champion.

"Ye shall know the truth and the truth shall make ye mad."

Aldous Huxley (1894-1963), brilliant and visionary British author whose most famous
novel is his 1932 satire *Brave New World*

Motivating and manipulating a Leo

"If you want to say it with flowers, a single rose says, 'I'm cheap!'"

Delta Burke (1956-), actress-turned-designer of plus-sized fashion

1 Realize that Leo vanity vies with bon vivant tendencies. They may need to be assured that Champagne is good for their skin before letting loose.

2 Like cousin Aries, Leo thinks the secret of their modesty is that they wear their greatness so lightly. There is simply no point in criticizing them for having an ego.

3 Leos like to be reassured of their brain power. They fear that their visual impact distracts from the depth and profundity of the amazing Leo persona.

4 Allow for an extra hour or so if going out. Even to the supermarket. Some people want down time, others quality time. Leo needs prep time.

5 Leo instincts are to conserve energy while looking fantastic. Don't frazzle the nerves of our Leo—it affects their hair and they really hate that.

6 Accept that Leos are pro-glitz. They need to camp things up a bit. All right, a lot.

7 No compliment or reassurance about the Leo hair can come too often or be over-effusive. More is always more.

8 They can be bought. Don't stingy the Leo. They like even their astral travel to be first class.

9 Let Leo think that they are getting the lion's share of everything because it is the Leo birthright.

"I often quote myself. It adds spice to the conversation."

George Bernard Shaw (1856-1950), Irish playwright and critic. His most famous play, *Pygmalion* (1913), became a musical and a film—*My Fair Lady*.

Leonine role models

"Imagination rules the world."

Napoleon Bonaparte (1769-1821), French soldier who became emperor

- Mae West—witty star of film and stage and sex symbol who became a by-word for sexy innuendo. Her self-written Broadway show, *Sex*, landed her in court and her play and film, *She Done Him Wrong*, was a huge hit. She is a Leo attention-seeker: "It is better to be looked over than overlooked."

- Bill Clinton—42nd president of the United States and lover of fine cigars. From poor beginnings he became a Rhodes scholar and Governor of Arkansas. Known for his trademark hair and purring smile. "You can put wings on a pig, but you don't make it an eagle."

- Amelia Earhart—glamourous American aviatrix and first woman to fly solo across the Atlantic Ocean. While setting records, she grabbed media attention with her photogenic looks and men's clothing. "The most effective way to do it, is to do it."

- Robert Redford—screen legend and star of movies such as *The Sting* and *Butch Cassidy and the Sundance Kid*. A total scene-stealer whose looks and flashing teeth set the standard for a generation of men. An ultra-Leo whose tawny hair resembles a lion's mane.

- J. K. Rowling—blond author who became the highest-earning woman in Britain with her Harry Potter children's books. A single parent, J. K. was living on welfare when she wrote her first book—a classic Leo link between creativity and children.

- Carl Jung—one of the founding fathers of modern psychology who invented the famous stream-of-consciousness concept. Theorized that one couldn't have a relationship with another until one related to oneself. "If you have nothing at all to create then perhaps you create...yourself!"

"Growing old is no more than a bad habit which a busy person has no time to form."

André Maurois (1885-1967), French novelist best known for his romantic-style biographies of literary luminaries Byron, Shelley, Balzac, and Proust

Chic Leo

"I have this sort of strange animal magnetism. It is very hard for me to take my eyes off myself."

Mick Jagger (1943-), lead vocalist of long-performing British rock band, the Rolling Stones. He's also famous for his flamboyant "romantic" entanglements.

Mirror, mirror on the wall, who is the...Hello? Clearly it is Leo who is the most whatever of all. Appearances are not everything for a Leo. They're more important than that. Leos can see into someone's past, present, and future with a quick glance at the way they've put themselves together. At least, they like to think they can.

Leo chic has a lot to do with designer labels. While budget-conscious Leos will buy at a chain store, they'll then go to their tailor to make the necessary alterations. They are brand-conscious as soon as they—or someone else—can afford to be.

They drop brand names the way groupies bandy about the names of drummers they've encountered. A Leo is expert at working any conversation around to their brand leadership. For instance, "Hey Pal, I think I left my Versace jumper in your Saab."

Sun signs

But, as all Leos are aware, nothing really works without the right hair. Other people have nightmares about their teeth falling out (fear of mortality, apparently) but Leos awake in a lather having dreamed all their hair fell out—that is, fear of losing social status. Or is it sexual potency?

Their scariest biblical scenario is not Revelations but Samson and Delilah. In the middle of even a massive argument with a Leo, you can distract them by saying something like "Oh, my God! Your hair is looking so shiny! Have you changed conditioner?"

They are not hypochondriacs, but they do worry about their hair luster and comparative buttock heights.

LOVELY LEOS Ben Affleck, Gillian Anderson, Lucille Ball, Eric Bana, Antonio Banderas, Halle Berry, Clara Bow, Sandra Bullock, Lynda Carter, Ben Chaplin, Robert De Niro, Estelle Getty, Melanie Griffith, Whitney Houston, Jennifer Lopez, Myrna Loy, Madonna, Steve Martin, Sean Penn, Pete Sampras, Christian Slater, Martha Stewart, Dominique Swain, Hilary Swank, Charlize Theron, Mae West

"Hair is your document. What's on top of your head says what's inside your head."

Douglas Coupland (1961-), Canadian writer, sculptor, and award-winning furniture designer who rose to fame with his novel *Generation X* (1991). He coined the terms "mac-jobs" and "accelerated culture".

Brilliant career

"I don't want to live. I want to love first and live incidentally."

Zelda Fitzgerald (1900-1948), glamourous, witty, and daring American novelist and writer. Her best-known work is her 1932 novel *Save Me the Waltz*.

Suitable careers for our Leo include acting, the arts, film directing, photography, music, news-reading, being part of the monarchy, being chairperson, or non-contributing editor of a lifestyle mag. Ideally, it should involve some form of creativity.

Leo is a shining superstar—not some serf—and being surrounded by dotingly gorgeous sycophants doesn't bother them at all. They can have problems reconciling the dancing, glam side of themselves with the limitations of a day job.

Leos love the idea that their pure charisma alone is capable of scoring venture capital. If only people would just relax and trust the brilliant Leo genius. But due diligence never goes out of fashion and Leo grudgingly adjusts to having to prove themselves. The executives in charge of Lucrative Promotions are suddenly barraged with a storm of compliments about how great their hair looks.

Although all Leos are enormously talented, gifted, and acclaimed people, they can run into problems on the day job. They can insist on berating co-workers with just how beneath the Leo the gig is. They are also good at soliciting everyone's opinion, then claiming the outcome to be the result of their own astonishing mind. Even despite any supporting evidence, they radiate a sense that they can out-do everyone. It's interesting that the twin brothers who invented *The Guinness Book Of Records* were Leos. The Leo resumé often resembles that book.

Leos do have leadership potential but, because Leo is also a fixed sign, some of them find it difficult to be flexible in their vocational reality. Leos willing to embrace change often do terrifically well. Madonna, for example, is always reinventing herself into, well, another version of herself.

"The shell must break before the bird can fly."

Alfred Lord Tennyson (1809-1892), British poet who was most famous for his highly

romanticized and sentimental works such as *Morte d' Arthur*

Fiscal reality

"I now had an Italian villa which I didn't need and couldn't afford."

Charles Handy (1932-), Irish social philosopher and management expert

A neo Leo is a beacon of radiant individuality and largesse. These people don't have time to read boring letters from the government. Rather than having an accountant, they would prefer to have a sort of slush-fund manager. They vaguely grasp that incoming funds (Yin) should ideally balance Yang or outgoing funds.

The sign of a Leo is often linked with self-expression, chivalry, and high romance. It's all done with credit. They can embody the classic Champagne-taste and beer-budget scenario.

Though they can easily ignore any chasm gaping between their actual income and their sense of self-worth, Leos are often good credit risks. They are careful to keep their fiscal reality vaguely under control because they never want to reach a stage where they can't say, "It's on me." Or, their fave, "Money is no object." Yes, their rich inner life does result in delusions of decadence, but this is actually one of the sweeter aspects of Leo.

The world needs glam, theatrical types clutching a platinum card with perfectly manicured hands as they bellow for more Bollinger. Or insisting that no date of theirs is going to get on an airplane and be made to turn right, into economy.

Leos are extravagant but they are also generous. They want you to have properly branded designer goods too, and, if they can afford it, they'll buy them for you.

Actually, they'll buy them even if they can't afford the mortgage that month. Leos who are temporarily down on their luck will often be infuriated that one can get charitable help for boring things like food but not for decent perfume.

But Leos are very rarely cash-strapped for long. They know, as (self-proclaimed emperor) Napoleon Bonaparte used to say to his troops, that "the money will come later."

"Luxury is not the opposite of poverty—it is the opposite of vulgarity."

Coco Chanel (1883-1971), founder of the French fashion house, Chanel

Chez Leo

"All that you have ever seen is always with you."

Henri Cartier-Bresson (1908-2004), French photographer—"the decisive moment"

Leo's home is their palace. Totally unafraid of opulence, Leos are naturally drawn toward quality brands and status-symbolic décor. Given an unfettered budget, Chez Leo would soon reflect a love of designer labels. Their exquisite taste aids them in picking objets d'art for art's sake, as well as for the all-important one-upping of inferiors. They can even sink to blatantly exhibiting evidence of their beauty, accomplishments, and celebrity contacts. Leo loves class indicators and is perfectly happy to forgo less important things, such as food and petrol, to ensure that their mini empire is as beautiful and groomed as its regal inhabitant.

Like cousin Aries, Leo appreciates a good dramatic statement—a chaise longue, a marble bathroom, or even gold-plated taps. There will naturally be an awesome array of thoroughly researched hair products, and flattering lighting is obviously a must.

For a Leo, the eyes aren't the mirror of the soul. The mirror *is* the mirror of the soul. In fact, the mirror is the Leo's self-development tool. There'll be several in Leo's home, rose-tinted and perfectly positioned for multi-angled viewing. Their fantasy fixture? Try a walk-in computerized wardrobe with stylist software.

"I don't believe in being humble when I don't feel humble."

George Hamilton (1939-), bronzed Hollywood actor and ladies' man

A Leo in love

"Love isn't an emotion or an instinct—it's an art."

Mae West (1893-1980), blonde bombshell, comic, actress, producer, and writer

Lusty, romantic, and requiring to be lavished in athletic devotion, the Leo libido is legendary. They are totally unafraid to honor their emotions. And, unlike certain other signs, they won't do so foolishly, such as phoning only to hang up when the object of desire answers.

Leos believe in saying certain things with flowers, scent, movie premiere tickets—whatever it takes. Is romantic love the "mystic flower of the soul" as postulated by psychologist Carl Jung? Or is it a stupid Darwinian social construct designed to keep the Leo libido from full bloom? Leos can have problems deciding but they are keen on the rules of attraction. They never tire of hair flicks, cute banter, or the sultry gaze held for just a heartbeat too long. Leos are often inordinately proud of their seductive powers and take sexual performance extremely seriously. It really is a performance and they are aware of an invisible audience. Memo to Leo: Mirrors in which one can see oneself from the bed are bad feng shui.

In love with love, Leos can wind up in the "date, mate, and hate school" of relationship management. When confiding their romantic history to a new lover—"I've never felt this way before"— the Leo can't decide between denouncing ex-lovers as insignificant slime or bolstering them up as an ego boost.

For an idea of the Leo relationship from heaven, watch any of the classic movies in the series that began with the 1934 classic *The Thin Man*. Leo actors Myrna Loy and William Powell play Nora and Nick Charles, a Dashiell Hammett-created, crime solving husband-and-wife team. They are a mega-glam duo who live in an amazing apartment, holiday in exotic locations, drink beautiful cocktails at amazing clubs, and emit an endless bubbling stream of sexy banter.

In real life, Leo has to accept that their partner may not always live up to the leonine ideal. Leos think an inch of regrowth is symptomatic of deep self-neglect. Failure to notice when they have had the hem taken up on their trousers means you have fallen out of love with them and they are justified in a revenge affair. They should, obviously, try and look a little below the surface.

"I am a deeply superficial person."

Andy Warhol (1928-1987), American iconic artist and film-maker who kick-started Pop Art. He also founded the ground-breaking magazine, *Interview*.

Leo-Aries

The Lion shall lie down with the Lamb? Get real. At first glance Ramzilla seems like a perfect new devotee. Aries energy could easily be harnessed into coddling and publicizing neo-Leo genius. Or could it? Aries is not as easy to dominate as Leo would like. In fact, if there's a power game being played, Aries likes to be boss. Leo and Aries love hard, fast, and often at first sight. Each adores the other's confidence and glamour. But, Leo is annoyed that Aries is not as clear on the importance of personal grooming as they are. Leo gripes about split ends and Aries freaks out about who's in charge. Leo says "I rule" and Aries says "Like hell." Aries thinks the Leo emotions resemble those of a spoilt show cat on heat. Leo wonders why Aries has to be so vulgar and direct. But really, these two are a heavenly match. Both are vital, outgoing, and hyper-energized. Aries mostly adores the Leo ego and self-expressive brilliance. Each inspires the other so long as the constant drool of drivel and flattery flows both ways.

Hot duos: Tipper & Al Gore, Eddie Fisher & Debbie Reynolds, Sean Penn & Robin Wright Penn, Norman & Brenda Schwarzkopf

Leo-Taurus

Taurus fancies Leo and vice versa—for a while. Taurus is capable of the unswerving devotion Leo requires of love slaves. Leo decorates Taurus' life. But Taurus likes moola, not to spend it, but for security. Leos like to spread around a little luxury. Leo is a work-in-progress, a would-be style icon in need of status artifacts to prove it. If it were left to Taurus to run the budget, Leo would look disgusting with unkempt hair and scabby shoes. Leo would be unable to go out in public. If Leo runs the budget, Taurus freaks out. Leo is so stubborn. Taurus is mega-obstinate. Neither ever gives in. Leo makes an entrance. Taurus doesn't notice. Leo makes a dramatic exit. Taurus tells the Leo to get a grip. Taurus likes to cocoon. Leo likes to be seen. Bedwork keeps them together as does an intense will to compromise. To win the heart of our Cow, Leo has to act like less than themselves and become a creature more in the strong, silent Scorpio mode. This couple could so rankle.

Hot duos: Mick & Bianca Jagger, Peter O'Toole & Siân Phillips

Leo-Gemini
Halt! Who goeth there, daring to hog the Leo limelight? Why it's Gemini—gorgeous, garrulous, and longing to mess with the Leo hair, or at least whatever's inside of it. Welcome to the madhouse of Leo-Gemini love. Leo likes to own their lover. Gemini ain't nobody's serf. Gemini flirtation gets revved up in rebellion. Leo sulks. But this is an awesomely compatible duo. Leo flirts too and Gemini doesn't care. Both are charismatic and artistic party types. Gemini loves Leo's glamour, style, and high-impact mode of living. Leo learns to let Gemini zoom off some place, without telling Leo where they are going. Gemini gets that the Leo ego needs to be honored nonstop. Leo loves that the more independence given to Gemini, the more Gemini can be controlled. Gemini realizes that, like themselves, the Leo is a dual character: Leo and the insatiable Leo ego that just can't hack Gemini being allowed too much space. Gemini changeability and Leo charisma keep each part of the duo endlessly infatuated.

Hot duos: Jacqueline & John F. Kennedy, the Queen Mother & King George VI, Norma Shearer & Irving Thalberg, Roman Polanski & Emmanuelle Seigner

Leo-Cancer
Crab People are cute, home-centered, and nurturing. Just the person to have waiting at home after a hard day fame-mongering. Even better, the Cancerian is by nature thrillingly compliant, only too happy to let Lion King/Queen rule. With Leo ruled by the Sun and the Crab by the Moon, this pair are sensually so compatible. But a major issue is most likely to blight loving, fun times: Despite being one of the most receptive and understanding types on the planet, Crab has a propensity for tempestuous scenes. But Leo thinks that if anyone's going to throw a temper tantrum, it'll be Leo. But Crab can easily outdo a Leo when it comes to being a drama-queen. Leo finds the

limelight hogged by this mood-swinger extraordinaire and this is not what Leo signed on for. But Crab points out that, if there are scenes being made, it's Leo's fault for not being demonstrative enough. Good loving is Leo's core competency. Art and love bring them together again and again.

Hot duos: Napoleon Bonaparte & Josephine Beauharnais, Kyra Sedgwick & Kevin Bacon, Jennifer Flavin & Sylvester Stallone

Leo-Leo
Two supercats are capable of taking up all the oxygen in a room. Is there room for two vibrant, theatrical glamour-pusses in one relationship? Should a third person be hired to fulfill a more traditional "helpmeet" role? How can Leo express noblesse oblige if Leo has to pick up someone's underpants? Can the two of you live with merely one mirror in the bathroom? Even the most profound emotions of Leo can be delivered as a series of dramatic clichés. They tend toward re-enactments of movie moments which moved them, sometimes without even knowing it. Sometimes the entire Leo romantic persona can be based on a celebrity they think is like them. This liaison can get weird. Both are charismatic people with an insane lust for attention. This brings them together or keeps them apart, as each Leo longs for a drabber partner who lets them own the huge glitz space. Both Leos like to flirt for precious attention. Both Leos are wildly possessive. Leo vs. Leo gets ugly without constant ego-tending.

Hot duos: Bill Clinton & Monica Lewinsky, Ben Affleck & Jennifer Lopez, Antonio Banderas & Melanie Griffith

Leo-Virgo
Leo loves that Virgo really gets the Leo fetish about details, even if it is only applied to Leo hair and entertaining. Virgo loves the glamour and positivity of Leo, which serves as an antidote to Virgoan fussiness and secret fears. Virgo lets Leo occupy the limelight

with pleasure. Leo loves the way Virgo sets up Leo gags and anecdotes. They find endless compatibility in bedwork and conversation. Trouble? Leo goes into the mirror space to create magic, not to have Virgo's nitpicking through the bathroom door about something so plebeian as being on time some place. Gentle Virgo can shrivel from the hyper-demands of the hot Leo ego. But Leo likes Virgo career and money advice just so long as Virgo stops short of bitching it up when Leo is in arty mode. Virgo gets that the Leo is also on a continual self-improvement trip. Leo loves how Virgos are so classically and elegantly sensual, yet without being glitzy enough to draw attention from Leo. The Lion must sometimes give full-on pep talks to Virgo to secure peace and harmony.

Hot duos: Madonna & Guy Ritchie, Isabelle Allende & Willie Gordon, Percy & Mary Shelley, Frieda & D. H. Lawrence, Amelia Earhart & George Putman, Edward Norton & Salma Hayek

Leo-Libra
This liaison is the coming together of two beautiful people to form an even more beautiful couple. Leo and Libra are Zelda and 1920s novelist F. Scott Fitzgerald. It's youthful actors Ben Affleck and Matt Damon getting their Academy Award for Best Original Screenplay in 1998. Nobody (hopefully), will get to see them carping away behind the scenes, lamenting what could be cellulite, micro-examining the hairline or rehearsing grand entrances. The sooner this delicious duo accepts that they are a pair of luvvies, the quicker the relationship reaches its glorious potential. They bond because they both care so much about appearances, art, and beauty. Libra falters into one of those Yin vs. Yang flip outs and Leo takes over as leader, telling them that the show must, no, that the show is going to go on. Libra knows just how to coddle Leo's giant ego. Each inspires the other into fulfilling their dreams. Each likes the other forever. The attraction is often instantaneous and totally undeniable.

Hot duos: Sam Mendes & Kate Winslet, Pete Sampras & Brigitte Wilson, Halle Berry & Eric Benet, Zelda & F. Scott Fitzgerald, Blake Edwards & Julie Andrews, Clara Bow & Rex Bell, Patty Scialfa & Bruce Springsteen

Leo-Scorpio Cue the cameras. The psycho-drama begins. This is a duo that relishes the more theatrical variety of life. Neither is completely comfortable with a romance that has settled into habitual patterns. Both make excellent scenes. Scorpio is stubborn and Leo won't move. Scorpio is so drawn to the Lion but wonders if Leo is slightly too shallow. Leo thinks Scorpio should tone down the intensity a little and maybe boof up the hair reality. The Lion helps Scorpio to become less paranoid and more able to enjoy the good life. Scorpio lets Leo be more forgiving of those with flaws such as nerdy clothing, less-than-dazzling dinner repartee, or snaggle-teeth and see into the person within. Scorpio provides insight into power dynamics, allowing Leo to become the player they secretly fantasize about being. Each is so jealous and possessive but both secretly get off on ranting about it. Given boundaries and/or an exciting dynamic of collaboration, this pair creates an intoxicating and addictive personal reality.

Hot duos: Louis XVI & Marie Antoinette, Bill & Hillary Clinton, John & Bo Derek, John Stamos & Rebecca Romjin-Stamos, Arnold Schwarzenegger & Maria Shriver, Nicoletta Braschi & Roberto Benigni

Leo-Sagittarius Leo and Sagg are one of the most beautiful, romantic combos of the zodiac. Both Fire signs, they constantly stimulate and lure the other by their very being. But Leo must realize that being bloody-minded and tactless is as vital to the Sagg as breathing. Sagg sees this trait as being more some kind of great seeker of truth. Leo sees only the most amazing clangers dropped in awkward

social situations. Leo doesn't relish Sagg wondering aloud whether the Leo career has stalled because the Leo hair is so thin and straggly. Leo likes artifice. Sagg has a reality fetish. Leo likes long, drawn-out sexual scenarios. Sagg wants to get on with it. Leo is a lounge lizard. Sagg is an adventurer. But, really, Leo inspires, exhilarates, and arouses the hard-to-get Sagg, taming their insane wanderlust. Sagg returns the favor via being a fantastic foil for neo-Leo radiance. Leo girds the ego and accepts Sagg for whatever it is they are, that day. Sagg is prepared to stand aside and allow this evening to be all about Leo's hair. Get a Sagg in a sporting contest, and they're incredibly competitive—but the glamour stakes? They don't even get it. Together they are smart, successful, and insanely in demand.

Hot duos: Charlize Theron & Stuart Townsend, Marcel Cerdan & Edith Piaf, Anna Scarpulla & Ray Romano

Leo-Capricorn
When Leo glitz combines with Capricorn elegance, the resulting duo is a power pair to behold. Both are aware of the value of appearances—that one can judge a book by its cover. Physically, Leo and Capricorn are awesomely compatible. Once it is decided who's going to play boss, they bond joyously in bed. And unlike many couples, they are unlikely to have disputes about your so-called budget. Each agrees that when something is worth doing, it's worth doing right. Obviously, those "come as you are" casual drinks must be catered. Status-aware Capricorn would never begrudge Leo that daily blow-dry and, of course, Cap dietary needs must be devised by a clinical nutritionist. Cap is unlikely to disappoint by developing cellulite, bad manners, or split ends. But expect power-struggling behind the public scenes of the liaison. Earthy Cap has never-ending "needs." Leo needs beauty sleep, along with grand public displays of lusty affection, not exactly the Cap's core competency. If the Goat can get that the supercat is essentially a star who must be given enough room to be brilliant and Leo remembers that normal sex is not exactly a case of "lights, camera, action," these two can bond.

Hot duos: Iman & David Bowie, Hilary Swank & Chad Lowe, James Cameron & Suzy Amis, Helen Mirren & Taylor Hackford, Simon Baker & Rebecca Rigg

Leo-Aquarius Opposites attract and Leo is sucked in by the icy Aqua beauty. Aquarius is secretly keen on a trophy partner and the game kicks off. Someone should nominate this relationship for a sitcom. Leo gets a fab new designer ottoman. Aquarius bitches up about how it's blocking the flow of Qi energy to the living room. Leo likes to live it up big and in luxury. Aquarius wants to go on some weird diet to suit their always weirder-than-thou biochemistry. Leo loves music, flowers, and gourmet food. Leo thinks they are the religion. Aquarius dabbles in many belief systems. Both have a gargantuan ego although the Aquarius ego often hides behind cant˜and strange bursts of wisdom gleaned from their latest email newsletter from their cult friends. But both brighten others' lives. Both are fussy about the sort of people allowed into their inner sanctums. Leo has to get that Aquarius usually cares deeply about skincare being organic. Aquarius needs to lighten up and not correctively nag our Leo. The Lion's theatrical nature inspires Aquarius. The future-is-now vibe of Aquarius turns on Leo, stopping them from being bored.

Hot duos: Whitney Houston & Bobby Brown, David Brown & Helen Gurley Brown, Gracie Allen & George Burns, Burt Reynolds & Loni Anderson, Emmanuelle Béart & David Moreau

Leo-Pisces Room for two drama queens? It depends on how doting the Piscean can manage to be. Leo can't possibly commit to someone unaware of how highly strung Leo is. Pisces is thinking exactly the same. Each is so intrigued by the other. Leo makes the mistake of thinking they can dominate Pisces. Pisces smirks and goes along with it. Pisces irritates Leo by racing around getting involved in everyone's life,

not just that of the Leo. Leo can't stand hearing Pisces prattle on about other people. Pisces tires of hearing Leo bang on and on about only Leo. Each requires demonstrative expressions of love and nonstop admiration. Leo thinks Pisces can be an idiot. Pisces fears that Leo is not esoteric enough for Fishy tastes. In this coupling, each gives as good as they get. Leo clams up without enough admiration. Pisces feels hurt and slips out with a secret admirer. Pisces doesn't like Leo's hair suggestions. Leo loathes Pisces hogging the limelight. Ideally, each accepts that both parties can be the superstar of the relationship.

Hot duos: Hugo Guiler & Anaïs Nin, Lucille Ball & Desi Arnaz, Angela Bassett & Courtney B. Vance, Terri & Steve Irwin, David Duchnovy & Téa Leoni

Are you really a Leo?

1 On the first day of an important conference, your hair has unaccountably gone straw-like yet greasy. You...

(a) Engage speed chic and skillful use of a hair product so you nonetheless project your usual suave image.

(b) Think, who cares? Your performance and results are your most eloquent statement.

(c) Cancel everything so you can get your hair properly cared for. After all, it's what's on your head.

2 Fame is...

(a) A societal construct which fails to recognize let alone reward those of true value in our community.

(b) Fickle and not to be trusted...it could go at any moment.

(c) An obvious outcome of slog and success—a commodity to be nurtured and yours for the taking.

3 Asked to think about spirituality or religion, you feel...

(a) That it is an intensely private matter.

(b) That the world is made up of many belief systems—whatever works.

(c) Bored. You literally can't imagine a superior being.

4 In the bathroom one morning you notice that your face looks gray and haggard. You...

(a) Decide that you really must watch your lifestyle—more sleep and water would be a damn good start.

(b) Are philosophical...beauty is skin deep, as they say.

(c) Go out to order a new mirror.

5 Mid-siesta, you are woken by an urgent-sounding knock at the front door. You...

(a) Ignore it and go back to sleep. Whoever it is can bloody well wait.

(b) Pull on whatever is closest to hand and grudgingly go to see who it is.

(c) Call out "Coming" and glamourously arrange a sheet around yourself, Greek god/goddess style, spritz on some fragrance, fluff up the hair, and glide out to answer the door. After all, you never know when opportunity could come knocking.

6 Your friends and/or partner conspire to throw a surprise party for your birthday. You are...

(a) Delighted! You love surprise parties!

b) Overwhelmed with emotion—they really, truly love you!

(c) Stupefied with rage. How dare they make you the guest of honor at something you haven't even been able to prep for?

Answers: If you checked mainly (c) answers, then you are an official Leo—a luvvie of the first degree, so chic, so sexy. If you checked (a) or (b) answers, you have other astro influences competing with your Leo Sun.

Virgo

august 24-september 23

Like a Virgo

"True life is lived when tiny changes occur."

Leo Tolstoy (1828-1910), Russian writer whose most famous work was the gigantic tome

War and Peace

Q: How many Virgos does it take to change a light bulb?
A: None. Virgo will just sit all alone in the dark and suffer.

At some point in their lives, most Virgos have been appalled to find out that their astrological symbol is the Virgin. They worry that it makes them seem prissy. The connotations of innocence evoked by the "V" word sit ill with the Virgoan ethos of worldly urbanity. But, when ancient astrologers referred to virgin, they didn't actually have a blushing maiden stereotype in mind. They were referring to Virgo's radiant purity and sexy self-reliance.

In the 19th century, dancer Lola Montez, who became one of the most talked-about women of her time, defied Virgoan stereotypes. A freewheeling femme fatale, she was famous for her erotic performances and her many affairs. Her lovers included King Ludwig I of Bavaria, French novelist Alexandre Dumas, and composer Franz Liszt. The point being that Virgo is not necessarily akin to being a virgin. The only thing pure and unspoiled about heaps of adult Virgos is their linen.

Like cousin Gemini, Virgo folk are ruled by Mercury, the brainiest planet of all. It is a gadabout little planet which flits through the skies making all sorts of connections in swift succession, much like a Virgo in networking mode at a function. Virgos are as mercurially minded as Geminis but more sensible and a little more grounded.

Geminis express themselves through the element of Air. Virgo is an Earth sign like Capricorn and Taurus. They are sensible, sensual, and straight. The astrological motto is the briefest possible summary of a Sun sign's ethos. It is a sort of mission statement. In the case of Virgo, their astro motto is "I analyze." And they do. Virgo has no problems with the clichéd "being unable to see the forest for the trees" scenario. They see the forest, trees, and early stages of leaf mold. Virgos get the fine print of life.

They are amazingly observant but awful to go to the movies with because they pick up on tiny little continuity glitches that nobody else notices.

Non-Virgo: It was [*sob*] so beautiful when he went back to her after...

Virgo: Yes, but his shirt had different buttons on it. How could that be when, in fact, he had...

Virgo definitely likes bitching it up but this trait must be put to productive use if Virgo is not to degenerate into a walking stream of consciousness, ranting about punctuation errors in unsolicited mail-outs.

Virgo on form is...

"It is far more impressive when others discover your good qualities without your help."

Judith Martin aka Miss Manners (1938-), witty American etiquette guru

HELPFUL Virgo is responsible for some awesomely practical and helpful innovations. For instance, Margaret Sanger, the nurse who started the world's first contraceptive clinic and gave us the term "birth control," was a Virgo. And, naturally, it took a Virgo, Samuel Johnson, to dream up the amazingly sensible idea of the dictionary. Virgos can always be relied upon for practical advice: think of this timeless piece from Joseph P. Kennedy (father of U.S. president John F. Kennedy): "Don't get mad—get even." When at a dinner party a Virgo asks, "Can I help?," they actually mean it, unlike, say, Gemini or Pisces who really mean "refresh my drink." They have a keen sense of duty and offer amazingly sensible advice for stressed-out friends. Virgos don't become hysterical, they are straight to the point with the best advice in the world and offer pragmatic assistance when appropriate.

WITTY Their unique brand of bitchy character analysis is hilarious. Virgo zooms in on the tiniest most revelatory details and expands them into a hyperbolic gush. They remember gags, anecdotes, and jokes and are able to tell them beautifully. Virgos are rightly adored across the known universe for their wit, humor, and observational skills. When told he'd have to "bite the bullet," Hollywood hunk Keanu Reeves replied "yeah, but I don't have to eat the whole rifle."

SUAVE Virgos of both genders have suave, cute, worldly-wise appeal. They always appear put together to just the right degree— not too over the top and contrived, but certainly not underdone.

POLITE Virgos are the original take-anywhere date. Blessed with exquisite manners and social perceptions, they know precisely how to behave with perfect aplomb in any situation. Though they live in fear of it, they never offend. It is quite common for Virgo to telephone after a party to ensure that they did not upset anyone when, in fact, they were the most functional and best-behaved guest in the history of socializing. They always remember to ask about *you.*

MODEST Virgos turn their analytical inclinations upon themselves with sometimes disastrous effects upon self-esteem. They can't fool themselves with the sort of comforting half-truths contrived by others to maintain serenity. Intimates of Virgo should try to remember to "stroke" their ego. That way Virgo won't be forced to fish for compliments or goad people into them. They are so aware that they are not doing a hamstring stretch while they clean their teeth, or whatever is their latest routine, that they forget what they achieve every day: civilized order in an often unruly world.

A PERFECTIONIST People belittle the Virgo for this but who do they screech for when something goes bung? That's right. Our Virgo, who knows where the receipt, guarantee form, and toll-free help number are filed. To totally thrill a Virgo, ask them to help reorganize the Rolodex and start a new, happier, and more organized version of life. Virgos are everyone's life coach. They know all the little tricks in the book: motivational tips, power naps, power showers, stain removal...

"The realisation of the self is only possible if one is productive."

Goethe (1749-1832), German over-achiever: poet, novelist, dramatist, geologist, lawyer, anatomist, physicist, revolutionary theorist, and philosopher

Virgo off form is...

"Life isn't a bloody popularity contest."

Sean Connery (1932-), Scottish actor, and the original Bond...James Bond

A FUSSBUDGET Inside every Virgo is a "school-sock" monitor waiting to get out. These people are so particular. Having handed you your drink, they then snap "that's all right" in sarcastic tones before you've even had a chance to say thank you. In fact, Virgo wanted you not to thank them. That's why they give you a mere two-second interval before bitching it up. The notorious mutiny on the Bounty in 1789 is a lot more understandable when we take into account that the captain of the ship, William Bligh, was a Virgo. He probably had one too many fits over the shocking state of the ship's baseboards.

GUILTING If anyone ever makes a horror film about Virgos it should be called *The Guilting*. All Virgos are elite, professional guilters. But it is not enough to be a natural-born quilter. Just as the world's best ballet dancers still perform the basic maintenance chore of a thousand pliés at the barre each day, Virgos are constantly honing their quilting skills. These can take the form of a dread silence, the infamous minute-long Virgo sigh or a clench-jawed "Seeing as you're too busy to make it over for Christmas, I'll put your nephew on to talk to you...I suppose hearing your voice will be some small comfort for the poor thing..." Whether they know it or not, most Virgos consider themselves to be saints. And what is the main occupation of most saints? That's right, martyrdom. The Virgo worship of natural fibers is really leading up to one obvious outcome, the hairshirt. It would add extra oomph to their "after all I have sacrificed for you" and "slaving over a hot oven" speeches. But martyrs also create miracles and there are many such manifestations of St. Virgo's powers. There is the St. Virgo "entertaining the in-laws at Easter" miracle, the "St. Virgo arising from their sick bed to hang out the washing" miracle and the "St. Virgo nearly breaking a bone dashing to answer the phone" miracle. Reserved for special occasions are the "St. Virgo marrying beneath themselves" miracle and "St. Virgo selflessly wrecking brilliant career for the children" miracle.

HYPOCHONDRIAC An estimated one in 10 people suffer from this ailment—a "state of mind in which the sufferer is so preoccupied with their health or with symptoms of ill-health that this preoccupation is in itself a disability"—and they are all Virgos. Everyone else gets a cold. Virgo is convinced they have Peking Virus X or whatever illness is most in style that season. Most people figure a strange rash will go away, Virgos can't help seeing themselves as the mysterious Patient X, afflicted with something so hideous it makes headlines in medical mags. With their whining, leisure-time reading of prescription drug manuals and surfing of symptoms.net, Virgos can make awful patients. The doctor says it's athlete's foot and Virgo demands a full toe scan. They can be germ phobic. For example, Michael Jackson wears a mask to avoid airborne bacteria.

NAGGING Okay, so old nun-face calls it correctional motivation. The point is that when Virgos are done badgering themselves closer to perfection for the day, they turn on whoever is closest or most susceptible. Even if a person is not at hand, they'll start picking through the cat's fur looking for fleas to kill. Virgo is so vile that they can't even see anything untoward with their conduct. To them, it is obvious that they can't commit their heart to a person so imperfect. They think casting aspersions on another's income-earning ability several times a day will inevitably result in the said person becoming more prosperous, or telling someone again and again that their sexual technic is so inept that an orgasm is nigh impossible will result in an ecstatic copulatory experience. A Virgo can always find time to stick a note to the fridge, whether it's for you or to nag themselves about whatever their gripe of the day is. Virgo is quite capable of taking a molehill and turning it into a whole new continent.

"I had a monumental idea this morning but I didn't like it."

Samuel Goldwyn (1879-1974), movie mogul who rose from being an impoverished glove maker to heading one of Hollywood's biggest studios

Motivating and manipulating a Virgo

"Curiosity is one of the permanent and certain characteristics of a vigorous mind."

Samuel Johnson (1709-1784), English author and lexicographer who wrote the first

English dictionary in 1755

1 Don't try and stop Virgo from compulsively cleaning. A Virgo on a household-filth purge is a Virgo in ecstasy. There will be big pay-offs later on in bed, you understand.

2 If Virgo is nervy, give them a task that involves inspecting something, like checking the wine glasses for specks of grime. This calms them more than any pep talk or chamomile tea.

3 Don't mess with the Virgo filing system. They know exactly what they are doing and may become hysterical if they can't place a document immediately.

4 Giving a gift to a Virgo? They only really like books. A good Virgo can never have enough books—the new Booker Prize nominee's offering, trashy cult novels from the 1940s, designer cookbooks, a weird history of some font—they don't care as long as it is a good book. If you buy them something which proves you have actually listened to their careful little hints, even better. You'll be in the good books.

5 Accept that, while Virgos do like spontaneous junkets and outings, they need at least three weeks' notice so that they have time to jot it into their busy schedule.

6 Don't bother telling them not to lie awake at 3 a.m. workshopping humiliating insults for some person they hate at work. They'd rather do that than be asleep which means they might dream. Most Virgos can't control their dreams and that irks them no end.

7 Realize that there is no point getting angry at Virgo. It'll just make them nag you about your blood pressure, temper, and/or lack of grammatical skills.

8 Never miss a Virgoan hint. They're subtle but nonstop.

9 Don't mispronounce words—Virgos think it's evidence of a slovenly and possibly substandard mind.

Virgo role models

"Life is not so bad if you have plenty of luck, a good physique, and not too much imagination."

Christopher Isherwood (1906-1986), British-born writer whose haunting 1939 novel
Goodbye to Berlin evoked the gathering storms of World War II

- Cathy Guisewite—super-talented cartoonist who created the *Cathy* series while sitting at home, dateless. Her column could be called the Daily Virgo, obsessing as it does on the minutiae of life. "Mothers, food, love, and career, the four major guilt groups."

- Sophia Loren—Italian film siren of the 1950s and 60s. She specialized in playing glamourous yet earthy love interests in epics such as *El Cid* and *The Fall of the Roman Empire.* She is frank on physical matters: "I'm not exactly a tiny woman."

Sun signs

- Siegfried Sassoon—brilliant writer, poet, and war hero. Standing on his principles, his article *A Soldier's Declaration* was published to great acclaim in *The Times* newspaper in 1917. "I believe that the war is being deliberately prolonged by those who have the power to end it."

- Judith Martin (aka Miss Manners)—highly successful American author and journalist. She turned an eye for detail into an etiquette column that is syndicated around the world. She also writes novels. She melds the two Virgoan traits of the natural writer and complete fussbudget.

- Karl Lagerfeld—famously eccentric German fashion designer. He sports a ponytail, uses a Japanese fan, and wears sunglasses indoors. Like many of his star signs, he's talented yet practical: "You can't have both the butter and the money for the butter."

- Samuel Johnson—pompous 18th century British writer who wrote the first English dictionary. He was a huge man who suffered from depression and strange twitches. His Virgo bonus points: he's a writer and a hypochondriac. "No man but a blockhead ever wrote, except for money."

"They say Virgos are not sensual and sexy. I feel sexy inside me. I just don't show it."

Kristy McNichol (1962-), American actress who starred with Tatum O'Neal in the cult 1980

film *Little Darlings*

Virgo in vogue

"Why not be oneself? That's the secret of a successful appearance. If one is a greyhound, why try to look like a pekingese?"

Dame Edith Sitwell (1887-1964), experimental English poet and visionary Virgo

If one is a Virgo, why try to look like some mad trendy Gemini or flash Leo? Looking like yourself—only better—is the Virgo style ideal. They tend to look excellent in clothes because they take such good care of their bodies. Even Virgos who don't give a fig about fitness are usually thin from worrying so much.

They have amazingly good taste. Keen to learn, they take advice from the best fashion dictators and have a wardrobe of classic separates to prove it. Even if a Virgo is fretting about a particular fashion statement, they always look relaxed and suitably put together.

Virgos naturally have organized closets with shoe trees, storage for out-of-season clothes, and an array of garb maintenance tools. They are rarely caught in the situation of having to dash out and buy an emergency outfit without sanity.

Virgo knows that the best prepared wins on the night. If they like something they sensibly buy three of them. Even a Virgo child will get up two hours early to iron their school uniform. Virgo is never ahead of the times but never behind. Virgo likes to be exactly on time.

They feel that being well dressed bestows order and peace upon what can at times feel like a disorderly and jangly world.

Virgo beauty is clean and lean; this is part brilliant bone structure, part ferocious grooming, and part earthy sensuality. Asked for her views on style, Hollywood legend Lauren Bacall said she liked clothes that didn't show the dirt. Actress Cameron Diaz will only wash her face in Evian spring water.

VA-VA VIRGOS Fiona Apple, Sean Connery, Harry Connick Jr., Cameron Diaz, Greta Garbo, Hugh Grant, Salma Hayek, Faith Hill, Sophia Loren, Rosie Perez, Ryan Phillippe, Jada Pinkett Smith, Jason Priestley, Keanu Reeves, LeAnn Rimes, Adam Sandler, Devon Sawa, Claudia Schiffer, Charlie Sheen, Shania Twain, Twiggy, Raquel Welch

Brilliant career

"The miracle is not that we do this work but that we are happy to do it."

Mother Teresa (1910-1997), high-profile missionary who was awarded the Nobel Prize
for Peace in 1979

Virgos do have a choice. They either brand themselves as being the solutions guru or as an anal-retentive grizzler with unresolved authority issues.

Virgos squawk for their rights, get almost everything they want, then bitch it up about their onerous responsibilities. Some say Virgos suit social work, where they can combine serving humankind with nagging. But Virgo can nag and guilt people on an amateur basis. The best career for our Virgo is writing.

Okay, so it took a Virgo to write the first dictionary, but they are also proportionately far more likely to become authors than any of the other signs.

Think: Leo Tolstoy, Frederick Forsythe, Alison Lurie, Martin Amis, Edgar Rice Burroughs, Ira Levin, Stephen King, William Saroyan, William Golding, Fay Weldon, H. G. Wells, Edith Sitwell, Roald Dahl, Taylor Caldwell, Agatha Christie, Jorge Luis Borges, A. S. Byatt, Shirley Conran, James Fenimore Cooper, Michael Ondaatje, Mary Renault, Jeanette Winterson, Mary Shelley, D. H. Lawrence. Virgos even swell the ranks of the better songwriters as in Leonard Cohen, Chrissie Hynde, Elvis Costello, Patsy Cline, and B. B. King to name but a few.

Can't write, won't write? Luckily, Virgo is one of the most employable signs of all. Not only are they capable and ambitious, they can radiate an air of ultra-efficiency even when dreamily evoking bedwork in their mind or scheming a shopping splurge.

Virgos are smart, hard-working, and clever at currying favor with bosses. But being a Virgo means getting used to a certain degree of vocational angst. They tend to fret about the path not traveled. Even famous Virgos need constant reassurance that their career is not a joke, and that their efforts do not go unobserved.

The better they do, the worse they can feel about themselves. They like the idea of success but fret about moving into a higher tax bracket, being recognized at the shops sifting through a pile of trashy lingerie or that someone will want to marry them merely for money.

Fiscal reality

"Spare no expense to save money on this one."

Samuel Goldwyn (1879-1974), a glove maker who became a movie mogul

Virgos are not immune to fiscal folly. They're just skilled at putting a better spin on it. So when another sign zooms out to buy organic-wood venetian blinds on some flimsy basis or to get their face resurfaced to impress a soon-to-be ex, that's extravagant. When our Virgin purchases an entire new spring wardrobe via so-called "dumb debt," it is ironic, a "homage" to society, and/or a sensible reaction to the economic climate. Virgos tend to agree with British comedian Spike Milligan that, while money may not buy happiness, it certainly brings a more pleasant form of misery. But Virgos tend to be poverty, rather than prosperity, conscious. They focus on what they don't have, or upon their fear of becoming the world's neatest and most-organized beggar, more than upon their own ability to create affluence.

Their perfectionist consciousness is so honed that poor Virgo is always aware of "shoulds." It's not easy combining an old-fashioned work ethic and modest expectations with a secret yen to live an international jet-setting life of incredible glitzy shallowness. Even Virgos who are saving up for their next tube of toothpaste will cheerily torment themselves by reading articles about the ins and outs of time-sharing a private jet.

They do experience the lust for things but only if the object in question is intensely useful. Unlike cousin Leo or Capricorn, they won't go madly into debt for an item that apparently symbolizes status. Virgo would rather splurge on wheatgrass juice, the ergonomic body-aligning chair to compose genius on, organic mascara that protects your eyes from computer rays, or a sage throat gargle.

"A fine wind is blowing the new direction of time."

D. H. Lawrence (1885-1930), British writer whose 1928 novel *Lady Chatterley's Lover* was banned in Britain and in the U.S. for being too risque. He loved to write "when feeling spiteful" as it was like "having a sneeze".

Chez Virgo

"What you practise is what you manifest."

Fay Weldon (1933-), British novelist and screenwriter who is known for her astute sense

of irony. She writes shrewd, analytical parables of relationships.

A gleaming model of extreme organization is the ideal Virgo home—not that they necessarily live up to it. The dream Virgo house has an infinite number of built-in cupboards for storage. No clutter shall blight the Virgoan sense of order. They really love that close-to-godly look of scrubbed floorboards with pure white curtains.

Virgos are, along with Scorpios, the compulsive cleaners of the zodiac. "It's filthy!," they'll shriek as they spot a stray speck of dust on a baseboard. Even the air inside a Virgo home will be purer than most, as many of them invest in negative ionizers or air-purifiers. While they admire the efficiency of stainless-steel, industrial-style kitchens, they're quite capable of throwing out the oven in an insane purge of household filth. They live in dread of grime and of being perceived as trying too hard to be trendy. Utterly non-faddy, Virgos can be scathing towards décor crazes, hence their constant gravitation toward clean surfaces with nothing on them. You don't find Virgo lurking in the latest fashionable furniture emporium, debating whether to get last week's sofa model or last month's. Virgoans are more likely to be seen in the furniture maker's studio or the upholsterer, where they spend hours poring over the fabric samples for that elusive "appropriate" covering.

Virgos' preferred decorating accessories are books—they can make quite fetching displays by simply shifting piles of them around. They love furnishings with slipcovers (which can be drycleaned every few days), any scientific advances in the field of pest control, and the timeless ease of muted beige.

A Virgo in love

"It is not always wise to appear singular."

Taylor Caldwell (1900-1985), fantastically prolific British-born American novelist who wrote best-selling potboilers. Her best-known works are *Dynasty of Death* (1938) and *Answer as a Man* (1981).

A Virgo in love can be a Virgo in denial, postponing bliss until the physique is chic, split ends mended, and the house more in line with the invisible Virgo ideal. Virgo is the most discriminating sign of all but, guess what? They give themselves a break when it comes to their own love life. They like the idea of providing form and function for an alleged creative genius or person with issues. Then Virgo bitches about being an unpaid muse, typist, and money-lender.

It's almost as if Virgo knows that the only chance they get to break out of their reputation for being a fussbudget is to have a torrid and dysfunctional love affair.

Ideally, they need someone who shares their values and enjoys correctional motivation. Like cousin Gemini, Virgo can lack intimacy skills but makes up for it in the sensuality stakes.

These folk are known as the closet kink artistes of the zodiac. So long as nobody minds them leaping out of bed to change the sheets after sex, they are renowned for bedwork skills.

It's the "us" chats which cause them the most concern.

Virgo's partner: I am so bitter and yet feel so lost and alienated from you. I really want you to...

Virgo: That's interesting. I was just reading this incredible magazine article about modern marriage by that author, you know, who also wrote the piece on the Sufi religion and...

Virgos are not often romantic in the clichéd flowers, scent, and chocolates sense. They think that sort of behavior is more suited to guilty adulterers and the like. Virgo prefers thoughtful small gestures like remembering the book someone was reading so they can ask how it was, leaving the toilet pristine and refraining from nitpicking if their partner is on the phone. Unlike the secret planner of other star signs, the Virgoan version is not about the Virgo. It's more of a comprehensive database listing every single transgression of their partner. Once they find their soul mate and are happy, Virgos are the (secret) best catch of the zodiac.

Virgo-Aries

Ramzilla thinks everyone who disagrees with their genius is a raving idiot. Virgo is more circumspect. Always willing to examine all aspects of a scenario, Virgo accomplishes much via careful evaluation. So what happens when Virgo force of reason crashes into Aries life force? Someone may need to compromise, not necessarily a problem with other signs but a possible deal-breaker with Aries. Debating is the core competency of Ramzilla. They love to argue and will go at it nonstop until they either win or fall asleep. Virgo is a skilled and vicious arguer. These two could spend a lot of time in verbal battle. If this is a big turn-on and bickering can be made an essential part of foreplay, love thrives. Aries officially deplores Virgo's addiction to petty detail but it's secretly admired. Virgo is freaked by how much energy Aries burns up stomping around trying to realize a totally unfeasible idea but winds up awed when it comes off. Aries loves that Virgo is so suave, sexily informed, and holistically put together.

Hot duos: Ryan Phillippe & Reese Witherspoon, Ben Lee & Claire Danes, Harry Connick Jr. & Jill Goodacre, Chris Evans & Billie Piper

Virgo-Taurus

Virgo and Taurus turn one another on from day one. As each is an Earth sign they share healthy libidos, a lust for things, and worldly goodwill. From the outside, this couple looks like a pair of besotted teenagers. Taurus adores Virgo self-containment and just loves calming those twitchy nerves with sensual attentions. Virgo enjoys teasing Taurus, testing the boundaries of an admittedly sometimes closed mind. This is one of the most officially delightful duos of the zodiac. Problems arise in friendly pastures when each gives in to their control-freak personas. Taurus tries to control the finely tuned Virgo mind. Virgo rebels and a Virgo in act-up mode is a scary sight. Virgo gets angry with Taurean mess and lack—apparently—of self-discipline. Then again, many Taureans like having a Virgo around to tell them not to put so much butter on their baked potato. The home of Virgo and the Cow becomes a haven of gracious living. Love lasts and lasts.

Hot duos: Mel Ferrer & Audrey Hepburn, Ingrid Bergman & Roberto Rossellini, Faith Hill & Tim McGraw, Christopher Isherwood & Don Bacard, Cherie Booth Blair & Tony Blair

Virgo-Gemini Virgo can be the Dr. Frankenstein of love, enjoying not so much a relationship as a human experiment. Virgo loves to nag, Gemini hates to be nagged. Virgos enjoy a spot of moralizing, Gemini can't bear being moralized to. If Gemini wants to be reminded to floss their teeth, they visit the dentist. Ethics? That's for the lawyer and accountant to figure out. Virgo is drawn to the carefree wit of Gemini and Gemini loves the mind—and body—of our Virgo. Both are brainy and enjoy word play. If talking were all it took to maintain a loving relationship, these two have it made. But Gemini amorality wounds the Virgoan sense of decency! Virgo can't believe how careless this sign can be with other people's feelings. Ever-observant Virgo is hurt by flirtation. Gemini is one of the most outrageous flirts of the zodiac. But basic tensions can be overcome via a strong mental and physical bond. Gemini gets that Virgo structure lends direction to their genius. Virgo loves the nonstop stimulation of Gemini. Each sparks off the other.

Hot duos: Prince Albert & Queen Victoria, Lachlan Murdoch & Sarah O'Hare, Hugh Grant & Liz Hurley, Sir Richard Attenborough & Lady Sheila Attenborough, David Arquette & Courteney Cox

Virgo-Cancer

Unbelievable as it can seem to Virgo, there are some personal dilemmas that logic is powerless to illuminate. The relationship with the Crab could be one of them. Virgo is not normally at ease with full-blown emotion. Crab emotes a lot. Virgo says get a grip and Crab loses the grip completely. These two seem like they're almost instantly married. It's as if they skip the "ripping off clothes" phase and move straight into afternoon strolls, nattering on about the price of everything. Sexual and mental compatibility are usually a given. It feels as if they're soul mates and nothing can tear them apart. What could? Guilting. Each party is great at guilting and blame-storming. Either or both can martyr themselves right out of an otherwise beautiful relationship. Crabs don't want to hear practical Virgo advice about nutrition and decluttering. Crab wants Virgo to feel their pain, not offer pragmatic stupid solutions.

Hot duos: Barbara Bach & Ringo Starr, Ben Bradlee & Sally Quinn, Ferdinand & Imelda Marcos, Jean-Michel Jarré & Isabelle Adjani, Oliver Parker & Thandie Newton

Virgo-Leo

Old-fashioned astrologers called Virgo the handmaiden to Leo. Scary? It is to Virgo. Leo kind of likes the idea. Maybe Virgo secretly does too—a demanding Leo character gives Virgo the chance to slip into a fetching little hairshirt. While Leo carries on like femme fatale Tallulah Bankhead or a banqueting Henry VIII, Virgo glides silently around emitting invisible guilting rays. Leos are big-picture people who see themselves as the director of their own life, with lavish production values, of course. They can skip over a lot of detail whereas Virgos are more keen on the minutiae of life. Leo hates that Virgo is really more sophisticated. Leo, despite the surface glitz, is a simple character who is often emotionally stuck in adolescence. Each complements the other so long as both pretend they are like the other. Huh? Virgo flatters Leo about their amazing analytical powers and Leo effusively admires Virgo's looks and sex appeal. When each opens to the other in collaboration, this duo is dynamic.

Hot duos: Guy Ritchie & Madonna, Willie Gordon & Isabelle Allende, D. H. Lawrence & Frieda Lawrence, George Putman & Amelia Earhart, Salma Hayek & Edward Norton

Virgo-Virgo
So many Virgos like to present as the anti-Virgo. "I'm so filthy and disorganized," they simper, pointing out a miniscule split end to prove their point. But when Virgo meets Virgo, the game is up. These two totally understand each other and are willing to go there with mega-analysis of the relationship and the other Virgo's foibles. There is not enough room on the high moral ground for two Virgos. You would imagine that two Virgos would be incredibly tidy, but no! It is almost as if they cancel one another out. Being obsessed with neatness, they both become enormously irritated with the mess created by the other Virgo. Their own disorder? A mere product of creativity and/or a busy life. Cohabiting Virgos should ideally have their own bathrooms and dressing rooms to allow for the fullest expression of fretting about their wardrobe and grooming. They truly understand one another, bonding in bed and by pointing out spelling mistakes together. Both really enjoy analyzing the quirks of their friends, family, and associates.

Hot duos: Dave Stewart & Siobhan Fahey, King Ludwig of Bavaria & Lola Montez

Virgo-Libra
St. Virgo loves to tackle the to-do list. Libra says "great" and books a manicure, or sits down to compose some poetry. Virgo and Libra have an excellent chance of living happily ever after. Each just needs to be prepped to tweak a few aspects of their core persona. Libra loves Virgo's sense of what is and what is not correct. Virgo loves Libra's aesthetics and fairness fetish. Virgo needs to go easy on the guilting and add more clichéd romantic utterings to the conversational repertoire. A query regarding the Libra's skin tone need not be met with brutal Virgo accuracy. A comparison to a peach or a

baby is just fine. Libra wants love sonnets. Virgo wants more bedwork. Virgo wants savings and security. Libra likes what Libra likes at that particular moment. Libra says a must-have and Virgo says a must-not. Libra heads off into smarmy charm mode on someone else. If these teensy barriers can be dissolved, these two bond on gossip, the intricacies of life, and the strongest feeling that each wildly needs the other.

Hot duos: Jada Pinkett Smith & Will Smith, Elaine Irwin & John Cougar Mellencamp

Virgo-Scorpio
Virgo is compulsive. Scorpio is obsessive. It works! Virgo gets off on being lean and clean. Scorpio likes to indulge all appetites and is a believer in the power of their unwashed pheromonal appeal. It doesn't work! Scorpio wants sex when Scorpio wants it. Virgo doesn't like to copulate without a proper flossing experience. But each person totally understands the other's intensity without being remotely freaked out by it. Virgo trains Scorpio to respond to Virgoan pep talks. Scorpio gets Virgo to think a little deeper. Scorpio says destiny. Virgo prefers the more scientific concept of synchronicity. This all gets talked out and what can't be talked out gets worked through in the sack. This pair can be so compatible that they wind up spending far too much time together, alone, developing a secret language and alienating others. But they don't care. Both agree that there is no point being in a relationship if it is not a matter of total immersion in the other.

Hot duos: Leo & Sonya Tolstoy, Antonia Fraser & Harold Pinter

Virgo-Sagittarius
Virgo's perfect but the world isn't. This annoys Virgo. Sagg loves the world at large, imperfections and all. That irritates Virgo. Two parts—each really cool—that can't create a sum? Two people, both raving on, who can't hear the other? It could happen.

Especially if Virgo nags Sagg about taking enough clean undies on their camping trip. Both see themselves as the teacher of the relationship. Neither is willing to play diligent pupil although they'll try when lust is fresh. Sagg can be too blunt for sophisticated Virgo. Sagg thinks Virgo is too realistic or—in Sagg lingo—self-limiting. But magic happens when the spark is too intense to be allowed to go out. Each agrees to take turns playing teacher and student. Sagg agrees to respect suave Virgo. Virgo abandons—temporarily, of course—caution and joins Sagg on a technically impossible mission. When this synergy is achieved, neither party is ever remotely bored. Each energizes the other and sensual satisfaction spins off the marriage of true minds.

Hot duos: Sophia Loren & Carlo Ponti, Conrad Black & Barbara Amiel, Jonathan Schaech & Christina Applegate, Hugh Franklin & Madeleine L'Engle, H. G. Wells & Rebecca West, Liam Gallagher & Nicole Appleton, LeAnn Rimes & Dean Sheremet

Virgo-Capricorn
Finally! The chance of a relationship with a sane life form. It's just too thrilling. Both are so wise and they know it. Virgo's healthy and the Cap's wealthy. Or, maybe it's the other way around. Whatever, this is the dynamic duo of love, sex, and work. Relishing one another's company, these two mutually inspire and stimulate in every respect. Both are Earth signs, willing to put in the slog for later rewards. Cap won't ring Virgo who's working late to screech about not enough time for "us." Virgo won't bitch at Cap for being emotionally unavailable. Cap loves Virgo's style and organizational skills. Each is respectful and supportive of the other. Bedwork is bliss. The idea of settling down together is heavenly. Mutual reverence for ambition may erode quality time together. Making space for reverie reminds Virgo and Cap of what else they share. Affection flows with simplicity and ease. Any disputes are settled with Earth-sign efficiency.

Hot duos: Cameron Diaz & Jared Leto, K-Ci & Mary J. Blige

Virgo-Aquarius

You're perfect, and the Aquarius—despite all evidence to the contrary—thinks they are perfect. Both are most particular about how life ought to be lived. They're a pair of raving cranks. Once Virgo learns to stop seeing their idiosyncrasies as awareness and the Aquarian's as bloody-minded eccentricity, these two can blend beautifully. Both are accustomed to having felt like aliens since an early age. Together they set up a mini Shangri-la, far from the madding crowds. Problems may arise due to the Aqua lack of libido. Compared to Virgo's earthy appetite, Aquarius can seem cold-blooded. But this is quickly solved with a comprehensive Virgo-style prenuptial contract. Virgo realizes that the Aquarius aura of being an ego-less guru is a pose and that Aquarius is like a New Age Leo. Snobbery brings and keeps them together. Both are loving and influential friends to a select crowd of people but secretly feel themselves to be above the masses.

Hot duos: Charlie Sheen & Denise Richards, Lauren Bacall & Humphrey Bogart, Richard Gere & Carey Lowell, Jeremy Irons & Sinéad Cusack, Baz Luhrmann & Catherine Martin

Virgo-Pisces

This is a union of astro opposites but neither cares. At first. Virgo can't believe that Pisces can so cheerfully lead such an eccentric and turbulent life. Pisces wonders what it is about "magical realism" that Virgo doesn't get. Pisces says "reincarnation"; Virgo says "DNA." Virgo in health mode says "no" to that breakfast croissant and opts for a brisk daily walk. Pisces eats "soul" food and then freaks out, doing Pilates one moment and Eskimo tribal dancing the next. Virgo stresses out. Pisces says, "So what?" But these two can be so good for one another. Each has something the other secretly needs. Pisces loves the freedom of being truly organized. Virgo adores how enchanted life can seem when seen through surreal fishy eyes. If each party in this love affair can learn to listen to and learn from the other, a weird merging occurs and both become more like the other, growing in the process.

Hot duos: Claudia Schiffer & Matthew Vaughn, Gloria & Emilio Estefan

Are you really a Virgo?

1 Watching a new movie release of a major novel, you are most likely to feel...

(a) Awed by the vision and keenly interested in how the novel has been interpreted.

(b) Whatever, you just go to the movies for entertainment.

(c) Frustrated, as there are just too many errors and glitches for you to hold in your mind to bitch about later.

2 In an impassioned rant, your lover accuses you of having failed them in nearly every sense. You...

(a) Are appalled—you listen, determined to set things right.

(b) Resist the tyranny—love is not a dictatorship.

(c) Helpfully correct their overworked lack of grammar—it's "should not *have* betrayed"—not "should of."

3 Stray hairs in food or the bathtub...

(a) Happen. So what?

(b) Are yucky.

(c) Freak you out totally.

4 Your bookshelves are...

(a) A mess but still a reflection of who and what you are.

(b) A fabulous resource which you never tire of.

(c) Alphabetically organized but will be classified according to the proper Dewey system when you get around to it.

5 A close friend's difficult relationship finally busts up. You say...

(a) Something to change the subject—you're so over it.

(b) That the gin is on ice—come over.

(c) I told you so.

6 You feel that a household towel collection should be...

(a) Color coordinated and fluffy.

(b) Set up so there is a clean towel available when needed.

(c) Sun-dried for health reasons and each towel should be able to double as a loofah.

Answers: If you checked mainly (c) answers, then you are an official Virgo—sexy, together, and always right. If you checked (a) or (b) answers, you have other astro influences competing with your Virgoan Sun.

Libra

september 24-october 23

Libra at large

"Sometimes I'm so sweet even I can't stand it."

Dame Julie Andrews (1935-), British singer and actress who starred in the hit films *Mary Poppins* and *The Sound of Music*

Q: How many Librans does it take to change a light bulb?
A: Er, one. No, make that two. No, one...if that's what *you* think.

Like cousin Cow, Librans are ruled by Aphrodite aka Venus, the goddess of love and beauty. Astronomically, this is a blue-green planet which is mostly swamp land and spends much of the year shrouded in mists. Very Libran?

Their Venusian rulership affords our Libra a keen interest in the arts of romance, seduction, and soft furnishings. These are tactile creatures, in love with beauty in all its sensual forms.

Libra's astro symbol is the Scales. Every other sign gets an animal or a person. Libra is the only one to be represented by an inanimate object. These are not the kind of kitchen scales where one weighs up Parmesan cheese for lasagna nor the sort that monitors the effects of the said lasagna on one's weight. Picture the old-fashioned type with bowls on either side that come into balance when equally weighted.

Striving for perfect balance is always the Libran issue. They may, in fact, not be well balanced whatsoever—some of them are about as well balanced as The Leaning Tower of Pisa—but their astro pursuit is to reach balanced opinion, budget, and balance of power within their relationships.

Ideally, a Libra is delicately poised between day and night, Yin and Yang, passive and aggressive. Suitably, their astro motto is "I balance" aka "I cooperate." Another version is "I seek myself through unity." Maybe it should be "I dither" because that is the inevitable result of their quest for equilibrium. Librans can make up their mind quickly in matters such as must-have mascara or the correct cufflinks but are often indecisive in other matters. They can always grasp the other side of any argument.

Due to this ability, Librans are sometimes portrayed as some kind of alluring jellyfish. The "Fixed" signs in particular—Taurus, Leo, Scorpio, and Aquarius—can't understand why Libra can't simply decide what they think and stick to it.

No, they didn't like that movie either. Yes, they can utterly understand why it's worth loving. The Libran yen for balance, along with their undeniable charm, makes them sought-after companions and guests. In certain circles—such as that of the recently divorced—the Libran inability to take sides can come in very handy. It is also refreshing to meet someone who doesn't have rigid views on something boring such as politics.

Libra is also an Air sign like Gemini and Aquarius. Mentally oriented, they like things sanguine and breezy. This gives Libra brain power and wit along with a slightly higher chance of going mad than non-Air signs. Not that Libra would care or notice so long as they were still invited out to places.

As well as all this, Libra is a so-called "Cardinal" sign, bossy and basically entrepreneurial like Aries, Capricorn, and Cancer. These people have ways of getting their own way. They are, as fellow Libra and former British prime minister Margaret Thatcher was once described, the "iron fist in a velvet glove."

"The test of a first-rate intelligence is to hold two opposed ideas in mind at the same time and still function."

F. Scott Fitzgerald (1896-1940), successful American novelist, who embodied the Jazz ·Age. He was celebrated for both his glittering hedonism and his literary genius. His best-selling novels include *The Great Gatsby*, *This Side of Paradise*, and *The Last Tycoon*.

Libra on form is...

"No matter how great a person you are, no matter how loving and honest you are, there's no guarantee that anybody else is going to be like that."

Alicia Silverstone (1976-), gorgeous, pouting star of the film *Clueless*

SWEET Everyone falls in love with Libra. Some never recover. People on public transport feel compelled to compliment Libran eyes. Children like Librans. Cats like Librans. Even parking police like Librans. Birds fly around the Libran so that they can excrete on somebody else's head. Librans are often only dimly aware that not everyone lives like this. They wonder why people are so mean about banks, when the manager is always so charming and helpful. They attract admiration and envy in equal measure. Ice-skater Nancy Kerrigan's sweetness and talent drove fellow skater Tonya Harding so mad she tried to have her hobbled. Nancy went ahead and won her medal, along with acclaim for her forgiveness of Tonya. Libran men can evoke doting service from the surliest waitress. Libra smiles and suggests that grouchier types should put lavender oil in their bath like the Libran does.

REASONABLE Librans specialize in unbiased counsel, a huge boon for everyone lucky enough to be in their orbit. Should a situation requiring mediation arise, Libra's already there, ready and able to hear and grasp the other person's point of view. Okay, so they do also agree with Irish playwright Oscar Wilde that "nothing annoys an enemy more than forgiveness."

BEAUTIFUL As is fitting for a sign that's all about balance, Librans tend toward pleasingly symmetrical features. A mind-boggling stat is that 54 percent of *Playboy* magazine playmates are Libran. So is a disproportionate number of official beauties.

Libran men are total smoothies who look as if they're wearing make-up even when they are not.

TACTFUL Librans find undue intensity in social encounters odious and are skilled at bringing hot-air-fueled conversations back to a bubbly and light level. If someone is midway through an interminable yarn about how someone nobody knows thought they had a disease and then didn't, Libra can be relied upon to deftly direct the topic away from the tedious. They are also the master of the social euphemism. For example, someone slept around until the other person broke it off? Libra says they drifted apart. The relationship was vile but with fabulous make-up sex? Libra says a passionate affair. Obese? Libra says generously built. Promiscuity? Libra says socially active. A cocaine addict? Libra says very vibrant.

LOVING Love really is like oxygen to our Libra. They are in love with love and with being coupled. All Librans want to have a soul mate. A Taurus prefers to be in a relationship but would make do with rutting around their entire life, if necessary. A Leo could be left alone with some Champagne and a Belgian-glass mirror and probably end up proposing. Loving is Libra's core competency. They believe life is most happily lived in tandem with another.

CHARMING When Libra turns it on, nobody can resist. They excel at making someone else feel as if they are the most important person in the world of Libra. When British novelist P. G. Wodehouse discovered an author he admired, he would immediately shout the person to lunch at a swank eatery.

"The universe is full of magical things, patiently waiting for our wits to grow sharper."

Eden Phillpotts (1862-1960), English novelist, poet, and playwright. His play, *The Farmer's Wife*, was one of Alfred Hitchcock's first silent movies.

Libra off form is...

"We must live for the few who know and appreciate us, who judge and absolve us, and for whom we have the same affection and indulgence."

Sarah Bernhardt (1844-1923), French actress whose career spanned 62 years. She became one of the first international entertainment icons.

SLEAZY Librans are grotesquely capable of almost knocking people over in their quest to stand beside the most famous and/or desirable being in the room. This is only slightly more healthy than the Leo tendency to assume that they always are that person. Spanish crooner Julio Iglesias branded a perfume called Only, "for all that women have given me, I wanted to give them something in return, something that would speak intimately to each and every woman the world over." Yes, they fancy themselves as the world's greatest lovers. British rocker Sting boasted about his all-night Tantric love-making techniques. The Libran woman doesn't have Call Waiting. She has Cad Waiting, just in case the current beau fails to completely fulfill.

HYPOCRITICAL Just do it...later. Librans procrastinate but they turn it into a strength-of-character issue. One moment they're raving on about their new carbohydrate-free diet, the next they're eating chips, sipping chablis, and citing moderation. The material known as pornography becomes erotica should a Libran find it of interest. Really pretentious Librans upgrade their smut to art: British novelist P. G. Wodehouse was living in the south of France when Germany invaded in 1940. He was never interested in what he called "keeping up" with the news so he continued to write, oblivious to what was going on in the world. Then the Germans found out he was British and locked him up. To score a better standard of living, P. G. agreed to make funny radio shows for the

Nazis about the lighter side of internment. As a result, he was imprisoned in a comfortable home and his show was broadcast to the U.S. and Britain. When journalist Malcolm Muggeridge was sent to spy on P. G., he came back with the conclusion that "the broadcasts are neither anti- nor pro-German, just pro-Wodehousian. He is a man singularly ill-fitted to live in a time of ideological conflict, having no feelings of hatred about anyone, and no very strong views about anything." Traitor? Or just very Libran?

TYRANNICAL Jim Henson, creator of *The Muppets* TV show, was said to have a "whim of steel." Anyone who thinks that Libra is more of a lifestyle concept than an actual person should shack up with one some time. If a Libra decides that a sofa, say, is suddenly unsuitable, it will be instantly redefined as trash. It doesn't matter what anyone else thinks because Librans have superior aesthetic instincts. Libra doesn't care if the offending item is the household oven. Libra doesn't care what you say because Libra listens selectively. Certainly, they demonstrate a plausible appearance of hearing—eyes focused on yours in tender bemusement, tennis-club smile plastered across their pretty face—but really, they're planning their next little aesthetic improvement. One moment the Libra is unleashing a tornado of invective about how disgusting the venetian blinds are, the next moment they're answering the telephone with that special, probably patented, Libran "company" voice—a dulcet croon designed to utterly disarm new acquaintances and potentially grumpy shop assistants.

A SOCIAL CLIMBER Moth-like, Libra flutters toward the light of what they imagine to be a higher form of society. To avoid offending touchy Librans, the term "social moth" was changed to social butterfly. It is also more appropriate as anyone who has seen our Libran emerging from the dysfunctional cocoon of home to attend a glittering event will attest. Librans love the idea of fiercely protective bodyguards hustling them through the adoring crowds. A Libra is capable of over-reaching and trying to invite minor royalty or a celebrity to some boring suburban barbecue. They can neglect their family for decades—"too tedious, darling"—only to experience a sudden surge of affection when it transpires that cousin Thing is now terribly important.

"Regret is an appalling waste of energy; you can't build on it; it is good only for wallowing in."

Katherine Mansfield (1888-1923), adventurous, free-spirited New Zealand writer who is
credited with revolutionizing the short story

Motivating and manipulating a Libran

"Forget what you need and think only about what you desire."

Donna Karan (1948-), U.S. fashion designer and diva of the New Age

1 Be gossipy but not coarse. Libra adores info-dissemination. They gather their intelligence, strain it through the chiffon layers of their psyche, and regale away.

2 Accept that Libra does not divide people into good or bad. They are either charming or tedious.

3 Don't resent Libra's ongoing campaign to make everyone on the planet like them.

4 Let them matchmake you as (a) Libra is very good at it and (b) Libra is going to do it anyway.

5 Don't make them live with ugly pieces of furniture on spurious budget grounds. Libra would much rather enter into a buy-now-cry-later-type credit deal.

6 Gifting a Libran? Aim for something that's scented, such as perfume, room sprays, scented candles, or potpourri. Librans are obsessed with fragrance.

7 Never, ever force Libra to take a side one way or the other.

8 Don't be afraid of romantic clichés. Libra loves love sonnets, flowers, beautifully thoughtful gestures like love-song requests on the radio...it can't be too gushy.

9 Don't expect Libra to hang out at home alone while you're off flouncing about town. Libra will invariably invite someone around for company...you understand.

"I just can't understand people who have ugly people working for them. I really can't. Just call me a pathetic aesthete."

Jade Jagger (1971-), beautiful British model and designer of ornate jewelry and

decorative accessories

Libran role models

"People just getting totally gushy and over the top—I love that!"

Sting (1951-), British singer/musician and environmentalist who started his career with
the New Wave group The Police

- Oscar Wilde—brilliant Irish playwright and poet. He made his name with plays such as *The Importance of Being Earnest* and *Lady Windemere's Fan* but was equally famed for his libertine sympathies and his leadership of the Aesthetic Movement. He was very Libran: "beauty is a form of genius."

- Brigitte Bardot—gorgeous French actress and model. In the 1956 movie, *And God Created Woman*, she became a legend as the sexually free heart-breaker let loose in the French resort town of St. Tropez. She retired from movies before hitting 40 and is now an outspoken animal-rights campaigner.

- Linda McCartney—multi-talented wife of former Beatle, Paul McCartney. She was a *Rolling Stone* magazine photographer, and then a member of her husband's band, Wings. She wrote bestselling vegetarian cookbooks and campaigned against the fur industry.

- George Gershwin—American Pulitzer Prize-winning composer. He wrote pieces as diverse as *Rhapsody in Blue* and the stage musical *Porgy and Bess*. As a child he was a sportsman and street-fighter—it was the beauty of the violin sound that lured him into music studies.

- ee cummings—celebrated American poet and playwright. Cummings changed the way poetry was written by subverting traditional grammar and syntax. He published more than 900 poems and most are concerned with love. He was married three times—the first lasted six months, the second, three years, and the third for the remaining 30 years of his life.

- Catherine Deneuve—iconic Venus of French cinema. She had a complicated love life involving overlapping love interests and children to different men. Once called the "frigid femme fatale," she plays an active part in a European campaign to stop capital punishment in the U.S.

"It's very important to have the right clothing to exercise in. If you throw on an old T-shirt or sweats, it's not inspiring for your workout."

Cheryl Tiegs (1947-), 70s and 80s American supermodel who has become a
homeopathic advocate and merchandising mogul

Chic Libra

"I hated grunge."

Catherine Zeta-Jones (1969-), beautiful and increasingly accomplished Welsh actress
married to fellow Libran and Hollywood actor Michael Douglas

If Librans were in charge of everything, cheap or artificial fragrance would be illegal. The streets would be washed down in essential oils of ylang-ylang or honeysuckle and all lighting would be very flattering.

Librans have no issues with beauty; they like looking at it and they like being it. Not that they'll necessarily own up to that fact. The female Libran is particularly prone to claiming that her entire beauty regime consists of soap, water, and thinking nice thoughts. Their authentic good looks and cunning make them mega-skilled at pulling off a glowingly natural look, guaranteed to have other, more overtly made-up types tensing their jaw.

The men infuriate rivals by appearing wholesome and hunky but really being accomplished seducers. While Librans follow fashion as part of a general interest in all forms of personal decoration and the arts, they do not really need it. Fashion needs Libra, the most beautiful Sun sign of all.

U.S. fashion designer Ralph Lauren is very Libran. Born Ralph Lifshitz, he has created a career out of clothes designed to hyperbolically emulate that upper-class white-Anglo-Saxon-Protestant-at-play look. Beautifully executed as they are, the advertisements are also an apt illustration of Libra's rich inner life.

Scarily, Ralph Lauren evoked the Libran "whim of steel" when he sued the British Polo Association for using the name of Lauren's "fitness fragrance" Polo. Hello?

LOVELY LIBRANS Brigitte Bardot, Sarah Bernhardt, Montgomery Clift, Matt Damon, Catherine Deneuve, Michael Douglas, Anita Ekberg, Richard Harris, Rita Hayworth, Charlton Heston, Julio Iglesias, Hugh Jackman, Lily Langtry, Heather Locklear, Carole Lombard, Viggo Mortensen, Gwyneth Paltrow, Guy Pearce, Luke Perry, Christopher Reeve, Susan Sarandon, Alicia Silverstone, Will Smith, Mira Sorvino, Eric Stoltz, Cheryl Tiegs, Naomi Watts, Sigourney Weaver, Kate Winslet, Catherine Zeta-Jones

"I never forget that a woman's first job is to choose the right shade of lipstick."

Carole Lombard (1908-1942), beautiful, witty comedienne during the 30s and 40s. She was a huge star of her time and was famously adored by her husband, Hollywood screen idol Clark Gable.

Brilliant career

"I have always believed in collaboration—some of my best work
has been when I'm vibing with others."

MC Lyte (1971-), American female hip-hop artist and actress

Harmony-loving Librans can be made literally sick by a
dysfunctional day job. An ugly workplace or bitchy colleagues
shreds their serenity and they will simply shut down.

Librans like to have a life—if their business or employment is
not their life, they can be very slack about honoring obligations.
The world is full of non-fulfilled Libras trying to get some quack to
diagnose a disease so they can go to lunch with an admirer or shop
for organic-cotton face washers.

Many Librans developed Repetitive Strain Injury when it was more
fashionable. Nowadays, they suffer from Sick Building Syndrome and
are allergic to cheap synthetic carpets and unflattering fluoro lighting.
These types of surroundings evoke such a violent reaction in the Libran
soul that they take to their beds for days, reading Tennyson's poems,
breathing in essential oils, and chanting affirmations.

Ideally, a Libran works at home or in some scenario where Libra
controls the surroundings. But remember that they loathe being
alone and function best in tandem. While Libra, like cousin Pisces,
is capable of subverting any routine ever invented, they like office
gossiping and stimulating company.

Their much-vaunted need to cooperate in harmony is not just
some scam. You know, for instance, that when Scorpios go on
about it they have figured out some ghastly means of achieving it.
Aries march in and demand cooperation or else.

Librans do wonderfully well in business for themselves, in a
position where their unique talents are adored and in industries
such as fashion where it is totally the done thing to throw a
tantrum over a bolt of fabric not being nice enough.

Their impartiality makes them fantastic lawyers and counselors but really they swell the ranks of the artfully employed, in areas where an atmosphere of beauty is mandatory.

"There is no human problem which could not be solved if people would simply do as I advise."

Gore Vidal (1925-), American novelist, playwright, and urbane social commentator who champions civil liberties

Fiscal reality

"I explained that I had simple tastes and didn't want anything ostentatious, no matter what it cost me."

Art Buchwald (1925-), American political humorist whose popular columns appear in more than 530 newspapers around the world

There's a time to save and a time to spend. And there is a time to phone the bank with the "there's been a terrible mistake" tirade, only to find out that one has been embezzling one's own funds.

Librans know this, but it doesn't stop them from being often on the verge of going to the police to report that a burglar keeps plundering their wallet while they are sleeping. How else to explain the mysterious disappearance of dollar bills when all Libra did was buy one lipstick? And one skinny latte. all right, three. And then there was that cellulite-dissolving soap. And that beautiful bedspread. And...

And so it transpires that Libra has not been robbed after all. "I haven't reported my missing credit card to the police," one-time tennis superstar said, "because whoever stole it is spending less than my wife." Anyone hooked up with a Libra could surely relate.

Libra *is* the ultimate must-have sign. When the going gets tough, they do go shopping. Their not-so-secret motto is Things R Us—skin-cream things that accomplish what molecular geneticists can't, bed things so they can pout in luxury, gadget things to remind them that not everything is dysfunctional.

Hilariously, lurking within the rich inner life of our Libra is a fantasy of themselves as ultra-minimalists, able to pack the entire essentials of life into one beautiful piece of luggage. In real life, they are like walking magnets for costly items. Even blindfolded and wearing nose-plugs, a Libran paw would alight upon the most pricey item in any array. Their idea of money management is "Oh, look! It says that the minimum payment is only $220 a month..."

When Libra considers the level of luxury, the object of lust for things is surprisingly affordable. Unlike some signs, who are always amazed and bitching about the cost of whatever, Librans adjust quickly and so everything *is* surprisingly affordable.

Chez Libra

"Either those curtains go or I do."

Witty Irish poet and playwright Oscar Wilde's last words (1854-1900)

Libra's home reeks to high heaven with the smell of fresh flowers, imported room fragrance, scented candles, essential oil, and the Libran's own signature aroma. Obsessed with scent, they make a lot of major life decisions based on how people, things, or houses smell. Thus, they spend as much energy on the aroma of their home as they do on their personal perfume.

Once the olfactory aspect of interior decoration has been satiated, the Libran gaze turns fondly toward the 1920s. For them, the Jazz Age and a copy of F. Scott Fitzgerald's lovelorn novel *This Side of Paradise* are reflected by Art Deco lamps, pink and black tiles, and pedestal bathroom sinks. Hopelessly in love with love, the Libran taste can go somewhat astray at times and arrive at the too-tizzy Barbara Cartland end of the design spectrum. Some of them could even wind up in counseling for an addiction to soft furnishings.

So-called coffee-table books, considered a relic by many, are the real speciality of Librans. Picture this: a low-standing oriental-style table graced with a vase of glorious gardenias, an oversized bottle of expensive perfume, and a huge stack of desirable books on art and photography. Ladies and gentlemen, a Libran is in residence.

A Libran in love

"I am not a prick. You don't have to explain nothing when you are in love."

Jean-Claude Van Damme (1968-), Belgian-born bodybuilder and karate pro who became a Hollywood action hero

Few Librans are ever single for an appreciable length of time. This is partly because they are so attractive but also because they will take anyone to avoid being on their own.

What to do if love starts to fade? Hating to be on the hop, they usually have their next relationship warming up and raring to go as the previous one dwindles. Not that the official partner of a Libran will necessarily know anything about this at the time. As Brigitte Bardot pointed out, "it is better to be unfaithful than faithful without wanting to be." Actress Susan Sarandon says she likes "in the moment, constant commitment."

When in love, that is, all the time ideally, Libra likes a highly charged level of erotic and romantic excitement. Too much chitchat about business, family, and tax sends Libra gliding off toward wherever the moonlit gardenias and tender frivolity await.

Ivan Pavlov, the Libran shrink, trained his dogs to salivate at the sound of a bell because they expected food. Librans can think of themselves as Pavlov with the lover as a version of Pavlov's dog. The bell is the Libran coo, causing the dog to salivate, ready to obey the whim of steel.

Other Librans see the lover as a mirror, reflecting back the Libra in a rosy halo. If you love something, set it free. Librans think that's sloppy thinking. They prefer, "if you love something, take it on holiday, buy it expensive gifts, and make expert, artful love."

Even the most happily coupled Libran still considers it good fun to make someone get a huge crush on them. The Libran may never intend to do a thing about it. They can exist for ages on the yearning and the love vibe radiating from the other.

Their love of love does not necessarily make them the ultimate platonic friend. They can be off the radar screen for months, devoted to the lover...only to re-emerge in a scented haze of gush, wanting to go to a discreet bar, to discuss our Libra's so-complicated love life, you understand.

Libra-Aries These two are astrological opposites, amassed against the other via a trillion little traits. Libra says "tomayto" and Ramzilla says "potato." Libra is Yin and the Aries is Yang. Aries is ruled by Mars and Libra by Venus. Each spends in such a way so as to send the cute couple sensationally broke but Libra browses, breathing in the retail ambience. Aries sees it as an in/out expedition. Aries likes to sweat. Libra likes yoga. Aries stirs. Libra makes peace. The Aries style of conversation sounds more like a hoony argument to Libra. Aries leaps to conclusions. Libra thinks things through or, as Ramzilla calls it, vacillates. But such a set-up creates a dynamic tension which can be

very exciting. Shared ideals along with stacks of space keep this relationship fresh, fun, and enduring. Libra is always aroused by the spunky Aries persona. Aries finds Libra amazingly alluring. Libra gives Aries stacks of advice which Aries secretly takes!

Hot duos: Danielle Spencer & Russell Crowe, Clyde & Bonnie, Nane & Kofi Annan

Libra-Taurus

Both are gorgeous Venusians, sharing sensuality, a penchant for sloth, and a love of soft furnishings. The physical bonding is breathtakingly physical, especially for Libra who tends to prefer romance to actual bedwork. Each helps the other harmonize their lives. Libra encourages Taurus to vary a few habits and be more accepting. Taurus gives Libra the reassurance and structure they need. But Libra is open-minded and objective whereas Taureans take years to change their minds. A tiny rift can gape out of all proportion if Libra sees Taurus as an intransigent old thing and Taurus thinks Libra is some fluff-ball with no real values. And then, in make-up mode, Libra aims for a beautiful love poem (preferably a haiku), flowery moments when Taurus expects (and gives) practical demonstrations of solid loving. This can be such a strong and perfect couple so long as each is capable of making a supreme adjustment to always see the other's world view, no matter how obviously nuts. And these two must utterly avoid viewing one another in a negative light.

Hot duos: Juan & Eva (Evita) Peron, Keeley Shaye Smith & Pierce Brosnan, Lord Nelson & Lady Emma Hamilton, Jermaine Dupri & Janet Jackson

Libra-Gemini

These two can't take their eyes off one another—unless it's to check out the competition circling around. Both want to head off to some bedroom and just stay there, together...forever. The crappiest pop song suddenly makes the most intense sense. Libra and Gemini are one of the most compatible couplings of the zodiac. Both are so used to having people fall wildly in love with them that they've become blasé. This relationship shocks both to the core. "I'm a cliché," thinks Gemini. Libra, so accustomed to doting and worshipful suitors, gets off on the hard-to-get Gemini. Physically, emotionally, and mentally, these two love everything about each other. Issues? Libra has a heart and Gemini doesn't...more or less. Libra definitely requires more classic romantic gestures from Gemini. Gemini doesn't get that some other signs see Libra as a ditherer. How dare they? It's called being flexible. Libra learns to wait elegantly should Gemini be off on some solo adventure. Gemini learns that Librans never wait alone.

Hot duos: Linda & Paul McCartney, Arthur Miller & Marilyn Monroe, P. G. & Ethel Wodehouse

Libra-Cancer Crab thinks it is so tacky to wield charm the way
Libra does, like a weapon, just so Libra can get whatever they want. Libra can't bear that the Crab turns on the tears, power-sulking, and general crap for precisely the same reason. Crab takes the high moral ground and Libra wonders why Crab doesn't lighten up...a lot. Crabs value security above and beyond anything else. On a day-to-day level, this translates into full-on stinginess. Crab can even resent Libra buying a few magazines for research purposes. Libra likes nice things and so what if they cost a bit? Crab goes on about saving for retirement. Agelessly cute Libra is aghast. Libra comes home with titillating gossip. Crab moralizes. Crab and Libra go out together and Crab grizzles about their issue of the day or some sad story which has gripped the imagination. Or so it seems to Libra. How this coupling can work: well, they do have things in common in that they are great organizers and are fantastic with start-up ideas for businesses and new opportunities. When these two can admit to their similarities and compromise a bit, this can be a fun relationship.

Hot duos: Heather Locklear & Richie Sambora, Mel Brooks & Anne Bancroft, William & Babe Paley

Libra-Leo

Leo and Libra love one another at first sight and sometimes forever. Each is a bona fide beautiful person, sensual, clever, and ambitious. Libra is smarter than Leo but smart enough not to let on to Leo. A Leo safe in the Libra's manicured paw has many advantages for our Libra. Leo does not merely tolerate Libran foibles, Leo *loves* them—except for when Libra hogs the limelight. That irks. Both are keen on scoring ego resources such as flattery, money, the lust of others (even when Libra and Leo don't care), even more beauty, status, and prestige and are happy to pull together in tandem. Libra does wonder what is up with Leo's conversational skills. Like, hasn't the big cat ever heard of asking about someone else? Libra sometimes thinks Leo is too demanding in the bedwork area. Leo has to realize that Libra likes feathery foreplay. Leo thinks Libra can be too wishy-washy but then Libra's dithery Yin vs. Yang—"oh God, you decide!"—brain is perfect for the bossy-boots Leo. The sexuality is compatible so long as the lighting is flattering and you do not mind the Leo penchant for stacks of rose-tinted mirrors.

Hot duos: Kate Winslet & Sam Mendes, Brigitte Wilson & Pete Sampras, Eric Benet & Halle Berry, F. Scott & Zelda Fitzgerald, Julie Andrews & Blake Edwards, Rex Bell & Clara Bow, Bruce Springsteen & Patty Scialfa

Libra-Virgo

Libra and Virgo share an idea that everything should be just so. When life swings too far from the other's inner vision of perfection, things get unpretty fast. Despite the air of nonchalance, Libra is a most particular person, who loves that Virgo understands this trait. Virgo doesn't think there is anything remotely fussy about Libra. Flighty, yes. Over-extravagant, yes. Louche?

Compared to Virgo. If high standards were all it took this could be such a beautifully compatible relationship that they may as well move in together right away. They could have hours of fun throwing away each other's stuff. But, yes, there are a few Virgo-Libra issues. Libra is horrified to discover that despite their air of refinement, Virgo is a grubby little Earth sign and, as such, prone to all sorts of (shudder) needs. A Libran who has applied their rejuvenating potions for the evening may not want Virgo pawing away. Virgo must also accept that Libra needs nonstop reassurance, rapport, mental intimacy, and...thoughtful gifts.

Hot duos: Will Smith & Jada Pinkett Smith, Harold Pinter & Lady Antonia Fraser, John Cougar Mellencamp & Elaine Irwin

Libra-Libra
If these two can stand each other at all, the relationship overcomes all obstacles. Both are beautiful charmers—smart, popular, and the most memorable of hosts. But when it comes to being clear with their partner, they can't hack the pace. They'd rather flirt their way out of any emotional issue. This is obviously a threat to an otherwise enchanted love affair. The anger beneath that seductive manner builds to boiling point until someone just has to...explode? Not at all. That would involve candor. Each is more likely to sneak off for a secret liaison with someone they feel will really "show" the other Libran. It's not nice, and at least one of them has to learn to express disenchantment as it occurs. Both being Venus-ruled romance addicts, they are sensually compatible in bed—it takes one Libra to know that the other Libra doesn't see roses, chocolates, and candle-lit dinners as a clichéd precondition for bedwork. The world's stocks of Barbra Streisand's CDs are depleting because of Librans in love. But do bear in mind that one reality-checking meeting with an accountant can make Librans frigid for weeks. The beauty of this coupling is that they understand and support one another's deepest romantic yearnings. That, along with the sheer physical beauty, of course.

Sun signs

Hot duos: Michael Douglas & Catherine Zeta-Jones, Susan Sarandon & Tim Robbins, Oscar Wilde & Lord Alfred Douglas

Libra-Scorpio

Scorpio tries to transfix Libra with their hypnotic gaze, refusing to activate under Libran charms. "What a weirdo," thinks Libra, tripping away from the very heavy character. Scorpio wonders if Libra is always so shallow and fluffy. Scorpio thinks everyone who is not as intense and definite as Scorpio is a flake. This is very tedious for Libra, especially when Scorpio gets onto conspiracy theories. Libra thinks, "where did I drop myself off?" Scorpio needs to get that Libra is a naturally vibrant and attractive person, hardly able to hack wallflowering around at a party just so Scorpio doesn't get ownership issues. Scorpio is sexual. Libra, while absolutely not asexual, prefers romance. Libra makes what they think of as a light-hearted snippet of pillow talk. Scorpio stays up all night, paranoid and bitching about the apparent deeper meaning of the quip. Yet, should each side of this duo be able to hack one another's unique traits, both can be so fulfilled. Libra gives Scorpio a (social) life. Scorpio fulfills desires Libra didn't know they had. The final verdict for these two? It can work—with work.

Hot duos: Gwen Stefani & Gavin Rossdale, Anne & Stan Rice

Libra-Sagittarius

The Sagittarian hype, bombast, and lack of responsibility can be stunning. So stunning that Libra fails to realize what a truly awesome love match this pairing could be. Sagg is initially so smitten by Libran charm and beauty that they plan to perhaps stay put for five minutes. All Libra needs to do is take advantage of this pause in the swirling Sagg consciousness. Sagg-training is not for the impatient or simple-minded. It takes someone strong enough to give Sagg space. Note: If nobody hears you scream in space then nobody will be able to hear the Sagg ranting either. Set Sagg free and they will soon be back to audition for a permanent placement. Then Libra has to let Libran diplomacy set Sagg an example of how hypocrisy can smooth the way. Sagg may well decide to make the re-entry. Once mated, this is a sweet liaison with lots of fun, sensual bonding, and late-night chitchat after the guests have left. For all their seeming clashes, this is what really binds them—Libra's romance streak wants someone like Sagg to make the running. And Sagg secretly adores retiring to the civilized Libran world after a day of adventures. They wind up being like the glamourous old couples driving sports cars in travel ads.

Hot duos: Sharon & Ozzy Osbourne, John Cowper Powys & Phyllis Playter, Soon-Yi Previn & Woody Allen, Catherine Oxenberg & Casper Van Dien

Libra-Capricorn Capricorn loves Libra on the spot, summing up Libra allure and cachet in a moment. Libra hesitates, intuiting that Capricorn may not be able to come up with enough romantic hype and gush to satisfy Libra. Cap moves in for the sell. Cap is hard-hearted. Libra is tender-hearted. Both are status-conscious. Libra is ruled by Venus and Capricorn by worldly Saturn. Libra needs more than a strong investment portfolio, structured life, and the ruttish Capricorn libido to keep them happy. Capricorn can find the Libran approach to socializing—"the future is here and it looks like fun, let's party!"—very irritating. Libra is an idealist. Capricorn is a realist. If they are willing to accept that the other has (gasp) a point, they learn vital love lessons from one another. This duo can boost their potential for relationship success by having planets in the same sign as the other's Sun. For example, Capricorn has Moon in Libra and Libra has Capricorn rising. The bonus is neither is likely to embarrass the other by making a scene.

Hot duos: Prince Edward & Sophie Rhys-Jones, Mira Sorvino & Olivier Martinez, Sting & Trudy Styler, Eugene O'Neill & Carlotta Monterey, Nia Vardalos & Ian Gomez

Libra-Aquarius

Libra and Aquarius can be true soul mates. Each is interested in truth and beauty. Libra teaches Aquarius to be more outgoing and giving to them and to others. Aquarius shows Libra how to be more compassionate of those who do not fit the Libran framework. Aquarius may be irked at times by Libra's go-anywhere, full-on charm. An Aquarius is more of the combative school of conversation, asserting something provocative or just plain irrelevant, just for a stir, and then waiting for a response. Libra thinks this type of behavior is so childish. Disputes ensue over how each relates to others. Aquarius must also be trained into providing Libra with the nonstop flattery and support they simply must have. This is such a beautiful relationship, consisting of two Air signs who are both rational and fair creatures. Of course, there is always the problem that each party is too civilized and real emotions are not recognized as such. In Libra-Aquarius heaven, each shares feelings without stressing out.

Hot duos: John Lennon & Yoko Ono, Carole Lombard & Clark Gable, Eleanor & Franklin D. Roosevelt, Kelly Preston & John Travolta

Libra-Pisces

Libra and Pisces bond over how beguiling they both are—and artistic, kind, and sweet. Both want to create a life in which they are free to follow their bliss. Both agree that they don't like money-grubbing straights. Libra and Pisces respect the talent, but they also have stupendous lifestyle needs. Nowhere in the zodiac is there quite the same degree of retail mania and reliance on "help" as there is with these two. To watch a Fish and Lib partnership fight it out over who has been embezzling the bank account—only to find it's both of them—is to witness a clinic in how *not* to handle personal finances. A business joint venture should be carefully thought through. They must take care not to fall into a competitive seductive sloth. When both are secure and in focus, Libra and Pisces agree on almost everything. A structure is ideally set in place so both can find fulfillment. Both are fabulous at seeing each side of an issue and working toward harmony. Both bring out the best in the other's social persona. Sensual bliss keeps them connected even when one or both has withdrawn to the sulking hut. Pisces can be a bit weird for Libran tastes. Pisces wonders if Libra is surreal enough, attuned to the alternative universes that are so much a part of the Piscean reality. Emotional rhythms can be so synchronized that each knows what the other is thinking.

Hot duos: Dorothea Hurley & Jon Bon Jovi, Gwyneth Paltrow & Chris Martin, Eminem & Kim Mathers

Are you really a Libran?

1 If feeling blue, you cheer yourself up by...

(a) Talking things through with a close friend.

(b) Exercising outdoors or taking a swim.

(c) Buying something scented: candles, essential oils, 10 bars of soap, designer scent, incense.

2 Arranging the guest list for your next party you have to cut numbers by a quarter. You strike off everyone who is...

(a) Not really that much of a true friend or someone you are not totally sure of. You prefer socializing to be among true intimates who can relax together.

(b) On second thoughts, a bit out of reach, not really in your circles. It's a party, not work.

(c) Plain, tedious, boring, coarse, or common—no matter who they are.

3 Your lover is going on a conference at a luxury resort but you're not invited. You are...

(a) Peeved at first but looking forward to a week off where you can live it up exactly how you choose.

(b) Keen to ensure that they maximize the career potential of this junket and not use it as an excuse to slacken off. You make plans to phone them every morning and evening and speak to them in life-coach mode.

(c) Crooning on the telephone to your most interesting "flirtee," explaining that you now have some free time, letting wistful little sighs hint that all may not be well at your place.

4 Your beauty therapist...

(a) Chatters too much. You wish she'd shut up and let you think.

(b) Changes all the time. You go to see whoever on the spur of the moment.

(c) Is secretly like a maid from medieval times—at least that's how you see her. She is your coconspirator in self-creation. Occasionally, you wonder whether she should sign a non-disclosure agreement.

5 Indecision indicates that one...

(a) Has a weak mind.

(b) Needs more information in order to make up one's mind.

(c) Is an evolved being.

6 People who don't like you...

(a) Don't bother you. You don't get along with everyone in the world either.

(b) Can get stuffed. It's their loss.

c) Need to be conquered as soon as possible; you're charmed and dangerous.

Answers: If you checked mainly (c) answers, then you are an official Libran—luscious, loved, and forever beautiful. If you checked (a) or (b) answers, you have other astro influences competing with your Libran Sun.

Scorpio

october 24-november 22

Scorp of ages

"Let them hate me so long as they respect me."

Tiberius (42 BC-AD 37), emperor of Rome for 23 years

Q: How many Scorpios does it take to change a light bulb?
A: Who wants to know?

Scorpio people are "ruled" by planet Pluto. For a long time, Pluto was called Planet X because nobody knew for sure whether it was really there or not. Nobody even knows if Pluto has an atmosphere. It is a most suitable sponsor planet for our Scorpio.

Astrologically, the main principle of Pluto is transformation. People with prominent Plutos in their birth chart are always regenerating themselves. To be born a Scorpio is to be constantly shedding old skins in preparation for the new.

Scorp is a Water sign, meaning that feeling is usually more important to them than anything else, for instance, intellect. But they are also what is known as a "Fixed" sign, that is, they are as stubborn as Leo, Taurus, and Aquarius. They live with the weird dichotomy of being an intensely transformative sign—that is, transmuting energy is their cosmic job but they are fixed in nature. At least they are not shallow.

The astrological motto is a sort of summary of a Sun sign's ethos. It is akin to a mission statement. In the case of Scorpio, it is "I desire," and they do.

Scorpions sting one another when they mate. Some scientists say that the toxic venom may contain sexy, falling-in-love type pheromones that bond the scorpions to one another.

Another explanation is that, like Scorpio the Sun sign, scorpion the insect is just kinky. Yes, the astrological symbol for Scorpio is the Scorpion.

Scorpions aren't among the most popular of creatures. Their most powerful instinct is to sting everything, including themselves, and they do seem to feature in a lot of biblical curses.

Scorpions seem really intense, mad, ruthless, in part because they will sting themselves to death if they think they are going to lose a fight. Scorpio people often radiate an impression that they would be willing to do something similar if someone even embarrasses them.

But Scorpio is such a complex sign that it has more than one symbol. It is also, for example, said to be represented by the mythical Phoenix that could be destroyed by fire and yet arise rejuvenated from the ashes.

Scorpios are old souls. As in totally ancient. Scratch a Scorpio and you will find some toothless soothsayer shaking a staff in warning. Or an aggressive amoeba similar to the unicellular beings we apparently all evolved from.

Some people go a bit over the top and suggest that Scorpio was the snake in the biblical Garden of Eden, thus exemplifying temptation, corruption, and the fall from grace. Was Scorpio the worm in the apple? Maybe Eve was a Scorpio?

Suffice to say that anyone who is strong, silent, and a bit scary is often a Scorpio.

"Do your damndest in an ostentatious manner all the time."

General George S. Patton (1885-1945), one of America's most distinguished military leaders, serving in World Wars I and II. He also represented his country in the pentathlon at the Stockholm Olympics in 1912.

Scorpio on form is...

"Oh Lord, give me chastity and continence but not yet."

Saint Augustine (AD 354-430), philosopher, writer, teacher, North African Bishop, and
Doctor of the Roman Catholic Church

INSCRUTABLE Mysterious by nature, Scorpio is the only sign which can carry off a chic yet compulsive-obsessive aura. Do they have hobbies? Stuff that they just dabble in? No. They tend toward deep and abiding interests in subjects to do with sex, the occult, and other people's money. Method-acting was invented by a Scorpio. So was the Rorschach ink blot test, where one's reactions to blobs apparently reveal all manner of deep issues. Scorpios don't feel the need to tell all. They can have whole years missing from their resumés and just shrug it off. Or they murmur, "No, thank you. You must understand that after that night in Morocco I can never touch gin again." Get the picture. Private is private.

DISCREET Unlike some signs of the zodiac, Scorpios do not stoop to scene-making under pressure. Someone naturally winds up on their secret crap list but they retain glacial serenity without grizzling. A secret confided to a Scorp is a secret forever safe. But, if you arouse their enmity, your secret could possibly wind up being posted on the Internet.

SEXY Scorps are the sexiest sign of all—sex appeal simply oozes from their every pore. They tend to go to extremes of being either wildly celibate or deeply immersed in sexuality. Think Prince Charles and his intended reincarnation as Camilla Parker Bowles's tampon, Larry Flynt who founded *Hustler* magazine, Helmut Newton's fetishistic fashion photography, Shere Hite's *Hite Report*, in which she provided stats on the length of orgasms and the number of sexual positions, Robert Mapplethorpe's nude photography, actress

Vivien Leigh's (Scarlett in *Gone With the Wind*) apparently legendary sexual appetite...Scorpios love to get it on. Actor Richard Burton was a celebrated rake who used a "throbbing sensation in my penis as a sort of barometer of when something important was going to happen." Fashion designer Oleg Cassini said of Princess Grace of Monaco: "She had a very powerful sexual personality." All Scorpios do.

STRONG A Scorpio can get blood from a stone. Scorpios are brutally self-aware. They don't flinch from self-examination. Nothing you can say gets to them because they've already thought of it. It's how they remain impassive in the face of the worst provocation. Feeling the fear and doing it anyway is what they do. The great explorers Captain Cook and Christopher Columbus just kept going until they saw land. Canadian singer kd lang grew up in a place where being a vegetarian was almost as difficult as being gay and somehow thrived.

SPOOKY Is the Scorpio spookiness nature or nurture? There is something profound about this lot. They have powerful instincts which they often obey. When Robert Louis Stevenson wrote his strange tale, *Dr Jekyll and Mr Hyde*, whose spooked psyche was he drawing inspiration from? Bram Stoker, the author of *Dracula*, or maybe Dracula himself? Because they have the ability to focus on other people so strongly, they can be highly intuitive regarding another person's needs, and can channel information that another person requires. Even the most seemingly placid Scorpio is on some level operating as a medium, transmitting light and energy to those in need.

PRINCIPLED Scorpios operate on an inalterable value system, one which remains in place despite vagaries of fashion, taste or common opinion. They are a noble people sticking to their own standards of what is correct, no matter what. The ancient Greeks saw integrity not as some nebulous goody-goody concept but as oneness, the very Scorpio trait of presenting exactly the same version of oneself to everyone, whether a pauper or a prince.

Scorpio off form is...

"Guilt is an emotion I don't really want to tap into."

Winona Ryder (1971-), Hollywood actress, Generation X icon—*Mermaids*

OBSESSIVE "I desire?" The astro motto for our Scorpio should be something along the lines of "I obsess." Ask Scorpios not to obsess and they obsess about not obsessing. They will stay up all night chanting a non-obsessive affirmation or sit there scrawling the words "I will be less obsessive" a thousand times in red ink. They will become secretly obsessed with getting to the psychological roots of their obsession. Their idea of getting over an ex-lover is to drive past their house *only twice* nightly. They can be vile dinner-party guests; they are so into their precious authenticity that they lose sight of how intensely they are boring everyone.

PARANOID Paranoid? Scorpio? Of course not, they scoff. Scorpio just wants to know who sent that big moth to fly in their window. That disappearing lunch box is a plot by their child to discredit them. Someone says, "you're looking well," Scorpio thinks it's a curse. Scorpio's social life can be conducted like a resistance movement—there are dozens of "cells" of friends, each knowing little or nothing about the other. They do a lot of snooping which, should you stoop to it, would count as a betrayal but is completely understandable on their part. They peer into bathroom cupboards, not like Libra or Pisces, to see what products you're using, but to find out about any medication or products having a possible sexual link. They micro-examine telephone bills with particular interest in mobile phone calls made when their partner was out of the house. They perform exhaustive Internet searches. They enjoy the concept of private investigation.

VINDICTIVE Scorpio's not-so-secret motto is "retaliate first," and they do. Their methods are subtle but devastating. They like messing with other people's emotions. They'll let you know that they know your little secret. They play games to incite jealousy. They draw you out to talk in vulgar terms about sex or money, then withdraw, a slight smirk of contempt playing across their manipulative face. Scorps can juggle a thousand revenge agendas in their minds. It's never too late. They can feed crap into other people's minds about you without anyone guessing a hint of Scorp's true and biased emotions. If a Scorp feels that you have violated their so-deep honor system, their ethics are then able to be ditched at the drop of a hat. It is because Scorps are so paranoid that other—perfectly nice—people are like them that they are so rigid about shredding credit-card statements, having people sign pre-dating agreements, and keeping love letters or erotic photographs stored in mysterious locked boxes.

GRUDGE-BEARING Okay, so not every Scorp takes up voodoo or looks for a bat to sacrifice when they want a credit limit increase or for their would-be lover to telephone. As any Scorp will tell you, they are not control freaks. They just completely freak if they are not in total control of everything. It is a miracle that, given their obsession with sex, they are not all professional S & M experts of some description. There is something so disconcerting about having a drink with an old Scorpio friend when you find out they're still in a stew about not having been made a school prefect. British historian A. J. P. Taylor said of Welsh poet Dylan Thomas that he "was a detestable man. Men pressed money on him and women their bodies. Dylan took both with equal contempt. His great pleasure was to humiliate people." Remind you of anyone? Maybe there was a slight personality conflict happening there, but it nevertheless sounds like a very Scorpionic syndrome.

Motivating and manipulating a Scorpio

"Calmness and irony are the only worthy weapons of the wise."

Emile Gaboriau (1832-1873), French classic mystery novelist whom some believe

invented the modern detective novel

1 They like to be thanked at length and preferably in writing with extra emphasis on how poorly off you would have been without the Scorpio's intervention.

2 Understand that a Scorpio gets sick of people instantly gazing at their crotch the second they admit to being a Scorp.

3 Accept that Scorpio has a finely calibrated personal point-scoring mechanism. If you give them a bowl of soup when they are sick, they bring you back one the next day, just so things are even.

4 Don't try to make Scorpio more sanguine or relaxed. They hate it.

5 Never pry into their personal affairs. If that invisible Iron Curtain seems to snap across Scorpio's face, change the subject fast.

6 Fascinate Scorp by letting them think you have a lurid secret.

7 You can never know too much about what is *really* going on; amuse Scorpio by outdoing their conspiracy theories.

8 Don't gossip lightly in front of them—they don't do anything lightly let alone anything so vital as sharing intelligence.

9 Even if you do consider being a nympho to be a form of mania, don't let on to Scorp. Scorpios consider sex and life force as one.

Scorpy role models

"I trust my opinions to give a lot of weight to what I want."

Sophie Marceau (1966-), beautiful, sexy French actress with a huge following in Asia.
Her films include *The World Is Not Enough* and *Braveheart*.

- Niki de Saint Phalle—amazing French artist and writer and, in her younger years, a model. Her huge surreal sculptures are often in the form of ridiculously full-bodied women; her men are demons. Her additional Scorpio credentials: she was into the occult and designed a sculpture park in Italy of enormous Tarot-card images. She coauthored and illustrated the book *AIDS: You Can't Catch it Holding Hand*s.

- Ennio Morricone—genius composer of creepy cinema scores as found in spaghetti westerns like *The Good, the Bad, and the Ugly*. Offbeat, hypnotic use of instruments such as whistling and harmonica. He is an obsessive worker with more than 400 film and TV projects since 1961.

Sun signs

- Peter Jackson—New Zealand cult director of weird splatter movies such as *Bad Taste* and *Meet the Feebles*. *Braindead* was his first professionally made movie. He is a driven film-maker who directed the "unfilmable" and highly acclaimed *Lord of the Rings* series in which he insisted that the armor be made as it was 600 years ago. He was born on Halloween.

- Anna Wintour—ultimate New York media queen and editor of U.S. *Vogue*. Her signature: sunglasses indoors, 1980s bob hairstyle, red-meat lunches, and sable coats. When animal-rights protesters once staked her out at a *Vogue* bash, she sent them a snack from the kitchen—rare roast beef.

- Magica de Spell—svelte Italian witchy duck who lives on the slopes of Mt. Vesuvius. She is seductive, bad-tempered, and obsessed with stealing Uncle Scrooge's lucky number-one dime. Her brother, Poe, was once transformed into a raven, and is now Magica's magical familiar.

- Carl Sagan—American Pulitzer Prize-winning astronomer, TV presenter, and debunker of superstitions. He spent his career looking for extraterrestrial intelligence. "A celibate clergy is an especially good idea, because it tends to suppress any hereditary propensity toward fanaticism."

"Most people have a conscious and a subconscious. Not me, I have a subconscious and a sub-subconscious."

Harpo Marx (1888-1964), American comic actor and elaborate mime artist who was a member of the Marx Brothers comedy act

Chic Scorp

"Life can be whatever you want it to be. All you have to do is make a wish."

RuPaul (1966-), American drag queen superstar, the world's first drag queen to become a spokesperson for a cosmetic company

It is very difficult to pinpoint the exact Scorp look. There are Scorpios who won't leave the house until they have approximated a movie-star look, that is, they will calculate the precise aura they wish to project, research how to do it, and get on with it. There are Scorps who will learn how to cut and color their own hair so expertly that they never again have to give over their precious control to somebody else. There are Scorps who will have every single hair on their body removed by painstaking electrolysis, dye their pubic hair to match the hair on their head, dye their children's hair to match theirs, and get up at 5 a.m to put on their first light "natural face" before anyone sees.

Obsessive about everything, if a Scorpio even vaguely decides to change their look they will totally transform it to the point where they are unrecognizable.

But Scorpio can also be the classic witch in sheep's clothing. Stacks of them slink around in tracksuit pants with unbrushed hair and still manage to seduce everyone. Scorpio sex appeal is not necessarily dependent on outward glamour. Some Scorpios are even against the socially sanctioned demand for deodorant. It's not just that they fear what aluminum in the deodorant may do to their lymph system—that's more Virgo and Aquarius—they genuinely prefer their own perfume. They believe in the power of their own powerful pheromones. A lot of people expect Scorpio to get around in fetish gear but they tend to save that sort of thing for home.

SEXY SCORPS Goldie Hawn, Julia Roberts, Veronica Lake, Meg Ryan, Vivien Leigh, Matthew McConaughey, Leonardo Di Caprio, Demi Moore, Lauren Hutton, Bo Derek, Jodie Foster, Hedy Lamarr, Dolph Lundgren, Ethan Hawke, Jaclyn Smith, Winona Ryder, Grace Kelly, Lisa Bonet, Loretta Swit, Tatum O'Neal

"Any girl can be glamourous. All you have to do is stand still and look stupid."

Hedy Lamarr (1913-2000), sultry Austrian-born Hollywood actress whose nude scenes in the notorious German film *Extase* caused a sensation in 1932. Her off-screen love affairs were equally scandalous.

Brilliant career

"To succeed in the world it is not enough to be stupid, you must also be well-mannered."

Voltaire (1694-1778), stylish, witty French author and philosopher. He drank 50 cups of coffee a day, even in his old age.

Scorpio focus, grit, and intensity helps them thrive in whatever realms they choose to pursue. But a Scorpio trapped in a career cul-de-sac turns into a catty megalomaniac and the Scorp sting is used to ill advantage.

Paranoia makes them excellent in work such as predicting and preventing violent behavior. They can work in government, private investigation, law, anything involving sexuality, the military, and any kind of auditing.

They are powerful and menacing, whether as underlings or bosses. Power-tripping is a constant temptation so Scorpios must be immersed in fulfilling tasks they can become completely obsessed with and/or have total control over.

A bored Scorp is a dangerous Scorp. An excellent career for a Scorpio is being a "sacred monster" like Spanish artist Pablo Picasso, that is, a complete creative genius who can behave monstrously but nobody minds because of their brilliance. Scorp sculptor Auguste Rodin also fits this mold. He apparently drove everyone who loved him absolutely crazy.

Once they have learned to cloak their naked power-lust and naked lust-lust, and mastered the art of light conversation, Scorpios are extremely successful. Mega-Scorp power-tripper: Microsoft boss Bill Gates.

"If they give me an Oscar, maybe I go naked. Why not?"

> Roberto Benigni (1952-), Italian-born failed priest and accountant who became an acclaimed actor, director, and writer. His film *Life is Beautiful* was based on his father's experiences in a concentration camp during World War II.

Fiscal reality

"Fortune favors the audacious."

> Erasmus (1466-1536), Dutch scholar who wrote *In Praise of Folly*

Scorpios are either huge spenders or huge savers. There is no middle ground in the fiscal life of our Scorp. If Scorp decides to spend it, they find a Libran or Piscean to encourage them and become a professional shopper. When in saving mode, Scorpio is utterly ruthless. They will walk everywhere and relish the fitness benefits, make their own lunch, give up coffee, alcohol—anything non-essential to Scorp well-being—borrow books from the public library, and work full-on hours seven days a week.

Whatever the goal, it will be met. Even Prince Charles makes an extra buck or two by selling his own brand of booze from his estate. Scorps crave control and they know that, while it may not bring happiness, money definitely bestows control. A Scorpio likes the sensation of knowing they can retain an elite lawyer, should they need to. Or fly to Nairobi to meet a hot new romantic prospect at the drop of a hat. Or spend a lot of money in a tiny amount of time on a complete personal makeover designed to make someone else very jealous indeed.

Scorpios are not afraid of money. If anything, money is scared of them. As Scorpios are always aware of the under-the-rock reality of anything, some of them flirt with the idea of suspending all ethics and going savagely on the drip, like collecting illegal debts for a living, becoming a card sharp, or even a con man.

But most Scorps play it super straight because, as everyone knows, being a Scorpio is about principles and control.

Never ever rip off a Scorpio. They take a homeopathic (like cures like) approach to such outrages. The sex-and-shared-finances syndrome can make Scorp funny with money.

How they feel about so-called "other people's money"—debt, tax, investment in Scorp Corp—is an indicator of where the Scorp is at spiritually. Resentment drains Scorpio's energy.

"Anything I've ever wanted to do, I've done. Anyone I've ever wanted to be with, I've had."

Calvin Klein (1942-), slick American brand icon and creator of contemporary hardcore-
underwear model culture. He also created scents such as Obsession, Escape, Crave,
and Eternity.

Chez Scorp

"The joy of a spirit is the measure of its power."

Ninon de Lenclos (1620-1705), beautiful French aristocrat and woman of letters. She
entertained a well-heeled circle of friends and lovers in her salon.

Scorpios are the official great seducers of the zodiac, aka the
stealth bombers of romance. Unsurprisingly, their abode can
resemble a sex den. Here's where you'll find the householder
nonchalantly leaving their merlot-stained copy of the erotic *Kama
Sutra* lying around. Scorpios enjoy watching their guests' reaction
to the very kinky Helmut Newton photograph in the toilet and
don't mind at all if you spot the school strap sticking out from the
end of the bed.

Subtle in persona, unsubtle in décor, favorite Scorpio themes
include faux leopard skin, black satin, red leather, ornate iron
candle-holders, and dark rooms with heavy curtains. In fact, their
aversion to light in the home invariably leads family and friends to
suspect definite vampire tendencies. Although some of these
people may experiment with the 1950s retro look at times, they're
all essentially Gothics. Their fantasy room? Eek! Dare you ask?
Seeing as you do, they quite like a home office evoking the vibe of
the wildly erotic Yves Saint-Laurent Opium perfume ads. Scorpio's
home will always reveal evidence of the inhabitant's obsessive
nature: a drum set, masses of fan magazines, a bong, a collection
of UFO-abductee case studies, or a secret store of cash.

"I do not seek—I find."

Pablo Picasso (1881-1973), flamboyant Spanish sculptor and cubist painter. He almost
single-handedly created modern art.

A Scorpio in love

"Assuming that prey capture and defence requirements are similar in both sexes, the best explanation is that the sting is more important for mating than it is for prey capture and defence."

Scorpion FAQ

Intimacy issues? Bedroom politics? The sex-money nexus? Hello? Scorp will go there. Because Scorp is a "Fixed" Water sign, many of their emotional fluctuations take the form of underwater currents, not visible on the surface. Scorpio spouses need storm warnings.

Scorpios know how to make someone feel mega-good about their sexuality and how to make someone feel very, very bad about their sexuality. The balance of power in a relationship is so incredibly important to Scorpios that they can indulge in megalomania without even knowing it.

They will cheerily initiate a zero-tolerance policy without a second thought. If accused, they say, of course, "Me? Manipulative? But I'm so direct." Never mind their ploys of getting the friends of their partner on side, mysteriously going off sex for a month when the other party disagrees with something Scorp says, and those subtle digs at someone's potency or lack thereof. And don't mention their tendency toward emotional blackmailing and/or undermining of their partner's self-esteem so they feel nobody but Scorp is ever going to love them again.

One thing Scorpio people do in a relationship is provide their partner with stacks of sex. If they've displeased them, however, Scorp brings out the hairbrush or whatever other punishment implement they're currently into. But a Scorpio will go all night in an effort to please their lover...whatever it takes.

As the official most highly sexed sign of the zodiac, Scorps have needs—lots of needs, constantly. But Scorpios can be completely celibate for years. They can even be frigid yet still be obsessed with sex. Scorpios like to love deeply or not at all.

Scorpio-Aries

Aries and Scorp are destined to learn from one another but do they like the lesson? Can they put up with one another long enough to glean any info? Scorpy mystique reels in Ramzilla. Aries energy intrigues Scorpio. Both share intensity, life lust, flair, and ambition. Scorpio can't stand the glib simplicity of Aries. Aries shows Scorpio how not to brood. Scorpio sets Aries an example of how to get needs met without ramming the gates and screeching about respect. Aries enhances Scorp reality. Scorpio deepens Aries reality. Power-tripping finishes off this relationship even more quickly than it began. Both parts of this duo have an ego and a temper. Ramzilla must go beneath the surface to get along with Scorpio but Aries fears this will slow the momentum. Scorpios simply fear for their sanity should they linger in the Ramzilla orbit for too long. This is not an impossible love affair—it's just it either lasts for what seems like a few moments or forever. The stakes are so high but so are the rewards.

Hot duos: Dermot Mulroney & Catherine Keener, Danny DeVito & Rhea Perlman, David Schwimmer & Mili Avital

Scorpio-Taurus

This life-altering love affair is never, ever a shallow fling. Either party can skitter into it with the most casually exploitative intentions and wind up being a soul mate. Scorp's drawn by Taurean beauty, sensuality, and stability. Taurean stubbornness mirrors Scorp's own and both see it as a sign of strength. Scorp adores the Taurean ability to nurture them—most other Sun signs are too freaked out to even imagine giving Scorpio that safe sensation. Taurus wants to soothe the rattled Scorp brow, put their feet up for a nice little reflexology massage, and make them some cookies. In return, Scorp gives Taurus the mind-blowing bedroom compatibility they've longed for. Each shares a deep, intense devotion. Taurus and Scorp are also socially compatible. Neither wants to be out for the sake of being out, or have some experience just because it's there. Each rejects what they see as fake fun. Anger arises when Taurus bags Scorp's wilder side. Scorpio simply will not have that and neither will budge.

Hot duos: Ethan Hawke & Uma Thurman, Sam Shepard & Jessica Lange, Marie & Pierre Curie, Louis Malle & Candice Bergen

Scorpio-Gemini
Gemini mind-tripping at first threatens hard-won Scorpio serenity. The apparently casual Gemini style of flirting irks Scorp no end. Scorpio wants to pin down the Gemini for an "us" chat. This doesn't work because Gemini loves Scorpio mystique—it offers what Gemini loves most, a challenge. These two are so different and yet so potentially compatible. The very intense Scorpio mind benefits from Gemini's lighter touch. Gemini, everyone knows, can definitely do with a depth charge of Scorpio reality. Each is accustomed to being so attractive to others and relishing the complications this brings. Trust is an issue to be sorted out as soon as possible. Scorpio likes to possess the lover. Gemini needs space as others require oxygen. Few social scenes are as ugly as the Scorp frog-marching garrulous Gemini out of a party, following a little too much Scorp-excluding shared laughter. But this can be a beautiful relationship. Gemini grows up and Scorpio grows young. Each is forever keen on the other's bedwork and insights.

Hot duos: Vivien Leigh & Sir Laurence Olivier, Sir Oswald & Lady Diana Mosley, Carl Sagan & Ann Dryan, Grace Kelly (Princess Grace) & Prince Rainier

Scorpio-Cancer
Scorp and Crab are instantly very sympathetic. This is one of the most astrologically compatible pairings of the zodiac. There is often a magical element—synchronicity? fate?—to their first

meeting. It feels so right. Scorpio is irresistibly drawn to the moodiness of Crab though appalled by their propensity for grizzling. Scorpio has turned "just getting on with it" into an art form. Crab can be emotionally petrified by the sheer weight of melancholy perception. Scorpio fixes that, imbuing Crab with their own sharky instincts. Crab gives Scorp the benefit of emotional wisdom and insights sometimes lacking in fixed Scorpio. Crab understands Scorpio in a way no other can. Each can find peace and happiness with the other, as never felt before. Scorpio must remember that Crab sensitivities do not respond to the scathing Scorp sting. Money and shared values can be a battleground. Sex and shared values are unlikely to be. These are true lovers, waiting for destiny to bring them together.

Hot duos: Laura & George W. Bush, Prince Charles & Princess Diana, Prince Charles & Camilla Parker Bowles, Harrison Ford & Calista Flockhart, kd lang & Leisha Haile, Kevin Kline & Phoebe Cates, Nick Lachey & Jessica Simpson

Scorpio-Leo
Leo shows off. Scorpio, also hot, glowers in the corner with a whip. It could happen. This is a strong, sexy, and yet tense, sometimes kinky, dynamic. It needs mega-compromise and neither the Scorp nor the most neo of Leos are good at giving in. Life in this love affair becomes hyper-real. Each is initially addicted to the other. It could turn into a cliché if both sides are not careful to honor the other's reality. Scorp literally can't believe the homage demanded by the Leo's ego. Leo wonders why Scorpio is so obsessive about things that don't matter. "Let's live it up," bellows Leo. Scorpio brings it back down to something very tedious to Leo. Denied oxygen in the form of flattery, Leo stalks off to a more hospitable part of the savanna. Made a gibbering fool of, Scorp demands revenge. Sex and drama work just fine but, for long term, it needs work. In Leo-Scorp Utopia, Scorp learns how to look on the sunnier side of life. Leo gains insight into life after their hair looking hot and making an entrance. They bond.

Hot duos: Louis XVI & Marie Antoinette, Hillary & Bill Clinton, Bo & John Derek, John Stamos & Rebecca Romjin-Stamos, Maria Shriver & Arnold Schwarzenegger, Roberto Benigni & Nicoletta Braschi

Scorpio-Virgo
Virgo compulsion meets Scorp obsession and everyone gets along—for a while. But maybe forever? Virgo loves that Scorpio goes deep into life. Scorp adores the keen analytical mind of Virgo. Both love each other in bed. Scorp doesn't resent Virgo leaping out of bed at dawn to steam-clean a few shirts or disinfect the toilet seat. It may even turn Scorpio on. Virgo dissects and unravels scenarios. Scorp does a deep probe. These two could talk for hours in between bouts of bedwork and fulfilling ambitions. Scorp gets annoyed at how Virgo likes to meet and bond with a variety of people. Scorp could quite happily consume much of their energy with those already known, always going deeper. Virgo can be a bit like a more sensible version of Gemini, a sign many Scorps have officially sworn off. Scenes of drama, especially public, alienate Virgo. They can't bear undue intensity. Scorp gets off on it. Work through such issues and they're together, forever.

Hot duos: Harold Pinter & Antonia Fraser, Sonya & Leo Tolstoy

Scorpio-Libra
Scorp is direct, unflinching, and uncompromising. Libra oozes charming euphemism. They specialize in being light and airy, not treading on delicate subjects or trekking off along difficult paths of conversation. Libra does small talk. Scorpio doesn't see the point of opening their mouth if it's not big talk. Scorpio can scorn the glamourous social life. To Libra, it's essential. Loving these little foibles assures the good life. Blissful sack synergy comes true. Libra, though infuriating, is good for Scorp. Life with Libra lifts sulky Scorp spirits and broadens that sometimes narrow mind. Librans can see both sides of a situation, something Scorps are notoriously unable to do. Libra's mental flexibility

helps jolt Scorp out of what can be a stagnant attitude. Scorpio sex appeal gets it on with Libran beauty. In return, Scorp helps Libra be less dithery and indecisive, less of a social chameleon, and more in touch with whatever it is they really do think.

Hot duos: Gavin Rossdale & Gwen Stefani, Stan & Anne Rice

Scorpio-Scorpio

For two Scorps to mate successfully, they must first neutralize their respective stings. Venom is not an appropriate bodily fluid for them to be exchanging. If things are not too compulsive and out of control, this is a beautiful relationship between two people capable of truly "getting" one another. Nobody else will quite understand Scorp depth and complexity so well as another Scorp. They are perfectly suited in bed and are able to use such activity to sort out any disputes. One potentially troublesome issue is their mutual propensity to take things to the limit. It would be horrid if, for example, they egged each other on to join a cult. Brinksmanship must be avoided and loyalty evoked. For bliss to manifest, they must strive to be a duo of positivity, embodying the beautiful Phoenix aspect of Scorpio, rather than the jealously bitchy vibe of the Scorpion.

Hot duos: John & Abigail Adams, Linda Evans & Yanni, Simon & Yasmin Le Bon

Scorpio-Sagittarius

They're so weirdly different from one another that it's almost crazy enough to work. Maybe. Scorp is a Water sign—deep, intense, and into emotions. Sagg is a Fire sign—vibrant, dynamic, and emotionally dyslexic. So, on the surface, there are a few things to work through. Scorp has to somehow let Sagg know that, for this thing to work out, Sagg has to stop shrieking and running off to the travel agent each time feelings are evoked. Scorp may also find Sagg to be as evasive when it comes to sex as they are with emotions. As an actual pastime with one's own lover, Sagg sex is hard to pin down. All this will be altered of course, if Sagg has, say, Venus in Scorp. Or Scorp has Mars in Sagittarius. Shared dreams also bond this duo over and above their foibles. Neither party must ever try to change the other's core persona. There lies madness.

Hot duos: Pablo Picasso & Françoise Gilot, Kate Capshaw & Steven Spielberg, Mike Nichols & Diane Sawyer

Scorpio-Capricorn These guys come together and create far more than the sum of their parts. Paranoia loops out of control at times, but this could be a meant-to-be relationship. Paranoia can always be managed but true love can't be beaten up out of nothing. Both are serious about romance. Casual dalliance is an idiotic distraction—a pastime for losers frightened of emotion. Cap can handle anything Scorp chucks their way, just so long as Scorp doesn't mess with their ambitions or respectability. This means no hysterical phone calls to Cap at work; no passing on gossip that isn't vouched for by a reliable source; no touching them too much in public, and no offering them a non-doctor-endorsed home cure. There are many don'ts in dealing with Caps and this could irk boundary-pushing Scorp. Cap loves Scorpio sensibilities, sensuality, and cool nature. Each admires the other so intensely that they can settle into a cozy rut. Quality time out for fun times is essential.

Hot duos: Georgia O'Keefe & Alfred Stieglitz, Lara Feltham & Pat Rafter

Scorpio-Aquarius When Scorp's see-all gaze first zooms in on Aquarius, Scorpio thinks they've found their dream super-being. Aquarians can often appear spacey and remote like a character from an Ayn Rand book. Scorpio loves this. It makes the conquest all the sweeter.

But Aquarius holds, if possible, even more fixed opinions than Scorp. Worse still, they are likely to be able to argue them into the ground, whereas Scorpios may have to concede that their position is held more on intense subjectivity. Assuming they agree on major policy points, this liaison is much more viable. The only other pitfall is Aquarian frigidity. With few exceptions, the Aquarian person is not exactly sex-obsessed. They could be more interested in intellectual aspects, such as a new translation of the *Kama Sutra*, than in being an actual practitioner. Scorp needs to explore this side of bonding before signing a 20-year Aqua lease.

Hot duos: Julia Roberts & Daniel Moder, Dwight Yoakam & Bridget Fonda, Brittany Murphy & Ashton Kutcher, Ben Harper and Laura Dern

Scorpio-Pisces Scorp mesmerizes poor little Pisces as if they

are a headlight-transfixed rabbit. Then, tee-hee, Scorp makes the mistake of thinking they hold the balance of power in the relationship. Pisceans are seductive and manipulative—expert at letting others feel they're in charge. But if Scorp can handle mind-tripping with the Fish, this liaison has all it takes to be The One. These two are so compatible it's ridiculous. The deep issues that Scorp spent years trying to explain to past lovers are understood by Pisces almost instantly. Fishy intuition is as powerful as Scorpy instinct. Once each starts feeling fulfilled on all levels, they're a pair to behold and a true-bonded couple. Pisceans can have issues with flirtation, responsibility, and/or money. They're sneaky and evasive in a sleazy way that infuriates Scorp. The truth issue is thrashed out. Even then, Scorp spends ages getting to know Pisces, only to realize that there are still secret corners of their psyche. Scorp loves that.

Hot duos: Goldie Hawn & Kurt Russell, Sir Richard Burton & Elizabeth Taylor, Demi Moore & Bruce Willis, Averell & Pamela Harriman, Guy Oseary & Eva Herzigova

Are you really a Scorpio?

1 On a stormy night, you rent a video for a big night in, but later, you find the video inside is different from the one in the case. You...

(a) Accept that mistakes can be made but exact a month's worth of free video rentals from the company.

(b) See it as a "message from the cosmos"—maybe this video is the one you should be seeing—and resolve to enjoy it.

(c) Go straight to the top. You send a 10-page fax to the CEO of the video company vowing to boycott the company.

2 Your most useful sexual asset is your...

(a) Enthusiasm and lusty libido.

(b) Ability to intuit what a lover truly needs.

(c) Knowledge of slipknots.

3 Your music collection...

(a) Varies, depending on whatever you're into at that moment. Once you're over the sound, out it goes.

(b) Is a suave assortment of past and present, always fashionable and appropriate.

(c) Vast, eclectic, weird, and not to be touched by anybody else, you understand.

4 At a party, you're most likely to be found...

(a) Dancing on some table to an audience of admirers...

(b) Holding forth on your latest genius views.

(c) Standing quietly in the corner, a charismatic spider awaiting the right person to wander into your web.

5 Revenge is...
   (a) Sweet.
   (b) Beneath you.
   (c) Your core competency.

6 Your partner is acting so weird, you are convinced that something sleazy is up. You...
   (a) Score some quality time and ask them bluntly what is up.
   (b) Do everything it takes to get their attention back to where it should be—on you and your gorgeousness.
   (c) Are intrigued and almost aroused. You turn private investigator, checking the phone for the last number dialed, investigating their computer cache for sites visited, quietly sounding out their maybe not-so-loyal-after-all confidantes.

Answers: If you checked mainly (c) answers, then you are an official Scorpio—powerful, seductive, and ever so charming. If you checked (a) or (b) answers, you have other astro influences competing with your Scorpio Sun.

Sagittarius

november 23-december 21

Saggability

"Why not seize the pleasure at once?"

Jane Austen (1775-1817), witty British novelist noted for her domestic novels of
manners—*Pride and Prejudice, Sense and Sensibility*

Q: How many Sagittarians does it take to change a light bulb?
A: The sun is shining, the day is young, we've got our whole lives ahead of us and you're inside worrying about some stupid burnt-out light bulb!

Sagittarians are ruled by Jupiter, aka Zeus, a fun-loving god who would roar around transforming himself into a bull, swan, statue, or even a tree, whatever it took to indulge his infatuations. He was also good-humored, kind, and devoted to the truth. It is from one of his pseudonyms, Jove, that we get the word "jovial"—also an apt description of our Sagg.

Jupiter gives Sagittarians their sporting love of the outdoors and philosophical broad-mindedness. Given his own conduct, Jupiter obviously had to be broad-minded. Hypocrisy is too mean a sin for gods.

Wherever Jupiter is in a person's birth chart is where they have innate good fortune and where they can expand. Sagg, being ruled by Jupiter, is expansive everywhere. The planet Jupiter is huge, 11 times bigger than earth but apparently with no solid surface. Some scientists even think it plays an important role in protecting us as its powerful gravity pulls meteors away from Earth. This fits in with Jupiter's astro image as the luckiest planet of all.

The Sagittarian astro symbol is the Centaur. That's right. Sagg is the only Sun sign to be represented by a mythical beast. Nobody who has lived with one of them would be particularly surprised. The Centaur is half back-end of a horse and half nude torso of a bearded guy. Some Centaurs were revered as poet-philosophers, while others galloped around worshipping Dionysus, the god of divine drunken debauchery.

Sagg is not an official Twin sign such as Pisces or Gemini but as half-horse and half-human is definitely dual-natured.

Some say that Sagg is the archer and the symbol simply an arrow "of truth" flying to its target but Sagg arrows don't necessarily fly straight. A symbol of arrows zinging all over the place wouldn't be nearly so cool.

The astrological motto is supposed to be a summary of a Sun sign's ethos. It is a sort of mission statement. The Sagg motto? "I seek." Sagittarians have a strong sensation of being on a journey or a quest. The other motto is "I seek the truth." Sagittarians are so into telling the truth that they can make one long for a compulsively fibbing Gemini, the opposite sign to Sagg.

Never ask a Sagittarian if your bottom looks big in the new jeans or whether your hairline is receding. If they have not already cheerily pointed out any flaws, they will be radically honest in response.

World War II British prime minister Sir Winston Churchill was renowned for his candor, aka tactlessness.

Woman: Winston, you are drunk.

Churchill: Madam, you are ugly but, in the morning, I will be sober.

Sagg candor has its happier aspect. They don't play games, you will always know exactly where you are at with Sagg.

Like Leo and Aries, Sagg is a Fire sign, flamboyant, active, and sensational at everything they do. So say the Fire signs and nobody wants to argue.

"I'm a Sagittarian—half-man, half-horse with a licence to shit in the streets."

Keith Richards (1943-), legendary British guitarist with the Rolling Stones

Sagg on form is...

"She had a rich and stimulating voice with a wide tone range, laughed a great deal, even though the point of humor might be obscure, and was an indefatigable talker. She could carry on an intelligent and logical discussion, for she had a varied flow of words and phrases. A woman of great physical courage, she was the first to ride astride a horse into the hills when few women were riding at all, and those who dared were riding English side-saddle on the Golden Gate Park bridle paths. She had a deep love of horses. Ambitious, both socially and intellectually, she worked hard to advance herself, and saved her money with which to take a trip through Europe, did a little painting on China dishes, tried hard to make progress each year over the last."

Description of U.S. novelist and ultra-Sagg Charmian Kittredge (1871-1955), who was
novelist Jack London's wife. Both wrote adventure stories.

SPUNKY Sagittarians are like the people in personal advertisements would be if they weren't lying. Sagg really is as comfortable in a ball-gown as in a pair of jeans, as happy bushwhacking as they are flying into an exciting new city. Even weirder, they're like people in television commercials. Sagg girls do come striding out of some shop, swing their shiny hair around, smile at the cute guy lurking behind their snazzy car that they managed to park right outside wherever they're at. Sagg guys wake up in the morning, looking hot, sing in the shower, bounce downstairs for a smoothie breakfast, and zoom off to tennis or sailing.

JOYOUS Saggs are keen to maintain a high level of personal optimism and glee in life. The one time a month they get around to cleaning the house, they will be deliriously happy with the way everything gleams. More dour types accuse them of being on drugs.

They're not. Oh, all right, maybe some of them are but their love of loving bubbles up from deep within them, like mineral water from a deep secret source at the base of a volcano. They're idealists so while they do angst about genetically engineered food and endangered wild animals, they keep it real and positive. They rant on to everyone they know, spreading the word, fire off letters and petitions and attend protests.

FUN-LOVING Like Spanish painter Picasso's Sagg lover Françoise Gilot, they think life is a one-way ticket...it can only be lived forward. British poet William Blake said the path of excess leads to the palace of wisdom. Sagg has a huge appetite for everything life has to offer. A Sagittarian would volunteer for a backyard cloning experiment if they were in the mood. Saggs love flying off to a great beach or going halfway across the planet for a fabulous party. A Sagg can be at a ski-resort toga party on the Saturday night and back in time for Sunday morning's aquarobics class before heading off to lunch.

CANDID Saggs can puncture the most pompous bore with a well-aimed quip. As novelist Mark Twain wrote, "power, money persuasion, supplication, persecution—these can lift at a colossal humbug—push it a little, weaken it a little over the course of a century; but only laughter can blow it to rags and atoms at a blast. Against the assault of laughter, nothing can stand." Incidentally, Twain once sent all his friends telegrams saying, "All is discovered— flee at once," and to his amusement many of them did. Writer Nancy Mitford created a huge stir with *Noblesse Oblige*, her best-selling guide to what is and is not upper class.

IN-THE-MOMENT Sagittarius loves to savor the moment, relishing the abundance of life whether they are skydiving, larking it up on a cocktail bar, or doing something as mundane as scraping a squashed snail off their foot. Like 19th century British novelist

Jane Austen (*Pride and Prejudice*), Sagittarians "think only of the past as its remembrance gives pleasure."

MOTIVATIONAL A Sagittarian's sheer delight in living inspires all around them to go for it and follow their own dreams. And Sagg's bawdy good humor enlivens everything.

Sagg off form is...

"No problem is so formidable that you can't walk away from it."

Charles Schultz (1922-2000), U.S. cartoonist and creator of the famous *Peanuts* comic strip. He was the most widely syndicated cartoonist in the world.

IRRESPONSIBLE Sagittarians can walk—or sprint more like it— away from any problem. And what is a problem to these people? Responsibility or, as they call it, "negativity." They can't hack the idea of being unable to cope, so they won't cope. See? It's a choice that Sagg has made—because they're dynamic, adventurous, and free-willed. Hey, they just didn't want to hang around and put up with that negative crap. Their idea of dealing with an issue is to make it your problem. Sagittarians are prone to storming out and telling someone to get their crap together even when it is clearly the Sagg's crap. Even worse is the Sagg who's done therapy: "I'm picking up that you're in a really resentful place right now..." before galloping out the door because "I don't want to go there with this negativity..." If responsibility was a place, Sagg wouldn't even be able to find it. Sagg would think it was like Narnia in the C. S. Lewis book *The Lion, the Witch and the Wardrobe*, where you had to go through the back of the magic wardrobe to find whatever you were looking for. Some Saggs don't even like the word "place." It sounds too fixed. They prefer "space." Sagittarians have spaces in their heart, not places. They have their *space* in the sun, and their moral-high *space*.

TACTLESS Sagg lack of tact is legendary. They drop the most amazing "did she just say what I think she said?" clangers and they don't even work at it. Never let a Sagg just wing it for a speech at a wedding, funeral, or christening. As everyone cringes, Sagg will smirk, thinking "at least I tell it like it is."

SELF-CENTERED You say ego, Sagg thinks self-esteem. Because so many Saggs have a bohemian aura, their ego can go undetected. It will be swamped in a sea of intellectual discourse, full-on raves about principle, and general Sagg swagger. But it's there, even if this lot do start off every second sentence with "I don't want to boast but..." They get frustrated when their support system slackens off. They don't get that it's not the done thing to screech "don't you know who I am?" at their own family like a has-been soap star being refused an A-list table. A Sagg can neglect to notice when the natives are restless. A Sagg can think the fact that their partner barely has the energy to do anything other than nod "yes, dear" is a good thing. It means the person is becoming more accustomed to being a valet or handmaiden to Sagg genius. Then they act all appalled when an outbreak of "negativity" occurs in their life. Many a Sagg has returned from a surfing safari with their ex-lover to find their home empty.

FULL OF CRAP It would be so cool if Sagittarians came equipped with a mute button. They go on and on and on. Ideally, like the characters on television, they would not know that they had been muted. They carry with them an invisible soapbox upon which they leap to deliver their interminable preachy raves. They can be so in love with their own righteousness that they don't even realize they are pulverizing someone else's psyche. Not deliberately, of course.

Our Sagg is totally into freedom and self-expression for all life forms. Well-brought up Saggs can actually manage to shut up and not interrupt. But all of them secretly think that the boring interval when someone else is talking is a mere gap for them to catch a breath while their mind boggles at their own profundity.

"Never complain, never explain."

Benjamin Disraeli (1804-1881), British politician and author of seven novels

Motivating and manipulating a Sagg

"You've got to look after your own legend."

Noël Coward (1899-1973), British playwright and sophisticated showbiz genius

1 Whatever it is you want Sagg to do, pitch it by saying something like, "Hey! Let's go! It'll be an adventure!"

2 Remember that Sagg is all about the big picture. Don't bug them with trivia; don't fence them in. They won't even bother to call you from the airport. Only a lunatic attempts to break the Sagg stride.

3 Want one to fall in love with you? Be more like them. Let them point out that you haven't been to bed for three days and say "So what?" Your unfinished screenplay? "So what?"

4 Get that the Sagg version of maturity is having enough credit cards and a passport so they can escape "negativity." They're okay

but you're negative. Whatever you're on about, couch it in very positive terms or else your Sagg will simply tune out. So maybe you say, "I know! Let's do some impulse-saving!"

5 Gifting a Sagg? They enjoy gifts of things they can do, such as theater tickets. This is the only sign who will not be remotely insulted by being given a gym membership.

6 To cheer one up, take them away or to the wilderness. Failing that, put the issue into a philosophical framework, the more vast, the better. You could compare them to Rome at its height, for instance. Incidentally, Roman emperor Nero was a Sagg.

7 Don't fight lack of tact with tactlessness; Sagg can dish it out but Sagg can't take it.

8 Don't try to nurture Sagittarius into behaving more responsibly. The more there's a parental-figure vibe in the affair, the more Sagg acts up in wayward-teen mode.

9 Never make the Sagg feel guilty.

"Forget inconvenient duties and then forgive yourself for forgetting."

Mark Twain (1835-1910), well-traveled, adventurous, and outspoken American writer who was controversial in his time. He wrote *The Adventures of Tom Sawyer* and *Adventures of Huckleberry Finn.*

Sagg role models

"I'm not radical—I'm just aware. I've come a long way, baby."

Billie Jean King (1943-), American tennis player who won 39 grand slam and
20 Wimbledon titles. She is also an outspoken women's rights activist.

- Aphra Behn—mega-popular British playwright of the Restoration period. She was England's first professional female writer. A beauty, she spied on the Dutch for Charles II and was then thrown in prison for espionage-related debts.

- Fritz Lang—big-thinking, larger-than-life film director who focused on the future and its possibilities. He left home at 20 to travel the world and was injured four times in World War I. His best-known film, *Metropolis*, was visionary and political, but it also bankrupted the studio.

- Snoopy—gorgeous, wise, and intrepid dog companion to "that round-headed kid," Charlie Brown. He has an enormously rich inner life—his daydreams make him a great writer and flying ace. He is adventure loving but averse to work: "It's better to sing and dance than do whatever it is you do on Thursday."

- Ozzy Osbourne—legendary heavy metal singer and now star of his own TV series: "All the bad things that ever happened to me were directly attributed to drugs and alcohol. I mean, I would never urinate at the Alamo at nine o'clock in the morning dressed in a woman's evening dress sober."

- George Eliot (aka Mary Ann Evans)—best-selling British author of *Silas Marner* and *Middlemarch*. She was Queen Victoria's favorite writer. George was alienated by her father as a youngster when she stopped going to church. She had Sagg

credentials: a keen traveler and pursuer of other women's men—
she had an affair with a married man in Victorian England.

- Bette Midler—multitalented comedienne, singer, Broadway diva,
  and Hollywood actress. She made her name with an outrageously
  bawdy comedy act in the 1970s New York gay scene. She has the
  Sagg ability to swing from prankster (The Divine Miss M) to
  preacher ("God is watching us," a line from her hit song *From a
  Distance*).

"It's never too late to be who you might have been."

George Eliot (Mary Ann Evans) (1819-1880), humane, insightful British novelist

Sagg in vogue

"What pisses me off is when I've got seven or eight record-
company fat-pig men sitting there telling me what to wear."

Sinéad O'Connor (1966-), radical Irish-singer/songwriter and priestess

Like cousin Aries, Sagittarians will boycott anything they're told is a
must-have. There is nothing that a Sagg must do, let alone have.
Some of the oddest looks at the Academy Awards have been as a
result of some Sagg sacking their stylist at the last minute.

But, although well immunized against the vagaries of the
fashion virus, Sagittarians can spread it. For example, between the
two of them, Sagittarian actresses Jane Fonda and Jennifer Beals
started the infamous legwarmer look of the early 80s. And fellow
actress Jamie Lee Curtis gave us the first buff-body fashion.
American teen pop star Britney Spears kicked off the bare-midriff
vibe. Hollywood hunk Brad Pitt gave us the "long-haired, straw

cowboy hat and torso" acting school of good looks. Italian fashion guru Versace brought whore-wear into vogue.

When planet Pluto went into Sagittarius in the mid-90s, what happened to fashion? In the cosmetics world, everything turned sheer which is very Sagg as it's outdoorsy and young looking. Sportswear became chic. Saggs are not the world's greatest carer for clothes. They think there is something so kinky about people who have shoe trees. Life is too good to spend all Saturday stuffing around in the laundry. A lot of them don't even wear underwear. Fancy lingerie doesn't go with their often sporty lifestyle, and feeling well ventilated is very Sagg.

The Sagg look is usually the appeal of hair, teeth, and often a totally buff body. Give them some clean jeans, freshly washed hair and they're off—just like some 70s pop song. They hate the word "can't" and are perfectly capable of using olive oil to get a fabulous tan and stuff what the so-called experts say. Their guiding principle is from British poet and Sagittarian William Blake: "exuberance is beauty."

SAGG SPUNKS Christina Aguilera, Christina Applegate, Tyra Banks, Kim Basinger, Jamie Lee Curtis, Brendan Fraser, Katie Holmes, Billy Idol, Don Johnson, Milla Jovovich, John Kennedy Jr., Ray Liotta, John Malkovich, Alyssa Milano, Jim Morrison, Brad Pitt, Anna Nicole Smith, Britney Spears, Ben Stiller, Kiefer Sutherland, Tina Turner, Katerina Witt

Brilliant career

"When a true genius appears, you can know him by this sign—
that all the dunces are in a confederacy against him."

Jonathan Swift (1667-1745), British novelist and satirist—*Gulliver's Travels*

Sagittarians have a very Zen approach to career matters. If a Sagg skips off work two hours early and nobody is there to notice, has Sagg really skipped off work? Slaving away doesn't really fit the natural genius image of Sagg. Colleagues complain but Sagg doesn't care. Sagg is a thoroughbred Centaur, not some draft horse. For best results, they need to be "spelled" in fresh, inspirational pastures.

The 40-hour work week was not really set up for Saggs. This lot take their weekends (and leisure) extremely seriously. Ideally, they need to start getting it together midweek, leave early on Friday morning and take Monday off to recover.

Their honesty gets them into trouble on day jobs that they don't really care for. They feel the compulsion to make sure everyone— that is, anyone in their right mind—knows how beneath the Sagg the job is.

Sagittarians, generous as always, also upset others with their choice of gift. They give people what they consider to be helpful, such as anti-hag cream, gym memberships, and books on how to stop stuttering.

Sagittarians don't believe that old wives' tale about not biting the hand that feeds you, so they come to hate how many banal, anal mediocrities are thriving just because they know how to play the game. Then Sagg decides to sell out but it's never subtle. They should avoid naked displays of power, especially if it's not really there. They need to avoid work where lying well is an advantage, such as PR, journalism, or the sex industry. Anything which involves preaching, iconoclasm, stirring, or coming up with brilliant ideas on the hop will suit Sagittarius.

Ideally, Sagg turns leisure into work and business to pleasure by becoming, say, a resort operator or professional athlete or something creative where one works as the spirit drives one, such as a vet, famous shrink to celebrities, explorer, or travel agent.

Fiscal reality

"If only God would give me a clear sign! Like making a large deposit in my name at a Swiss bank!"

Woody Allen (1935-), U.S. film director and actor, known for his cynical offbeat humor—

Why Men Shouldn't Marry, Anything Else

When Sagittarians open their credit card bills, they go into shock mode. It is at this point that the awful truth sinks in: garnering all those Frequent Flyer points actually costs one something in the first place. Sagittarians are supposed to seek truth, not debt. Not that Sagg stays stressed for long. There's always another adventure to be had.

Saggs do sometimes set out to educate themselves on the straighter aspects of finance. This is always an enlightening process: "Disposable income? What other kind is there?"

Sagg sees money as a means to several ends. They are not remotely fixated on things and prefer to blow their cash on experiences or going places.

If Sagg decides to improve their sailing skills by crewing on an ocean-going boat, off Sagg goes. Should Sagg realize that a convergence of planets can be best observed from a remote village in Mexico, off Sagg goes. If Sagg does get an attack of lust for things, it will most likely be temporary. Next week, when the novelty has gone from the electric toothbrush, portable fountain, or tapestry, Sagg gives it away to whoever asks about it.

Some sad Saggs—and this is relatively rare—wind up being amazingly stingy. This is the kind of Sagg who resents every single encroachment upon expenditure as a violation of personal space, like electricity bills, children's school uniforms...all manifestations of negativity designed to annoy the Sagg.

"Why are we here? What is this about? What does this mean? What do we feel? What are our dreams? I've been engaged in those kind of explorations for as long as I can remember."

Jennifer Connelly (1970-), American actress—*A Beautiful Mind*

Chez Sagg

"I'm trying to break the border between chic and shock."

Gianni Versace (1946-1997), Italian fashion designer to the glitterati

Don't fence them in! Fresh air is the focus of the Sagg home. Restless and sportive, these blithe spirits require constant reminders of the adored outdoors. Their ideal home has the surfboard, skis, tennis racket, golf clubs, and whatever else all ready for action. And you'll find the passport on the hall table, just in case they want to jet off to Samoa for the weekend.

When in residence, Saggs require easy-care everything, a massive spare room in which to hide all those things they can't be bothered dealing with right now, an intelligent TV to record their friends' small-screen appearances, and a machine capable of washing, drying, and folding their workout clothes.

These natural-born optimists periodically paint the town red and their own home in spring/summer colors that are symbolic of the Sagg joie de vivre. How bright? Their house can look like something a parrot would relish. They'll also festoon their base camp with mementos of their fun-loving life, such as a photo of them laughing their heads off on that Yugoslavian snowboarding junket; a funky jacket from Nepal; a ripped-off street sign from Bangers. Their favorite interior decorating themes? Austin Powers-style psychedelia will do it.

"Reporters ask me what I feel China should do about Tibet. Who cares what I think China should do? I'm a f***ing actor. I'm here for entertainment. Basically, when you whittle everything else away, I'm a grown man who puts on make-up."

Brad Pitt (1963-), studly American superstar who was voted Hollywood's "sexiest man." His films include *Troy*, *Ocean's Eleven*, and *Spy Game*.

A Sagg in love

"The sense of living is joy enough."

Emily Dickinson (1830-1886), wilfully weird U.S. poetess

On the surface, Sagg seems quite simple to please. They like a lover they can have fun times with, like going skiing, dancing, or on junkets to exotic destinations.

They prefer it if their partner is not into turgidity, tiresome emotional demands, or other manifestations of the dreaded negativity. Some Sagittarian spouses come to feel that just living with Sagg is a variety of extreme sport. But Sagittarians of a certain age don't mind being bonded as a pair like this. They just don't like having to stay home and relate to their partner. And sometimes Sagg thinks love is having to grovel your head off just to get some personal space. Remember that Sagg thinks groveling is letting someone else finish a sentence.

Like cousin Gemini, they are also often fairly hopeless at dealing with high emotion. They don't realize that saying something like "chill, babe, you're getting hysterical" is not especially helpful.

Although Sagittarians have contributed a fountain of wisdom to the world, sage advice dealing with deeply tricky emotional situations is not usually forthcoming from them. "A good many dramatic situations begin with screaming," actress Jane Fonda helpfully noted.

Sagittarian seduction techniques are fairly simple. They'll give it a go. But getting one of these folk to fall in love with you is fairly simple. Just study everything you can on the Gemini genre and behave like one of them. A Sagg with a soul mate is a vision of love and supportiveness; this is one person who will never ever stand between you and your most grandiose dreams.

"I love Mickey Mouse more than any woman I have ever known."

Walt Disney (1901-1966), U.S. film-maker and animator. He created Mickey Mouse, Donald Duck, and Goofy and films include *Fantasia* and *Pinocchio*.

Sagittarius-Aries It should be obvious that Sagg and Ramzilla are absolutely fantastic together. This duo exhilarates each other—fiery optimism dictates the Sagg conduct. And in Aries the Sagg may have found one of the few people who will not only let Sagg be Sagg, but will actually jump up and down cheering. It's a perfect match intellectually, energetically, and physically, assuming both can stay in the same place long enough to actually mate. This could easily become one of those alpha couples, supportive of one another's dreams and ambitions, taking turns to hog the limelight. The catch? Sagittarians do need to work on the supportive bit. This is not going to be a long-haul relationship if either party declares superior status, or that they have the most demanding ego-needs. Ideally, they thrash out issues of power and prestige early on in the affair. Aries may need to tone down the famed Sagg candor. Ramzilla is probably not ready for the unvarnished

truth about the great Aries screenplay, or the bid to become an astronaut.

Hot duos: David Furnish & Elton John, Sir Winston & Lady Clementine Churchill, Miranda Otto & Peter O'Brien, Talisa Soto & Benjamin Bratt

Sagittarius-Taurus
Sagittarians are initially stunned by the Taurean combo of physical beauty and financial stability. How can someone so attractive lead such an apparently non-turbulent life? Sagittarius raves about the Taurean strength, sexuality, and an attribute that can only be referred to as being centered. This often happens when a Fire sign (like Sagg) meets an Earth sign (such as our Cow). Sagittarians will tend to find sanity quite the novelty at first, but soon they'll begin to long for some of the old delirium. These two drive each other to new heights of "good in bed" and Taurus feels compelled to impress with great performances. But everyday relating can send Sagg running. All Sagg lovers—of whatever gender—can wind up running around being silly while the Bull plays the role of supportive dullard. It can work so long as Sagittarius stops messing with the Cow Person's head. Memo to Sagg: Don't move their things. Don't touch their things. Don't sell their things. Don't knock their bodies.

Hot duos: Noël Coward & Graham Payn, Kathryn & Bing Crosby, Ralph Fiennes & Francesca Annis, Jake Gyllenhaal & Kirsten Dunst

Sagittarius-Gemini
Astrologically, Gemini signifies the so-called lower mind while Saggs represent the higher mind. That's right! The Gemini brain is chock-a-block with trivia—they tend to be way up on new music or breaking Hollywood info, but not so informed on the profound issues pondered by higher-minded Saggs. And yet these two are so compatible. The Gemini adds dash and sparkle to the Sagg wit,

while Sagg contributes desperately needed depth to the Gemini riff. This duo is so mentally stimulating to one another that they could live happily for years on a conversation-only basis; in fact, they may have to. The Gemini libido, though famously kinky, is also sporadic. Note: The way for Saggs to fire it up is by constantly changing the themes of their rants. Boredom sets in quickly if the Gemini isn't kept challenged. Saggs may also have to put up with high-level flirtation aimed elsewhere. Both crave attention; both are heartbreakers who, once they've lost interest, scoot off without compassion. These two deserve each other.

Hot duos: Percy Gibson & Joan Collins, Joe DiMaggio & Marilyn Monroe, John Cassavetes & Gena Rowlands, Erskine Caldwell & Margaret Bourke-White, Jennifer Connelly & Paul Bettany, Joan Didion & John Gregory Dunne

Sagittarius-Cancer Sagg is a swinger—the Crab Person is just a mood-swinger. By the time the Cancerian has made up their mind to be vaguely human again, Sagg is out the door. No time for negativity. No patience for people who walk around like those cartoon characters with little black storm clouds over their heads. Sagg can't possibly visualize a future with someone so unstable and clingy. Or can they? It could be time to grow up. And, if emotional maturity is the goal, the clever Crab Person could be the ideal lover for Sagg. And, of course, Crabs are also often very attractive. Sagittarians will have to get used to talking about their emotions in the candid mode Crabs say they like, but all the time making sure to lie enough so their feelings aren't hurt. You'll know by now that the Crab is sensitive, prone to feeling sorry for everyone even when it is their own fault. They must have their compassion, but Saggs shouldn't let themselves be guilted for one second. This is not because you don't deserve it, but because it will insidiously undermine this love affair. The big bonus of this relationship? Saggs get the support; Crabs get a blast of air.

Hot duos: Rita Wilson & Tom Hanks, Joel Coen & Frances McDormand, Diego Rivera & Frida Kahlo, Don Gummer & Meryl Streep, Judi Dench & Michael Williams, Liv Ullmann & Ingmar Bergman

Sagittarius-Leo

This is one of the most desirable couplings of the zodiac. This may very well be "meant to be." Sagg and Leo make each other look even better than they are naturally anyway. Sagg is candlelight to the Leo's complexion—a rose-tinted mirror for the giant Leo ego. Sagg contributes fun and youthful vigor to what might otherwise be an overly ostentatious existence. In return, Leo simply adores Sagg, providing structure and a solid frame of worshipful support for the genius. These two get along in bed and out, during good times and when the crap hits the fan. Both are naturally optimistic life-enhancers. They tend to agree about the important things—who is and isn't a pain, what is or is not music, and how to while away a beautiful Sunday. But to truly cement this relationship, Saggs must tame the leonine ego. It's a beast of a thing, demanding an endless flow of flattery in order to function. Saggs must find a balance between boosting the Leo vanity and keeping their own genius intact.

Hot duos: Stuart Townsend & Charlize Theron, Edith Piaf & Marcel Cerdan, Ray Romano & Anna Scarpulla

Sagittarius-Virgo

A relationship between Sagg and Virgo is one of the weirdest known to humankind. Both envy aspects of the other that equally repel them. Sagg admires Virgoan efficiency and their holistic togetherness, yet secretly suspects them of suffering from anhedonia (the inability to experience pleasure). What Saggs don't know is that, when the Virgo carps on about having to disinfect some cupboard or cull the book collection, that is their pleasure. A Virgo guilting over how big their bottom has become is just Virgo enjoying decadence. The Sagittarian role in this is to engage that famous Sagg candor and say, "yes, your bottom has grown kind of sideways, but it's more low-slung than usual, and it appears to be developing cellulite." This could be a ruthless, S & M of the mind-type relationship, especially as Virgo can apply analytical skills (of which Sagg has few) to studying Sagg fecklessness, lack of application, and scattered energies. And does Sagg want to hear such negativity? No, no, no!

Hot duos: Carlo Ponti & Sophia Loren, Conrad Black & Barbara Amiel, Christina Applegate & Jonathon Schaech, Madeleine L'Engle & Hugh Franklin, Rebecca West & H. G. Wells, Nicole Appleton & Liam Gallagher, Dean Sheremet & LeAnn Rimes

Sagittarius-Libra
If Saggs can get over their tendency to tell the truth then this could be true love all the way. These two are blessed with soul-mating potential, given a slight temperament alteration from Sagg to begin with. Libra finds Sagg ludicrously attractive—and this Libran may be the most alluring being that Sagg has ever set eyes on. One prob: Saggs are known for candor (aka bloody-minded tactlessness) and Librans prefer appealing fallacy to fact or at least a highly varnished truth. There is no room for bumbling oafs in Libra's life, and nor can Saggs expect to get away with the rants that they claim are conversation. To win the Libran heart, Saggs must become mannered. Once you're back from finishing school, this relationship tends to flow smoothly. Libra loves the expansive Sagittarian intellect and boundless optimism. There are endless subjects to gossip about and when all the social and intellectual life is exhausted, there's a happy tumble in bed. Note: If Sagittarian shacks up with Libra, the bed will have to be color-coordinated, flattering, and osteopathically approved.

Hot duos: Ozzy & Sharon Osbourne, Phyllis Playter & John Cowper Powys, Woody Allen & Soon-Yi Previn, Casper Van Dien & Catherine Oxenberg

Sagittarius-Scorpio

Sagg has noticed, for someone who swoons on about being so into "seeking" the truth in everything, this Scorp friend is freaking out when actually hearing any truth. One of the good things about the Sagg-Scorp tryst is that Sagg will never have to worry whether they're weirder than the Scorpio. It's a given. And the Scorp will rarely bore Sagg, except when they flip out into possessiveness, which can be on several occasions a week. Unless they're totally soul mated, the Sagittarian attitude toward love and relationships could politely be described as cavalier. Sagg certainly doesn't enter into relationships just to be nagged and made to feel negative. Heck, no. If that's what's going to happen, Sagg will just go out that door, and old Scorp can hiss on about facing up to stuff on a solo basis. Shudder. When Saggs have fallen wildly in love with a Scorpio, they may have to have a few words to them about this. Constant scrutiny is not something that Saggs thrive on, especially if the Scorpio has charged the detective agency to Sagg's credit card.

Hot duos: Françoise Gilot & Pablo Picasso, Steven Spielberg & Kate Capshaw, Diane Sawyer & Mike Nichols

Sagittarius-Sagittarius

It could be hard for these two to get down off their soapboxes long enough to actually relate. Sagittarians love to get together and just rant the night away about their various issues: politics, eco-activism, education, art...whatever. Sagg and Sagg make an absolutely gorgeous couple. They roam the world inspiring each other and every person fortunate enough to socialize with them. But they may be so busy having civilized fun that they omit the harder emotional work of a relationship. And when one does finally admit to feeling something non-intellectual, the other is prone to waving it away in a fit of pique at having to deal with such negative stuff. This couple can live together in a state of blissful denial. Identifying this tendency is the first step to eradicating it and establishing intimacy. Two Sagittarians really bond by respecting one another's need for space and not taking (too much) offense at bloody-minded Sagg candor. Few other signs can tolerate Sagittarians for too long. This is a heaven-sent match.

Hot duos: Billy Connolly & Pamela Stephenson

Sagittarius-Capricorn
The Sagg-Cap pair brings two disparate personalities and molds them into an unbreakable unit. First, Saggs have to respect their Capricorn mate, resisting the temptation to screech "Straight!" at them just because their Cap is trying to stop their partner from becoming one of the sad Saggs sitting in some bar, fingering their sacred crystals. Saggs have big dreams and a stunning breadth of vision. Cap can help make this all happen, but there will be a price—the Sagg nomadic spirit may be tamed by Capricorn's sexy stability. Sex, if the Sagg can stay still long enough, is sensational. And in comparison to Sagg, Cap can be boring and prosaic. Saggs wanting to get serious with the canny Goat Person will have to play against type and learn to compromise their full-on personalities. And what does the Goat have to give up? For a start, sanity, as far as the Capricorn understands it. The Sagg is a total liver of life and is excited by the kind of risks that canny Cap spends a lifetime avoiding. Capricorns must decide early to channel this energy, not destroy it. Capricorn and Sagg can be so powerful—the Goat brings the calm ability to work the system and Sagittarians have the intellect and energy to build a money empire if only they can bring themselves to listen to Capricorn.

Hot duos: Frank Sinatra & Ava Gardner, Charmian Kittredge & Jack London, Maria Callas & Aristotle Onassis, John Kennedy Jr. & Carolyn Bessette, Julianne Moore & Bart Freundlich

Sagittarius-Aquarius
These two could almost have been genetically created for one another, cloned and programmed to titillate

one another. At first meeting they can't believe how alike they are and how fast they can power-bond. This coupling has the potential to run forever, especially once it's agreed that trifling differences of opinion should not creep into the socio-sexual reality. It is very sad to see a Sagg-Aqua couple turn celibate just because someone bought clothes made by sweatshop labor. Saggs are more flexible and candid than their Aquarian partner. The Aqua can be a bit of a hypocrite, a raving snob, and yet an armchair anarchist. A Sagg's opinions may be fickle, but at least they're honest about their principles being a work in progress. The Aqua is often the kind of person dubbed a bo-bo—half-bohemian, half-bourgeois. They torment themselves with middle-class ideals of how to live, and then feel guilty for not being ethical enough. Saggs are more the genuine wilderness article.

Hot duos: Brad Pitt & Jennifer Aniston, Imran Khan & Jemima Goldsmith, Walt & Lillian Disney, Bruce Paltrow & Blythe Danner, Leonard & Virginia Woolf

Sagittarius-Pisces This is a misalliance waiting to happen; a dangerous *liaison dangereuse* that has the most chance of flourishing when both parties live on separate continents, meeting up occasionally for "discreet fun times." It could also work out if Sagg has significant planets in Water signs or the Fish person has strong Sagittarian influences. Saggs are the most active sign of all—say the word and they're off on that snowboarding junket. Pisceans are generally creatures of the chaise longue. Too much activity stifles the flow of Fish-Person whimsy. They don't like group sporting action and, no, they will *not* sit patiently at home awaiting the Sagg's triumphant return. The Pisces will probably invite around one of their still-doting former lovers to entertain in the Sagittarian absence. Then there's the small matter of candor. Sagittarians are candid by nature but the Fish just fibs for leisure. Fish People will drive Saggs insane through being needy, dishonest, and passive, yet *they* will act most devastated (not

remorseful) by the break-up and, of course, it will all be the *Sagittarian's* fault.

Hot duos: Jane Birkin & Jacques Doillon

Are you really a Sagg?

1 Someone at a party is regaling the crowd with their adventure trek through Tibet story. You...

(a) Are interested—you love it when banal conversation turns to cool tales of derring-do.

(b) Are totally bored—you'd rather get back to joining in the latest gossip.

(c) Explain that you went there and did that yonks ago, before it was spoiled by yuppie tourists...Or did you?

2 Your ideal pet is...

(a) An animal companion—cute and furry is a big bonus—that you truly adore.

(b) Quirky, unusual, and definitely a conversation point. The rarer the better.

(c) Some loud and boisterous creature—large dog, horse, falcon—requiring untold exercise in wide open spaces.

3 At midnight on New Year's Eve you are usually to be found...

(a) In bed. It's just a date and you love to confound by being the one non-sleazy person kicking off the first day of the new year clear and glowing.

(b) With close friends or family, mulling over the year that has been, a little bit sad but relishing the chance to re-affirm your core values.

(c) Wherever the best fireworks and biggest party are at.

4 The adventure vacation is...

(a) So not you. You're a resort, sun-lounge, and cocktails kind of person.

(b) A growing market segment catering for people unfulfilled by everyday life.

(c) Booked and—nearly—paid for...sort of.

5 Nobody ever really gets that you are...

(a) So much more sophisticated than you are actually given credit for.

(b) Truly creative albeit slightly gaga.

(c) Genuinely not settling down and succumbing to societal crap, thank you very much.

6 Your love affair reaches a point where you are having relationship counseling. Asked to list what you would improve about your partner's relating, you write...

(a) Better intimacy, more understanding of your mutual goals, and trust.

(b) Nothing. You hate this sort of thing and prefer to sort out issues on your own.

(c) Blonder, bigger breasts/biceps, more sex, less nagging.

Answers: If you checked mainly (c) answers, then you are an official Sagittarius—untamed, free, and unbelievably stunning. If you checked (a) or (b) answers, you have other astro influences competing with your Sagittarian Sun.

Capricorn

december 22-january 20

Capricornia

"Nobody can give you wiser advice than yourself."

Marcus Cicero (106-43 BC), Roman orator, politician, and philosopher. His writings are
still relevant to modern-day politics.

Q: How many Capricorns does it take to change a light bulb?
A: None. They don't waste their time with childish jokes.

Capricorns have an eerie trait of looking increasingly youthful as
they age. This is one of the gifts bestowed upon them by Saturn—
aka Chronos, the Lord of Time—the sponsor planet for Capricorn.

Saturn represents limitations and restrictions that must be
overcome in order to be absolutely brilliant. Another name for
Saturn is the Karmic Taskmaster.

Everyone gets their own personal brush with Saturn during an
astro syndrome known as the Saturn Return. It first occurs—ready
or not—when one is about 29 years old and then every 30 or so
years after that. This wake-up-and-smell-the-maturity growth
passage is why people even just a few minutes over the age of 30
are so distinctly different from those yet to go through their
Saturn Return.

As Capricorns are ruled by Saturn, they are basically born with a
Saturn syndrome, giving them an ultra-realistic take on life right
from the start. Saturn makes Capricorns prone to melancholy and
yet also super-successful. In early youth they can seem like young
fogies fretting about work, status, power, and prestige at what
seems like a ludicrously young age.

But then, just watch Capricorn scale the heights, getting more
carefree and youthful-looking the more successful they get.

The astrological motto is a sort of summary or mission
statement of a Sun sign's ethos. In the case of our Capricorn, it is "I
use." Yes, it does sound slightly ruthless. You probably wouldn't see

it on a school's coat of arms or featuring as a corporate motto. But Capricorns are here to utilize all that is available to them. They bring people together, they start businesses from scratch, they use their pragmatic natures to effect real and lasting change in the world. They are never ones to overlook a talent. They use whatever they were blessed with.

The astrological symbol for Capricorn is the Goat. Astrologers often point to the animal's renowned tenacity.

Astro Goat is the mountain goat, poised precariously but apparently comfortably at a 90-degree angle, occasionally adjusting their hoof hold and munching on rare alpine daisies.

Like the Goat, Capricorn is comfortable scaling huge heights and so enjoys the view from the top.

Each Sun sign is either of the Fire, Earth, Air, or Water element. Along with Virgo and Taurus, our Capricorn is an Earth sign, giving them a practical nature, grounded quality, and a lustfulness most politely referred to as "earthy sensuality."

Capricorn is, of course, the most worldly of the Earth signs. Like Aries, Cancer, and Libra, Capricorn is also a "Cardinal" sign. It means they get things going, that they like to be boss, and that if there isn't a hierarchy happening, Capricorn will create one, with guess who at the top?

"I don't mind being called a dumb blond. I know I ain't dumb and I know I ain't blond."

Dolly Parton (1946-), American country and western singer and actress. Her hit songs include *Here You Come Again, Jolene,* and *Coat of Many Colors.* She starred in the hit films *Nine to Five* and *Steel Magnolias.*

Capricorn on form is...

"Derive happiness in oneself from a good day's work, from illuminating the fog that surrounds us."

Henri Matisse (1869-1954), French painter, sculptor, and graphic designer. The bold forms and bright colors of his works shocked the French art world.

SMART Capricorns can hound offspring to find lost library books, plan menus for the dinner party, and compose a speech to the nation, all at the same time and all without the slightest stress to their mind. They have a lengthy to-do list dancing around in their head at any one time and, unlike certain other signs, all are feasible. All get done.

SEXY Capricorn appeal is modern, snazzy, and always together. Already a sensual Earth sign like Taurus and Virgo, Capricorn adds the worldly wit and magnetism that is the gift of Saturn. Capricorns are elegantly ribald and able to conduct flirtations and romances in an appealing grown-up and sophisticated style. They get more attractive the more mature they get.

AMBITIOUS No matter how well certain Capricorns (comic actors Howard Stern, Jim Carrey, Tracey Ullman) disguise themselves as ditsy free spirits imbued with divine carelessness, they are extremely pragmatic. Weirdness is a well-considered career move. They are expert at energy conservation and will not get worked up about anything unless they're going to get really worked up. Then they reach out and sue someone. Capricorns are here on earth to create structure. They do it in their day jobs, they do it in their ultimate career plan, and they do it in their daily life. They have an awesome ability for grind, toil, mentoring, and that science of networking.

CLASSY Capricorns find salvation in the details. Flowers say so much about a person, particularly if they are just that moment in season or very difficult to grow. A Capricorn CD rack is not usually clogged up with cover-less *Greatest 80s*-style discs, scratched from being chucked about at the latest party. Instead, it will feature a selection of favorably reviewed contemporary musical items and non-cheesy classics. As Quentin Crisp, author of *The Naked Civil Servant*, wrote, "most people are at present content to cherish their mere identity. This is not enough. Our identity is just a group of ill-assorted characteristics that we happen to be born with. Like our fingerprints, if they are noticed at all, they will probably be used against us. You have to polish up your raw identity into a lifestyle so that you can barter with the outside world for what you want. This polishing process makes your life so formal that, by comparison, the life of a Trappist monk is an orgy."

COOL These people are blessed with enviable calmness. They can cope with the most full-on stress event without stressing out. It's one of the reasons they're so sought after and successful. The stiff-upper-lip ideal was coined with Capricorns in mind. They're glacially cool and always in control.

TENACIOUS No matter what the conditions are like at the beginning, Capricorns can claw their way out of some swamp to create the life most desired. Many of them have astonishing "before" pics tucked away. Or, more likely, destroyed.

"If there is a Supreme Being, he's crazy."

Marlene Dietrich (1901-1992), iconic and charismatic German-born Hollywood actress
and singer. She was the star of such films as *The Blue Angel*, *Blonde Venus*, and
The Lady Is Willing.

Capricorn off form is...

"You can't learn too soon that the most useful thing about a principle is that it can always be sacrificed to expediency."

Somerset Maugham (1874-1965), British novelist and dramatist. His best-known novels include *Of Human Bondage* and *The Moon and Sixpence.*

CREEPY What do you say after you say hello? Capricorns could try not saying or implying "what have you done for me lately?" Or, "I'd like to take a few minutes of your time to discuss an exciting business opportunity..." A Capricorn can literally act as if you did not exist for years. And then, when you hit the news with your invention which would have sold for an undisclosed amount of money believed to be in the vicinity of trillions, guess who's first to make contact? Remember that the Capricorn motto is "I use" and they will. They are particularly good at harboring their own resources while shamelessly cadging off those of others. They get away with this by giving off straight vibes and making everyone else appear quite flaky in comparison. When asked for help, they won't help. But they'll always have a variety of sensible excuses. You feel embarrassed for even asking.

DISHONEST They can justify anything. Embezzlement of funds? Just an unauthorized loan. Faked your doctorate? They were simply trying to better themselves. That lollipop? The baby dropped it. Capricorns are enormously judgmental about the foibles of other people, but blessed with deep reservoirs of understanding for their own less-than-candid outings. They lie in order to bolster their own position, avoid some nasty truth about themselves emerging, get out of giving you back the book they borrowed ("Oh no, that's not your book—it's mine, I've had it since I was a child!"), undermine an opponent, destabilize a lover's self-confidence, or aggrandize their career. The one thing they don't do is lie for leisure or to embellish a story and make it funnier. Capricorns always have a motive, which excuses the fib in their own computer-like minds.

SELFISH Capricorn self-interest is so over the top that it can be literally alarming. Should you or your agenda not fit the vicious Cap world view or clash with an ambition of the Capricorn's—guess who's suddenly enemy number one, to be rolled at the earliest opportunity? That's right. You. Everyone knows about fight or flight; Capricorns have elaborated the choice to fight, flight, or groom themselves to mate with the victor.

SNOBBY Caps work so hard to be somebody. They replace shabby friends just as ruthlessly as they edit their underwear drawer. Hollywood legend Cary Grant used to be Archibald Leach. Note how his roles carefully branded him as a wealthy, witty, and well-bred catch. There is no such thing as casual Capricorn entertaining. It simply does not count as an occasion if it doesn't involve catering, sandblasting, unsustainable debt, and an anxiety attack. Even if their job requires them to wear a name tag, Capricorn will still be completely full of it, judgmental, and petty about people's position in life. Whether it's name-dropping, paranoia about whether or not Capricorn is "keeping up," or naked attempts at social one-upmanship, Capricorn is there.

"When the president does it, that means it isn't illegal."

Richard Nixon (1913-1994), the 37th president of the U.S. who served from 1969-1979.

He resigned in 1979 as a result of the infamous Watergate scandal.

Motivating and manipulating a Capricorn

"I'm an old soul—I was a menopausal 16-year-old."

Tracey Ullman (1959-), British singer, actress, and comic with her own TV show

1 Be born rich.

2 Do boast about accomplishments.

3 Don't lose control.

4 Recognize that, to Capricorn, sometimes "no comment" is the only comment. They so respect you being circumspect as opposed to being authentic.

5 Forget that nonsense about how it doesn't matter if you win or lose but simply how you played the game. Capricorns like winners.

6 Gifting a Capricorn? Go for something that affords prestige such as the best seats at the opera, an original painting by a recognized artist, or a sports car.

7 They like lovers to be hands off in public but wildly insatiable behind closed doors.

8 Be acclaimed, either in a higher social class or be powerful.

9 Have famous friends.

"I somehow instinctively knew it would be better to win."

Susan Lucci (1947-), American soap star and TV icon—*All My Children*

Capricorn role models

"I'm kind of a paranoiac in reverse—I suspect people of trying to make me happy."

J. D. Salinger (1919-), reclusive American novelist—*The Catcher in the Rye*

- Susan Sontag—American new intellectual and writer. She started university in California at the tender age of 15. Susan subsequently became a successful academic, journalist, art critic, polemicist, novelist, and film-maker. Sontag fulfills the Capricorn elements of being worldly, witty, and wise.

- David Bowie—once-androgynous English rock legend. A sax player in 60s mod bands, he later gained mega-success with song "characters" such as Aladdin Sane, Ziggy Stardust, and Major Tom. Cap credentials? Was the first songwriter to float himself on a stock exchange.

- Tiger Woods—golf prodigy. He won a career grand slam of the four major titles at age 24. He delayed turning professional so he could graduate at Stanford University. He is one of the world's richest athletes and famously does not like to party with other golfers. "I just try to win."

- Marlene Dietrich—fabled ice queen of 1930s and 40s cinema. A Berliner who left her husband and child behind when offered the chance to make movies in Hollywood. When the movie gloss faded, she turned to singing and cabaret and then became a recluse. "I am not a myth."

- Kahlil Gibran—Lebanese artist associated with the beginnings of the New Age. An illustrator and painter, he became a poet while being supported by an American woman. He typifies the

Capricorn in that he wrote his book, *The Prophet*, which became a hit in the 1920s and its re-release in the 60s, making him a wealthy mega-star poet.

- Christy Turlington—first of the supermodels to turn modeling into a successful business. This American beauty has the longest-running contract in the modeling world (with top New York designer Calvin Klein). Works just 12 days a year for her multi-million dollar Maybelline gig. She has her own brand of skin products as well as yoga wear.

"I don't waste any time. If they invented a nine day week, I would work nine days a week."

Steve Allen (1921-2000), U.S. TV host and creator of *The Tonight Show* in 1954

Chic Cap

"Style, in the broadest sense of the word, is consciousness."

Quentin Crisp (1908-1999), flamboyant British writer and performer who referred to himself as "the stately homo of England"

Nobody is actually sure who really said "You can never be too rich or too thin." It is variously attributed to the Duchess of Windsor, U.S. society queen Babe Paley, and even novelist Truman Capote.

But regardless of who first uttered the phrase that is doomed to be forever recycled by fashion hacks, it is very Capricorn.

Capricorns are the sort of people who do ab-strengthening exercises at every red light. And, as you might imagine, there are stacks of Capricorns racing around trying to project that rich look. One refreshing trait of Capricorn is their readiness to admit how hard they work at it. Unlike Geminis, they don't slink around, lying that they can eat whatever they want or that they "just got out of bed and dragged a comb through my hair."

If a Capricorn gets her hair blowdried at a ritzy salon each morning, she will tell you. Actress Faye Dunaway is frank about the fact she hasn't eaten a tidbit of white flour for decades.

Cosmetics queen Helena Rubinstein once said, "there are no ugly women, only lazy ones." Even a totally unblessed-by-nature Goat Person will nevertheless surpass practically anyone with sheer grooming. If thrice-weekly manicure appointments, blowdries, and oxygen facials are what it takes, then by Saturn, that's what the Capricorn will do! Their bodies are probably too scared to sprout unsightly hair. They have excellent fashion sense. Unlike many Sun signs who use fashion magazines as something to put them in a filthy mood and give them an excuse for a drink, Capricorns use them as their reference.

They know when to splurge and what they can save on. None of them seem to have a stockpile of faddy acid citrus, chocolate, or aquamarine clothes hidden in their wardrobe. Their look is ultra-clean. They are the only people in the world who can wear an all-white outfit and pull it off without spilling a drop of red wine or pesto on it.

CAPTIVATING CAPRICORNS Kate Moss, Jude Law, Carolyn Bessette Kennedy, Ricky Martin, Annie Lennox, Val Kilmer, Donna Summer, Christy Turlington, Mel Gibson, Victoria Principal, Elvis Presley, Faye Dunaway, Eartha Kitt, Cary Grant, Estella Warren, Ava Gardner.

"Being in prison with no skincare really does a number on you."
Heidi Fleiss (1965-), notorious Hollywood brothel madam. Among her clients were allegedly many well-known stars. She's not telling all...yet.

Brilliant career

"Diligence is the mother of good luck."

Benjamin Franklin (1706-1790), U.S. statesman, scientist, inventor, and visionary

Golfer Tiger Woods made it to the cover of *Time* magazine at the age of 21. Elvis Presley is dead and getting more successful every second. Sci-fi writer Isaac Asimov wrote a book a week in the last year of his life. Capricorns have a lot to live up to.

Worse, because they are always so age-obsessed, they can sink into deep melancholy on hearing that someone younger than them has somehow surpassed the Capricorn achievement. "Born in 1978? Surely, he'd still be at school...?"

They quietly reassure themselves that the person is bound to go *mad* before long anyway. Capricorns, no matter how stressed, never go mad.

Well, if they do, nobody notices. There are thousands of Capricorn sociopaths chirpily running their companies and writing management "how-to" guides.

Capricorns also don't subscribe to the concept of success somehow being bad for anyone. Novelist Somerset Maugham put it succinctly: "The common idea that success spoils people, making them vain, egotistic, and stupidly complacent is erroneous. On the contrary, it makes them for the most part humble, tolerant, and kind."

Capricorns tend to favor expediency over risky innovation. They work brilliantly within systems. They are arch experts at suck-up maneuvers, power-tripping, and any form of workplace real politics. Never ever try to out-shaft a Capricorn person on the day job. Their parking space? Forget it.

Capricorns will return the favor 10-fold even faster than they destroy unflattering photos of themselves, shred incriminating documents, and quash unsavory rumors. But, although they are like some maniac out of an Ayn Rand novel, you have to admire their triumph-of-the-will approach to work. Capricorns can do anything. They can take the proverbial sow's ear and turn it into a Gucci clutch bag.

"It's no good running a pig farm for 30 years while saying I was meant to be a ballet dancer. By that time, pigs are your style."

Quentin Crisp (1908-1999), British writer and "the stately homo of England"

Fiscal reality

"There is a gigantic difference between earning a great deal of money and being rich."

Marlene Dietrich (1901-1992), iconic and charismatic German actress and singer

Capricorn is the sign of money. Even cash-challenged Capricorns are somehow attuned to the money market. They are type AAA personalities and a dodgy Dow Jones index sends their stress levels into the stratosphere. Always terrified of ending up as a bag person, despite all indications to the contrary, the classic Capricorn will manage to both amass status-infested objects and have some loot tucked away in case of inclement weather.

They handle money the same way they handle everything else in life—by taking charge. When a bank teller whines something like, "Well, what do you want me to do about it?," the Capricorn is capable of actually suggesting an innovative and/or startlingly obscene solution. But this rarely has to occur. Goat People are all into money management and are the Sun sign most beloved of banks. They can slither into the bank and somehow make the staff act as they do in advertisements. Tellers beam benevolently and the bank manager emerges from his office like a lovelorn bull ant.

Even Capricorn junkies somehow look like pretty good credit risks. But they are horribly given to what they call negotiating. They are capable of crowing over a "real bargain" that they haggled out of some poor soul in a manner that definitely belies their pretensions.

"Chance favors the prepared mind."

Louis Pasteur (1822-1895), French chemist who developed pasteurization and a

vaccination for rabies

Chez Cap

"Success is the best deodorant."

Howard Hughes (1905-1976), U.S. tycoon, a bon vivant who became a recluse

Capricorn's home is always ready for its close-up. Goat People like their domicile to convey bourgeois respectability by conforming to well-established precepts of good taste. They like a space that categorically says "up yours," especially to all those people who choose to underestimate the youthful Capricorn.

Instead of slavishly following homeware fashion, Capricorns purchase the best classic pieces they can afford. Having sought out the highest style advice that money can buy, they then stay very quiet about the source of their design expertise. This lot is fascinating in that they will all—no matter what their background—have an innate grasp on old-fashioned money principles. They dislike going into debt, but will spend stacks of money where it counts—their sofa may cost them as much as a down payment on a house, but it will last and can always be updated to reflect the times.

Goat People are a canny bunch. If the house has but one painting, you can guarantee it will have been cleverly chosen with an eye to profit. Their secret fantasy interior-design statement? Apart from a tennis court and pool, they want a killer view—a vista as spectacular and expansive as their own ambitions.

A Capricorn in love

"One cool judgment is worth a thousand hasty counsels."
Woodrow Wilson (1856-1924), 28th president of the U.S. from 1913 to 1921

Capricorns are lusty and romantic creatures but heaven help the person who fails to meet the expectations of the Goat Person they have shacked up with. A jug of wine, a loaf of bread, and thou—it's just not enough for Capricorns.

They can express their deep and bitter disappointment with the way their partner has turned out with just one vile glance. Or a quick jibe. Think the TV show *Married With Children*: Peg Bundy rarely let an opportunity pass to remind Al that if she had married the college quarterback, she would not now be stuck with a shoe salesman.

Capricorns know that you don't have to love yourself in order to attract love. They can be riddled with self-loathing and still attract, well, someone.

But, as physicist Isaac Newton pointed out, "for every action there is an equal and opposite reaction." Capricorns often see this played out in their own relationships. The Capricorn says tomato and their partner doesn't say tomayto—they say zucchini. Or something that isn't even a vegetable. This is partly because Capricorns are drawn to the total opposite of themselves. They like the idea of bringing order to the life of sexy hysterical types and then wonder why they end up with someone demented. Then again, Goat People are often so rigid that the emotional range of an average person can appear deranged. Living with a Capricorn has also been known to induce a form of insanity.

Clever Capricorns know how to perform relationship crisis management. They work at making their relationships successful with the same diligence applied to everything else they want to thrive at—that is, everything. If you are with a Goat Person, you won't have to worry about your place in society. It's assured.

Capricorn-Aries

Technically, this pairing is supposed to be incompatible. But, in real life, Rams and Caps can find an enormous amount to admire about one another. Aries can't believe how cool, sexy, and competent their new best friend is. Remember that Aries is a sign with a shocking attitude to authority. The very fact that Capricorn can survive— let alone thrive—in an organization awes the Arian. These two share a love of pragmatism, both of them loving to hear it how it really is. Nevertheless, Aries will accept any lie if it is flattering to their ego. And because Capricorns are such unabashed realists, there's a good chance they may not wish to put in the slog of maintaining the Ramzilla "sense of self." In fact, Caps could find it hard to believe that someone so exciting and dynamic could be so insecure. Sensually, these two will always blend well. As a business partnership? Once power-struggling is out of the way, both parties have the potential to raise one another's prosperity.

Hot duos: René Angelil & Céline Dion, Chris Robinson & Kate Hudson

Capricorn-Taurus

This can be one of *the* best astro couplings of all. The Goat-Cow pair dilutes one another's less-appealing foibles and evokes the absolute best—they're loving, supportive, and productive. Taurus adores Cap's strength and ambition, while Capricorns appreciate the centered stability of their Taurus. Both are keen on prosperity, harboring no illusions about the slog required to reach umpteen goals. Neither is averse to forgoing short-term goals to help bring about a far more desirable outcome. Who needs French fig-scented candles or a flashy stereo now, when they can organize a nifty little joint-property portfolio for later? If there *are* any problems with this often meant-to-be relationship, it will be early on as they experiment with annoying one another. Caps do so like to test the quality of someone's devotion. But once officially bonded, they'll get down to making money and staying healthy. Another blessing: Capricorn and Taurus are hugely compatible sensually. Even when disagreeing on some stock options, they'll always be able to resolve matters in the sack.

Hot duos: Dolly Parton & Carl Dean, Dr. Martin Luther King & Coretta Scott King

Capricorn-Gemini The Capricorn in this combo may have got onto the one sign of the zodiac that isn't going to call them cold and unfeeling. Because by the weird standards of Gemini, the Goat is warm and giving. These two may bring out the worst in each other but the compatibility rating is very high. Gemini likes Cap's competent, corporate-sharky air of amorality. It turns them on and, before they know it, they're embroiled in a hot romance. Accept that it's all work and sex play. Capricorns are not used to being so intrigued by anyone, and they can often struggle to ensure that they're the dominant player in the relationship. Tips for Goats: Show too much devotion too soon with a Gemini and it's all off. Don't struggle—Gemini gets off on insouciance. Be amusing—Geminis have the lowest boredom threshold of all and they will swap mental stimulation for security any time. Capricorn banging on about banks or the tax department night after night won't do it for Gemini. Don't fence them in. Just as Capricorns can't stand turgid emotional scenes, the Gemini loathes to be asked what they're up to.

Hot duos: Jude Law and Sadie Frost, Simone de Beauvoir & Jean-Paul Sartre, Nigella Lawson & Charles Saatchi, Kate Moss & Jefferson Hack, Vanessa Paradis & Johnny Depp, Elvis & Priscilla Presley

Capricorn-Cancer

If this relationship doesn't degenerate into emotional sadomasochism right away, it has a wonderful chance of success. The Goat and the Crab Person are astrological opposites with completely distinct core competencies. Capricorns are traditionally more worldly and adept with success, while the Cancerian is more at home in the realm of feelings—doing the emotional work of a relationship, creating a cozy nest for the Goat Person. It sounds like an antique gender-role division, but it need not be. Yes, the Cancerian has more emotional wisdom than Capricorn, and the Goat's pragmatic mind benefits from Crab intuition. But remember that the Crab is also amazingly canny with money and investments. This is one of the couples most likely to be prosperous—it's just that healthy, wealthy, and insane is probably not the ideal lifestyle. Capricorns and Crabs need to ensure that they thrive together by benefiting from the differences. Capricorn can provide emotional as well as material security for the Crab. In return, Caps can demand that Crabs stop saving string; Goats can stop calling their partner paranoid.

Hot duos: Yvan Attal & Charlotte Gainsbourg, Diane & Prince Egon von Furstenberg, Kid Rock & Pamela Anderson

Capricorn-Leo

At last, a star sign that supports Capricorn's desire for things to look good. Not all Leos are movie stars but they do like to look like one. But despite the sexual and mental compatibility in this tryst, both sides need to remember that Leo is a living-out-loud Fire sign. Caps and Leos may both be control freaks, but Leo needs to emote as theatrically as possible. Goats just want stuff done; Leos dramatically and suddenly contract repetitive strain injury when asked to empty the dishwasher. And, although both are raving snobs, Leo is more apt to indulge in decadence. Caps who are simply being themselves can suddenly find themselves cast as the mean mommy or daddy figure to Leo's gorgeous, freewheeling, in-touch-with-inner-teenager self. Also potentially tiresome is Leo's desire to feel lusted after by practically everyone. But, if Caps can learn to channel the Leo libido into art, and learn to become slightly more artistic themselves, this is a beautiful liaison.

Hot duos: David Bowie & Iman, Chad Lowe & Hilary Swank, Suzy Amis & James Cameron, Taylor Hackford & Helen Mirren, Rebecca Rigg & Simon Baker

Capricorn-Virgo This relationship is a miracle of time and efficiency in motion. Love and poetry will also get a look-in, but Caps will always admire the first two most. Virgo is the only sign that takes one look at the Goat and instantly *adores* what they see. Both are lusty Earth signs so the sensual stuff works fine. Both are also able to bond in all senses. In career realms, Virgos can be supportive while retaining their integrity; their advice is pithy and pertinent and, like Capricorn, Virgo wants a relationship that cures old childhood wounds while fulfilling adult potential. These pairings often involve the two becoming each other's life coaches, happily egging one another on to more triumphs (even if Virgo is also egging Cap on to do something about the grubby baseboards). Yes, Virgos are major nags. It springs from their robot-like observational skills and base levels of anxiety. Capricorns, wanting a more peaceful life, need to transmute the Virgo anxiety into creating mutual happiness.

Hot duos: Jared Leto and Cameron Diaz, Mary J. Blige & K-Ci

Capricorn-Libra Do Caps and Libras really want to go here? Yes, the Libran beauty is eye-catching and their charm lures even jaded old Goat People. But this is fated to be tricky, even if it is fulfilling. Librans

are quite capable of using darling Cap to engineer their social-astronauting plans. Librans—just as Capricorns do—take social life seriously. It's a kind of extension of their career. It is not enough to merely relax and catch up with a few old friends. One is either on or off form, and one is either entertaining or not. If Libra and Cap can agree on who is and isn't desirable socially, it can be an extremely fulfilling relationship. The catch? Well, there's the Libran craving for frivolity, which somehow always involves money and the spending of it. Sadly, the average Libran is perfectly happy to sacrifice long-term gain for short-term comfort, something that infuriates all Caps that ever lived. If the Libran actually had a libido it could all be worked out in bed. But they don't...unless they're seducing someone else's husband or wife.

Hot duos: Sophie Rhys Jones & Prince Edward, Olivier Martinez & Mira Sorvino, Trudie Styler & Sting, Carlotta Monterey & Eugene O'Neill, Ian Gomez & Nia Vardalos

Capricorn-Scorpio Caps fall fast for Scorp, and the Scorp, though not letting on, tends to be smitten instantly with the Goat. This is a love match in the making: Caps adore the fixed intensity of the Scorpio gaze, the certainty about practically everything. Scorp loves the Cap worldliness and the way they seem to manipulate systems to suit themselves, which, of course, Scorps can't resist knowing all about. On the physical level? The answer is yes. Mentally and emotionally, this duo needs to be aware of tramping on one another through being so similar. This affair needs to install an objective third person, trusted to be the paranoia monitor, and whose decision must be abided by. Either that, or both must vow not to accuse one another of flirting, or undermining the other's career, 10 times a day. These two can dominate the sex-and-money space in any social scene. Not everyone may love the Cap-Scorp duo, but everyone is scared of them.

Hot duos: Alfred Stieglitz & Georgia O'Keefe, Pat Rafter & Lara Feltham

Capricorn-Sagittarius
Is this an officially fascinating odd couple? Despite outward appearances to the contrary, Caps and Saggs are likely to have stacks in common via planets in each other's sign. But they also benefit from one another's influence. Capricorn gives the Saggs valuable "getting on" skills, helping them package their talents and selling them off to the highest bidder. Caps also help Sagg with achievement and boosting resources. Saggs help Goat People get back their freedom and relaxation—taking them out of their self-imposed grinds and off for a surf lesson, a hike through some mountains or a fully themed bar crawl. But it's important that Capricorns don't let Sagg occupy the official *enfant terrible* space while they cast Cap as the authoritarian parent figure. Cap says "you must"; Sagg says "I shall." It could turn bad if either side stops listening.

Hot duos: Ava Gardner & Frank Sinatra, Jack London & Charmian Kittredge, Aristotle Onassis & Maria Callas, Carolyn Bessette & John Kennedy Jr., Bart Freundlich & Julianne Moore

Capricorn-Capricorn
Anecdotal evidence suggests that Capricorn with Capricorn is an extremely popular combo for couples. Why? Perhaps it takes a fellow Goat Person to make another feel truly at peace? Caps do, after all, have a lot in common. They're always on heat, always on the make, and both Goats tend to improve with age. That's right. Unlike other signs whose beauty and/or accomplishments can peak early, Cap-and-Cap relationships are in it for the long haul. They may not be the cutest young couple in the room, but they'll shine as the most sophisticated, mature duo. These partnerships can quietly plot a pleasant future. If an issue is to blight Capricorn's home, it will most likely have to do with conflicting ambitions or perceived laziness. Caps can be so hard on Caps, and they must ensure that career or business considerations do not creep into what ought to be quiet, nesting moments. Scheming in tandem is a favorite romantic pastime for this pair but they should also attempt some form of lovelorn cliché for best results.

Hot duos: Cary Grant & Dyan Cannon, Tiger Woods & Elin Nordegren, Helena Christensen & Norman Reedus

Capricorn-Aquarius

This relationship requires more slog than most. The Capricorn modus operandi is to figure out the rules of whichever society they find themselves in, and excel. The Aquarius seeks out the status quo in order to stuff it up. A Capricorn is a highly skilled political animal, adept at corporate game-playing, power-socializing and business. The Aquarius has no idea how to do anything except buck the system. Caps say "I use"; Aquas say "I abuse." The erratic Aquarian behavior means it is hard to take them any place serious. Capricorns can be bored senseless with Aquarian rants about the Cap's mink coat, new digital television set, and dietary regimes. The Aquarius won't listen to a word of the Goat Person's hard-won wisdom. Why? Because, despite all evidence, Aquarians think they know it all. It would be nice to say that sex is an ameliorating factor, but guess what? The Aquarian sex drive is about as strong as the Capricorn's innate sense of anarchism. If nothing else, you give each other a lot of wry laughs.

Hot duos: J. R. R. Tolkien & Edith Bratt, Nicholas Cage & Lisa-Marie Presley, Christy Turlington & Edward Burns

Capricorn-Pisces

Capricorns beware! Pisceans drive all sorts of people barking mad. It's one of their core competencies. It's not their occasional inanity or extreme flirting that bugs Goat People, because a spot of Goat discipline soon sorts that sort of nonsense out. It's more the slippery Piscean avoidance of responsibility. Just when Caps think they've got their Fish set for a spot of corrective nagging, the Piscean eyes have gone kind of vacant. But if Caps can free themselves of the desire to control the Pisces, this can be a most rewarding relationship. The Fish intuits a Cap's deeper psyche and artistic potential, as well as satisfying sensual needs. But Capricorns who are serious about this tryst need to realize that their own personal prescription for worldly success may not suit surreal Pisces. At the same time, Caps should be aware of the kind of Fish who think they will simply suck up any material largesse before wafting off like the Cat in the Hat. Hint: the Cap needs to become more arty and the Fish more straight.

Hot duos: Marlene Dietrich & Rudolph Sieber, Andrew Taylor & Rachel Griffiths

Are you really a Capricorn?

1 Gordon Gekko, the "greed is good" character in the film *Wall Street*, was an example of...

    (a) An ethical vacuum.

    (b) Michael Douglas in his best role ever.

    (c) Your role model.

2 Your favorite holiday is...

    (a) A trip to some place that's not conspicuous, like off the beaten track.

    (b) Anywhere that truly triggers your relaxation hormones.

    (c) Anywhere that's paid for by the company.

3 A business meeting that goes wildly awry is...

    (a) Quickly brought back into order by your outstanding leadership skills.

    (b) A nuisance. People should respect other people's agendas.

    (c) Unlikely to happen if you have anything to do with it.

4 The absolute one thing guaranteed to put you off a potential lover is...

    (a) Infidelity, or even just full-on flirting with others. You like to be so doted upon and adored.

    (b) Inappropriate decadence. You've worked too hard to get your own life in order.

    (c) Lack of means.

5 At a party, you naturally gravitate toward...

   (a) The Beautiful People...you're an aesthete.

   (b) Wherever the most noise and fun seem to be happening.

   (c) The most powerful person in the room. If there is no such person, head toward the most potentially useful.

6 Aging...

   (a) Freaks you out so much you can barely think about it.

   (b) Is a natural part of life and you're okay with it...sort of.

   (c) Is cool—every year you get better and better in every way.

Answers: If you checked mainly (c) answers, then you are an official Capricorn—sophisticated, chic, and so successful. If you checked (a) or (b) answers, you have other astro influences competing with your Capricorn Sun.

Aquarius

january 21–february 19

Age of Aquarius

"Emancipate yourselves from mental slavery."

Bob Marley (1945-1981), Rastafarian musician, visionary, and "king" of reggae

Q: How many Aquarians does it take to change a light bulb?

A: Well, you have to realize that everything is energy, so...

The astrological motto, a summary of a sign's ethos, is "I know" for Aquarians. While this is obviously supposed to refer to Aquarians' amazing breadth of brain power, "I know" is also their most overused phrase. It is almost impossible to tell these people something they don't already know. Even if they've never heard of it they feel as if they might know something about it. Vaguely, you understand.

Within five seconds of hearing a new theory they can extrapolate so well that you think maybe they do know something about it. But some Aquarians don't even bother to extrapolate. They just start crapping on with extreme savoir faire.

Aquarians are "ruled" by Uranus, planet of enlightenment and liberation. Although, like the average Aquarian, little is known about it, most scientists think that Uranus has an atmosphere composed almost entirely of methane gas. Uranus represents ultra-fast intuition. An Aquarian is someone attuned to life and the world in all its manifestations. In someone's personal chart, Uranus is the great awakener, an astro influence that forces people—ready or not—to bring in positive changes.

In many ways, Aquarius people act this out; they can walk into someone's life and electrify it within five seconds. Uranus is also the wine glass sent crashing to the floor with an over-the-top gesticulation. It's what makes U.S. astronaut Buzz Aldrin say, "Neil Armstrong was the first man to walk on the moon—I'm the first man to piss his pants on the moon." It's former Russian president

Boris Yeltsin spontaneously doing a little jig in front of his own military parade.

The astro symbol for Aquarius is the Water Bearer; some see it as Hebe, cup bearer to the gods, but this character is more often shown as a youth of no particular gender—very Aquarian—clutching a jug. Does it contain water of life? Knowledge? Mead? Opinions vary. But Aquarians do feel a certain responsibility to nourish everyone's apparent thirst for their brilliance.

Like Gemini and Libra, Aquarius is an Air sign: light, breezy, sanguine, and detached. But Aquarius is also a so-called "Fixed" sign like Taurus, Leo, and Scorpio. They can be stubborn and slow to change. This does not sit well with their other reality of being a freewheeling, futuristic, and visionary genius.

Aquarians can be like slugs. An Aquarius can be committed to progressive social change and yet eat exactly the same lunch for two years in a row. It's not particularly easy being as lazy as, say, Taurus but highly strung to boot. They are full of contradictions, like Irish novelist Brendan Behan claiming to be a "daylight atheist" or feminist Germaine Greer's constantly controversial statements of belief or Lisa-Marie Presley's ongoing marital scenarios.

Aquarians are ultra-sensitive to memes, those units of cultural thought that some scientists feel are transmitted like a virus only positive. Meme theory explains how concepts, jokes, and jargon flash around the world in a mere twinkle. Aquarians are the meme carriers.

Aquarius on form is...

"I am an Aquarius—high spirited, love animals, swimming, the beach—that's definitely me."

Paris Hilton (1981-), party-hopping Hilton Hotel heiress

ORIGINAL Aquarians don't give a toss about the generally accepted version of reality. They don't march to the beat of a different drummer—they march to the beat of an instrument that hasn't even been invented yet. Throughout history, Aquarians have been the mystics dabbling in alchemy, the mavericks insisting that the earth is round or that it revolves around the sun when everyone knew that our world was the center of the galaxy. Astronomer Galileo got excommunicated and placed under house arrest yet still managed to invent the telescope, among other things. Aquarians are nearly all inventive by nature. It is a rare Aquarius who has not got a few mind-bending concepts tucked away.

VISIONARY The future is here and it looks like fun, says the fearless Aqua. Aquarians enjoy visualizing a Utopian new world order. They secretly vibe to the words of *Age of Aquarius*: "Harmony and understanding...mystic crystal revelations."

REVOLUTIONARY Even the most seemingly straight, sheepish, gray-tracksuit-wearing Aquarius person you know is quietly subverting society. They don't necessarily need green hair or extensive body hair to do it. These natural-born radicals tend to live ahead of their times. The world needs them because they believe in changing the world and empowering practically everyone. They'll happily take a day off from whatever it is they officially do to get involved in a protest campaign. Aquarians believe in consumer power and put their money where their mouth is. An amazing proportion of them are vegetarians and no matter what the temptation, they tend not to buy products from companies with abhorrent politics or environmental non-policy. To an Aquarius, there is no such thing as a minority and even if there is, why is that an excuse to ignore it?

STUNNING Aquarians are stunning in a space-age way. Their face has the symmetry of Libra but with an alien air. Their charisma is wired, hyped, and capable of literally changing the energy in a room. They tend to polarize people, producing emotions of either extreme attraction or actual repulsion.

HILARIOUS Aquarians are extraordinarily funny. Their iconoclastic sense of humor and lack of regard for conventions produce an apt flippancy like nothing else. As someone once said of U.S. actress Tallulah Bankhead, "Tallulah never bored anyone and that is humanitarianism of a very high order indeed." An accomplished stage, movie, radio, and TV performer, she even starred in the original *Batman* TV series. An openly bisexual, cocaine-snorting actress, she had affairs with people as diverse as actors Gary Cooper and Greta Garbo. "Daddy warned me about men and booze but he never said a word about women and cocaine."

ELECTRIFYING They are the all-time greatest networkers—they matchmake soul mates and casually perform career-altering introductions. Aquarians alter someone's life for the better without even noticing they're doing it. Sometimes they'll find you something before you even know you need it. If they can be bothered tuning in to you for five seconds, the advice is superb. But bear in mind that five seconds is the base unit of Aquarian concentration. That's as long as it takes to say "here is the number of my genius osteopath" or "you should be working with my friend Thingie, I'll email the company tomorrow."

Aquarius off form is...

"Sentiment is emotional promiscuity."

Norman Mailer (1923-), iconoclastic, anti-establishment American writer

ERRATIC Aquarius can completely freak out at something as innocuous as a wedding invitation but put a note in their planner to overthrow the pharmaceutical industry complex next Tuesday. In social life they go way beyond playing devil's advocate. The Aquarian will tell outrageous fibs to bolster their suddenly held view that the world has, in fact, been flat all along. Why? Because they can. Blessed with a highly active sixth sense, Aquarians have problems tuning into the usual five senses. They see things that aren't there, hear voices when nobody is in the room, and get electric shocks from things that aren't even electric. They get the giggles at momentous occasions. Aquarius is officially associated with groups but, like so much to do with this sign, that's really more of a concept. In real life, Aquarians often dislike groups. Belonging to one would mean they'd have to cooperate or, as they call it, compromise their principles.

BOMBASTIC An Aquarius does not just clean the house. They find that sort of stifling bourgeois convention too tiresome. Instead, the Aquarian rearranges the furniture, sandblasts the floors, tears a wall down if possible, gets the place feng shuied, and buys new linen. Though they are the opposite sign to Leo, they share the huge ego. An Aquarius languishing from lack of attention takes it just as hard as Leo. But Leo knows how to suavely switch the spotlight back onto themselves. Aquarius starts saying the most dreadful things, regardless of whom they alienate. Aquarians have two social speeds: focused suck-up mode for people worth impressing and maverick-genius-goads-intellectual-inferior mode.

290

COLD Due to their oft-adopted glacially cool detachment, it can be difficult to tell what an Aquarius person is feeling. Why? Because they have no feelings, at least, not as normal people know them. They feel that an overt display of actual emotion is almost wanton. If you confide an important secret to an Aquarian, just be aware that they are already thinking of you as Subject A, or as something akin to a lab rat. Aquarius ponders the correct response, wondering whether to issue the verbal equivalent of a rat food pellet or weensy electric shock. This "life is a laboratory" approach garners valuable information for Aquarians' ongoing research into humanity project and gives them clues for how they might best fake a feeling, should circumstances require it.

ARROGANT Aquarians love humanity but loathe people. They can easily work up more emotion on behalf of beggars in the street or battery hens than they can for their own nearest and dearest. Those who do not know them well often call Aquarians hypocritical. Those who are close to an Aquarius can expound upon the topic at length. Nobody does armchair anarchy or chardonnay politics as well as Aquarius. Aquarians are free spirits, unfettered by bourgeois convention. Don't fence them in but heaven save you should you want your space. It was said of actor John Barrymore that he was "given to sudden fits of generosity and equally fitful moods of self-centered arrogance." Think that could apply to any old person? Perhaps, but you have to remember that the Aquarian version of being generous is giving away practically their entire library to a stranger on some whim. Their fits of self-centered arrogance defy belief. Their genius will not be stifled by some idiot, that is, you.

"Mad, bad, and dangerous to know..."

Lady Caroline Lamb (1785-1828), British novelist, speaking about her former lover, romantic poet Lord Byron. Their brief affair shocked England.

Motivating and manipulating an Aquarius

"The more you know the less you think you know."

Lewis Carroll (1832-1898), British novelist—*Alice's Adventures in Wonderland*

1 Don't bother bugging an Aquarian about time. Living in their very own time zone, they don't care whether it's three o'clock in the morning or not.

2 Gifting an Aquarian? They like ethical presents such as a voucher signifying that on the Aquarian's behalf you have purchased a Third World family a goat.

3 Want to get rid of one? Bitch it up about them not fulfilling various bourgeois conventions. For example, "Where is my dinner?" "Why aren't you dressed yet?"

4 They won't admit this, but so what. They get off on people who are glamourous and confident. If in doubt, channel our Leo.

5 Betray no personal alarm at the Aquarian rant. They'll so love that you haven't flipped out. Yet.

6 Understand that the Aquarian concept of socializing is to bring a diverse bunch of people together, add wine, and start an inflammatory argument on unions or capital punishment.

7 Accept that they like their little ailments to be above the hoi polloi. They will blame their mood swings or itchy bottom on an allergy to something such as bread that plebs can eat without causing ill-effects but the Aquarius just can't eat.

8 Manage your expectations about the Aquarius attending official functions and the like. They truly do not give a damn.

9 Encourage their inventiveness. There is genius in the Aquarius and maybe you'll wind up with a few primary shares in the very first time machine.

"The most common way people give up their power is by thinking that they don't have any."

Alice Walker (1944-), American poet and novelist who wrote the Pulitzer Prize-winning

novel *The Color Purple*

Aquarian role models

"I don't get along with too many people. Not because I am difficult but because I'm different."

Nastassja Kinski (1959-), German actress whose big break came with the film *Tess.* She

was a poster pin-up girl, posing naked with a live python.

- Oprah Winfrey—incredibly influential American talk-show host, humanitarian, and entertainment billionaire. She is smart, intuitive, and forever espousing new causes. "I was raised to believe that excellence is the best deterrent to racism or sexism. And that's how I operate my life."

- Helen Gurley Brown—legendary writer and editor of U.S. *Cosmopolitan* magazine. She made a career out of empowering single girls to get a man and a career. In her seventies, she released an autobiography entitled *I'm Wild Again: Snippets from My Life and a Few Brazen Thoughts.*

Sun signs

- Colette—amazingly prolific French novelist. Her early "Claudine" schoolgirl tales gave way to more mature literary works. She exposed a breast during a brief stage career. She was married three times but reputedly had gay affairs. "If I can't have too many truffles, I'll do without truffles."

- David Lynch—the only avant-garde film-maker still making Hollywood movies. Weird films like *Eraserhead* and *The Elephant Man* made his name, but his commercial work, like the cult TV series *Twin Peaks*, is still strange. He even composes the music for some movies—"It's so beautifully abstract."

- Jules Verne—visionary French writer and the "father" of science fiction. He brought into the popular imagination the idea of the submarine, moon exploration, and globe-trotting travel. He wrote his first short story at age 35. "Anything one man can imagine, other men can make real."

- Matt Groening—rebellious and brilliant cartoonist, publisher, and producer. He brought animation back to prime-time TV with the hit series *The Simpsons*. "When authorities warn you of the sinfulness of sex, there is an important lesson to be learned: Do not have sex with the authorities."

"I don't remember anybody's name. How do you think the 'dahling' thing got started?"

Zsa Zsa Gabor (1917-), Hungarian-born Hollywood glam actress who collected eight
husbands along the way

Aquarius in vogue

"It's such a bloody responsibility having to look cute."

Minnie Driver (1970-), British-born Hollywood actress—*Good Will Hunting*. Her partners include Tom Cruise, Matt Damon, and Josh Brolin.

As everyone knows, a lot of people can put together an amazingly avant-garde look and then blow it the second they open their mouths. Stacks of Aquarian folk are so radical they don't care at all for fashion as a form of self-expression.

In fact, many Aquarians are so scared of their inner weirdness that they compensate by dressing in an incredibly traditional way.

Some Aquarians even entertain secret fantasies, which they are very ashamed of, that everyone on earth would have to wear a uniform with only a badge or something giving away one's official status.

Crystal Aquarius, of course, uses fashion to indicate their *inner* convictions. This is where one sees the ethnic influence. Aquarians do so like to support their little oppressed friends in wherever it was their little multicolored vest was woven.

Crystal Aquarius likes non-exploited worker-crafted hippie bags, hemp jeans, purple aura-enhancing T-shirts, and psyche-supporting gemstones. Radical Aquarius prefers to leave everyone in no doubt as to their convictions via a T-shirt or a little guilt-inducing badge. It's really bizarre how smug this often makes them.

It's not as if anyone is going to go around wearing something saying they're against Amnesty International and anti-literacy.

Radical Aquarius will often make something like a bicycle their biggest fashion accessory. That's right, the Aquarian bike guy thinks there is something so irresistibly right on about his bicycling stance. As Aquarius is a so-called "Fixed" sign, some of them get totally stuck in whatever look worked for them when they were about 22. They don't realize that there is something scary about a man in his forties stomping around wearing a 70s rock band "Crew" T-shirt. Or a woman with a totally perfect ash-blonded, matt-faced, wedge-shaped blusher, dragon-red lipstick, early 80s look, who is not doing it retro style.

ALLURING AQUARIANS Paul Newman, Bridget Fonda, Rutger Hauer, Geena Davis, Diane Lane, Clark Gable, Michael Hutchence, Elijah Wood, Heather Graham, James Dean, Farrah Fawcett, Jennifer Jason Leigh, Jennifer Aniston, Stockard Channing, Sheryl Crow, Christina Ricci, Chris Rock, Kim Novak, Denise Richards, Rene Russo, Brandon Lee, Jane Seymour

Brilliant career

"What exactly is success? For me it is to be found not in applause, but in the satisfaction of feeling that one is realizing one's ideal."

Anna Pavlova (1881-1931), ethereal-like yet incredibly athletic and strong Russian ballerina who became the most celebrated dancer of her time

Aquarians have a definite preference for being the ideas person. Diligence is not normally their core competency and they prefer to work in seemingly erratic fits and bursts of hyperactivity.

They are better known for dreaming up wizard ideas (for example, why not give people who file their income tax return by a certain date the chance to win a lottery? There would be no more compliance problems!), or sitting back to let themselves "develop" and planning their Booker Prize acceptance speech.

For people so resolutely future-oriented, Aquarians can be very slothful when it comes to dull old planning for it. Their work life can consist of a series of dramatic endings and rebirths. Luckily, they like it that way. They either succeed in something wildly idiosyncratic or become noble "I'm not cosigning the system's bullshit"-type slackers.

Aquarians resent any routine imposed upon them and react as if it was some sort of fascist dictatorship with them as the glamourous freedom fighters. Aquarians who are somehow forced into following someone else's schedule often suffer from naked-at-work nightmares. Even Aquarian suits are alarmingly prone to blithering on about smashing the system.

Aquarians under stress can also be prone to dipso or deluded behavior on the day job, such as tantrums, ill-deployed coups, a few tranquilizing shots of tequila before their television appearance, or impressing the boss with their initiative by catching them at home with their request for a pay rise.

Their other major career enemy is procrastination. Their astro motto is supposed to be "I know" not "I put everything off until...whenever."

But, obviously, someone has to compose overwrought letters to editors only to shred them the next day. And somebody needs to buy ragged, recycled twig notebooks to use as dream diaries for two days before they decide it's a stupid idea.

"Achievement is largely a product of steadily raising one's level of aspiration and expectation."

Jack Nicklaus (1940-), veteran American golfer who's won over 100 major titles worldwide. He's also scored a whopping 18 holes in one.

Fiscal reality

"A bank is a place that will lend you money if you can prove that you don't need it."

Bob Hope (1903-2003), British-born American comedian and actor. He entertained
troops during World War II and the Korean and Vietnam wars.

Any Aquarian worth their organic sea salt crystals has a hatred of banks. Why not? They represent everything anti-Aquarian: bureaucracy, faceless authority, money-grabbing, and unaccountable inefficiency.

Aquarians are always flirting with system-subverting fiscal stratagems. The idea of a nationwide Buy Nothing Day, or all employees demanding (as is their right) to get paid in cash daily. That would show them. Them who? *Them* them.

Aquarians have principles and are wise enough to know that one of the quickest ways to demonstrate such is via the consumer dollar. These people don't usually give a stuff about bargain hunting. They're perfectly happy to spend three times as much on the biodynamic potatoes, or the organic coffee beans grown on a plantation where the workers get paid a decent buck for their labors.

But Aquarius people also know that honoring their genius requires certain props. If a snazzy new electric toothbrush will imbue them with a sense of oral godliness then that is what they will obtain. If there is a feng shui problem in their house and they have to go out and buy hundreds of dollars worth of wind chimes to counteract it, they will. The bills can be dealt with later, once the household Qi energy has been fixed.

It is, obviously, good if Aquarian brilliance can shine without being encumbered by power cuts, credit malfunctions, and repossessions. In their younger years, these folk can also have a problem with possessions. It's amazing what can slip through their fingers without them even noticing it. Aquarians can wake up gasping, "I have a lounge-room suite! Who did I lend it to?" Once they learn to respect objects as resources, they're fine.

"The cross is the symbol of torture. I prefer the dollar sign, the symbol of free trade and therefore of a free mind."

Ayn Rand (1905-1982), Russian-born U.S. novelist and individualist. Her most famous works are *The Fountainhead*, *Atlas Shrugged*, and *We, the Living.*

Chez Aquarius

"There is no such thing as security—there never has been."

Germaine Greer (1939-), Australian academic and feminist. Her first book *The Female Eunuch*, written in 1970, was a runaway bestseller.

The original manifestation of bohemian chic, Aquarians are also ahead of their time. They were, for example, onto that Santa Fe terracotta craze way before everyone else. They threw out their first futon when the masses didn't even know what one was. Now they're keen on a space-age kitchen with a fridge that purchases missing ingredients online.

Mad for all that's ethnic, they often reject Anglo-American design philosophy and adopt an Afro-Asian fusion of styles. But just when you think they've actually conformed to a theme, Aquarians go and add a characteristically maverick touch to the mix. They enjoy making faux-anarchic ironic design statements out of simple, utilitarian objects such as ironing boards or kettles. But somehow, no matter what their mood, the Aquarian's home interior is always thoroughly modern.

Consistently inconsistent, they'll eschew curtains for tie-dyed cotton sheets, then blow a month's income on an orthopedic bed and pillows. With the future in focus, favorite Aquarian fantasies include an autonomous robo-vacuum cleaner.

"I try to catch every sentence, every word you and I say."

Anton Chekhov (1860-1904), Russian doctor, journalist, comic writer, and playwright.

His plays include *The Cherry Orchard* and *Uncle Vanya*.

An Aquarius in love

"It doesn't matter what you do in the bedroom so long as you don't do it in the streets and frighten the horses."

Mrs Patrick Campbell (1865-1940), British actress. Playwright George Bernard Shaw

wrote the part of Eliza Doolittle for her in his famous play *Pygmalion*.

Aquarians in love fancy themselves as being fantastically easy to please. After all, they desire only best friendship, euphoric romance, mental rapport, and craven worship.

Yes, they need to be doted upon by a Svengali or muse-style character who allows them space when required. Their partner must also be enough of an official catch to ease secret Aquarian fears of not being cool enough.

Unfortunately, Aquarians can't often conceptualize the conflict between their varying needs. They demand the freedom to act like someone in a cheap perfume advertisement when the mood takes them. But they must have a cozy childhood-scar-healing and genius-respecting home base.

The Aquarian's partner should behave supportively and with total dignity at all times. Or else.

The Aquarian is obviously free to stain the bathroom forever during a henna-dabbling frenzy, drink Pernod alone in the study while composing unreadable stream-of-consciousness crap, or screech about how their brilliance is always being undermined by societal demands.

Aquarians do have trouble finding that elusive soul mate. Ideally, the Aquarius learns how to fake some semblance of normal human emotion, acts vaguely like an earthling and lures in a genius-nurturing partner. And that, so far as Aquarians are concerned, is often that. But they are always astounded at how much care and attention a relationship demands.

Many of them can't help comparing their love affair to their house plant or budgerigar and wondering why it can't be as simple in its needs. Yes, the little things one does for love can be very irksome indeed to an Aquarian. And, before you know it, they are lurching around pontificating about what a bourgeois notion commitment is.

Once they have their soul mate, the Aquarian is very loyal and never ever dull.

"It's really hard to maintain a one-on-one relationship if the other person is not going to allow you to see other people."

Axl Rose (1962-), heavily tattooed frontman of U.S. band Guns N' Roses. He was the tight-leather-trousered rock god of the 90s.

Aquarius-Aries Stop the world! Aquarius and Aries want to change it. Mutual ranting unites this pair with a fantastic mental rapport. Each side of the combo is exhilarated with a rapid flow of ideas, opinions, and cant. Aquarians' out-there ideas thrill Ramzilla and the Arian energy inspires Aquarians to high-octane originality. Together, this is one of those "it" couples that others just love to be around...in relatively short doses. These two are united by a spectacular knowledge of what is good for the masses, aided by the fact that between them they know everything worth knowing. This can easily be a mutual adoration society, or it could be an emotional battlefield of

temperament and ego. Aries says "respect me" and Aquarius says "earn it." The Ramzilla pomp and bombast can infuriate the more elegant Aquarian. The inability to nail down Aquarians to a single viewpoint could look flaky to Rams. But, if they can stop talking long enough to indulge other basics, they find that they excite one another on all levels.

Hot duos: François Truffaut & Fanny Ardant, Bess & Harry Houdini, James Joyce & Nora Barnacle

Aquarius-Taurus
The Bull and the Aquarian? The most stubborn, immovable sign of the zodiac shacking up with the most fleet-of-thought? On the surface of things, the quicksilver so-called mind of the Aquarian should simply addle and annoy the more contemplative Taurean. Bulls never make a decision until they are totally ready while Aquarians can be talked into most things so long as it has an air of novelty, modernity, or originality about it. Of course, these signs are compatible—in a counter-weighting sense. Taureans may lack the Aquarian brilliance, but having someone to put quality controls on the flood of Aqua-genius could be a very good thing all around. Aquarians may not be as stable or self-loving as Cow folk, but they will intellectually challenge everything, including the Bull's complacency. The Aquarian says "I doubt" and the Bull says "I trust." Sex? The Taurean's "always up for it" approach is poles apart from the Aqua indifference. But too many ranty arguments will see Aquarian sleeping on the sofa anyway.

Hot duos: Andrew Upton & Cate Blanchett, Gertrude Stein & Alice B. Toklas, Natalie Imbruglia & Daniel Johns

Aquarius-Gemini
Aquarians are deep and Geminis are shallow? Well, so what? Actually, sometimes Geminis make more sense with their glibness than Aquas do with their ponderous drivel. This is

certainly the relationship that can drag Aquarians into the real world. Aquarians can have problems with self-doubt and lowered expectations. Geminis shatter this problem with their shallow belief in superstars and with simply adoring their partner. The Aquarian says "my play isn't working" and the Gemini says "you are just so brilliant!" This is one of the best pairings ever—if there's a physical or mental connection at first meeting, things could click forever. There may as well be nobody else present at whatever arty-farty thing these two meet at. Despite the glib vs. deep differences, these two signs are fast and inventive thinkers who are driven spare with people who think slowly or make statements of the obvious. They will never, ever bore each other which is important to both of them. Both prefer amusement to honesty. The bonus points are that neither sign can abide horny displays of public touching. These are two people who trust one another *not* to start groping in the box-office queue.

Hot duos: Anthony LaPaglia & Gia Carides, David Lynch & Isabella Rossellini, Prince Aly Khan & Kim Novak

Aquarius-Cancer This is one of those technically incompatible unions. Aquarians say "stay cool" and Crabs say "I'm so f***ing bitter!" But, for a theoretically unsuitable couple, there are a lot of them around. What could lofty Aquarius and the sub-hysterical Cancerian have in common? Lightning-speed intuition, for starters. Both just know things, without surface logic or actual information. Both take this gift for granted and are used to being thought weird because of it. The rub? The sensitive Crab Person can destroy all the Aqua defenses and have the Aquarian emoting and bonding like a normal person within moments. No wonder the Aquarian runs away! But the Aquarian brave enough to embrace intimacy with the Crab can be rewarded with a more groovy, 21st-century kind of persona. Aquarians help their Crab lovers by drawing the intensity off their worst emotional excesses. Aquarians' relatively even emotional keel helps bring the Crab to a more consistent flow. If both are prepared to make small but constant adjustments, this can be a beautiful relationship.

Hot duos: Ronald & Nancy Reagan, Adrian Edmondson & Jennifer Saunders

Aquarius-Leo

Early warning for this relationship: Leos care very deeply about their hair yet Aquarians often have better hair than Leos (think actresses Farrah Fawcett and Jennifer Aniston, both are Aquarians). Aquarians make the mistake of thinking that this is so superficial that it couldn't possibly impinge on an adult relationship. But even cynical Aquarians should be on the lookout for weird hair dynamics in the relationship. These two signs are officially opposite one another in the zodiac, and a happy union has to reflect this. Aquarians are rebels who often decide to transcend the official reality. But Leos want to be so accepted by the official reality that they are honored in public. When Aquarians think of people, they think ignorant suckers, while neo Leos think people are the adoring masses thumping on the tinted windows of the stretch limo. Leo may be happy entertaining some society dentist, while Aquarians are going on about amalgam fillings causing mercury poisoning. Aquarians don't want to be a brand soldier fulfilling some fashion corporation's marketing plans. But Leo is a logo showcase.

Hot duos: Bobby Brown & Whitney Houston, Helen Gurley Brown & David Brown, George Burns & Gracie Allen, Burt Reynolds & Loni Anderson, David Moreau & Emmanuelle Béart

Aquarius-Virgo

Aquarians look at a bunch of trees and see a forest; Virgos see the mess that all those leaves are making. This is a case of big-picture people (Aquarius) vs. small-detail (Virgo) types. Yet, if they don't at first drive one another sensationally insane, the Aqua-Virgo union could be a beautiful relationship. Both are signs operating on raw brain power who'll initially bond over how smart they both are. They're both readers and culturally literate—just don't expect any intellectual conclusions to match. As a duo they'll love applying their sneering intellects to films that don't measure up, yet Aquarians see the themes and feel of the movie while Virgos get twisted out of shape by tiny continuity problems. Aquarians see their intellectual life as something that connects to everything else and Virgo just sees Aqua's clothes on the floor. Virgo is a champion guilter whereas Aquarians don't know what guilt is. Sex? The grubby Earth signs find it hard to slow their considerable sex drives down for the more torpid Air-sign libido. This partnership has a chance, if the differences are salved with humor. However, the burden for the laughs will be shouldered by Aquarius.

Hot duos: Carey Lowell & Richard Gere, Denise Richards & Charlie Sheen, Humphrey Bogart & Lauren Bacall, Sinéad Cusack & Jeremy Irons, Catherine Martin & Baz Luhrmann

Aquarius-Libra Aqua-Libra is a sweet, fizzy, and yet good-for-you designer soft drink, which is much the tone of this relationship. Both are Air signs and thus basically compatible on all levels. Unlike some of the more crass Earth signs, Libra isn't going to drive an Aquarius mad by crawling around shrieking for sex all the time. Money, dinner parties, and resort holidays? Well, that's another story! Librans stimulate Aquarians and stretch their already wide horizons while Aquarians inspire Libran creativity. But they should ensure that one doesn't always play Muse to the other's artistic genius. Potential for misery? It is slight, but it is there. Libra can dither, driving the more certain Aquarian mentality to distraction. An enjoyable debate with a Libran can confuse an Aquarian because Libra will argue anything, without any actual beliefs. Aquarian rebels could also be left cold by the Libran desire to socialize and be liked. Aquarians don't need applause or even to inspire envy to be happy. The secret bond between Aqua and Libra? Aquarians are closet snobs and the Libran elitism allows them to live it all vicariously.

Hot duos: Clark Gable & Carole Lombard, John Lennon & Yoko Ono, Franklin D. & Eleanor Roosevelt, John Travolta & Kelly Preston

Aquarius-Scorpio

This relationship works at its best when Aquarius and Scorpio share some sort of obsessive belief. A typical bonding could be over a mutual dislike of compulsory fluoridation in council water supplies, or a fervent appreciation of solar-energy-powered cars. Antique turntables and LP records? An anti-antiperspirant stand? Both these signs are raving eccentrics and may, in fact, be vastly relieved to meet one another. It'll seem as if they can finally relax with a true peer. Or can they? Those couples who live together despite working for opposing political parties are not Aqua-Scorp couples. When they disagree on some major principle or other, it will be very difficult to advance the relationship. Both these signs care enough to want to convert the other person—ready or not. If Scorpio is a plastic-slide-wearing vegan and the Aqua is a defiant fur-attired, raw steak and vodka imbiber, don't bother going there. But if both are on the same self-discovery track, this could be one of those great relationships.

Hot duos: Daniel Moder & Julia Roberts, Dwight Yoakam & Bridget Fonda, Ashton Kutcher & Brittany Murphy, Laura Dern & Ben Harper

Aquarius-Sagittarius

The Aqua-Sagg duo is an officially compatible astro pairing. Both signs share a love of idealism and truth. Seeing straight through media constructs and fake values, this is a right-on couple with attitude. Sagittarius falls more or less instantly in love with Aquarius, only to spend the first few years of the relationship freaking about the fact that someone has "got" them. Aquarians are easily able to detach and give Sagittarians all the freedom they are always on about. Then, guess what? All that space sends them loopy. Sagg is so used to muttering "just don't fence me in, babe" as they slip out the door to the open road that the famous Aquarian non-possessiveness is a surprise. They get their precious space, only to realize that in space nobody can hear them ranting on. They come blithering back to Aquarius, amazed at the coolness. There is awesome rapport here, especially in discovering conspiracy theories, but there is also tension—both signs think that they are right. Sagittarians take the soapbox, Aquarians hog the pulpit...and neither feels truly heard. Together these two can get quite hooked on conspiracy theories.

Hot duos: Jennifer Aniston & Brad Pitt, Jemima Goldsmith and Imran Khan, Lillian & Walt Disney, Blythe Danner & Bruce Paltrow, Virginia & Leonard Woolf

Aquarius-Capricorn
The Capricorn ethos is to maintain the status quo. They have been doing this for millennia and are very good at it. The Aquarian raison d'être is to highlight what's wrong with the world and, by living about five years in the future, show the masses a better way of living. Aquarians are anti-logging activists, vegans, or committed to an out-loud gay life. They are walking poster kids for their own belief systems—the last of the red hot radicals. Capricorns? They want security, sex, money, and power as soon as possible, and they don't care where or how they have to shut their mouths in order to get it. Aquarians are surprised that these things are even issues to someone. Aquarians say "think outside the box" and Capricorns say "inside the box is where my bonus and corner office are at—I like the box." The big bonus of the Aqua-Cap relationship is in what each "alien" can teach the other: Aquarians learn that ideals can coexist with material gain and Caps can learn a new way of thinking...if they can just refrain from calling the police first.

Hot duos: Edith Bratt & J. R. R. Tolkien, Lisa-Marie Presley & Nicholas Cage, Edward Burns & Christy Turlington

Aquarius-Aquarius

A meeting of the celibates? For Aquarians who have tired of being hit-on by grabby Earth-sign types, this has the makings of a perfect relationship. Because both people are prime examples of humanity vibing at its highest level, social popularity won't be a problem—and both will enjoy each other's company. The Aqua-Aqua relationship should mean neither side having to explain themselves since weird and erratic behavior barely registers with other Aquas. Unlike those folk who try to act zany, the Aquarius has been accustomed to being seen as odd since a very early age. It's only as they become more mature and comfortable with themselves that they can relax and *be* themselves. Two Aquarians together are perfectly happy to continue acting straight but they will also give one another freedom to be their true selves. And, come on—the sex life is not non-existent, it's just that Aquarians tend to place friendship above torrid times. Aquarians believe in the "best friend" model of marriage and they find infidelity abhorrent. Should this liaison linger past the critical first few months, it will probably be there for the long haul.

Hot duos: Shakira & Antonio de la Rua, Rene Russo & Dan Gilroy

Aquarius-Pisces

Despite untold similarities between Aquarians and Pisceans, there is one *huge* difference: Aquarians are low maintenance and the Piscean is high maintenance. Pisceans need their lovers to be a combination of life coach, courtesan, doting servant, and best friend for 24 hours a day, seven days a week. They give back, of course, but this kind of hyper-relationship is not for everyone, especially not Aqua. Aquarians are so enlightened and understanding that they just want to let people be. So when the Piscean storms off to a "silence" retreat just to get some attention, Aquarians are likely to wave a fond farewell and wish their Fish lots of serenity. But there are plenty of points of compatibility. Both signs are perennially misunderstood by people in general; both exhibit frequent flashes of everyday genius;

neither is a popular-culture pleb but is a fastidious, rigorous individual. To make it work? Aquarians need to get cozy with the Fish and try to become more doting. The Fish has to be less clingy and less needy. Hint: get some domestic help as soon as possible.

Hot duos: Paul Newman & Joanne Woodward, Oprah Winfrey & Stedman Graham, Chynna Phillips & William Baldwin, Federico Fellini & Giulietta Masina

Are you really an Aquarius?

1 An ugly argument about the politics of cloning threatens to wreck a peaceful social occasion. You...

(a) Elegantly attempt to change the topic to something lighter.

(b) Try to put a reasoned yet informed point of view.

(c) Started the whole thing and aren't going to stop until you've won.

2 You receive an invitation to the wedding of the year at an exotic location and between two people you adore. You...

(a) Immediately begin to plan what to wear, find out who else is going, and what social synergies you can organize around this fabulous occasion.

(b) Burst into tears of bliss. How beautiful and romantic!

(c) Totally stress out. You hate big dates that are booked in advance and you hate socially sanctioned crap. You'll break the couple up if that's what it takes for you *not* to have to go to this wedding.

3 Your household sheets absolutely must be...

(a) Cheap. Hello? You've got better stuff to spend your dollars on than boring old sheets.

(b) High thread count and a designer brand name—what you sleep between says a lot about you.

(c) Organic and unbleached cotton or, even better still, hemp.

4 Your favorite color is

(a) Burgundy.

(b) Aquamarine.

(c) What a fascist question—all colors are equal and deserving of acclaim.

5 Spontaneous combustion, where a human being just catches on fire and burns for no apparent reason, is...

(a) Utter rubbish.

(b) Something you hear about from time to time, but really...?

(c) Your greatest fear.

6 The story of the *Titanic* is to you all about...

(a) Human tragedy of immense proportions. Why weren't there more lifeboats? Why did the first-class passengers get out before all the others? And why did Leonardo DiCaprio have to die in the movie?

(b) An act of violence and a harbinger of World War I.

(c) A boat.

Answers: If you checked mainly (c) answers, then you are an official Aquarius—an awesome person of charismatic character. If you checked (a) or (b) answers, you have other astro influences competing with your Aquarian Sun.

Pisces

february 20-march 20

Fish People

"I believe in fate and destiny and karma. I believe in God. I believe in Buddha, Allah, and the Druids."

Drew Barrymore (1975-), U.S. actress and Hollywood wild child. She hit the big time at age seven after her godfather, Steven Spielberg, cast her in *E.T.*

Q: How many Pisceans does it take to change a light bulb?
A: None. Only the inner light matters.

People are often mystified by Pisceans. They can initially come across like the men and women from Atlantis; or as if they arrived from another dimension via some sort of wormhole in space.

As weird as they may be, it is amazing how many people think they get away with describing Pisces as some kind of advanced dish cloth. Pisces is secretly the most advanced sign of all. They are cool, scarily psychic, and blessed with surreal allure. As the last sign of the zodiac, they combine the best (and admittedly also the worst) traits of the eleven Sun signs before them. It is for this reason that they are sometimes unfairly described as the "trash can" of the zodiac. Holy grail of the zodiac would be a more appropriate term.

The astro symbol for Pisces is two fish entwined together and yet swimming in opposite directions. Apart from Gemini—the Twins—it is the only sign to be represented by two distinct entities. Some say that Pisceans are a more emotive version of cousin Gemini. And just as with Gemini, people can get overwrought talking about the duality of Fish People: The saint! The sinner! The madonna! The whore! The Yin! The Yang!

Fish People learn to handle the polarity within themselves and wind up exactly who they are at any given moment. Just don't ask them to explain it.

Astrologers sometimes say that there are two types of Piscean—the shark and the dolphin, or the whale and the dolphin. They tend to pick dolphin, then something less appealing to contrast. But, really, the Piscean is both Fish at once—the dolphin and the piranha or whatever.

Fish People are ruled by nebulous Neptune, ancient god of the ocean. Blame Neptune for the fact that Pisceans are so otherworldly. They can sometimes transmit or pick up on energies just floating around in the ether.

The astro motto of a Sun sign is a sort of mission statement or a summary of its ethos. In the case of Pisces, it is "I believe." And they do. Faith—in love and peace—is their core competency. Never be too ready to dismiss Fish People and their theories. It is eerie how even their utterly unscientific hypotheses turn out to be correct.

Fish People are of the Water element, feelings-oriented and, like cousins Crab and Scorpio, artistically inclined (think artists Michelangelo, Renoir, and Botticelli, who were all Pisceans). But they are also a "Mutable" sign like Virgo, Gemini, and Sagittarius. These signs all share a certain flexibility. They are swift to process info and adapt but some call them fickle. As a "Mutable" Water sign, Pisceans can be millpond serene one moment and the perfect storm in a teacup the next. Unevolved Pisceans love paying telepsychics for clairvoyant advice. Clever Fish get that they have their own repertoire of occult wisdom and can tap into their psychic genius.

Pisces on form is...

"When genius interacts with mediocre minds, expect violent opposition."

Albert Einstein (1879-1955), German physicist and genius who found fame with his theory of relativity. He was awarded the Nobel Prize for Physics in 1921.

AMAZING Pisceans pull off the miraculous every day. Whether it be something spectacular, turning water into wine like Jesus Christ whom scholars think was more likely to be Pisces (that is, born in early March) than a Capricorn (who would have become chief carpenter to Pontius Pilate rather than have himself crucified), turning around their own life or brightening that of another, their presence can be a constant reminder that miracles are all around us. French tightrope walker Charles Blondin was the first (and last) person to successfully cross Niagara Falls on stilts.

ALLURING Their charm is supernatural. They tune into the subtle needs of people around them, providing whatever is required at that moment. They effortlessly project sensual innocence, a trait capable of making certain types fall instantly in love with them. In others, Pisces induces a besotted state by bringing out their bawdy hedonism or deep understanding.

COSMIC Pisceans don't believe in the universe. They believe in a "multiverse." Pisceans aren't futuristic like Aquarius. They are past, present, and future concurrently. Pisceans are said to be big on forgiveness and this gentle aura can confuse the more predatory people around them. They think Pisces looks like a walkover. Pisces smiles and says "I forgive you," and they do! What the predator doesn't get is that the cosmos doesn't forgive. Pisces knows how to "register" the insult at a higher level and walk away.

COMPASSIONATE Piscean kindness is legendary. They can be utterly saint-like in their gracious taking in of the lost or lovelorn. Expecting no thanks, they give, give, and give again without weirdo motives. It's like they think it's their duty. Maybe it is?

EMPATHETIC Unlike Virgos who can't resist a quick little "told you so," Pisceans do not sit in judgment. Other signs pretend to listen with lots of little coos but butt in with a "something like that happened to me once!" Pisceans get it. Their eerie empathy shines out in the Fishy aura with the result that people start telling them stuff even when the poor Pisces is a child. The Fish kid is the one picked out by the tipsy adult to hear all about the failed marriage, desire for liposuction, fear of mortality...whatever. And the desire to confess to Pisceans never stops. Fish folk grow up thinking this is normal. Naturally, it can be a blight on Pisces' life. When it's all too much they need to channel cousin Capricorn and learn how to snarl "it's not convenient."

A MAGICAL-REALIST Even as children, so many Pisceans believe they have been here before. While other kids are busy acting out the latest juvenile culture thing, Pisces is doodling hieroglyphics or interpreting their dreams. They see the enchantment in everyday life, scrying the white noise in between-channel moments of the television for cosmic clues, divining oracles in birds or graffiti, or seeing the beauty of the flowering weed pushing up through the footpath. Whether they consciously know it or not, they are aligned with the occult (aka unseen powers) of the worlds around us.

Pisces off form is...

"Reality is something you rise above."

Liza Minnelli (1946-), American singer and actress. She has earned an impressive three
Tony awards, an Oscar, an Emmy, and a Grammy.

IMPOSSIBLE One moment Pisces is playing worldly wise citizen of the world. The next, they've tuned into their always-close-to-the-surface inner teen and are consulting the I-Ching for insight into some hopeless crush they've managed to develop, or seeing how their kissing style feels on the inside of their arm. Or, if forced out of their bedroom and into attending a social function, muttering angrily into their mobile. Pisceans are perfectly happy to sit there chain-smoking and sculling gin while bitching about the evils of white flour. Their seedy state the following morning is quite clearly due to a food sensitivity, you understand. Probably from something *you* cooked them. If a Pisces manages to vaguely eschew their preferred lifestyle of feckless hedonism for five minutes, they're enormously self-congratulatory. A Pisces who conducts a civilized relationship for three weeks, buys new clothes without a hyperventilating anxiety attack in the middle of the store, or speaks to an authority figure without dissolving into hysterical giggles is a Pisces on the verge of organizing a lecture tour to share the secrets of their success.

SNEAKY Pisceans go online and offline but nobody ever notices. If your energy doesn't vibe with theirs, they *are* offline but the hype and gush continues unabated. Then if, believing it, you call to ask the Pisces to a dinner party or something, they accuse you of stalking them. Their need to be all things to all people can turn ugly. Even mega-pagan Pisces still wants the priest to be impressed at the Piscean's innate holiness. Trying to pin them down on some moral issue is almost impossible. Pisces simply figures out which character they are supposed to be playing and goes within to find their motivation. For people who ostensibly believe so much in beauty and truth, they are horrifyingly good liars, embellishing everything to suit their agenda. Only the agenda slides around and only Pisces has any hope of keeping track of it.

SLEAZY Yes, the Pisces is non-judgmental. But that's partly because they elicit so much more juicier info that way. Beneath that Fishy "I'm okay, you're okay" smirk is a Rolodex brain rifling through all the possible connections and ramifications, flipping out with glee. They adore interfering in other people's lives. Should Pisces decide your lover is beneath you, Pisces will helpfully—in their mind—start looking for your true soul mate as well as doing their best to undermine the apparently inferior scenario. Pisceans believe in freedom of choice and that nobody should ever, ever interfere in another's right to live their life how they choose. Unless it's the Fish who's doing the interfering. That's okay, of course, because Pisces is such a blissed-out cosmic child of the "multiverse." The Pisces' "do what thou wilt" theories evaporate the second it doesn't suit them—that is, if it's you doing what thou wilt.

UNREALISTIC This lot can be so not into reality that they wind up as utter cadgers, sponging off the "straights" they expect to look after them while honoring the Piscean genius. For Pisces to be able to create, they need a clean and serene environment. Someone—not the Pisces, obviously—needs to rise at dawn to perform space-cleansing in preparation for Pisces (who has been in a lengthy dream-analysis session, aka sleeping in) and be the graciously living creative person. Pisces wants a towering pile of glossy magazines to trigger the brilliance, and Pisces gets. Or else. Ditto, the jag of throwing out all the music to start again. Or, the special trip away so that Pisces doesn't need to think about boring old bills. If anyone made a sci-fi film about a Pisces, it would be called *The Procrastinator* and feature a time-traveling droid with red eyes gliding around telling people its spaced-out excuses for not completing...anything. Pisceans believe in everything in moderation, including—obviously—moderation itself.

"F**k them. Remember, this is the shortest prayer in the world. F**k them."

Gary Oldman (1958-), British actor best known for his diverse choice of roles

such as Beethoven, Sid Vicious, and Dracula

Motivating and manipulating a Pisces

"I don't know, I don't care, and it doesn't make any difference."

Jack Kerouac (1922-1969), American novelist and one of the leaders of the

Beat Generation

1 Accept that they can't be fooled, even if they let you think they have been for some spooky ulterior motive of their own.

2 Never, ever write one of this lot off. They can emerge from the most incredible crises sweeter and more gracious than ever.

3 Don't pry. Pisceans like pretending to be shallow but they have oceanic depths of personality, hiding untold secrets.

4 Accept that there is no use trying to fix the Piscean personality. They need to be all things to all people.

5 To charm a Pisces, listen deeply to whatever they have to say; they are so used to being the listener, they adore being truly listened to and understood.

6 Gifting a Fish? If it's an official occasion, forget it. They only really appreciate spontaneous, of-the-moment gifts.

7 Remember that Pisceans see you as an unsupportive brute if you do not go along with their flow, like extravagant wine fests or mega-health festivals with optional colonic irrigation.

8 Let them flirt their heads off with whoever (even you), without pouncing. Like cousin Gemini, they enjoy the swoon, not necessarily anything real. Moralizing merely makes them act up, or take off out the door.

9 Send them appropriate poetry—your homespun haiku, their fave poet or Tennyson's greats. They love any poetry.

"Life shrinks or expands in proportion to your courage."

Anaïs Nin (1903-1977), American writer born in Paris and famous for her revealing and controversial diaries

Piscean role models

"Imagination is a spiritual quality that, like memory, can be trained and developed."

Luis Buñuel (1900-1983), surrealist Spanish film director whose works challenged the establishment and scandalized society

- Elizabeth Barrett Browning—English glamour poet of the 1800s. She wrote her first poem at age four and penned epic verse in four books at age 11. Forbidden to marry by her insanely possessive father, she wed poet Robert Browning in secret, then fled with him to Italy. "Since when was genius found respectable?"

- Aragorn—hero of the novel *The Lord of the Rings*. He is a gifted fighter and leader who leads the race of men against the dark forces. Like many Pisceans, he is extreme in his pursuit of love, a swashbuckling poet, and deep romantic. Aragorn is in love with Arwen Evenstar, an Elf.

- Anaïs Nin—French-born American writer of erotic fiction. She married a banker and set about a lifetime of bohemian infidelity with men and women—and kept diaries. The real and imagined have never been completely separated in her work, but she did gain the moniker of the female Casanova.

- Michelangelo—great Italian sculptor, painter, and architect. He carved the famous statue of *David* in 1504. The personalities of his staff enraged him, but he wouldn't fire them. He was a social climber and entrepreneurial landlord. He hated painting, especially the repaint of the ceiling of the leaky Sistine Chapel in the Vatican: "I'm in no good place, nor am I a painter."

- Dr. Seuss (Theodore Seuss Geisel)—genius creator of kids' books. Originally a magazine humorist, he won Oscars for animation and for writing a documentary film. He produced cult books such as *Cat in the Hat* and *Green Eggs and Ham*. He kept the cat as his publishing symbol—a fitting tribute to the Piscean point of view.

- Elizabeth Taylor—beautiful, violet-eyed Hollywood diva. The oft-married star of *Cleopatra* and *Who's Afraid of Virginia Woolf?* drove men crazy with her endless demands, tantrums, and diamond fetish. Welsh actor Sir Richard Burton—whom she married twice—named her "Ocean." She counts superstar Michael Jackson as one of her closest friends. "I have a woman's body and a child's emotions."

Pisces in vogue

"Best be yourself, imperial, plain, and true!"

Elizabeth Barrett Browning (1806-1861), celebrated English poet of the Romantic period.

She married poet Robert Browning and settled in Italy.

When actress Elizabeth Taylor sets off on a junket, how is her 16-piece luggage set labeled? E. Taylor? Diva? No, the cases all have "Mine" written on them in purple sequins. That is the ultimate definition of Piscean style.

Pisceans are not so much into status symbols as status experiences. For example, they would rather visit an amazing spa hotel than own a designer suit for the sake of it.

However, Pisceans are always keen to purchase objects that help them cope in an often non-Fish-friendly world. Huge sunglasses, for example, are a personal fave of Fish People. They like the protection from the sun and their hangover, obviously, but they are totally into the incognito-celebrity-hoping-to-avoid-the-paparazzi look as well.

But the essential Piscean look is disheveled. Think of *enfant terrible* actress Drew Barrymore at a film premiere: totally tousled hair, falling bra straps, no jewelry, and a little butterfly tattoo. Or Hollwood actors Bruce Willis and Rob Lowe in singlets. They look wrong in overly structured clothes and look their best in just-out-of-bed mode. Even British actor Michael Caine looks better in a dressing-gown than he does in a suit. All Pisceans do.

In seduction mode, Pisceans will pour themselves into whatever cliché does the trick: Pisceans look their best when they are in rude health. Because so many of them already have a debauched air about them at the best of times, being officially dissolute makes them look extremely odd.

PISCEAN PULCHRITUDE Ursula Andress, Drew Barrymore, Thora Birch, Jon Bon Jovi, Glenn Close, Cindy Crawford, Fabio, Andy Gibb, Jean Harlow, Elizabeth Jagger, Queen Latifah, Rob Lowe, Rudolph Nureyev, Bernadette Peters, Kurt Russell, Antonio Sabato Jr., Dominique Sanda, Sharon Stone, Elizabeth Taylor, James Van Der Beek, Vanessa Williams, Bruce Willis, Billy Zane

"Don't worry—be happy."

Meher Baba (1894-1969), Indian spiritual master who observed silence for 44 years as he traveled the world to work with the poor and share his teachings

Brilliant career

"You can only sleep your way to the middle."

Sharon Stone (1958-), charismatic Hollywood actress and cultural icon. Her films
include *Basic Instinct*, *Casino*, and *A Different Loyalty*.

Pisceans know that everything is interconnected. A Tahitian butterfly flutters its wings and Pisces gets split ends. They are practitioners of synchronicity, able to have both big-picture eagle vision and minutiae-focused mouse vision as required. But for Pisceans to succeed in life they must master the time-space-money continuum. They spend a lot of time trying to get all three into perfect balance.

The first thing they have to confront is the employer who would love to hire the Pisces but would like them to come up for a few drinks and perhaps a nice cuddle in the hotel room they have hired. Pisceans really have to watch out for this sort of thing. They give off strange sensual vibes without even realizing it.

Also, because the Fish Person's astro motto is "I believe," they want to trust and believe in people. They want to feel that their agent is doing the right thing by them with the nude shopping-mall appearance. But the Pisces usually sorts this sort of thing out and can then get on with realizing their vision.

Pisceans, as we know, come in many flavors. There are Pisces people always on the lookout for the next fat-burning, miracle diet tea that they can sell, and there are Pisceans like media tycoon Rupert Murdoch busily amassing might, wealth, and power. There are Pisceans living on alfalfa sprouts and art-gallery-opening canapés as they work toward their big break in whatever form of creative genius they are devoted to. There are also Pisceans who set their alarm at 3 a.m. so they can wake up and monitor their dreams for Lotto-number clues.

Whatever they are, if they are even vaguely successful, the Piscean will have to learn to cope with casual hatred.

Why do some people loathe them on sight? Because they manage to make their success seem effortless. Pisceans always appear like the most unambitious souls on earth. They're too insecure to boast about every single little achievement, so others tend to underestimate them.

"People hate me because I'm a multifaceted, talented, healthy, internationally famous genius."

Jerry Lewis (1926-), American legendary comic actor, teamed with crooner Dean Martin in a string of hit films and starred in *The Nutty Professor*

Fiscal reality

"Necessity has the face of a dog."

Gabriel García Márquez (1928-), Colombian writer of magical realism who won the Nobel Prize in Literature in 1982

Duty is an offensive four-letter word to most Fish People. They can easily see the elegant necessity behind, say, an outsized and mega-priced flask of French perfume and they can certainly justify it in terms of their feng shui and personal Qi.

But stupid final demands for commodities like water? When the Pisces has cut their shower time down to half an hour twice a day? Ridiculous!

Fish People are often supposed to be too other-worldly to worry about money. This is not true. They only give the impression of not worrying about it when they are hanging onto someone else's for a tad too long.

But they are totally attuned to New Age ideas about lovely lucre. Pisceans know that money is an energy. And that, like any energy, spending it helps to shift that energy and create more.

You can see Pisceans doing "energy work" at the luxury goods counters of department stores any day of the week. They don't need New Age guru Deepak Chopra to tell them about creating affluence by flying first class so that the Universe kind of thinks you're rich and responds in kind. They do need to realize by a reasonable age that being responsible with money will ultimately bring them the freedom they crave.

Like Librans, Pisceans are the sort of people who are always shrieking, "There's been a terrible mistake and you are going to pay..." speech at bank-tellers, only to realize that they have been embezzling their own accounts.

No wonder, when the Piscean budgeting technique often involves buying a bread-making machine to save money on bread, or enrolling in a DIY designer shoemaking class. They'll do anything, as long as they can still afford proper Champagne, prestige face lubricant, and the rental on the satellite phone.

Chez Fish

"Good things happen to those who hustle."

Anaïs Nin (1903-1977), U.S. writer whose affairs were as famous as her work

Pisces is the most cosmic sign of the zodiac and, naturally, their home is where you can expect to find a fully themed, New Age domestic reality. Those little pots of stones around the toilet aren't there just to look cool—they're the feng shui cure to keep Piscean prosperity flowing. As for that rose quartz by the bed? Well, there could be a pronto divorce without it. Then there's that integral "every day I am growing more confident, powerful, and secure" affirmation tacked to the bathroom mirror—

anything to help out with confronting the results of a demanding lifestyle.

When Pisces isn't in macro-cosmic guru mode, they like to drift away from everyday ennui with the aid of their Zen bubble bath, a box of organic chocolates, a bottle of good Champagne, and a trippy music collection.

If Pisceans were to choose but one item of furniture, it would most likely be the bed, the secret center of their existence. Apart from physical bonding and precious cell-renewing snoozing, Pisceans also work, eat, and do dream analysis from bed. Their fantasy domestic design accessory? A shiatsu-trained maid. A Piscean's home is also their day spa, you understand.

A Pisces in love

"Luck affects everything. Let your hook always be cast. In the stream where you least expect it, there will be fish. Venus favors the bold."

Ovid (45 BC-AD 18), Roman poet who enjoyed widespread fame. He wrote poems based on erotic love, mythology, and exile.

Roman poet Ovid, aka Publius Ovidius Naso, was a fantastic wordsmith but also an excellent example of the Piscean in love. Some academics struggle with the way he manages to portray himself by turns as "a faithful lover, a promiscuous Casanova, the world's greatest stud, and an impotent neurotic."

But this extreme type of mood swing in self-perception is really quite normal in a Fish Person.

Pisces people are traditionally lauded as being into universal love. This can mean (a) they are disgustingly indiscriminate with the sexual ethics of a cane toad or, (b) capable of imbuing the most fleeting of friendships with spiritual light. Or both.

The classic Piscean is always on the lookout for, as Mills & Boon authors put it, "delicate flames springing to life inside their stomach." They are quite capable of making a shocking scene just because their lover refuses to wear the duck suit to bed. They are very good at murmuring "hold me" to their partner to get out of an awkward confrontation.

If they are ultra-manipulative, it is not particularly surprising. Most Pisceans have been swotting up for their romantic life since they were about 12. They've studied everything from *The Joy of Sex* and bodice-ripper books to the philosophies of Machiavelli and Edward Albee's play *Who's Afraid of Virginia Woolf?* Edward Albee was a Pisces so he knew what he was on about when he wrote a scene. Pisceans deeply believe in love. By the time they find it they have usually sown enough wild oats to feed the Third World. They will thus be perfectly happy to leave the hurly-burly of the chaise longue for the deep, deep peace of the double bed. Once they have a soul mate, a Pisces is forever an ultra-date.

The Piscean needs to find someone strong enough to keep them from the slutting around that they call mild flirting and yet gentle enough to respect the Piscean genius. Their partner should bear in mind that a Pisces person who is not paid enough strict attention will start thinking about doing an Anaïs Nin, that is, having "artistically inspirational" extra-marital dalliances.

"Music speaks for me when I can't put my feelings into words."

Fabio (1961-), blond, muscle-bound Italian hunk, who was once dubbed "the sexiest man in the world" by *Cosmopolitan* magazine

Pisces-Aries

It's lucky Pisceans are so good at looking enraptured and pretending to listen. Ramzillas do go on and on and on—all about themselves, of course. What to do? If this relationship has the basic goods, then the Fish will already know that it's one worth hanging onto. Aries totally gets the Pisces' fresh-start mentality and is excited by their ability to cull a few friends and just move on. Aries is one of the few signs that will not only listen to a Piscean's wilder or more ambitious dreams, but will actively support them. When Aries action meets Piscean genius, things happen. Fanatical about loyalty, Ramzilla will also meet the Fish's need for total trust. Aries ranting is the price paid. Bear in mind that the classic Aries pattern—not unlike the Piscean's—is to madly slut around in early youth and then become the paragon of committed respectable relationship. Hmm...this might just work. Very important hint: Pisceans ought to be tactful about some Ram follies. The Fish says "windmill tilting" and the Ram says expedition.

Hot duos: Freddie Prinze Jr. & Sarah Michelle Gellar, Claire Booth Luce & Henry Luce, King Ferdinand & Queen Isabella

Pisces-Taurus

Can a Piscean make sure they haven't attracted the kind of Taurus who's entire modus operandi is to make the Piscean change as soon as possible? For example, "I love you for your creativity and vision, but wouldn't it be better if you took this steady job at the Tax Office?" Taureans can be insanely stuck, whereas Pisceans go with the flow in life. Taureans will flip out if their toothbrush mug is moved to the other side of the bathroom cupboard. "That's where it goes" is a common response in the Taurus home. The Fish knows that objects must be moved, culled, and/or reinvented so life and opportunities do not stagnate. Taureans, remember, suffer terribly from lust for things. At the same time, Cow People can impart a lot about making life's structures more compatible with Piscean dreams. This partnership can create beauty from the most arid possibilities. Pisceans and Bulls are deeply compatible in the sensual sense, although budgeting meetings sometimes resemble a Jerry Springer episode. At the very least, you'll have no problems with intimacy.

Hot duos: Barbie & Ken Doll, Elizabeth Barrett Browning & Robert Browning, Edna St. Vincent Millay & Eugen Boissevain, Juliette Binoche & Benoît Magimel

Pisces-Gemini This would be a great combo for a pair of con
people. Both Pisceans and Gems are scarily seductive, charming, and amoral people able to mess with one another's pretty little heads. Both are dual-natured and fluid; both are used to attracting attention and evoking fierce emotions from others. Gemini and the Fish Person see themselves as simple creatures and can't understand the trail of chaos left behind them. Fickle? Not at all. They're like the weather—variable with the occasional cold front. So, if they're so similar, where's the problem with hooking up? Actually, they're too similar and the one big difference doesn't enhance compatibility. Gem is like a Pisces, but with no emotions. Pisceans are in touch with their feelings. Try emotion with a Gemini and they'll run. If it can't be turned into a gag or some gossip, Gems don't want to know. Pisceans toy with the idea of Gem, but Pisceans need someone able to cope with their feelings.

Hot duos: Vita Sackville-West & Violet Trefusis, Sharon Stone & Phil Bronstein, Lou Reed & Laurie Anderson, Drew Barrymore & Fabrizio Moretti

Pisces-Cancer This pair often experience love at first chat.
Neither one can believe that someone else could radiate so much wisdom and empathy. All those feelings the Pisces finds overwhelming are sorted and expressed by the Crab Person. It gives Pisces a secure feeling even though Fish People are very skilled at playing the wild child. This is one of the most compatible duos of the zodiac and one in which the duo has the

natural potential to be soul mates. Warning: Pisces may find the Crab to be cloying. Pisces are skilled at the art of moving on and dumping friends or situations that bore them. The Crab clings and clings. Nostalgia horrifies Pisces, which means trouble when the Crab detours into a bunch of old photo albums or, worse, expects Fish to sit still and put up with some blast-from-the-past rant. The vibe can be good between these two, as long as Crab doesn't push the Piscean boredom switch. Crab says "the past" and Pisces says "the tedium."

Hot duos: Kurt Cobain & Courtney Love, David Thewlis & Anna Friel, Nancy Wilson & Cameron Crowe, Frédéric Chopin & George Sand

Pisces-Leo

This isn't a fatal attraction but it can get a bit sickly sweet. Fish People have to be careful not to sacrifice themselves and their needs to stronger, bigger egos. Pisceans thinking about a big-cat romantic experience should first observe the leonine super-ego at close hand. These people are quite capable of taking the Pisces' brilliant idea and turning it into their genius. Even weirder, Leo will genuinely have no idea that this is what has occurred. But, of course, this can also be an absolutely gorgeous love affair. They're both party people, wits, and connoisseurs of the good life. They play off one another to create an environment others yearn to be part of. Ideally, Pisces convinces the Leo that the Fish ego needs to be coddled. Once galvanized, the Lion King or Queen is steadfast, loyal, and capable of eternal pair-bonding. Their flirting won't really be any more ridiculous than the Piscean surreal attempts. And if the Fishie sometimes feels like some kind of slave or subject—well, quite a lot of Pisceans kind of like that.

Hot duos: Drew Barrymore & Tom Green, Anaïs Nin & Hugo Guiler, Desi Arnaz & Lucille Ball, Courtney B. Vance & Angela Bassett, Steve & Terri Erwin, Téa Leoni & David Duchovny

Pisces-Virgo

Virgos don't admit this in a hurry, but they take one look at a Piscean and see a sinner in need of reforming. The St. Virgo stint may seem to be going a tad too far sometimes, but it's the Fish who brings it out in them. So, what to do? It depends whether Pisceans really want to check into St. Virgo's Special Treatment Center for the Criminally Disorganized. Pisces can benefit from a touch of Virgo in their lives and this could even be *the* relationship. And, indeed, Virgo will be happy to take all that scattered Fish genius and potential, bring it together, and mold it into a neo Pisces, capable of practically anything. In return, Pisces enchants Virgo's life, healing their many secret vulnerabilities. Somehow, creativity is always the result of this sort of coupling. One or the other is driven to brilliant poetry or painting. True love can spring up fast with these two—whether it stays is dependent on how much the duo is willing to morph together, to really blend. If both want to stay polarized, it won't work.

Hot duos: Matthew Vaughn & Claudia Schiffer, Emilio & Gloria Estefan

Pisces-Libra

Accomplished seducers, these two are drawn together fast. Pisceans enjoy practicing their enticing wiles on an appreciative expert, loving the diverting conversation, the double entendres and full-on compliments. Pisceans love the sex—so much so that if they could run this relationship as a kind of perpetual honeymoon, they would. Once the Pisces-Libra liaison lands back on earth, there are a few differences to contend with. Librans are intensely conscious of their appearance, in a way that alienates the naturally gorgeous and unpretentious Piscean. The Fish People are perfectly happy to go out bare-faced and non-blowdried; and Librans imagine they're about to expire from sheer embarrassment. Libra wants to throw a party and invite only the right people. Pisceans don't see why they can't ask their entire monster-mash of friends, family, and acquaintances. They can also vague each other out via passive aggression. So, apart from hiring a Virgo social-secretary-cum-bookkeeper, this relationship will be enhanced by both embracing the art of being direct.

Hot duos: Jon Bon Jovi & Dorothea Hurley, Chris Martin & Gwyneth Paltrow, Kim Mathers & Eminem

Pisces-Scorpio
Because both Pisces and Scorpio have potential for cheerful depravity, there is often a whiff of deviousness about this relationship. Onlookers find the vague references to handcuffs and midnight trips to "hotels" rather seedy. In fact, there is an element of compulsive obsession with the initial Fish-Scorp meeting. But once they settle down and get into some everyday relating, this coupling can be one of the most compatible of the zodiac. Being a Water sign like Pisces, Scorp understands all the myriad emotional complexities that go with the territory. Pisceans don't feel dried out or insecure with Scorpio, as they so often do with skittery Air signs. Scorps and Pisceans are always willing to do the emotional work of a relationship with each other. Clash potential? It may be because the Scorp is a "Fixed" sign, prone to truculence and a stuck attitude, whereas the Pisces is fluid and able to adapt quickly to change. Fish will have to cajole Scorpio into flexibility and the Piscean culling makes Scorps nervous.

Hot duos: Kurt Russell & Goldie Hawn, Elizabeth Taylor & Sir Richard Burton, Bruce Willis & Demi Moore, Pamela & Averill Harriman, Eva Herzigova & Guy Oseary

Pisces-Sagittarius
Romancing the rock head? Fish People are delicate aristocrats, highly attuned to every nuance of nature and society. Sagittarians are thundering galahs, oblivious to all but their own reality. Before anything gets going, the Piscean aura could be too easily shattered by Sagittarian's lack of tact. The Sagg person may find it hard to grasp that when the Fish asks for an honest answer about,

say, their figure, they are not seeking the actual truth, but more of a flattering reassurance. Even if Pisceans don't demand the truth, Sagittarians will dish it up without dressing. What to do? Well, Pisces could try joining Sagg on one of their interminable sporting jaunts. (Hmm, perhaps not.) But this couple can bond over a mutual love of chat and philosophy—so long as everyone realizes that Sagg is better at talking than listening. Lucky that Pisces is so skilled at seeming to listen attentively, murmuring occasionally, "you're so insightful." This, plus sexual compliance, is all that's required for the relationship to work.

Hot duo: Jacques Doillon & Jane Birkin

Pisces-Capricorn This liaison is particularly successful when the Fish Person is willing to play ingenue to Capricorn's Svengali. Yes, even if Pisces is officially the most accomplished half of the pairing, it's the way Goat People like it. But it's also true that many Pisceans get off on acting all coy and submissive, even if it is all a raving act and they do exactly what they please anyway. Some Fish like to think of Capricorn as the person who's going to straighten them out and, indeed, it will be most difficult to be so spendthrift and fickle once a Goat has finished the lecturing. Pisceans amuse and inspire Capricorns and, in return, the Goat provides more structure in the Pisces' life. Pisces get more secure and happy—Capricorns get a new sense of what is possible. Things only go awry if a Pisces attracts one of the Lower Capricorns—someone whose modus operandi is to be a total user. Given the Fish Person's compulsion to give, this can be an ugly scenario. Pisceans should ask: how much is the Goat truly listening to my dreams?

Hot duo: Rudolph Sieber & Marlene Dietrich, Rachel Griffiths & Andrew Taylor

Pisces-Aquarius

Aquarians and Pisceans are often drawn together through their mutual eccentricities. They are both accustomed to having been seen as weird since an early age. As the last two astrological signs, they are also similar in that they're both highly evolved beings. They share an interest in realms beyond the obvious, and are both kind of ahead of their time. They share a surreal sense of humor—if mental rapport were all it took, these guys could be soul mates. But classic Pisceans need extremely focused and loving attention just to get out of bed in the morning. The Aquarian focus is more diffuse and not necessarily centered on the Fish Person nonstop. In fact, Aquarians may not be emotionally equipped for the hothouse atmosphere preferred by the Fish. Pisceans may need to give their Aquas warmth-training, lest they find themselves flopping around gasping for romantic attention. Pisceans think "I need" and Aquarians think "I need to breathe."

Hot duos: Joanne Woodward & Paul Newman, Stedman Graham & Oprah Winfrey, William Baldwin & Chynna Phillips, Giulietta Masina & Federico Fellini

Pisces-Pisces

Fish People are the true romantics of the zodiac. No matter how snide or cynical they seem, they yearn to be soul mates. So what happens when two of these beautiful people come together? They first test out the other Fish to see how much they can mess with their pretty head. No, it's not a nice sight. Yes, you could, in fact, call it dysfunctional. The problem with Pisceans is that they are all terribly attractive. Since a very young age, they've been luring folks without even trying. This leads to all sorts of trying situations and it's the rare Piscean who reaches a vague semblance of maturity without stacks of psychic baggage. When two of them bond, they can't help trying out the last umpteen methods of partner torment they've learned from a troubled past. The key to domestic Pisces-Pisces bliss is being a sane, stable, and non-escapist grown-up.

If a Pisces can catch a Fish at a stage where their worst life lessons have been learned, then they have a chance of a serene and sustained love.

Hot duos: Sir Richard Burton & Isabel Arundell, Shakira & Michael Caine, Heather McComb & James Van Der Beek

Are you really a Pisces?

1 Talking about street lighting, you and a neighbor suddenly bond to the extent that you invite this person in for a drink. They confide an awkward detail to do with personal sexuality. You...

    (a) Pretend not to hear—this is way out of line.

    (b) Take it as a cue to discuss Third World politics.

    (c) Get another bottle of wine and one-up by going more lurid and more deep.

2 The movie, *The English Patient*, was about...

    (a) Love in a time of war.

    (b) Passion and betrayal.

    (c) Some idiot who left his girlfriend in a cave.

3 Your spouse's best friend makes a pass at you. You feel...

    (a) A bit creeped out.

    (b) Totally outraged at the breach of trust.

    (c) Flattered.

4 You think new disco versions of old songs are...

    (a) Fine...if you're at a nightclub.

    (b) An abomination—it lacks the integrity of the original.

    (c) The only version that counts.

5 The one indispensable item in your house is...

    (a) The oven—a person has to eat.

    (b) The TV and DVD player.

    (c) The chaise longue.

6 When someone lies, you...

    (a) Demand an explanation.

    (b) Vow never to believe them again.

    (c) Trump them with a doozy of your own.

Answers: If you checked mainly (c) answers, then you are an official Piscean—perceptive, pulchritudinous, and powerful. If you checked (a) or (b) answers, you have other astro influences competing with your Piscean Sun.

soul
mating

For "Us"

"The minute I heard my first love story

I started looking for you not knowing
how blind that was.

Lovers don't finally meet somewhere.
They're in each other all along."

The Minute I Heard My First Love Story—Rumi

For your eyes only! Top-secret astro info

Whether solo or duo, blissfully bonded or longing for love, we are all interested in the concept of soul mating. Do you ever feel as though you just know that your soul mate is out there and wonder what nature of person he or she could be? If in a relationship, do you wonder if your lover is truly The One? Or just the seat-warmer? Wishful thinking wise, wouldn't you love to know how the object of your adoration really feels about you?

This section offers all the inside info about love, romance, and, of course, finding your soul mate. Armed with just the date of his or her birth, you can quickly and easily find a person's ideal lover—maybe before even they figure it out—and their soul secrets!

This info is far above and beyond the usual Sun sign compatibility guff. Hello? Don't we all know supposedly so-incompatible Sun signs that are as happy as hell?

Think he's hot? Look him up here. Or have fun figuring out your own subliminal love motivations. Eeek?

Got any friends whose love life defies belief? They could probably do with a spot of soul mating analysis as well! Celeb relationships? Are Reese and Ryan soul mates? You and Ryan? What does Colin Farrell really want in a woman? Is your so-secret love persona the same as Uma's? Or are you more like Nicole?

Confused by Mr. There But Not There? Sneak a look at his ideal woman, as determined by the cosmos, for the real facts. So in love? Check out the astro-soul mating potential of your liaison! You can do it all through this section!

This secret astro love biz is so simple to learn. Anyone can do it. And you'll be wowed by how freakily accurate it is!

Have fun and blessed be.

Mystic Medusa xxx

Love in a
logical climate

"Launcelot loved Guenevere
from the moment he first beheld her."

King Arthur and the Knights of the Round Table–Doris Ashley

Love in a logical climate

P hysicist Albert Einstein once said that gravitation is not responsible for people falling in love. Love may not make the world go around but it sure feels like it sometimes. Yes, even an official genius like him could grasp that love ain't logical.

Yet the emergence of psychology as a science has also made us suspicious of love. Maybe we feel those first pangs of love and think, "Eeek, is this some sort of dysfunctional complex?" Somehow, this narcissistic object choice has set off an infantile need for ongoing company...theirs only! Or maybe the dizzy sensation signifies a wheat allergy? That's it, for sure. It's all to do with insulin levels. No more grains, rice, or pasta. No sugar.

Then again, that woozy feeling could be some sort of endocrine disorder. What else but hormones going crazy causes sudden lust attacks in the middle of a workday? Or perhaps an osteopath may be able to fix you up.

Sudden blissful experiences alternating with nervousness? There's medication for that, isn't there?

Shrinks talk of love in terms of codependency, conflict management, long-term relationship, boundaries, working at it, foreplay, bonding...making love sound as though it's some sort of hideous day-job gig! Then there is the socio-biology mob who say love at first sight has to do with our pheromones and the hip-to-waist ratio of females. Just as apes are drawn to one another by the

Soul mating

baring of bottoms, revelation of mammary glands, and a show of strength, humans enact complex but essentially banal mating rituals.

Romance, apparently, is just a ploy to ensure population growth. We have no real affinity with a partner and instant attraction is hardwired into our genes—it's simply a tribal impulse. So we're tricked into breeding and then have to somehow forge a productive social unit with our partner.

Another modern love theory is the idea that attachment to another lowers one's higher mind. Romance is simply a low-rent yearning that stops us merging with the Cosmos. Better by far to stay pure through yoga, meditation, and celibacy.

Finally, there is the cynical "romance as sport" belief system. Love is a competition and the best prepped—that is, the most toned, educated, rich, good at sex, etc.—scores the best catch. Until, that is, a better contender comes along to challenge our position and take our "trophy."

However, most of us have too much poetry in our hearts to subscribe to the above clinical schools of thought. Love is not a dysfunction, a competition, the privilege of mammals, or a distraction from our high-falutin' spiritual goals.

Love is all about feelings and emotions. It's the hook that keeps us interested, that adds meaning to the most banal of pop songs and lifts us above the usual round of health warnings, cosmetic color trends, mismatched socks, geopolitics, cellulite, past use-by dates, and letters from the council...

And romance is still the pivotal point around which our personal worlds revolve. The sudden "zing" of connection with another, that swooning sensation and so scary, "Wow, I'm in love" realization that is essential to human well-being.

True romance turns life back into a fairytale for grown-ups. Falling in love not only feels magical, it elevates our entire being. The euphoric ideal of happy ever after sustains us through the peaks and (yes!) lows of everyday loving.

It's why even the most jaded and louche among us secretly cherish the concept of having a soul mate.

So, what's it all about, this thing called love? And what exactly is a soul mate?

"Whoever loved that loved not at first sight?"

Hero and Leander—Christopher Marlowe

Soul mating
101

"As soon as I met David, I thought, 'I want to marry this person, grow up with this person, learn things about life with this person, and have a family.' I surprised myself."

Former Spice Girl Victoria Beckham on her husband, soccer star David Beckham

S urprisingly, not every dictionary acknowledges the word soul mate. The ones that do tend toward the dry definition of he or she being a person of "shared temperament."

So let's delve deeper and look to history for a more meaningful explanation. Plato's theory of soul mating is probably the best known definition. The ancient Greek soldier-scholar postulated the idea of one soul being made up of a male and female. Split apart, we wander the world, seeking our "other half" so we may be whole again. This twin-soul motif has recurred in all sorts of belief systems and myths over the centuries.

In the 20th century, Edgar Cayce, one of the world's most famous clairvoyants, popularized the concept behind the "haven't we met before?" sensation of déja vù. Edgar felt that strong attractions to another were linked to subconscious memory patterns of having been with this person in previous lifetimes.

His theory was that such connections feel "pre-ordained" because, in fact, they are. You and Mr. or Mrs. Previous Lifetime are destined to keep on meeting up and working through, er, issues. Hmm. A good excuse for the nonstop bickering dynamic?

Edgar Cayce believed that the feelings aroused go instantly beyond a mere physical attraction (not that we don't love that, too) and are about the other person utterly enlivening us, physically and mentally as well as spiritually.

Soul mating

So your soul mate is a person you're destined to be with forever and you recognize him or her right away. Other New Age theorists take that a step further. They say that we have whole soul tribes—bunches of people whom we've known before and whom our soul immediately recognizes.

Whether or not you subscribe to reincarnation dogma, something is definitely up. We do meet people we simply adore on sight! The relationship instantly feels as though we're just picking up on a conversation started elsewhere.

And, yes, this can happen with or without the sex urge—there are plenty of soul mates who are simply best friends. There are others who are lucky enough to be born equipped with soul mates in their family.

That such instant love exists—and I know for sure that it does because I knew I was going to marry my now husband the moment I saw his photograph in a magazine and experienced extreme hot and cold "flushes"—is all the proof I need.

The story of how British actress Joanna Lumley met her husband is one of my faves and is a perfect example of "physical impact" soul mate recognition. The Emmy Award winning star of two hit TV series, *Absolutely Fabulous* and *The New Avengers,* locked eyes with a man sitting at the church organ and was seized with the strangest sensation.

"It was like someone had pushed me sharply in the chest with a great bang," says Joanna in her autobiography, *Stare Back and Smile* (Viking, 1989). "I felt as though I'd had some kind of electric shock. It wasn't a matter of falling instantly in love, it was the impact of a colossal shock, completely memorable."

The fellow who set off this reaction was Stephen Barlow. This former chorister at Canterbury Cathedral, who would become one of the world's foremost musical directors, was eight years younger than Joanna. The pair had a mutual friend at the time who lived in the country. As a 21-year-old, Joanna was staying at the friend's home when they were expecting Stephen to arrive.

"For some unknown reason, he never turned up," says Joanna. "I can remember feeling terribly disappointed that I wasn't going to meet this boy. But even then that struck me as odd. I was eight years older than this child and I had never met him. But the name Stephen Barlow burned into me or it came from me as though it was a memory from the future, if you can imagine something as strange as that."

A little more than a decade later, the star was attending a marriage in the same country village. As she stepped through the porch into the church, the organist turned, looked straight at her and their eyes locked. Stephen and Joanna had finally met.

They met again in London several years later when Stephen—now 30—was rehearsing near her home. He dropped by one day.

"Finally, we got to know each other and it became apparent, we both agreed, that it was exactly as though each of us had found our other half," Joanna says.

The couple married in 1986 and, like so many soul mates, they are best friends who adore one another's company. They have long periods apart but they either call each other every day, or they fax one another in handwritten notes.

"With Stephen, it was not only a case of eyes meeting across a crowded room but also something deeper as well," Joanna explains. "An inner voice told me he was the one and when that happens you've got to go with it because your heart is open and you feel marvellous.

"If you're lucky, and I guess I am, romance continues wildly after marriage because you're wildly in love. I know that other people get bored stiff [with their marriages] and go off and have affairs. Not me, babe."

When love walks in the door, consciousness is suddenly raised sky-high, the heart opens, and you do feel marvelous, as Joanna says. You become a magical realist by default.

Soul mating is not necessarily socially convenient. Love's history is littered with unfortunate folk, cast off by those lovers who meet one another and leap heart-first into a whirl of complications and entanglements. Here is one such story.

French writer Bernard-Henri Levy first met his actress wife Arielle Dombasle when she was at one of his book-signings. She had pursued

Soul mating

her literary hero after falling in love with his dust-jacket photo. "It was the most moving face I had ever seen, full of pain, femininity, gravity," Arielle says.

During a brief exchange, Arielle tried to lure Bernard-Henri into seeing a play she was appearing in. But it was Bernard-Henri who was in awe.

"I went rigid with fear," explains Bernard-Henri. "I said to myself, 'This is impossible. She looks too bizarre, too beautiful, too this, too that.' It was too dangerous, too complicated. I was thunderstruck by her beauty, her gaze, her voice, her oddness, and I didn't want to be thunderstruck—I was a libertine!"

Bernard-Henri didn't take up the offer of the play—he moved on and married another woman.

Two years later, the pair met again in Milan, Italy. In an interview with *Vanity Fair* (January 2003) Bernard-Henri said they spent the afternoon together and then the night at his hotel.

"I was bludgeoned with joy," he says, but he also decided not to see her again (his wife had just given birth to his child).

Meanwhile, Arielle, who was also married at this stage, was holed up in her apartment, refusing to eat or to see anyone. After a month of stand-off, Bernard-Henri had to go to Italy.

"I called Arielle and she joined me in the plane, and we've been together since then," says Bernard-Henri.

"I felt this was exactly the woman I had been waiting for, who was right for me. I understood that if I attached myself to her I would never leave her, that she would make all the others redundant, fill all the available space for passion and feelings, and that's what scared me. I didn't believe in love, did not think it existed, and if it did, that it was just an illusion, and I didn't want an illusion to be the center of my life."

"I feel as though I've met the one who you think about as a child, searching the world over and finding the one, the right one. I feel very blessed to have her. I feel like I've been given my destiny."

Actor Johnny Depp on partner, actress Vanessa Paradis

Star-crossed lovers

"All this time I have been thinking of nothing but you. I live only in the thought of you. I wanted to forget, to forget you. Why, oh, why, have you come?"

The Lady with the Dog—Anton Chekhov

Star-crossed lovers?

I t is said of the most major love affairs in the world that they seemed meant to be or are simply "written in the stars." Astrology is about the Cosmic law of "as above, so below." This means that patterns formed by the position of the stars at our birth are akin to a celestial blueprint of our potentials in every respect. So it has always been about divining destiny and thus it is inextricably linked to the idea of fated romance.

True lovers sometimes talk of the bizarre synchronicities that brought them together—on a whim, actor Ryan Phillippe gatecrashed (his now wife) Reese Witherspoon's party. And when the magic happens, it certainly feels as though the planets have aligned in our favor.

A duo is said to be "star-crossed" when certain astro scenarios are revealed in their respective birth charts. Astrologers look for strong soul mating indicators but simple Sun-sign compatibility (Can an Aries be happy with a Taurus? Will my Aquarius lover understand me?) is the most common and best-known use of the ancient Zodiac.

Sun-sign compatibility is basic, but it's a definite start because it shows the interaction of our core personalities.

Then, if you want a little more detail, you could check out a whole range of planetary movements that can influence your love life. For example, the Moon's contacts between your chart and another's reveal the emotional ease between you; the involvement of the Moon's Nodes

Soul mating

is said to imply a fated aspect to a love affair; the placement of Saturn often shows whether there is a long-term potential in a structured relationship; and the planets Mars and Venus measure gung-ho sexual attraction—that sexy, little "Hello, I love you" spark.

However, it's those dashing asteroids—Eros and Psyche—that have become most linked to soul mating and true love. Never heard of them? You soon will. They are the power players of the love game. These two are the most accurate astro indicators of our most secret selves and the soul mating potential of any relationship.

Before finding out how the asteroids Eros and Psyche affect your love life and romantic destiny, it is vital to understand the legend behind them. These asteroids were named after the eternal lovers of ancient mythology!

The story of Eros and Psyche has survived over the aeons because it strips the saga of "us" down to the essential elements. Whether we are youthful and trembling at the threshold of first love, sophisticated and worldly, just married, or gay, this tale speaks to the part of us that yearns for love and will do whatever it takes to get it...

"When you realize you want
to spend the rest of your
life with somebody, you
want the rest of your life
to start as soon as possible."

Billy Crystal to Meg Ryan in *When Harry Met Sally*

The legend of Eros and Psyche

"When I met him, I was definitely shocked
that I was so in love with him."

Actress Kate Hudson on her husband, musician Chris Robinson

There once was a princess called Psyche. The youngest of three sisters, she is blessed with extraordinary beauty, wit, and compassion. Studly suitors vie for her attention. Word of her wisdom and kindness to others spreads across the land. Her renown becomes such that the people begin to worship her in favor of Aphrodite, the goddess of love and beauty.

Peeved by this slight, Aphrodite sends her son Eros to teach Psyche a lesson. Eros, the offspring of his mother's fling with the war god Ares, is the most handsome man of all. He is the god of erotic love and his gold-tipped arrows evoke unquenchable desire in all who are struck by them.

Eros must abide by his mother's wishes and sprinkle a potion on Psyche that will make her fall in love with the ugliest man on earth. But upon seeing her, Eros becomes so overwhelmed by her beauty and sweetness that he pierces her as well as himself with one of his own arrows.

Soul mating

Fearful of his mother's rage, Eros flees. And when Psyche awakens she is sick with love for the beautiful boy who came to her, seemingly, in a dream. She knocks back all offers of marriage, inconsolably yearning for Eros.

In desperation, Psyche's mother, the Queen, consults an oracle who tells her that Psyche is not fated to marry a mortal. She must be left alone on top of a mountain where she is to meet her destiny. Psyche's family are convinced that she has been cursed to marry some kind of monster.

But, instead, she finds herself whisked off by the wind to a glorious palace on top of a mountain. Invisible servants waft around, ready to cater to her every whim.

Come nightfall, Eros dutifully goes to Psyche's side, declaring his love for her. He tells her that it was him she "dreamed" of that night. He explains to her that she must never set eyes on him otherwise the spell will be broken. And if the spell was broken they would no longer be together.

And so the lovers spent night after blissful night with each other. And every night Eros would flit out of their bed before dawn to avoid being seen by Pysche. Psyche doesn't know that Eros is a god.

One evening, Psyche confides to her dream lover that she longs to see her sisters. She wants them to come to the palace to visit her. Eros prevaricates, knowing in his heart that this could wreck everything. However, he eventually relents because it upsets him to see his precious Psyche feeling so sad.

The next day the sisters arrive and are suitably impressed by the opulent palace that sits atop its own secret mountain.

However, several hours later, they become jealous of her happiness. In the pleasure gardens, they ask: "What type of 'man' is he who won't let Psyche even see his face! Don't you remember the rumored curse? You're so naïve that you're sleeping with a monster and don't even know it!"

At first, Psyche argues with her sisters but, eventually, they win her over with their logic. Psyche agrees to break the rule set down by Eros. Her sisters provide her with a candle with which to see for herself the monster she loves.

That night, when Eros is sleeping, Psyche quietly sneaks off and returns with her candle aflame. Under the soft glow she sees that her lover is neither monstrous nor beastly but the man with the golden arrows—the most beautiful man in the world and the one she adores.

When the hot wax drips onto Eros's chest, he awakens in horror, knowing that the spell has been broken and their idyll of love has gone forever. He flees and Psyche faints. When she awakens, she finds herself in a barren field, alone.

Soul mating

Psyche is lost in the wilderness for months. Her heart is broken. One day she comes to one of the temples of Aphrodite and decides to go in and ask the love goddess for guidance.

Aphrodite eavesdrops on Psyche as she explains her story to one of her aides. She is furious that her son has disobeyed her. She appears before Psyche and says she can only have her heart's desire by completing four tasks. Psyche agrees, not knowing that the tasks she's about to be given are impossible...

The first task is horrendous. She must sift through a seemingly sky-high pile of grains—food for the sacred doves of Aphrodite—and sort them into different colors. The doves were suddenly *that* discriminating! Psyche freaks out, realizing the hopelessness of her situation. Psyche knows all too well that Eros is the only man she will ever love and yet she can't have him.

An insistent voice rouses her from a fit of despair. It's not Eros, but it's an ant sent by him to help her. Trillions of ants work all night to help her and, by morning, Aphrodite is astounded—and suspicious—to see that the impossible job is done.

The second task is worse than impossible. It will almost certainly result in Psyche's death! She must steal a snippet of golden fleece from the rams of Ares, the god of war and the father of Eros. These are no ordinary sheep but a bunch of macho beasts that charge around day and night. If she crosses their path she will be crushed.

Psyche asks them for a snippet of their fleece but they are unable to hear her amid the thundering of their hooves. Even if they could, it is doubtful they would help. Their golden fleece is not to be given away.

Once again, Psyche is beside herself. She flops to the ground and weeps, feeling utterly lost in her despair.

Soul mating

A short time later, Meander, the god of rivers, appears and offers to help. He is sympathetic to lovers, having finally scored his own hard-won heart's desire, the love of a tree nymph. He points out to her that, in their excitement, the golden rams leave snags of their fleece on the low branches of the willow trees that overhang the river.

Psyche walks into the river and, as she does, Meander raises the water so that she might snatch a snippet of golden fleece.

Aphrodite is furious when she hears that Meander, her ally, has helped Pysche.

Next, Psyche is asked to fetch a cup of water from the river Styx, a river that's not under the domain of Meander. It flows from the Underworld!

Worse still, she must get the water from its source, a waterfall gushing from a rocky cliff. Even if she could climb that high, how does she bring the cup down without spilling it? She can't do it.

At that moment, a majestic eagle flies to Psyche and offers to help her. With that, the bird whisks her up to the rocky cliff, where she fills the cup, then flies her safely back down again.

From whom does this aid come? It is a mystery to Psyche.

Soul mating

Even Aphrodite is impressed at what Psyche has achieved. She is starting to admire this potential "daughter-in-law." But, she decides to set Psyche one final task before she may win Eros's love.

This time she must venture into the Underworld and bring back a sample of beauty cream from Persephone, Queen of the Underworld. Psyche knows this task is impossible—no mortal returns from here.

Demeter, the fertility goddess, advises Psyche on how to approach her daughter, Persephone, a woman with her own romantic history who slowly grew to love her Underworld lord.

Unbeknown to Psyche, Eros has come to her aid. He is constantly (albeit invisibly) by Psyche's side and guides her through the murky paths to this other place.

Persephone, perhaps looking forward to her annual spring/summer sojourn in the sunlit lands above, is sympathetic to Psyche and her romantic dilemma.

She gives Psyche a pot of her special beauty cream. She also gives her permission to leave the Underworld without any hassles. But, she warns her never to open the pot of beauty cream—it would be fatal for a mortal woman to use it.

Having completed the task, Psyche begins the journey back to Aphrodite's abode to report to the goddess. She desperately yearns to be in the arms of her true love Eros.

The forthcoming reunion with Eros turns her mind's fancy to seduction but Psyche knows that she looks a bit worse for wear. Completing the four tasks has wreaked havoc upon her good looks and equilibrium. She does not yet realize that Eros loves both the outer and inner Psyche.

Disobeying the dictum from Persephone, Psyche opens the pot of beauty cream and instantly falls into a deep faint. Some say she dies at this point.

Besotted Eros flies Psyche immediately to Zeus, the king of the gods. Eros speaks of his love for her so eloquently that Zeus is moved to intervene, restore Psyche to life and make her immortal. He then marries the couple on the spot. And Psyche is now the goddess of the soul.

When Aphrodite sees how happy her son is, she softens toward the union and indeed learns to like Psyche for herself.

Eros and Psyche live happily ever after with their three children, aptly named Bliss, Pleasure, and Ecstasy.

Together 4 eva

"You had me at 'hello'."

Dorothy (Renée Zellweger) to Jerry (Tom Cruise) in *Jerry Maguire*

Together 4 eva

The beating of utterly ludicrous odds in order to score true romance "4 eva" forms the basis of the greatest love stories. Never mind the tragedies such as *Romeo and Juliet, Antony and Cleopatra* or the thwarted romance between Rhett Butler and Scarlett O'Hara in *Gone with the Wind*.

The biggest blockbuster movies are about the love that overcomes all obstacles, including distance, war, and even death itself. Think *Casablanca, Doctor Zhivago, Titanic, Ghost, Sleepless in Seattle, Love Story*. Even full-on action sci-fi *The Terminator* has at its core a hero who travels across time to save the woman he loves.

Real-life classic film star passion? Katharine Hepburn and Spencer Tracy, Elizabeth Taylor and Richard Burton (they were married twice to each other), Humphrey Bogart and Lauren Bacall.

"How can one change one's entire life and build a new life on a moment of love?" asks Greta Garbo as Marguerite in *Camille*. "And yet, that's what you make me want to close my eyes and do," she says to her lover Armand. How indeed? It's a similar dilemma to that of Psyche.

The legend of Eros and Psyche is the original version. Over the centuries, it has naturally been analyzed nonstop. Mythology historian H. A. Guerber says that Eros is the Sun God seeking in Psyche the Goddess of the Dawn. So Eros can't rise to full light without her. He can't even really be. And without the light of Eros to shine upon her

Soul mating

inner beauty, Psyche can't be complete. Each needs the other and, unlike the players in many a myth, they wind up happy ever after.

The story of Eros and Psyche is clearly about the manifestation of true love after trial and tribulation, the struggle to become the "other half" and the certainty that people who have found their soul mate can act in ways that make absolutely no sense to those around them.

Psyche also does most of the work in this myth so it is more the female's journey toward love than the male's. But, really, it's about the metamorphosis evoked by love.

The sisters who insist that Psyche is sleeping with a monster may have a point, from their perspective. Yet does real love require a second opinion? Our heroine risks her own true love by trusting the lights of those who are not in love!

In darker versions of this myth, Psyche goes off and sleeps with a few monsters before discovering Eros. Ahem! Who among us can relate?

You could say that the helpful eagle character is lofty perspective and scoring some golden fleece under difficult conditions is about subverting male systems with sneakiness. Maybe the sorting of the grain is to do with engaging our logical "ant mind" to sift through the received opinion that so often comes between us and our emotions?

Could the beauty cream picked up in the Underworld be a metaphor for the knowing radiance to be gained—afterward, of course—from a vile relationship?

Whatever we take from the legend of Eros and Psyche, it is undeniably a wonderful love story as well as an allegory for our own progress toward love serenity.

"I really wasn't meant to be at the dinner but destiny lured me there. Justin was flirting with my girlfriend at the other end of the table, and when he came to sit next to me, I reacted really badly. We were fighting for the next two hours, screaming at each other. He was drunk. I was drunk and everyone was laughing. His best friend said: 'Look, Justin's found his wife'!"

Model Natalia Vodianova on meeting her husband, artist Justin Portman

His view on the relationship? "I think we've been married from the moment we met."

Soul mating a go-go: the how-to of love witchery

"Medicine, law, business, engineering, these are noble pursuits and necessary to sustain life. But poetry, beauty, romance, love, these are what we stay alive for."

Teacher John Keating (Robin Williams) in *Dead Poets Society*

Soul mating a go-go: the how-to of love witchery

Y ou don't need to be a scientist, doctor, shrink, or a spacey New Ager to discover the secrets to soul mating, compatibility, and true love. Anyone can do it. It's that easy. All you need is a birthday.

The great thing about the Eros and Psyche signs is that they can tell you a whole lot about your love life—like who is your ideal man or woman, how your partner really feels about you, and what type of person makes the better soul mate for you. This is "personalized" soul mating at its best. It's a fast-track to finding true love and it eliminates all that time-consuming guesswork.

At the back of this book are the astrological tables (ephemerides) of Eros and Psyche. The tables tell you the astrological sign that these two were in for any date of birth.

Here's how to get started. You first look up the date of birth of you and your partner in each of the tables. This will tell you what Sun sign Eros and Psyche were in at the time of your birth. Once you're done deciphering the romantic soul secrets they reveal, you can start cross-referencing via the soul mating maps on pages 490–493 to discover the compatibility of a relationship via Eros and Psyche.

Let's say you're a girl with the hugest crush in the world on Mr. Maybe. You look up your Eros sign to find out the kind of guy you really need, like it or not! Then, for an insight into Inner You—your secret (soul-driven!) romantic persona, look up your Psyche sign to see what you're really all about.

Soul mating

Now comes the love-witchery part, the bit of the book that enables you to seemingly get inside the head of Mr. Maybe, wowing him even more than you probably already have.

You look up his Eros sign and get a full-on glimpse of his secret lover-boy self. Hmmm? Interesting? Then you can discover his Psyche sign, the truest astro indicator of his ideal woman.

Mr. Maybe? Or Mr. Forever? Now that you know him (and yourself) a little better, why not see how your Eros and Psyche signs get along? Check out His Eros with Her Psyche and Her Eros with His Psyche. Follow the symbols to read the two soul mating interpretations. Why two? Because, believe it or not, in the magical astro world, these two are always in relation to one another. Looking up (say) only his Eros with your Psyche will give you just half of the picture.

When in complete harmony, Eros and Psyche add up to fated love. That's right! If you believe in the previous lifetimes paradigm, it's a definite indicator that this full-on-feeling dynamic is actually a reunion of two lovers who have already known one another...before.

Let's examine the secret personas and soul mating potential of two major celebs, just to make sure you're on the right track.

Bodacious Ben Affleck was born on August 15, 1972. On the face of it he is a strong and egomaniacal Leo. This is so fitting for a latter-day matinee idol whose presence can "open" a movie. However, when we look further, we see that his Eros is in Pisces. His secret "lover-boy" self is akin to Prince Charming, burdened—bless him—with romantic idealism that few real-life relationships can live up to.

Cool. But Ben's Psyche, which reveals his ideal woman, is in Virgo! So he's a discriminating fussbudget, judging every detail about his girl. Compare the Eros and Psyche signs of this guy and you wind up with someone who wants to enjoy unconditional love from a super-control-freaking perfectionist. Maybe he and Jennifer Lopez make sense after all! Let's check her out.

Another multitalented Leo, she was born on July 27, 1970. So her Eros (which reveals her ideal man) is in Capricorn (for Jennifer, it really *is* about the money, honey, along with a hefty dose of status and prestige) while her Psyche (which reveals her secret romantic persona) is in Gemini. She's just so-o-o fickle and yet demanding!

Now for this couple's soul mating potential. Looking at the ephemeris, we see that matching his Psyche in Virgo with her Eros in Capricorn makes this a diamond relationship—classic love at first sight sizzling between two superstars. Her Eros and his Psyche are symbolized by the Sun. This means they will always be able to renew their love. Even if they're split up, they'll remain friends. Neither of them will want to be the one who loves less (or more!) for one second. It has to be utterly equal so let the psychodrama begin! Could this be you and your love? Or are you the slow-burn, long-haul "love that dare not speak its name" type of love affair?

Now you can investigate you and yours! Or amaze friends with your astro-analyst soul mating skills and even make astounding celebrity love predictions!

Happy soul mating!

His Eros reveals… his secret lover-boy self!

"You cannot think how my feelings are alive toward you, probably more than ever and they never can be diminished."

Lord Horatio Nelson, in a letter written to his lover, Lady Emma Hamilton

His Eros reveals...his secret lover-boy self!

In astrology, Eros represents the smitten heart. The Eros sign of a man shows us how he truly wants to be in love. It's like the "in his dreams" best romantic expression of himself.

By tuning into this particular persona—which he may not be that consciously aware of himself—you effortlessly access an off-limits area of his mind and heart.

It's an aspect of his male identity that may not even have been awakened yet. Yet, like the Eros of myth, he can only rise and shine via the expression of his Eros sign.

Even the most callow boy or hardcore womanizer (perhaps especially him!) has a secret fantasy guy hiding inside. Understanding his Eros personality takes you beyond the realms of Sun sign astrology.

It's great that he is (say) a suave Libran but if it's romance you're after, you'll get where you want a lot quicker by relating to his (for example) conspiracy theorizing and intensity-craving Eros in Scorpio!

Real-life celeb example? Colin Farrell. This guy's a Gemini and sure lives it up like one. However, despite the wild partying et al, he's already a dad and seems most truly happy in this role. His Eros is in solid Taurus and he has Psyche in clucky Cancer. To put it really simply, play to his Eros sign and he will feel truly understood, fully a man. Wanna know it? Read on!

His Eros is in...

"Her face
so fair
first bent
mine eye

Her tongue
so sweet
then drew
mine ear

Her wit
so sharp
then hit
my heart."

Her Face—Sir Arthur Gorges

"We met at my 21st birthday party, and we immediately hit it off. But he left the next day and was gone for two months. So we wrote each other letters and really got to know each other more through correspondence and talking on the telephone than any sort of physical attraction. It was so romantic; he wrote me these wonderful letters. And, after he came back, it was like we were an old married couple. We were so comfortable with each other. I really believe I was meant to find this person in my life, and he was meant to find me, and we were meant to be together. I feel very corny talking about it, but I am just overwhelmed with a sense that it chose us; we didn't choose it."

Actress Reese Witherspoon on meeting her husband,
actor Ryan Phillippe

Aries

march 21 - april 20

Cosmically activated by the scent of ginseng and
musk, "sporty" fragrances, even sweat. He loves
it that you appreciate his au naturel reek. To
trigger his Eros, lay it on thick.

He wants to hear: Save me!

He is love's daredevil. In his mind, he gallivants around Camelot, the bravest knight of all and official rescuer of distressed damsels. He needs a quest to motivate him. His gigantic ego won't let him admit it but he wants to work in scoring your unconditional love. Give him the chase that he craves and somehow forget to call it off. Even if you've been blissfully bonded together for 20 years, Eros in Aries is mission-oriented. Engage his protective instincts with a "he did me wrong" tale of woe...he likes to shine in comparison with other lesser males.

Richard Burton, Ewan McGregor, Kid Rock

Taurus

april 21 - may 21

Cosmically activated by the smell of freshly cut grass and any similar fragrance. Woo him in the wilderness, walk through a field. The term "roll in the hay" was invented for this guy.

He wants to hear: I'm yours

A stayer, Eros in Taurus most values sensual compatibility. Seemingly insatiable, he is best won via bedwork and appeals to his so-tactile nature. Once truly in love, he is possessive, doting, and demanding, lavishing his lover with athletic devotion. Despite an often-intense, sexing-it-up phase in youth, he yearns to be placed on a perfect husbandly pedestal. His libido waxes rather than wanes with a long-term love affair. Stability really turns him on...he sees soul mating not as metaphysical but as metabolic, part of his very physical being.

Russell Crowe, Colin Farrell

Gemini

may 22 - june 21

Cosmically activated by ever changing scents.
He always likes to be surprised. Flip him out with
a hot Latin scent one moment, then blast him with
a fresh, clean soap smell the next.

He wants to hear: Come here, go away!

The laughing cavalier of love, Eros in Gemini can't engage his heart without a strong mental affinity. He's aroused by new info, gossip, and jokes that he hasn't heard yet. He gets bored with moralizing and emotive ranting. So just keep him interested with lots of chitchat. He'll love that you change the subject before he can. Whether he's happily soul mated or not, this guy needs to feel as though he's with a variety of people. Feel free to show off the myriad aspects of beautiful you to him. Reassure him by remaining unpredictable and always elusive.

Antonio Banderas, Colin Firth, Hugh Grant, Ryan Phillippe

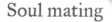

Cancer

june 22 - july 23

Cosmically activated by scents that remind him of Mama, whether he admits or not. If in doubt, always go mega-girly and classic. He's lured by the odor of a time past that maybe never was.

He wants to hear: Hold me!

He is the prince of tides, a mood-swinger, and manipulator of hearts. He's easily enslaved by sentimental gestures. Tread tenderly around anything to do with Mama. The way to his heart really is through his stomach—or massage. Bored by trivia but blessed with granite strength and serenity for real challenges, Eros in Cancer really understands the feminine mind. Accustomed from birth to gaga-gushing attention from females, beauty moves him. He abhors sleaze and vulgarity and will not be remotely amused by coarse stories.

Matt Drudge, Guy Pearce, Gavin Rossdale

Leo

july 24 - august 23

Cosmically activated by officially difficult Diva scents. He likes a luxury brand fully layered via the trappings of body and bath versions. He just loves a smell that says, "Hello, I am here."

He wants to hear: I love the real you, beneath the fame

The sultan of love, Eros in Leo wants unconditional worship. Nonstop sycophancy is an optional extra. His heart is gracious, regal, and giving if perhaps too easily ensnared by hardcore glamour. Like Eros in Aries, he appreciates the chase aspect of romance but with added theatrics. He gets off on the grand gesture. For example, the ritual destruction of love letters from past suitors is now rendered irrelevant. His fantasy of true romance can be annihilated by the split ends of everyday life. Don't undermine his dignity. The queen of his heart must act the part.

David Arquette, Pete Sampras, Justin Theroux

Virgo

august 24 - september 23

Cosmically activated by clean, clean, clean. Loves the pure smell of soap, freshly scrubbed skin, and recently washed hair. The Virgo Eros is utterly freaked out by over-the-top scents.

He wants to hear: I trust you

Eros in Virgo equals love in observation mode. He has a details fetish so he relishes every little tidbit of info on his object of desire. He likes to be taken into your confidence. He loves that you ask for his advice. Mystery is not a major turn-on. He wants a companion. But Eros in Virgo comes with a strong moral kick and a code of correctness. He'll happily sit and listen to you whine about work, talk about your technique for making toast—whatever. But he'll flip out big time at any hint of dishonesty or tacky conduct.

David Beckham, Enrique Iglesias, Prince William, Luke Wilson

Libra

september 24 - october 23

Cosmically activated by classic florals. He has a highly discerning sense of smell and hates tricky fragrances, synthetics, and over-application. He could easily have a fetish about body lotion or scented lipgloss.

He wants to hear: You are so beautiful

Eros in Libra fantasizes about a total merger of heart, mind, body, and soul. Once soul mated, he gets off on nonstop togetherness. His romantic ideals are lofty. A relationship should be nothing less than poetry in motion. He can be enraptured by the idea of woman—adoring of the concept, less taken with the everyday reality. A natural-born aesthete, he thrills to beauty, philosophy, and talent but is appalled by banality. Keep it real? No way. Make it surreal. The elegant euphemism is preferable to au naturel.

Edward Burns, Tobey Maguire,
Adam Sandler

Scorpio

october 24 - november 22

Cosmically activated by the smell of you, genuinely.
For example, daub some "body fluid" behind your
ears. He likes pure essential oils [not cheap fakes]
and is a secret admirer of musk.

He wants to hear: Wow! how do you know that?

Eros in Scorpio loves on two different levels. The first is dalliance—he has an enormous capacity to fool around without his hard-to-get heart even being involved. The second is true romance, which he is wary of, knowing his capacity for deep involvement. This man harbors unbelievable depths of emotion. He secretly reveres the concept of his Twin Soul but is also a game player, stopping only with the woman secure enough to call his bluff. He fantasizes about the grand passion that is strong enough to linger for lifetimes.

David Bowie, George Clooney,
Ralph Fiennes, Ian Somerhalder

Sagittarius

november 23 - december 21

Cosmically activated by the smell of something sporty such as liniment. If he isn't into the locker room scene he may instead crave something spearminty. Think grassy or fresh.

He wants to hear: Don't fence me in!

The philosopher of love, Eros in Saggo craves candor. Incapable of sneaky behavior or mind games, he likes to express feelings freely, on his terms, and in an expansive context. He sees love as a trip and this guy is an inveterate traveler. He loves the idea of two total individuals together on the same journey. His heart engages only after a fun and life-enhancing friendship has been established. He likes to hear you say "come away with me." Romance is his escape and not a necessary component of mundane life.

Jake Gyllenhaal, Hugh Jackman, Prince Harry, Will Smith, James Van Der Beek

Capricorn
december 22 - january 20

Cosmically activated by the sweet smell of success.
He likes the whole package to be clean like Virgo
and non-vulgar like Leo, but so understated like the
faint waft of professionally blow-dried hair.

He wants to hear: Financial independence
turns me on

The player of love treats romance with respect. Whether he lets on to her or not, he is auditioning applicants for the position of life partner. Eros in Capricorn is into strategic courtship. Watch for his *Princess and the Pea*-style tests. Worldly and assured, he's after a liaison that not only fulfills his lusty sensual requirements but is mutually supportive. His true soul mate is, above all else, appropriate to where he feels he is heading in life. Chaos tempts him not. He loves the idea of the couple that schemes together to rise above, becoming more than the sum of their parts.

Christian Bale, Matt Damon,
Ethan Hawke, Owen Wilson

Aquarius

january 21 - february 19

Cosmically activated by the weird fragrances,
the avant-garde, hard-to-find scents that are
talking points in themselves. Eros in Aqua loves
metallic and/or fruity fragrances.

He wants to hear: You're not like the other guys

Socially progressive, Eros in Aquarius believes in love Utopia. He can appear unfeeling because his romantic ideals involve mind enmeshment. His heart only softens with intellectual equality. He is capable of playing loyalty-testing games to ensure that he is able to let his guard down. The cant of romance bores him senseless. Eros in Aquarius can forget your birthday, let alone love anniversaries, but show the deepest tenderness in unexpected ways. He is easily bored with social convention—drive him away quickly by making such obligations an essential part of your relationship.

Johnny Depp, Heath Ledger, Brad Pitt

Pisces

february 20 - march 20

Cosmically activated by ylang- ylang essential oil.
Unlike most men, Eros in Pisces is interested in
complexity and mystery. If in doubt, try anything
that's oriental. But make sure you use it sparingly.

He wants to hear: I'm so in love with you

Eros in Pisces is the king of love and is the most romantic sign of all. He yearns for the all-enveloping romance, one that annihilates walls between the lovers and fulfills his childhood dreams of The One. This man is capable of unconditional love and acceptance. Wildly compassionate, he can't fall truly in love with a woman who's mean-hearted. Cynical arrangements or the merely "convenient" relationship harden his heart. Yet, because he believes so utterly in love, he can easily be hurt by those who fail to grasp his inner goodness.

Ben Affleck, Matthew Broderick, Jude Law, Sam Mendes, Freddie Prinze Jr., Ben Stiller

Her Psyche reveals... her romantic persona

"She croons, like a cat to its claws;
Cries, 'I'm old enough to live
And delight in a lover's praise,
Yet keep to myself my own mind;
I dance to the right, to the left;
My luck raises the wind.'

'Write all my whispers down,'
She cries to her true love.
'I believe, I believe, in the moon!–
What weather of heaven is this?'

'The storm, the storm of a kiss.'"

Her Words—Theodore Roethke

Her Psyche reveals...her romantic persona

The sign of a woman's Psyche reveals her inner "girlish" emotions regarding romance. It is here she shows off her secret self. Her Psyche sign may be the same as her Sun sign, in which case the search for true love is likely to be an integral part of her life. Or it could represent a hidden aspect of the self—an aspect that a woman most needs to have accepted.

In fact, a woman's Psyche sign—the planet in which she has Psyche—is often an accurate indicator of the dreams she abandoned at puberty, a "self" that was covered over in childhood or a deeper yearning of the soul that she has decided to hide.

So expressing her Psyche sign will always provide peace of heart for a woman. When she is soul mated, it allows the perfect excuse to let that spirit run free. Romance will never fully work if the Psyche sign is somehow unable to shine.

This is where soul mating and its indicators, Eros and Psyche, are so powerful for women. A partner who sincerely desires that a whole part of a woman be repressed to fit his fantasy is not The One. He's also not the one who disrespects her dreams and achievements or who subtly undermines her by insisting that she dress in a particular way.

When a woman's Psyche is evoked she feels as if something from long ago is unfurling within her. It often materializes as an almost pre-adolescent feeling, akin to that first flush of love before sex got involved in the scenario. It is as if, no matter what the usual trials of love, she feels finally free to be herself.

The word Psyche means both soul and butterfly and so, along with being the goddess of the soul, she also represents our little flitting dreams of romance, freed from the drab chrysalis at last.

When a woman's Psyche is triggered, it's as though a light has been switched on inside her. Whether it is a new lover or simply the discovery of a new best friend, that inner glow is probably the expression of the true self.

Her Psyche is in...

"I thought this was probably an illusion
that was going to go away. But, it didn't.
We started calling each other, then we saw
each other, and I realized that I was in love."

Actor Antonio Banderas on his wife, actress Melanie Griffith

"St. Antony's Dance: fell down the steps, and seem to have fallen in love with J. We didn't dance much."

Novelist Iris Murdoch's diary entry for 3 June, 1954

"We talked without stopping, endless, childish chatter, seeming to invent on the spot, as we talked, a whole infantile language of our own."

Her husband John Bayley's version of the encounter

Aries

march 21 - april 20

Cosmically activated by crimson flowers of all
types like roses, tulips, gerberas. She likes
anything that's boldly burgundy. With her, you
should say it large, say it with scarlet.

She needs to know that she is feminine

Psyche in Aries is the warrior queen. Headstrong, a thrill-seeker, and imbued with a strong sense of entitlement, she charges young into romance. The initial approach to love is combative and her high demands scare many men off. Psyche in Aries can be too strong, sticking in a vile relationship because she is "not a wimp." Truly in love, she learns that a love affair need not involve a constant power struggle. She needs, more than most, someone exciting and "tough" enough to earn her respect but who is also tender with her well-concealed dreams of love.

Naomi Campbell, Uma Thurman

Taurus

april 21 - may 21

Cosmically activated by wildflowers gathered
just for her. Try dandelions, moss, herbs,
flowers with therapeutic meaning.
The ultimate? Something you've grown yourself
or perhaps something you can drink?

She needs to know that her allure is working

Psyche in Taurus is the natural-born seductress who trusts her sensual instincts above all. Her vital indicators of love are the scent of her mate and pleasurable skin-to-skin contact. However, if the fingertips don't zing off one another at first touch, she turns off. Flighty, on-off-on-again guys need not apply. However, these types will still swarm around her, longing to be soothed by that grounded aura. A true sybarite, she is drawn to abundance. Nature and stability of affection evoke her deep inner serenity.

Liz Hurley, Iman, Angelina Jolie, Jennifer Lopez, Kristin Scott Thomas, Brooke Shields

Gemini

may 22 - june 21

Cosmically activated by a surprise posy. She officially thinks flowers are a cheap romantic trick. But, if you pull out the totally unexpected, for-no-reason bouquet, she melts.

She needs to know that she will be amused

The muse of love and a sparkling wit, she is able to spin the mundane into sparkling fresh vistas. Psyche in Gemini is comfortable with romantic ambiguity to the point of perhaps even preferring it. She trusts her mind, staying where the stimulation is, needing both to amuse and be amused. Her romantic ideal is to be a coconspirator in love, the true companion and confidante of her soul mate. She quickly realizes that Mr. (You-Figure-It-Out) Taciturn is not for her. Complex and beguiling, she is literally terrified of dull people.

Christina Aguilera, Jennifer Connelly, Danielle Spencer, Charlize Theron, Shania Twain, Rachel Weisz, Reese Witherspoon

Cancer

june 22 - july 23

Cosmically activated by waterlilies. To trigger
the nurturing but complex depths of the
Cancerian Psyche, bring anything that grows in
the water, or November lilies. Think lush.

She needs to know that she is safe

She is the empress of hearts, a woman of profound nurturing instincts and compassion. Some wince at the "lame duck" guy—she sees only the swan-in-waiting. Her all-understanding mien attracts many not-so-suitable suitors. Spookily, she is able to morph into whatever guise feels most appropriate for the circumstances. Yet this Psyche must take care to stay attuned to her own true needs and avoid wandering around lost in the desire-driven projections of others. Highly emotional and intuitive, she needs a lover to cherish her extreme sensitivities.

Natalie Portman, Princess Diana

Leo

july 24 - august 23

Cosmically activated by yellow flowers such as
sunflowers, marigolds, daffodils, yellow roses.
The Psyche in Leo girl is at the center of her
universe. Maybe the Sun Goddess rose...

She needs to know that she is the star

Psyche in Leo is the showgirl at heart, needing admiration from more than just one-quarter of the male population for true happiness. A born creative spirit, she flees fast from mediocrity. She makes men giddy and she fancies the idea of being dizzy with love. The first moments of a crush are heaven for Psyche in Leo. But herein lies the problem. She craves a love beyond all others, the greatest love show on earth. But what relationship can actually live up to that? Easily bedazzled by good looks, her heart's true fulfillment lies in manifesting her own star quality.

Beyoncé Knowles, Jada Pinkett Smith

Virgo

august 24 - september 23

Cosmically activated by rushes, river grasses, or one of those lettuce arrangements. She likes anything that's green. Her vampish knowingness and grasp of nuance suggest an arrangement of kale with sword ferns.

She needs to know that it's more than good sex

Psyche in Virgo is the vamp of love and the mistress of nuance. Whatever her lover's unspoken fantasies or secret motivations, she's onto it. She's slinky, suave, and so totally together that it's holistic. But Psyche in Virgo frets, yearning for someone to show the same grasp of her details. She wants to be finessed, to have someone remember her favorite poem or the thread of the conversation from three months ago. Utterly sensual, she is nonetheless most enticed by a deep mental affinity, by someone who understands her with no explanations needed.

Pamela Anderson, Kirsten Dunst, Sarah Michelle Gellar, Melanie Griffith, Jade Jagger, Nicole Kidman, Sarah Jessica Parker, Meg Ryan, Britney Spears, Elizabeth Taylor, Liv Tyler

Libra

september 24 - october 23

Cosmically activated by pink flowers. The Psyche in Libra woman is girl-girly in love and she prefers subtle shades. Think pink: fuchsias, pink gerberas, coral carnations.

She needs to know that she will be allowed to breathe

Psyche in Libra is the dream girl of many but her own heart remains somehow detached—a skillful romantic player but somehow disengaged from the action. So sophisticated in the arts of love, she is also too smart for many of her would-be lovers. The Libran Psyche requires someone with her own depth of sophistication and worldliness. She can't handle too much emotional intensity or someone who sees a relationship as simply a socially convenient unit. Rife with ambiguity, she wants to be doted upon, yet at the same time afforded her precious personal space.

Cameron Diaz, Brittany Murphy, Gwyneth Paltrow, Rachel Ward

Scorpio

october 24 - november 22

Cosmically activated by something growing. It
has to be viable, alive, and a bit different from the
run of the mill. A cactus? A feng shui money plant?
She also has a soft spot for berries.

She needs to know that she will not be lied to

The enchantress of love, Psyche in Scorpio is a strategist. Preferring to bewitch rather than be bedazzled, she moves in quietly and presents herself in many different guises. Her ultimate love goal is the "nothing but you" paradigm. Should she be involved in a mere fling, her standards are almost impossible for anyone to live up to. She is a super control freak, running the dalliance on her terms, like it or not. The lover who betrays her trust to even the teeniest degree is out that door, forgotten in a moment. She knows her journey is to find The One.

Ashley Judd, Madonna, Vanessa Paradis, Audrey Tautou, Naomi Watts

Sagittarius

november 23 - december 21

Cosmically activated by plants that make a political statement. She loves natives, especially the ones that have been ousted by exotics over the years. She adores the eco dimension.

She needs to know that she will not be forced to be someone else

Psyche in Saggo is the adventuress, the most free-spirited lover of all. She is at her most ecstatic during a "You understand me, you really do!" moment with a new love interest. In her soul she is a child at play in the sometimes too-grown-up world of adult relationships. There is always a wild child in the heart of this woman. She would throw over a sensible liaison in two seconds—even if only in her mind—just to experience the bliss of the moment. No matter how fixed her reality, her heart may only be unlocked by a fellow visionary wanderer.

Helena Christensen, Catherine Deneuve

Capricorn

december 22 - january 20

Cosmically activated by a mauve journey of
status. Psyche in Cap is switched on by nature's
finest like orchids, tulips, and dahlias...but not in
red. Stay elegant and stick to lavender.

She needs to know that she is The Trophy

Worldly and assured, Psyche in Capricorn is the prima diva of love. A true trophy bride for a hero, she is adept at scoring the guy that no-one else can get. Until Mr. Perfect comes along, her heart is often a no-fly zone. Her secret soul is well enclosed, protecting her from exploitation. Mature love often becomes her more than the games of early youth, where her gifts can be overshadowed by some tougher competition. She is a work-in-progress, learning from life as she goes along, honing her extreme sensuality and insight.

Jennifer Aniston, Fanny Ardant,
Jennifer Love Hewitt, Kate Moss,
Mena Suvari, Christy Turlington

Aquarius

january 21 - february 19

Cosmically activated by the Zen approach.
Psyche in Aqua leans heavily to the simple
yet powerful. Think bamboo, ikebana…but not bonsai.
Watch her thrill to the perfect origami.

She needs to know this is for real

From an early age, Psyche in Aquarius knows that she is unconventional in love. The druidess of romance, she is euphorically independent, unwilling to be "grounded" by any but the most ideal of men. The source of her power lies in her refusal to be anyone but her authentic self. Her dream relationship is a true companionship, mutually supportive beyond the dreams of most love affairs. Breathtakingly frank, she has no time for playing games and typical romantic cant. Her only true love is the man strong enough to let her be her utterly complicated self.

Victoria Beckham, Claire Danes,
Kate Hudson, Jewel, Elle Macpherson,
Pink, Hilary Swank, Catherine Zeta-Jones

Pisces

february 20 - march 20

Cosmically activated by white flowers.
Whether they're conspicuous gardenias, sexy
jasmine, or mysterious Apache plumes, this girl
adores the intricate scent of such blooms.

She needs to know that her sensitive side is
also acknowledged

Jaded as she may pretend to be, Psyche in Pisces is love's princess, the most romantic of them all. This is a woman who never gives up on her girlhood dreams of true love. Compassionate and blessed with the magic gift of being able to love unconditionally, her kindness can lead her up many a wrong track. Underestimate this woman at your peril. She likes to project vulnerability but is actually the Psyche sign most capable of reinvention. She needs a lover sensitive enough to see beyond the myriad personae that she tries on for fun and to nurture the sweet "child" within.

Drew Barrymore, Natalie Imbruglia

His Psyche reveals... what he wants in a woman

Arwen: "Do you remember the time when we first met?"
Aragorn: "I thought I had strayed into a dream."

from the film *The Lord of the Rings, The Fellowship of the Ring*

His Psyche reveals...what he wants in a woman

There are many ways to a man's heart. One of them is investigating his Psyche sign as it will reveal his secret ideal woman. A man's Psyche sign operates on a more clandestine level than a Sun sign. Even though it signifies the kind of female energy he needs in order to feel truly fulfilled, his Psyche could be operating subconsciously, lost beneath the roar of a full-on planet like Mars.

Interestingly, actors Catherine Zeta-Jones and Michael Douglas have their Psyches exactly in conjunct. This means that her innermost femininity matches his female ideal. The acting duos of Ben Affleck and Jennifer Lopez and Sarah Jessica Parker and Matthew Broderick also have strong Psyche-Psyche links.

When a man meets a woman who sets off his Psyche energy he feels instantly liberated. He also senses immediately that this is going to be a huge relationship. His romantic and protective instincts can't help but be awakened. He becomes the best version of himself that he can be, leaving old flames astounded.

How many times have you heard the tale of the girl who apparently "tamed" some bad boy? Nobody can believe how the one-time heartbreaker is now swooning around. The reason? His Psyche has been activated.

The Eros-Psyche phenomenon is so strong that it doesn't have to be an exact Eros-Psyche link. A Psyche-Psyche link, or even a woman's Sun sign being in the same sign as his Psyche, can't help but evoke love.

So, yeah! Another little bit of secret astro biz! If your Psyche sign is the same as his Sun sign—whoa! But just getting his Psyche sign is a valuable insight into his inner feminine ideal.

His Psyche is in...

"You must allow me to tell you how ardently I admire and love you."

Mr. Darcy to Elizabeth in *Pride and Prejudice*—Jane Austen

"It was quite shocking to me to
fall in love. I was completely
not beyond having an affair.
I thought that was a great idea.
But falling in love? I didn't
see it coming at all. I thought,
'This is fun,' and then, bam!"

Actress Uma Thurman on her partner, actor Ethan Hawke

Aries

march 21 - april 20

Cosmically activated by a powerful bass riff. He turns onto music via the beat and this is the way to his heart. He knows how to vibe in a sophisticated way, but he's a closet metal-head.

He needs to know that he will not be lied to

His dream girl isn't even a girl—she's a dominatrix. This guy is fearless and in no way intimidated by the strong female dynamic. He is confident enough about his masculinity to flip things around and become playful or even passive if he feels like it. He falls for women other men would consider officially difficult. This man is not remotely threatened by her success, opinions, or charisma. But he can't bear to be lied to and will always honor his lover's candor. He loves the energetic and positive woman.

David Beckham, Enrique Iglesias

Taurus

april 21- may 21

Cosmically activated by the music of his youth.
The Psyche in Taurus man lives in a world of
how things should be. He needs you to totally "get"
the tunes he is most loyal to.

He needs to know that frequent sex is not an issue

Psyche in Taurus is the guy in love with a figment. Okay, a time-tested classic ideal of beauty and femininity. He secretly yearns for the swimsuit-model type who'll cook him a carb-loaded dinner or the mogul woman, wealthy in her own right but who trusts his financial advice. Yes, it's tricky, all right, but easier to handle once you remember that he's enraptured by his sensual urges, an utter lover of beauty and aesthetics. No matter what his prowling habits, he longs for a settled and stable love existence. Once he is taken, he rarely gazes into other pastures.

Joshua Leonard, Tobey Maguire, Scott Major

Gemini

may 22 - june 21

Cosmically activated by whatever he has not heard before. Don't bother this guy with songs of meaning, just amaze him with something gimmicky. With his fickleness, he loves compilation albums.

He needs to know that change is okay

The guy with Psyche in Gemini will put up with sly and fickle vixenly types. Actually, he prefers it that way. If a woman wants to mess with this guy's mind he tells them to go ahead. He loves it. In fact, without a willing partner in his innuendo, wit, and sibling-combative-banter games, this love affair won't even begin. A variety buff, his true love is a multifaceted minx-witch type, never the same persona for two days running. His true love is complicated. However, she is neither boring nor a whiner nor into making turgid emotional demands. Remember, his Psyche is symbolized by The Twins.

Antonio Banderas, Matt Damon, Colin Firth, Hugh Grant, Jake Gyllenhaal, Ethan Hawke, Ewan McGregor, Ben Stiller

Cancer

june 22 - july 23

Cosmically activated by emotive music. It
could be classical or New Age, perhaps Ennio
Morricone. What does it for Psyche in Cancer
is a musical piece from their belle époque.

He needs to know there's a safe place for his feelings

The sign of Cancer is linked to the goddess Psyche, so the man with Psyche in Cancer seems to have a direct line into the female soul. Combine that with his deep subconscious drive for total security—that is, back to the womb—and he can be the classic womanizer. His relationship with his mother or a key maternal figure is intensely important and provides the key to his romantic self-expression. His feminine ideal is totally womanly, soft, and giving. She is a natural-born nurturer of both children and animals, a total girl's girl, and spontaneously artistic or creative.

George Clooney, John Cusack, Colin Farrell

Leo

july 24 - august 23

Cosmically activated by glitzy music. He may
have a secret collection of songs from the
New Romantic period. Or he adores over-the-top
pomp like the *1812 Overture*. Make sure it's grand.

He needs to know that everyone else wanted her

His inner ideal of the ultimate woman is a superstar—gorgeous, acclaimed, and his. The man with Psyche in Leo fantasizes about—or has!—a life of success and luxury of which his woman is one of the most important indicators. He likes the glitz, glam, and psychodrama of love, someone who is a personage in her own right, a prima diva by nature and yet also warm, generous, and talented. Frankly, he needs to feel that she is an "object" of some worth and status. His inspiration is old Hollywood movies. Think golden, think bombshell.

Pete Sampras, Adam Sandler, Luke Wilson

Virgo

august 24 - september 23

Cosmically activated by clever, even difficult music. Don't think that just because he's into jazz, it means he wants to dance. When he says "jazz" he means goatees and berets.

He needs to know that details count for something

The man with Psyche in Virgo longs for someone to understand him on every level. But this trick must somehow be accomplished with a high degree of sophistication. He loves the woman who can draw an intelligent conclusion without him having to spell things out. His Ms. Ideal is meticulous without making a big fuss of it, and someone who is together, worldly, and witty. Eschewing mess and living an out-there lifestyle, she is clean-living and discreet. Intensely moral, Psyche in Virgo appreciates a "good" woman who respects his need for privacy.

Ben Affleck, Matthew Broderick,
James Van Der Beek, Prince William

Libra

september 24 - october 23

Cosmically activated by elegant quartets and
beautiful singing. Gorgeous music is perfect for
the Psyche in Libra; it reaffirms his love of
beauty while letting him stay distant.

He needs to know that she is a mystery

Psyche in Libra likes mysterious beauties. Familiarity can create contempt with this guy and perhaps the next step is longing for new stimuli. He can wind up in love with the general concept of "woman" but, really, he is ducking the challenge of true romance. His other method for avoiding the nitty-gritty of reality? Being madly in love with another man's woman. If her situation changes he may lose interest faster than he loses her phone number. His feminine ideal is lovely, supernaturally elegant, and smart. She stays forever just a few steps in front of him, creating that elusive quality he prizes so highly.

Guy Pearce, Gavin Rossdale

Scorpio

october 24 - november 22

Cosmically activated by intense, brooding
pieces with eerie instrumentals or featuring
depressing "poetry." He often selects his music
based on how the musician lived…or died.

He needs to know why another man's photo
is in her wallet

Bring it on! Psyche in Scorpio engenders the man who is ready for the big challenges. His ideal woman is intense, complicated, and difficult. He can be the biggest womanizer on earth but, secretly, this guy yearns for the grand passion, for the female who awakens every cell of his being. His ideal girl is spiritual, creative, bold, and beautiful, as amazed by the Universe as he is and just as much of an "extreme-o-phile." He's totally into true togetherness. Once in love, he wants to merge. Despising sycophants, he loves the woman who is first true to herself.

Ed Burns, Johnny Depp, Ralph Fiennes, Jude Law, Guy Ritchie, Will Smith

Sagittarius

november 23 - december 21

Cosmically activated by loud rock 'n' roll
or gratuitously "free love" hippie music.
The Psyche-in-Saggo guy sees himself as a free
spirit who needs a sexy soundtrack.

He needs to know that she is untamable

The return of the lotus-eater; the man with Psyche in Saggo loves the woman who expands his horizons, blows his mind, and then flits off unencumbered. His ideal girl is fun-loving, utterly uninhibited, and able to relate to anyone. He is incapable of setting boundaries for the woman he loves—the louder and more vivacious she is the better. In his mind he wants to be in Shangri-la with his fun-loving adventure girl and someone who says about the impossible dream, "Let's just do it!" She is completely candid—this man can't handle manipulators—and feels that she is as unlike "the others" as he does.

Hugh Jackman, Ozzy Osbourne, Brad Pitt, Ian Somerhalder, Owen Wilson

Capricorn

december 22 - january 20

Cosmically activated by Top 40 soft rock. Not a
man who likes to be sidetracked, Mr. Psyche in
Cap keeps to the musical straight and narrow.
If in doubt, check where his car radio is tuned.

He needs to know that the pursuit of success will be
mutual

This is the alpha guy in love. The dream girl of the guy with Psyche in Capricorn is a classic Type-A personality: vibrant, demanding, and ambitious. He is most easily turned off by the victim stance or by a woman who wants to coast along on someone else's slog to success. His ideal female has poise, goals, and a plan on which to structure her life. He likes the ones who don't need him. In fact, icy indifference inspires his ardor far more than over-the-top declarations of needy emotion. He fantasizes about being one part of a dynamic duo. These two are an unbeatable power couple.

Kieran Culkin, Ryan Phillippe

Aquarius

january 21 - february 19

Cosmically activated by German synthesizer
bands and symphonies played entirely with drums.
He has odd tastes in music: do your homework
before giving him a Céline Dion CD.

He needs to know that his mind
will be stimulated

Luckily, for some women, the man with Psyche in Aquarius is a connoisseur of female eccentricity. His ideal woman is a clear-thinking, way-ahead-of-her-time type of individual. A natural-born feminist sympathizer, he is not particularly keen on the usual "tricks" of seduction and instead relishes the "great minds thinking alike" paradigm. He likes it when a lover can challenge his preconceptions and turn him on to new ways of thinking about "the obvious." Though a romantic player when he wants to be, his soul mate must first access his mind and form a friendship.

Russell Crowe, Michael Douglas, Prince Harry

Pisces

february 20 - march 20

Cosmically activated by sexy, maybe even tarty girl bands and female singers. He's openly interested in sex and the idea of the sexy chanteuse. Loves female musicians being raunchy or naughty.

He needs to know that she is cuddly but difficult

Psyche in Pisces wants the impossible in a woman—an intriguing blend of vixenly cunning and baby-like innocence. His fantasy of the perfect woman is the most idealistic of all and can easily keep him from forming a real-life romance. His soul mate has to be someone fluid of personality, forever in flux, and yet also firm enough to keep a grip on herself amid the changing projections of Psyche in Pisces. Easily beguiled by beauty, he can also be at risk of falling in unrequited love. What better way to ensure that the excitement and allure he craves do not become overly real?

Luis Buñuel, Travis Fimmell

Her Eros reveals...
her ideal man

"This relationship with David has taken
me totally by surprise, a wonderful surprise.
I have found my soul mate in him, my friend.
In him I have found my lover, my companion.
[He is] the person I was looking for—my other
half. I hope everyone in this world finds their
other half as I did mine."

Über-model Iman on her husband, rock star David Bowie

Her Eros reveals...her ideal man

Put simply, a woman's Eros sign shows us the man she dreams about. Our masculine "type" is so often formed fairly early in life, perhaps from a mish-mash of family and cultural influences—that childhood crush or (eek!) father figure.

But her Eros reveals the guy who can truly make her happy...the one she needs as opposed to wants. Imagine a worldly and sophisticated Capricorn woman, predestined—she feels—for an official catch, a "suit" if you like. But should her Eros be in bohemian Sagittarius, her real masculine ideal is more likely to turn up in surfer-dude guise.

It is vital that girls get to grips with their Eros sign as it represents the true lover. Only a man with at least some of the Eros "cred" can totally ensnare her heart. The sign placement of Eros reveals how the woman's idealized lover figures above and beyond her more prosaic, real-life concerns.

The placement of Eros of actress Jennifer Aniston is exactly conjunct with the Eros of her husband, actor Brad Pitt. The same applies to actress Uma Thurman and her husband, actor Ethan Hawke. So the erotic ideals of these women are displayed by the choice of their men.

For ultimate happiness in love and to feel truly soul mated, the Eros sign must be able to find full expression along with the yearnings revealed by the sign placement of Psyche. The idea is to read both signs and gain more insight into what may be going on subconsciously, far beneath the so suave and sensible romantic persona du jour!

Her Eros is in...

"I always had this dream of meeting an artist, an artist girl who would be like me. And I thought it was a myth, but then I met Yoko and that was it."

Former Beatle John Lennon on his wife, artist Yoko Ono

"She is wild and innocent, pledged to love
Through all disaster; but those other women
Decry her for a witch or a common drab
And glare back when she greets them.
Here is her portrait, gazing sidelong at me,
The hair in disarray, the young eyes pleading:
'And, you, love? As unlike those other men
As I those other women?'"

The Portrait—Robert Graves

Aries

march 21 - april 20

Cosmically activated by the fire of a bloodstone.
Her fiery nature is triggered by firestones, rubies,
and garnets. Burning red is forever her hue
du jour. She sizzles.

She wants to hear: I want you

Her dream lover? The wild-at-heart studly type whom only she seems capable of conquering. Up for a challenge, the Eros-in-Aries woman appreciates strength and success in men more than any other female. She likes to mess with the head of Mr. Hard-To-Get, making him crash through new barriers of love and adoration. Far from upsetting her, healthy competition arouses her fighting instincts. It's vital that she feels superior to those who may have gone before. Once soul mated, her guy becomes the hero of her heart. Her loyalty is unsurpassed just as long as he first jumps through the hoops.

Pamela Anderson, Nicole Kidman, Madonna, Elle Macpherson

Taurus

april 21 - may 21

Cosmically activated by green from the Earth. The Eros-in-Taurus girl is brought alive by emerald, jade, greenstone, green tourmaline, and peridot. Think like her, think green.

She wants to hear: I'm here to stay

The woman with Eros in Taurus longs for a man who is the epitome of assurance and stability. She comes undone easily with jittery guys, tantrum-throwers, and manipulators of girls. The man of her dreams must relish the nonstop slog to score his goals and feather their nest. Her fantasy is that of the insatiable sensualist at home and the dignified patriarch type everywhere else. She is naturally drawn to the mature, manly end of the male spectrum as opposed to the rowdy or uncertain iconoclast.

Britney Spears, Hilary Swank

Gemini

may 22 - june 21

Cosmically activated by pearls and pearls only.
The milky baubles are traditionally so-o-o lucky
for the Gemini woman, and for her only. Light
up the Eros-in-Gem girl with a special gift.

She wants to hear: I'm changeable,
very changeable

Eros in Gemini falls for the witty, silver-tongued guy. She loves the super-smart, mind-challenging man and is turned on by innuendo-laden gossip, over-the-top flirting and amazing new info. She's keen to try new things and will never allow dullness to darken her love life. Given this set of prerequisites, it is not surprising that the woman with Eros in Gemini is also known to crave variety in her menfolk. At some point it occurs to her that one man may not be able to satisfy her continual need for stimulation. The one who can is her soul mate.

Beyoncé Knowles, Mae West

Cancer

june 22 - july 23

Cosmically activated by moonstone, water sapphire, clear quartz crystal. Her favorite gemstones symbolize the power of pure clarity and illumination. She's a person of sensitivity— her stones must be as clear as her lover.

She wants to hear: I need a muse

It is almost impossible for the woman with Eros in Cancer to fall in love with a man who is not sensitive and creative. Men who are hardened to life, in an effort to fit in with the system, leave her cold. She idealizes the artist, the musician, and the writer—the guy incapable of mortgaging his dreams for the sake of respectability. But, she is also very security conscious so her ideal soul mate is the one who somehow attains wealth by following his bliss. Highly intuitive and compassionate, her true lover is gentle and nurturing, never macho or blustering.

Drew Barrymore, Iman, Natalie Imbruglia, Courtney Love

Leo

july 24 - august 23

Cosmically activated by gold! The yellow
metal is warm like the Sun and as precious as
the Leo sense of self. Give the gift of gold and
watch her fabulosity come to life.

She wants to hear: And you can be my queen!

Eros in Leo needs nothing less than a superstar of love. She is truly admiring of talent and success. Her ideal guy is a highly acclaimed limelight-hogger with a super ego, immense confidence, and an extreme belief in himself. She always checks out the talent in a social situation, overlooking the less impressive man in favor of the most gorgeous and over-the-top stud. Her idea of love involves grandiose, never-ending romance and the luxurious life. She simply can't warm to someone who is insecure, shy, or even vaguely undemonstrative.

Kirsten Dunst, Gwen Stefani,
Audrey Tautou, Catherine Zeta-Jones

Virgo

august 24 - september 23

Cosmically activated by lapis lazuli. Cool
and beautiful, just like the Eros-in-Virgo girl,
the ultramarine rock has associations as an
aphrodisiac and a health charm. Make her glow!

She wants to hear: I've already cleaned it

She likes the cute quirky guy who, closeted like Superman, turns into a very suave alpha male. Immune to braggart gesturing and shallow displays of affection, her heart is won by the insightful compliment, the truly thoughtful act of kindness. But her ideal man is above all witty and funny. Eros in Virgo falls in love with the brilliant raconteur, the guy who can make a hilarious morsel out of even the most banal detail of everyday life. She is not at all interested in the guys who alternate from wild flights of fancy to crashing insecurity. This woman appreciates sanity and urbanity.

Melanie Griffith, Angelina Jolie,
Jada Pinkett Smith

Libra

september 24 - october 23

Cosmically activated by diamonds. When a woman has Eros in Libra, her heart yearns for harmony and enduring balance, on a highly sophisticated scale. The diamond she wears is aptly distinguished.

She wants to hear: I love you for your beauty

The girl just can't help it—she's a lover of male beauty in all its forms. And the man interested in hooking up with her has to acknowledge that she won't stop noticing the glory of masculine pulchritude just because she's soul mated. Eros in Libra adores not only good looks and charm but also the man of a philosophical bent, someone who can detach and consider both sides of an argument. Scenes and disharmony send her skittering away. An aesthetic creature at heart, she can't abide a man who makes scenes or who is ballsy and macho just for the sake of it.

Jade Jagger, Ashley Judd, Rachel Ward

Scorpio

october 24 - november 22

Cosmically activated by the dark stones. This woman's love nature is mysterious, which is not completely apparent on either the first or 10th meeting. Bring her the brooding malachite and black opal.

She wants to hear: You consume me

Eros in Scorpio doesn't even bother dating unless her knees tremble at the sheer sight of the guy. It's either intensely passionate or she's not there—literally. Her ideal man is super-focused on his brilliant career and his interests. One of his interests—her—could be better classified as an obsession. She is quickly bored with the guy who is too light-hearted about an affair and ditto the "just good friends" dynamic. She already has plenty of friends, thank you. Her soul mate cares deeply about the world and is capable of being deeply moved by emotion.

Catherine Deneuve, Princess Diana, Charlize Theron

Sagittarius

november 23 - december 21

Cosmically activated by the blue-green rock.
As changeable as the Eros-in-Saggo girl
herself, turquoise is also about things that
don't change, such as love and loyalty.

She wants to hear: If it's the truth, it can't
be embarrassing

The woman with Eros in Saggo admires the independent man who makes up his own rules as he goes along. She also prefers the company of rugged idealists and bohemian dream boys. Her ideal man gives her stacks of space in which to develop by herself and hang out with her friends. A jealous or possessive male is like a bad nightmare. She needs someone secure in his own right to let her shine her own light in peace. Trust is her biggest motif in love and also the belief that "truth is beauty."

Christina Aguilera, Liv Tyler,
Naomi Watts, Kate Winslet

Capricorn

december 22 - january 20

Cosmically activated by success without drama.
She craves status without gaudiness, which is not
always easy. The clean, successful statement of
silver and sapphire meets the brief.

She wants to hear: I'll look after this

Eros in Capricorn can't help but be drawn to the self-made man. A guy in charge of his destiny, the boss man, the rainmaker—all these are her archetypes of maleness. Luckily, she tends to scare off those she would consider dilettantes or wimps, leaving the field clear for her alpha-male ideal. Oddly enough, her preferences are often even more clearly delineated by early romantic experiences with immature men who bring only chaos and mess. This makes her even more certain that the love she craves must take place in a defined structure with rules.

Sarah Michelle Gellar, Jennifer Lopez,
Jennifer Love Hewitt, Kate Moss,
Brittany Murphy, Meg Ryan,
Danielle Spencer, Mena Suvari,
Uma Thurman

Aquarius

january 21 - february 19

Cosmically activated by amethyst, aka "metamorphosis." She is working at an elevated psychic level, so give her the rock that converts energies from low to high. Heavy stuff.

She wants to hear: This is about us, it's not about the rules

Her lover ideal is a rebel, nonconformist, and politically progressive free spirit. She cares not for convention and often recoils from socially sanctioned lovers. Her dream is that she can have a relationship of equals, unmarred by fuddy-duddy ideas of what a love affair ought to be. The sexist or patronizing male does not stand a chance with this woman. Her heart is essentially free and the true lover of Eros in Aquarius is the man who wouldn't want to fence her in, even if he could. She's willing to wait for as long as it takes for that one guy who understands her on the spot.

Jennifer Aniston, Jennifer Connelly, Kate Hudson, Gwyneth Paltrow, Pink, Christy Turlington

Pisces

february 20 - march 20

Cosmically activated by a stone that enhances her interest in the metaphysical. Eros in Pisces is connected to other worlds, and aquamarine's oceanic association is a great balancer.

She wants to hear: You have a temper?
I hadn't noticed

These girls are after Mr. Unconditional Love. "Do what thou wilt and I'll still adore you, darling" has to be the motto of he who would score her love. She is a frank admirer of men who are visionary, genius, or artistic. Normality sends her shrieking off into the wilderness. Ditto what she considers to be petty judgments and silly expectations. Most of all, she wants to be with the guy who is truly compassionate. The harsh and cynical man is anathema to her tender soul. Naturally, the singer of love songs or the writer of beautiful poetry has a huge head start with her.

Victoria Beckham, Cameron Diaz,
Missy Elliott, Elizabeth Hurley,
Vanessa Paradis, Sarah Jessica Parker,
Michelle Pfeiffer, Brooke Shields,
Shania Twain, Reese Witherspoon

Eros and Psyche in love—the soul mating maps

"I awake filled with thoughts of you. Your image and the intoxicating evening that we spent yesterday have left my senses in turmoil. Sweet, incomparable Josephine, what a strange effect you have on my heart."

Emperor of France, Napoleon Bonaparte, in a letter to his wife, Josephine Beauharnais

"My dear Nora,

It has just struck me. I came in at half past 11. Since then, I have been sitting in an easy chair like a fool. I could do nothing. I hear nothing but your voice. I am like a fool hearing you call me 'Dear.'"

Irish novelist James Joyce in a letter to his wife,

Nora Barnacle

Soul mating

His Eros is in...

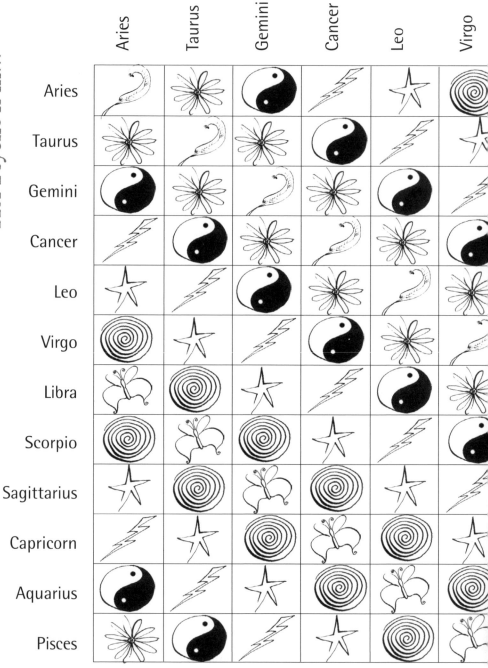

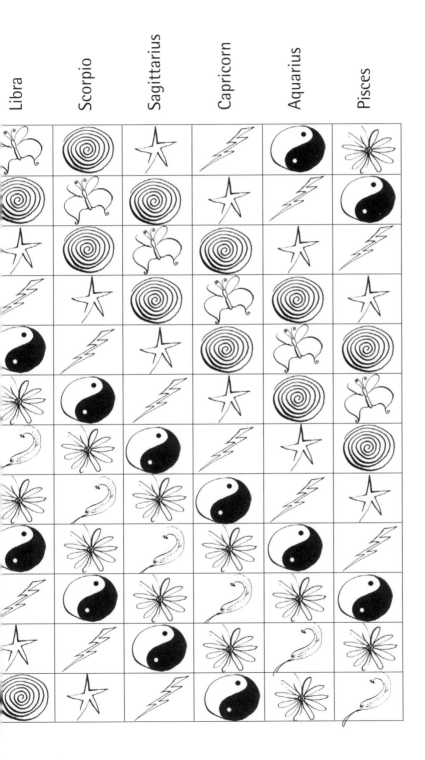

Libra	Scorpio	Sagittarius	Capricorn	Aquarius	Pisces

Her Eros is in...

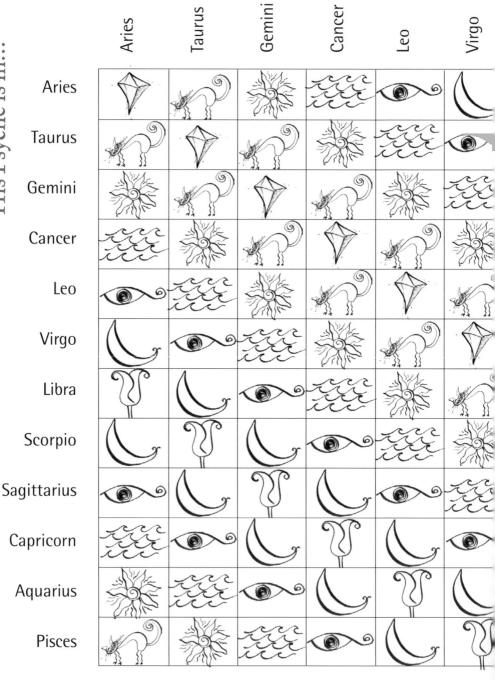

His Psyche is in...

	Aries	Taurus	Gemini	Cancer	Leo	Virgo
Aries						
Taurus						
Gemini						
Cancer						
Leo						
Virgo						
Libra						
Scorpio						
Sagittarius						
Capricorn						
Aquarius						
Pisces						

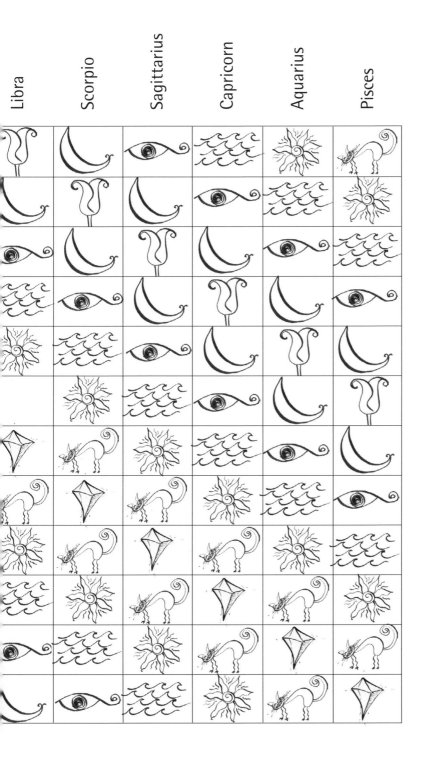

His Eros—her Psyche

"It was like the old cliché where you see somebody, lock eyes across the room, and time stands still."

Actor Chad Lowe on meeting his wife, actress Hilary Swank, at a party

"We didn't date before we married at all. We
made *Bugsy* together and, at the end of
the movie, I asked Annette if she wanted to
have dinner and have a baby and she said yes.
And we did that night…"

Actor Warren Beatty on meeting his wife,
actress Annette Bening

Feather

Instantaneous combustion!

Wow! This is the classic love-at-first-sight scenario! So often it seems as though fate genuinely conspires to bring these two together under the most bizarre of circumstances. For example, she shouldn't have been there that night but she was and so she met him! When these two soul mates get together, each feels as though they are somehow coming home. It's similar to the sensation felt by a child, bored at a totally adult party, suddenly meeting another kid! No matter what the differences or even the geographical and cultural distance between them, they bond on the spot and forever at some level. Even if this duo meets but once, they will never forget one another and *that* encounter. And yet, this is the most likely relationship to go the distance, no matter what. Both people can't help but immediately sense the significance of the chemistry between them. They can run and they can hide but never deny the attraction.

Ryan Phillippe & Reese Witherspoon
Chris Henchy & Brooke Shields
Federico Fellini & Giulietta Masina
Liam Gallagher & Nicole Appleton
Ben Harper & Laura Dern

Daisy

The Weirding!

Ready or not, these two mess with one another's minds from the second they meet. They quite often start out with an official "hate each other's guts" dynamic going on. They challenge each other to a strange "who are you really?" duel of wits. Cosmically, they are destined to alter the other's reality to such an extent that, no matter what happens, life will never be quite the same again. Oddly enough, they tend to meet via normal circumstances. Perhaps they have even heard mention of the other for some time and vowed something like "That person is so not me!" Yet, when they do meet up, they're irritated yet intrigued. Someone says one little thing and the other is like "WHAT, did you say THAT?" This liaison often lends itself to on-off-on-again shenanigans as each person must make huge adjustments to fit into the life path of the other— madly in love as they may be.

Richard Burton & Elizabeth Taylor
Guy Ritchie & Madonna
Russell Crowe & Danielle Spencer
Daniel Johns & Natalie Imbruglia

Yin-Yang

Collaborators in love

Serendipity strikes hard and fast as these two suddenly wake up to the fact that they're fully in love. Yes, this couple is the most likely to already know one another—perhaps they are even the clichéd "just good friends," when suddenly one night, IT happens. Oh, dear. They're so naturally compatible and happy together that they often bond on a purely platonic level, knowing right from the start that this person is someone they want to have in their lives indefinitely. Consciously or otherwise, they don't want to blow it via some psychodramatic lust scenario. So? So they suppress their real feelings. Should true love run its destined course, this couple is a teamworking duo, evoking sustained mutual stimulation to help them ride out the ruts of long-term love. The best expression of this relationship is that of real partnering. They're mates in every sense of the word.

Bryan Brown & Rachel Ward
James Joyce & Nora Barnacle
David E. Kelley & Michelle Pfeiffer
Graham Payn & Noël Coward

Lightning Bolt

Oh, God! I'm so in love!

Let's be quite clear about this one. It so often kicks off when one or both of the lovers are otherwise involved. Or, for some reason, the entire thing is utterly impossible. They meet, sense the heat, and feel the fear. Each falls insanely in love and decides to ride it out like a kind of exotic flu. They frequently come across one another when every little thing goes against their romance. There is an initial encounter or two and then nothing. Yet something brings them back into contact with one another and it's all on—ready or not! Should they be wild enough to go ahead with this rollercoaster romance, they become the couple to watch. Each eggs on the other to fully follow their bliss. They take up all the oxygen in any room—the passion, the bitchery, the ego-conflicts. The sheer heat generated by this pair bonding is beyond belief.

Ethan Hawke & Uma Thurman
Johnny Depp & Vanessa Paradis
Antonio Banderas & Melanie Griffith
Sam Mendes & Kate Winslet
Michael Douglas & Catherine Zeta-Jones
Ed Burns & Christy Turlington
Ralph Fiennes & Francesca Annis
Matthew Broderick & Sarah Jessica Parker
Pete Sampras & Brigitte Wilson

Soul mating

Star

Haven't we met before?

From the first moment they meet they're convinced that they know each other. And, in fact, this relationship is the most likely to begin with a massive confession session in which each feels compelled to tell ALL to the other. Afterward, neither can believe the inner *merde* they just told this person for no apparent reason. The soul link is profound and often signaled by a strong physical sensation. But it is not remotely lust-driven. It is, rather, a palpable shock of recognition—not the "You ARE me" feeling generated by some of the other connections. It's a feeling of ease and luxury, like leaping into a hot opulent bath after battling through a long and stormy day of mundane crap. They feel understood as if for the first time and all of the ancient angst seems suddenly solved. This is one of the most likely "together forever" soul mating scenarios.

Stephen Barlow & Joanna Lumley
Willie Gordon & Isabel Allende
Dario Franchitti & Ashley Judd
Will Smith & Jada Pinkett Smith
Oscar Wilde & Lord Alfred Douglas

Butterfly

Opposites attract but first repel!

Your friends suggest therapy as soon as possible but you don't give a damn what the shrink thinks. Nobody from the outside ever really gets this love affair but the people involved don't care. Not for one second. It is most likely to begin via an act of rebellion from one half of the pairing. Somehow, one of them is in riot about society and its expectations, so disillusioned and over love that it's not funny. This romance pops up as the proverbial bolt from the blue and each heals the other. It can even materialize like this: a brief encounter, a few words spoken, and someone heads home to his or her life. The practical details of being together on a day-to-day basis bore this pair. They often seem to wind up in a dynamic that encourages them to polarize like a long-distance romance or some reason why they can't be too involved with one another's family. That's how it goes. And, as you might expect, this is an attraction that can quickly blow over. But, when it doesn't? It lasts forever and a day. And still nobody understands.

Freddie Prinze Jr. & Sarah Michelle Gellar
Spencer Tracy & Katharine Hepburn
Bernard-Henri Levy & Arielle Dombasle
Jack London & Charmian Kittredge
Kid Rock & Pamela Anderson

Spiral

Married already!

Hello, you must be my husband! Wife? Whatever, this duo knows quick smart that they're on, or off. They either get it on from the start or neatly avoid one another. Another way of putting it is that there is either no chemistry whatsoever between them or it is on from the literal second they see each other. If it's an on situation, they are so prone to skipping the usual courtship stage that it's ludicrous. People can't believe that these lovers haven't known one another since childhood! They often even look similar! They are the couple most likely to nauseate others via an extreme public intimacy dynamic. Speech, gags, and even sexual preferences seem like suddenly shared secrets. If one, the other or both are accustomed to full-on tension between lovers, this relationship will freak them out at first. The comfort zoning is immense. Warning: Even if these two do break up, they never truly split up, you understand.

David Beckham & Victoria Beckham
Ben Lee & Claire Danes
Royston Langdon & Liv Tyler
Danny DeVito & Rhea Perlman
Ben Stiller & Christine Taylor
Tim McGraw & Faith Hill

Her Eros—his Psyche

"But we had talked for 10 hours without noticing the time passing. I let myself into my apartment thinking elatedly, 'I have met the man I want to marry.' Gone were doubts about the existence of real love. I wasn't anywhere near understanding it yet, but I was full of joy."

U.S. novelist Madeleine L'Engle on meeting her husband, actor Hugh Franklin

Rochester: "1 knew you would do me good in some way, at some time: 1 saw it in your eyes when 1 first beheld you; their expression and smile did not...strike delight to my very inmost heart so for nothing..."

Jane: "1 had not intended to love him; the reader knows 1 had wrought hard to extirpate from my soul the germs of love there detected; and now, at the first renewed view of him, they spontaneously revived, great and strong! He made me love him without looking at me...Reader, 1 married him."

Jane Eyre–Charlotte Brontë

Diamond

Immortal lovers

A single mad moment often defines this love affair, probably the one with the highest soul mating potential of all! The second these two encounter each other, there is no room for anyone else. Memories of past lovers flee from their suddenly addled minds. They realize immediately that nothing, no matter what the complications, is going to stand between them and their goal to fulfill this liaison. One of the most surreal aspects of the diamond relationship is that one or both of the "adorees" will have dreamt of it beforehand, perhaps even repeatedly. So it feels like it is the most déjà vu thing ever. There is often some sort of sign or significant something worn or uttered in the initial meeting and neither will ever forget this conversation. Ready or not, they meet and realize that (eeek!) this is likely to be one of the most significant romances of their lifetime! Another cosmic clue: They are destined to deeply inspire one another creatively.

Edna St. Vincent Millay & Eugene Boissevain
Helena Christensen & Norman Reedus
Laura Dern & Ben Harper

Cat

Mind mates!

These two enjoy a love affair that gets better and better with time. Gossipy intimacy and shared dreams bring them closer together. Upon first meeting one another, they feel—if not a striking moment of lust—a strong sensation of friendship. It's like the trust and familiarity of good mates is with them right from the start. There seems little need to explain much to each other. This is also the couple most likely to succeed together. They totally "get" one another's mindset and let nothing erode their mutual loyalty. In fact, it is often work or business of some sort that brings them together at first. They weave around them a tight little web of friends and family, ensuring that their own romancing does not inhibit a broader social push. Together they are easily more than the sum of their parts. Astro ick factor: They could wind up vibing more like close siblings than lovers.

Rachel Ward & Bryan Brown
Danielle Spencer & Russell Crowe
Sharon & Ozzy Osbourne
Ashley Judd & Dario Franchitti

Sun

Déja vù!

Love comes quickly as neither party in this magical pair-bonding can believe their luck. They are often introduced by mutual friends who seem to sense their extreme compatibility well before the Sun couple gets it. Somehow, a bizarre factor seems to come between these two at first—there is always a challenge to overcome. Perhaps the strong presence of an ex-lover? Domineering or disapproving family? Total fear of succumbing to the passion? Whatever it may be, the couple either race off in different directions (yet never quite forgetting the feelings evoked by the other) or become much closer by joining to dissolve the love obstacle. Get between these two at your own peril. More than any other type of couple, they deeply admire one another and will do whatever it takes to protect their romance from toxic emotions or outside interference.

Brad Pitt & Jennifer Aniston
Iman & David Bowie
Kirsten Dunst & Jake Gyllenhaal
Naomi Watts & Heath Ledger
Gwen Stefani & Gavin Rossdale
Danny DeVito & Rhea Perlman
Christine Taylor & Ben Stiller
Jada Pinkett Smith & Will Smith

Waves

Karma drama!

These two are totally destined to meet and make a maximum impact upon one another. This cosmic scenario naturally makes for some tempestuous scenes along with the classic make up/break up dynamic. Just as waves allow the ocean to craft a relentless change to a coastline, the Waves relationship is about long-term transformations. These soul mates often have to face challenges to be with their lover and then the affair becomes its own pressure cooker of change. It's as if, despite their deep and abiding attraction toward one another, neither can be in the relationship as they are. The romance thus proves cathartic with each party ringing in profound changes: personality, beliefs, goals, lifestyle—even looks. The most instant manifestation of this so-destined love affair is that each person seems to begin a process of metamorphosis. Some call it crazy love but this destined duo doesn't give a damn.

Elizabeth Taylor & Richard Burton
Melanie Griffith & Antonio Banderas
Denise Richards & Charlie Sheen
Elin Nordegren & Tiger Woods
Christy Turlington & Ed Burns
Sarah Jessica Parker & Matthew Broderick
Brigitte Wilson & Pete Sampras
Faith Hill & Tim McGraw

Soul mating

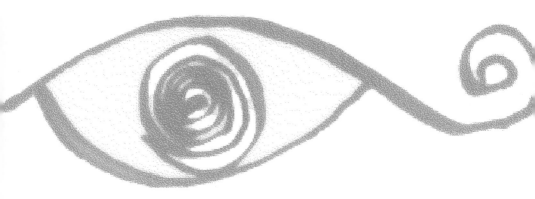

Eye

You are my everything!

This tender romance has the potential to be the clingiest of all! Once pair-bonded, this couple can be almost inseparable. They literally find being parted from one another to be *that* irksome. Some have love at first sight, others get a bolt from the blue; peace relationships are often built on emotional and social togetherness before any passion sneaks in. This doesn't mean there isn't any excitement—it just means the tension builds to the heat of that first kiss. These guys know each other by the way each feels serene and kind of blissed out by the whole thing. Life itself seems to conspire to bring them together. It's as if they can see all the "fragile, handle with care" areas of other relationships and not only tread around them but actually heal the psychic scars from any ancient angst.

Vanessa Paradis & Johnny Depp
Fanny Ardant & François Truffaut
Reese Witherspoon & Ryan Phillippe
Amelia Earhart & George Palmer Putnam
Jennifer Lopez & Ben Affleck
Natalie Portman & Gael Garcia Bernal
Francesca Annis & Ralph Fiennes

Moon

Always on my mind!

Always evolving, this relationship is perpetual poetry in motion and a nonstop work in progress. It is as if each "adoree" must make constant—if tiny—attitude adjustments in order to let the love affair shine. If one or the other gets too stuck in a certain paradigm, the whole liaison starts to stall and, if they are not careful, bog down. It is amazing how often this romance is characterized by one of the parties loathing (or at least not much liking!) the other person. Yet, if this is the case, there will nonetheless be a kind of incessant buzz at the back of their mind. Once sighted, these guys are never out of one another's minds. Another astro clue: They often meet each other at a time of personal crisis. The mutual emotion is like "Whoa! And now this!" They are also highly likely to be a "rebound" affair—albeit one that may go on forever!

Uma Thurman & Ethan Hawke
Kate Hudson & Chris Robinson
Gwyneth Paltrow & Chris Martin
Charmian Kittredge & Jack London
Natalie Imbruglia & Daniel Johns

Tulip

We may never come this way again!

The dynamic tension generated by this pairing is truly something to behold. Often they are officially the complete opposite of one another. No? Something is bound to be diametrically opposed. They get it on via an instant emotion of not "Wow, we are so similar" but of "You complete me." Happier than any other kind of couple to not just tolerate but relish the differences between them, they give one another "free to be me" room. They're also suave, modern, and worldly about gender expression, caring not about who seems to be "in charge." Deeply private and always discreet, they keep the real passion and power politics to themselves, to be played out in private. This is because, cosmically, this duo always has something hot to be, er, worked through.

Hilary Swank & Chad Lowe
Yoko Ono & John Lennon
Kate Winslet and Sam Mendes,
Madeleine L'Engle and Hugh Franklin
Candice Bergen & Louis Malle

How your Sun sign gets it on with Eros & Psyche

If you are an Aries...
march 21 - april 20

You are a self-actualizing and upbeat egomaniac. Nobody tells you what to do or how to do it. Over the top? For sure. As ultra-Aries fashionista diva Diana Vreeland said, "exaggeration is the only reality." You believe—along with (brilliant painter, sculptor, architect, engineer, musician etc.) Leonardo da Vinci—that "every obstacle yields to stern resolve." You're hyper-competitive in love, needing both a full-on challenge and nonstop drooling adulation. Hard to get? You bet. Difficult? You're officially impossible. You can be so prone to seeing even a much-adored lover as a mere blip on the radar of your genius. But whoever wins your love will be assured of an almost insanely loyal life partner.

and your Eros is in...

Soul mating

ARIES

Okay, so you're an Aries by nature and an Aries in love! The good news is that there is no conflict between your core persona and the character you become when smitten. But, wow! Are you aware of how mega-demanding you can be? You ideally take steps to ameliorate bolshie tendencies. Admitting the occasional vulnerability does not render you a gimp. You can also be impatient with other people's displays of "weakness."

To do ASAP: Learn the art of graceful apology and how to at least fake sympathy. Say "sweetie."

TAURUS

Own up! You are secretly turned on by displays of status and/or economic prowess. You notice those luxury cars. But, yes, you come across as a hell of a lot more dependable than the average Sun sign Aries. You're also more in touch with your physical self and sensual needs. Aries says "You want me or not? Because if you don't, there's plenty who do!" You apply clichéd seduction techniques. And you know they work!

Astro speciality: You love mood music, especially those cool DIY compilations. You are the DJ of love.

GEMINI

The Aries part of you is direct. But Eros in Gemini makes you relish the art of mind-gaming. Aries is morality driven and *très* harsh on those deemed to be sleazy. Eros in Gemini is incapable of judgment, especially about anything to do with love, lust, or soul mating. So your love life is about constantly reconciling the contradictions that make you so cute. Vow now: Forgive and forget yourself. Love thyself as a so-complex creature, forever in flux and loving it!

Your astro alibi: Mild mendacity retains your mystique.

CANCER

Aries doesn't give a damn about security. Your Aries Sun part of you is willing to throw everything away on a "Respect me or else!" whim or to fulfill a feral crush that hit five minutes ago. Your Cancerian Eros craves comfort zoning and continuity of experience. What to do? Accept that when it comes to romance, you are a far clingier creature than the "average" Aries. You are also kinder and more emotionally intelligent.

Astro witchery: Create the coziest boudoir in the world. Satisfy that Aries ego by thinking "pouncing pit."

LEO

Who can hack the heat of your radiant charisma! Eros in Leo adds feline grace to your Aries Sun schtick. You're a natural-born show-off diva, the performance artiste of love. So what alienates wannabe lovers? Grandiose vanity? Insatiable ego? Hmm. Yet you are also glamourous, inspirational, and giving of yourself. Don't deny dramatic tendencies. Exaggerate!

Cosmic love tips: Learn several romantic poems off by heart for reciting to rapt potential adorees. Candlelight is your at-home equivalent of airbrushing.

VIRGO

"Don't bug me with details," barks Aries, whirling off in a haze of bliss-following genius. But Eros in Virgo does bother about the details, especially with relationships. You fall instantly in love, start "creatively visualizing" the romance and then, before anything has even happened, you panic about where the two of you are going to live or indulge a "what if the in-laws hate me?" fantasy.

Celestial mission: Please don't undermine your sexy and suave worldly love style via low-rent neurosis. What's it to be—crow's feet or laughter lines?

Soul mating

LIBRA

As an Aries, you can make up your mind about anything in two minutes flat. Quick and decisive, you're a legend. Or are you? Eros in Libra likes the multi-view. The Aries you despairs at this dithering but it helps make you human! You can deal with romantic ambiguity. You score big time in the dishing-out-(good-)advice stakes. You are the confidante, not the dictator, of love.

Astro bonus: You are far more sophisticated than "normal" Arians. Just don't tell them. But you can't wait to find one and boast! See? You are an Aries.

SCORPIO

Who cares what the shrink thinks? Not you. With the Sun in Aries and Eros in Scorpio, you're a free-wheeling individualista. You've got the gung-ho gorm of Aries blended with Scorp inscrutability. Ideally, Aries, positivity, and self-belief enlighten the sometimes melancholy Scorp persona. Then, let the Scorpy depth of perception inform the oft-shallow Aries' world view! Voila! Meaningful and deep Aries spunk with attitude. Scary astro fact: You're too busy ranting on to notice how seductive you are. Mirror, mirror?

SAGITTARIUS

Sweet candor? Or bloody-minded tactlessness? As both Aries and Sagittarius place high value on honesty, you find it almost impossible to deceive. This works for and against you. Yes, people trust you. And no matter what your chronological age, you come across as forever young and breezy. No, they don't necessarily enjoy hearing your unpolished version of reality.

Cosmic lesson du jour: Truth is not necessarily beauty—well, certainly not in a relationship. Finessing a compliment is not an ethical betrayal of principles.

CAPRICORN

You're a seductive force to behold. Eros in Capricorn gives a grown-up, sophisticated kind of allure. Your Sun in Aries can dazzle anyone. But Aries is the baby of the Zodiac and Capricorn the know-all ancient. These influences can work at odds against one another. For example, you vibe arch old fogy when a breathless "Oh, golly!" would work wonders. But, then you come off sounding anarchic and callow in a chat about income tax brackets. Reverse that paradigm and pull!

Cosmic sex flash: Love on the job is always an issue.

AQUARIUS

As an Aries, you're simple and demonstrative in love. However, Eros in Aquarius complicates the scenario. An aspect of you is practically robotic, able to grasp romance in theory but not wanting to "lower" yourself. Intimacy issues? "I love you" says Mr./Ms. Maybe. You change the subject to some article on human cloning law you read.

Astro romance resolution: You know all those meaningless bourgeois gestures? Flowers? Extravagant compliments? Moonlight declarations of intent? Love song requests? Just do them.

PISCES

You are both the macho warrior king or queen and the prince or princess bride. Thing One and Thing Two? Aries is ultra-assertive and strident. Eros in Pisces operates on a subliminal level, intuiting realities way below the radar of optimistic but brash Aries. People go ape for this combo of confidence and modesty. How do you pull it off? You have no idea. But you're at your best au naturel—hideous when contrived.

Cosmic memo: Retain your idealism. Try not to ring your ex-(or future) lovers for moral support during a date.

Or your Psyche is in...

ARIES

Do you have sky-high expectations in love? Inner you and outer you are a perfect match! Blessed with a strong sense of self-worth, you are also prone to sudden insecurity crashes. How to reboot? You need flattery and stacks of it. Your motto: Life's too short to be subtle. But do bear in mind that with this placement comes rabid antagonism. You're also argumentative.

Astro flash: MAD (Mutually Assured Destruction) is a geopolitical concept, not a romantic policy. Got it?

TAURUS

As an Aries, you're often hyper-boho. Screw convention. The only system you're interested in is your own Aries-archy. But Psyche in Taurus counteracts that gung-ho attitude. You like things to be done right. You need relationships to follow a prescribed path. People who don't appreciate your boundaries are quickly ousted.

What to do: Eschew tacky scenarios. Casual sex creates casual enemies. Accept your "inner straight."

GEMINI

You're flash, swank, and fickle, the playgirl/playboy of love. If someone's easy on the eye, you'll wink. You say whatever it takes to make the point du jour. People are so confounded by the complexity beneath your cultivated air of simplicity. Aries keeps no secrets—why bother? Psyche in Gemini has stacks. For inner peace you need privacy of mind, that "something stupid" go-nowhere flirtation, the frisson with someone so off limits.

Cosmic love task: Reread the fable about the goose and the gander.

CANCER

Aries is anti-nostalgia. Officially, you abhor sentiment. Everyone knows that you live in the now. So, how do you justify your Cancerian Psyche? The part of you that reveres the past, tradition, and sentimental keepsakes? No way are you going to shred those erotic love notes from yesteryear! You're torn between getting on with it and wallowing in ancient angst from some long-gone, doomed-before-it-even-began excuse for a love affair.

Hot astro hint: Always reroute that clandestine slushy emotion into the current love reality.

LEO

You are a "no frills" simple soul. The psycho-theatrics of love do not intrigue you. Like hell they don't! Eros in Leo equips you for the most lavish production of all—the pure weight of your heart—and its diva demands. Aries and you screech on about honesty. Psyche in Leo likes the mega-scene. Your entrance makes the paparazzi go wild. All eyes are upon you. Even when you're technically losing it in sensual ecstasy.

Karma drama: The specter of the Elizabeth Taylor/Richard Burton superstar relationship.

VIRGO

Bolshie Ballet? Psyche in Virgo makes Aries and you fantasize about perfect poise. You guilt yourself for saying the wrong thing, not saying anything. In an extreme self-guilting orgy you're angry at yourself for just being: Let your Aries Sun reassure Psyche in Virgo over-analysis. Yet it is also this Psyche of yours that bestows supernatural self-assurance and observational skills beyond the ken of the "average" Aries.

Cosmic love cure: Seek a second opinion for self-diagnosed personality deficits. Judge not lest you know this one!

LIBRA

You can go it alone anytime. It's a point of major pride, your core competency, and complete crap. With Psyche in Libra, you seek love's paradise. Suave as always, you go along with the general hoo-hah but your heart yearns for life lived in tandem with a truly significant other. Pretend your pretty head off but please don't undermine yourself by mixing with people who disrespect you and your not-so-secret true romance agenda.

Cosmic love mission: To avoid mixed messaging. Tame the ego ASAP. Be open to all options.

SCORPIO

The Aries you is like the nightclub of love. You're raunchy, ready to get it on, and damn the consequences. But, beyond the "shiny disco balls, late-night calls" reality, the tide of your heart is always high. Admit it. You're a romantic. Psyche in Scorpio runs so deep that you're constantly tweaking different acts—Brave New Aries and Scorp of Mystery.

Astro flash: Stop alternating between being brash in situations of bona-fide intimacy and hyper-intense when it's not appropriate. Naïvete is so non-you. The one you love arrives quietly.

SAGITTARIUS

The performance-driven Aries You wants to score at all costs, whether it be for a minute or a lifetime. It's all about Brand You and ego on the sleeve—where is the heart? Your Psyche in Sagittarius is light-in-love, able to seize the passing joy without seeking to conquer. You'll dutifully shoulder the factory worker "burden" of everyday relationship while cherishing the blissful fantasy of some fleeting attraction.

Astro love karma: To merge your romantic-escape artiste dream with an actual real-life romance. Flirt! Even as you do your tax together!

CAPRICORN

"Do what thou wilt"—you want the one you love to be happy, no matter what it takes. Non-profit yoga someplace dingy? Hmm. Maybe not. Psyche in Capricorn kicks in and so it should! Worldly, wise, and wealthy is the comfort zone of your soul. Your true love is as ambitious and on-message as you. Relaxation doesn't relax you. Only accomplishment creates the serenity you dream about. You and your soul mate scheme in harmony.

Astro nightmare to avoid: Needing a note from his/her accountant before you date.

AQUARIUS

In love you are your partner's biggest fan ever. You're utterly supportive in every respect. Except one. Sucky flattery. You love to receive it and, in fact, contrive matters to ensure that your ego is lavishly serviced twice hourly. In public, you're adoring and doting spouse-ish. Behind the scenes, you pull major "Don't you know who I am?" stunts, then quickly retiring to your "den" whenever the conversation gets too real.

Cosmic love lesson: To grasp the idea that you—lovely *you!*—may actually be emotionally dependent upon another.

PISCES

You're so straightforward, you take no crap—what you see is what you get. Or is it? Beneath that flashy Aries exterior lurks Psyche in Pisces, the most idealistic and toxically flirtatious of all! Yes, you. Own up! You love to be the off-limits object of desire almost as much as you yearn to be faithfully, slavishly adored. Whenever your love life weirds out, just know that it's you being surreal—yet again.

Astro karma: To own your own magic, to be psychically faithful, and to meet someone just like you. Fresh linen rebirths you.

If you are a Taurus...
april 21 - may 21

You're ruled by Love Goddess Venus and an official cutie-pie but, à la actress Penélope Cruz, you're "more tough than sweet." Yes, along with Goddess-given allure comes a hefty dose of grit. You're a long-haul success machine, always willing to put in the extra slog to secure your aims in life. You're dependable, physically and mentally robust, but so stubborn that your personality can verge on tyrannical. You are perhaps the ultimate marital catch. Few other Sun signs can match your combo of sensuality, devotion, and dedication to life goals.

The ick factor: You can become stuck, overly obstinate, and quite fearful of change. As Hollywood hunk George Clooney says, "Trying not to be a dick takes work."

and your Eros is in...

ARIES

You think you're so straight but you're really a flake! At least, you are the second your heart gets engaged. The Taurean You believes in The Rules. Eros in Aries says "stuff the rules—let's go there!" and you do. You'll throw over years of sensible achievement (maybe even a logical but non-fulfilling relationship) to pursue someone you met just once. Taurus values steadiness. Eros in Aries wants the zing! This so freaks you out.

Astro destiny: Long-term supportive and sensible love affair plus sexual bliss and excitement...who? Dreams tell all.

TAURUS

Both your Sun and Eros are ruled by Venus. Your luscious gorgeousness and radiantly long-term loyalty potential reels in would-be lovers like no other earthly creature. You say "hello" and they hear "I love you." You spend a lot of time quelling misconceptions about your availability. In your mind, you run forever free in some grassy pasture, holding out for the ultimate. It happens the second you get over yourself.

Celestial love lesson: The soul mate is (apparently) immune to your beauty...you bond mentally.

GEMINI

The Taurean You seeks civilized stability, the no-explanations-needed, relax-at-last comfort zone of home. But the Eros-in-Gemini You enjoys destabilizing anything that's settled. Not that you will admit to this dynamic. So, if you're home in your zone and exchange glances with the cute tradesman, the Taurean You will guilt out for days. However, Eros in Gemini *milks* it for fun and extra-teasing potential within the core love relationship.

Astro karma drama: You go for the Suit archetype but, really, you need a silver-tongued split persona à la secret you!

Soul mating

CANCER

Taurus says "just give me the facts"—the Cancerian Eros wants to know "how did you feel?" You can't fancy anyone without getting a huge blast of where they are at emotionally. It's concurrently your liability and asset. You see behind the props of macho bluster or that awkward bombshell pose. It's a blessing for true love and friendship, an immediate sop upon any form of casual flirtation.

Cosmic love lessons: Do not waste your pearls of wisdom on swines who just don't get it. Do not phone every half hour just to check that they still love you.

LEO

As a Taurus, you are the most adequate sign of all. A dependable force for stability, you don't like to make "a fuss" about anything. But your Eros in Leo demands fuss. That scene? Flared nostrils, raised perfect brows, and beautiful hair? That was not the Taurean You. It was luvvie Leo, demanding proper attention. In love, you need to seduce like a Leo and that means a little drama. No way will you be overlooked for even a moment.

Celestial solar hotness memo: Beautiful hair sets the scene. The moment is all. Vanity *is* Zen.

VIRGO

One burp and it's all off! This happens the moment you fall in love, lust or when your Eros in Virgo steps in, just to make sure that your Taurus self is not too trusting. Taurean You vibes off physical impressions (scent? gorgeousness quotient? body tone?) but your Virgoan Eros seeks sanity, decency, and productive function in society. No matter how mysterious or joyful the encounter, Eros in Virgo is there as the police officer. Yes, this can be a barrier between you and love.

Astro memo: Think discrimination—not random nitpickery.

LIBRA

You're criminally cute and, worse, cosmically hard-wired to run several lovers at once. Yes, of course you can settle down with just one but he or she would have to be extremely, er, multifaceted. The Taurus You is uni-minded and definite. Eros in Libra finds serenity by never making up his or her mind...for sure. The path of pleasure and fun lies in remaining always open to possibilities or another point of view.

Celestial love lesson: To accept that your love life is supposed to be a mental expansion trip for you!

SCORPIO

What's weird about your love life? There's drama-disdaining You, so correct and proper that you verge on pod-personage. Then there's your sensation-seeking Eros in Scorpio.

What to do: Ideally, accept that you require a certain degree of intensity and mystique in romance. Deny this longing and it blows back at you in the form of high mega-maintenance lovers. That's right. If you're dating a string of crypto-hysterical nympho compulsives, you are, in fact, attracting repressed aspects of yourself! Don't deconstruct *them*! You?

SAGITTARIUS

Being a Taurus is about certainty. But Eros in Sagittarius is a wanderlusting free spirit. Someplace in your mind is a secret island where attractive and undemanding natives worship you as God or Goddess. But, you also want Mr. or Mrs. Reliable, someone who actually gets off on your anal control-freaky to-do lists and endless crusading recommendations re food, dining room furniture, fingernails...whatever. Get a grip?

Good romance karma: Non-vocational "just because" courses of study, especially if exotic travel is involved.

Soul mating

CAPRICORN

The good news is that Taurus (your Sun sign) and Capricorn (your Eros sign) are both Earth signs and thus extremely compatible. You have little conflict between your core persona and getting-it-on character. You're strong, sexy, and hideously ambitious. Success is a huge turn-on for you along with people who are physically toned and together.

The astro weirding: You can have this compulsion to shack up with someone completely unlike you and then turn him or her into a *clone of you* via corrective nagging. Ugly.

AQUARIUS

The Taurean You is a sensual beast, renowned for insatiable libido and hardcore money-grubbing. You'll do whatever it takes to feather a secure little nest for you and yours. But Eros in Aquarius switches off sexually when in love! Yes, this can translate into a rather tedious Madonna-Whore/Prince-Bastard complex. You're unintentionally cruel, the benevolent dictator of love.

Cosmic task: Realize that lust at first sight rarely works out for you. The friendship must be allowed to form first. Hint: But don't hit on friends unless your intentions are pure.

PISCES

This cute little astro combo makes you captivating beyond reason. You are poetry in motion. Or, okay—because this is Taurus, after all—poetry slacking off on the couch. The joy of being a Taurus with Eros in Psyche is that you come across like some wild romantic, convinced that every object of your lust is the reincarnation of a past life lover (you gotta watch this!). But then, when things get real, you are fully present, sensual, and aware! You are the magical realist of love.

Astro nightmare: Dutifully sticking with someone who's inferior.

Or your Psyche is in...

ARIES

You claim to crave the peaceful life but really you're just after a good scrap! No, this does not have to be a dysfunctional dynamic. Think more that apart from the usual Taurean life mission (a comfy castle with adoring family, respectable position in society, et al) you've got an internal quest going on. You're a person of purity and such lightness can attract muddier types in early love life. You may find heart's ease via the not-so-scenic gutter detour.

Astro flash: Your soul mate is adoring but takes no crap.

TAURUS

Taurus You and your Soul sign (Psyche in Taurus) are in sweet agreement. The way you project is how you are! Your Taurean Psyche values loyalty above all else. You are a moral person, capable of cutting off another person forever, should they not live up to your ethical code. This, while admirable, can create difficulties.

Astro lesson: To not miss out on following your bliss by being overly judgmental—that is, you're a thundering bore mid-rant.

GEMINI

Congratulations! This is one of the Sun sign-Psyche sign combos most likely to drive lovers utterly bats! Not that you'd notice. You're a blend of "go hard or go home" material demands—your ideal person is successful or else—and a secretly quixotic, fickle little heart. It's like you get a banker partner and then use some of the money to fund your secret anarchist lover. That's an extreme example but, admit it! You don't *want* to be understood!

Celestial hint: Weave variety into the structure of la vie en Cow.

CANCER

Okay, so you're a hoarder and maybe your house does remind people of an ill-curated museum but you have the potential to be such a holistically together person! Just keep on talking to yourself. Not in the mad-mutterings-on-street sense but via attunement to real emotions. Taurus is prone to taking things on face value. Your Psyche sign is clairvoyant: you intuit people's hidden motivations. Access your inner druid/druidess dude!

Cosmic love secret: Your ideal lover relates to the spiritual you as well as the rest of you.

LEO

The Taurean You may be super-sensible but your Psyche in Leo is not! Taurus can say "Yes!" to a less-than-thrilling relationship paradigm, perhaps even to keep (eeek!) the peace. You can get stuck in a tedious scenario, just because it's familiar. But your Psyche sign needs to be worshipped! You will never be truly content in a lukewarm love affair...Happiness lies in honoring your Leonine Psyche's desire for glamour and beauty.

Stellar spell: Believe it or not, beautiful hair is the beginning of unfurling your Leo self.

VIRGO

Taurus is one of the most sensual signs of all and Psyche in Virgo is a successful seducer/seductress by dint of being able to zoom in on another's every personality foible. So, you're so suave in love. But the "curse" of Psyche in Virgo is that penchant for self-guilting. You judge yourself by standards you would never dream of applying to friends et al, let alone the lovers who swarm around you. It's true. Would you say to a friend who's freshly fallen in love: "What if you undress and he hates your thighs?"

Cosmic coupling: First love thyself.

LIBRA

Love me for whoever I am, dammit! One moment you want your hard slog and professionalism to be admired. Then, the next moment, you're whining about being adored in spite of it. The Taurus You finds a center and stays there. Some would say that you get *stuck* there. Psyche in Libra needs to alter his/her position several times a day. It bugs you? Imagine how it affects lovers. But, guess what? It's you. And, by trying to become too fixed, you lose something precious.

Astro flash: You're Yin-Yang, Yang-Yin, Yang-Yang, Yin...

SCORPIO

There you are, trying to get it on with Mr./Mrs. Suitable when someone so freaky but gorgeous seemingly dives into your life. It's going to keep on happening! Your Psyche in Scorpio wants more than Sun in Taurus. You want more heat, passion, and mystery. More, *more*. To honor your Scorpy Psyche, try tarot card reading, kung fu, super-modeling, deep-sea diving, advocacy work for victims of sex abuse, bodybuilding.

Cosmic love lesson: You will never be satisfied with a merely convenient liaison. It's soul mating or nothing!

SAGITTARIUS

Taurus is the most settled Sun Sign of all. Psyche in Sagittarius is restless—mentally, emotionally, and, yes (!), physically. Go too much with the Taurus aspect of yourself and you risk becoming stultified, prematurely aged, and prone to random bitchery. No matter how much in love you are, your spiritual well-being relies upon frequent escapes to the wilderness, thought leadership, and/or just the simple scoring of solo Q-time.

Astro hint: Acknowledging your independence flushes out the true pair-bonding that you need.

Soul mating

CAPRICORN

Your Sun Sign (Taurus) and your Psyche Sign of Capricorn are ultra-compatible. Your core persona and your soul are admirably in sync. Success in every area is, you feel, your birthright. And, you're so right! You tend to attract partners who can and will make you happy! And your discriminatory powers are so honed that you rarely waste precious time and energy on non-you lovers.

Possible ick factor: To be orgasmic or else. You're mega-sensual. Like it or not, sexual compatibility must be paramount for long-term satisfaction in a relationship.

AQUARIUS

Taurus is a huge fan of the status quo. Aquarius seemingly exists to stuff around with it. You're both! What to do? Some people with this fascinating combo act it out by becoming, say, a corporate lawyer who dates an anti-globalization activist. But, deep down, you know that the solution lies in being both yourself: you somehow need to fulfill your yearnings for comfort and respectability while also letting radical you express him/herself.

Astro flash: Your ideal lover is a BoBo (Bourgeois-Bohemian), just like you! You're so modern.

PISCES

The secret of being a Taurus with Psyche in Pisces? Not going too far into either paradigm. You need to be free but within boundaries. Your Taurus side flourishes via routine and money! The Pisces You rebels against societal demands. It's the part of you that wants to stay up all night wearing retro-lingerie or polka-dot pajamas, scribbling poetry, throwing the I-Ching, and contemplating the crush du jour. Taurus needs to get up at 6 a.m. to make the gym before work. You send people absolutely gaga with this kind of behavior. Lucky you're so alluring.

If you are a Gemini...

may 22 - june 21

There's two of you! Yes, you're born under the sign of the Twins. So Twin One is blithe, amusing, and always informed. Twin Two is a heartless and amoral flake. Light-hearted, easily bored, and seemingly able to process any emotion whatsoever in five minutes flat, you're the heartbreaker of the Zodiac. Some call you fickle but you go along with the Chinese sage Confucius (another Gemini) that "only the wisest and the stupidest never change." Irked as you can be by the demands of everyday love, you can be up for the unrequited romance or secret frisson that is never quite kept at an exciting boil.

and your Eros is in...

Soul mating

ARIES

It's you! You're the person people grizzle to advice columns about. You come on strong and then, wham! You've forgotten their name! Eros in Aries adores the chase and the thrill of making a maximum impact. That first falling-in-love phase is like heaven to you. But then your contradictory ("so self-aware, so full of shit") Gemini Sun kicks in. A hint of "Where were you last night?" and you go demoning off into the sunset.

Cosmic flash: Your soul mate has an even lower boredom threshold than you. He/she changes the subject before you.

TAURUS

Your Taurean Eros (lusty, robust, dependable) attracts people who are totally unlike the Gemini ideal. Your Sun in Gemini likes mind-gaming and manipulative, complicated conversations. You specialize in triple entendres and multilayered flirtations. But Eros in Taurus indicates a more traditional love nature. Those who are drawn to your steady Taurean side get a hell of a fright when they confront your "don't fence me in" Gemini self.

To do: In your rush to bedazzle the latest "victim," try not to tell more than three fibs.

GEMINI

Sun and Eros in Gemini? Do you have a social secretary simply to handle all the requests for dates? A shrink on standby to counsel the broken hearts? You are alarmingly charismatic. This combo also gives you the gift of being light-hearted in love. Laughter and wit are your turn-ons. You're able to "kiss the joy as it flies," preferring the fleeting beautiful moment to the day-in-day-out doldrums of domesticity.

Celestial love lesson: To stop exercising your skills by setting your heart on romancing monstrosities just as a challenge.

CANCER

You'll come to their emotional rescue. At least, that's how your Cancerian Eros manifests itself to potential lovers. You're so adept at talking about your feelings, intuiting the unspoken demands of your partner, ultra in touch with where you're at. Running an emotionally responsible relationship is important to you. Yeah, and then there's your Sun in Gemini side—blessed (cursed) with the lowest boredom threshold on earth and loathing any kind of interaction that is not informative or amusing.

Stellar spell: Own up to this ASAP.

LEO

Given your urbane and glossy surface gleam, nobody need ever know about your secret persona of true romantic. Yes, that's right! Your Sun in Gemini treats love as a game. Life is your laboratory and you're interested in people's drooling, practically Pavlovian responses to your gorgeousness. But Eros in Leo indicates a person who believes utterly in love. This part of you wants to swoon. So you're into both elegant detachment (Gemini) and the idea of hopeless devotion (Leo). Now you know.

Your "type": A superstar.

VIRGO

As both Gemini and Virgo are mind-centered, observational signs, you could be at risk of analyzing yourself out of love. You see everything! From that teensy white lie to the ill-dyed hair. You believe in love but insist on what you call discrimination. Would you accept that your standards are pretty extreme? You can also be at risk of letting your gregarious Gemini self embarrass your Eros in Virgo and then the Virgoan side of you overcompensates by guilting you.

What to do: Evoke the energy of Water: ocean, spa, pure emotion.

Soul mating

LIBRA

With the Sun in Gemini and Eros in Libra, you like love that takes your mind to new places. True romance is, to you, inextricably linked with the expansion of your personal horizons. Art and creativity are always close at hand when you're smitten.

Cosmic flash: You are highly likely to meet your soul mate by following some form of artistic bliss! As Gemini and Libra are such compatible signs, you have few internal conflicts.

Potential ick factor: You could be in danger of over-intellectualizing romance. Airy-fairy? Ground yourself.

SCORPIO

Your Gemini self is adept at light-hearted love. When the scenario turns turgid, your motto is "Let's move on" and you do! But the part of you that is Eros in Scorpio desires intensity and profound level communication. Gemini can take or leave love. Scorpy has the potential to be completely compulsive-obsessive about even the most casual of affairs. So you say you want to keep things casual and then call 10 times a day.

What to do: Accept that this is an officially complicated dynamic. Try not to swing wildly between the extremes.

SAGITTARIUS

Sun in Gemini with Eros in Sagittarius? You need space and stacks of it. Your ideal lover could even be in another country. Maybe he/she outdoes you by only letting you have the mobile phone number. You never get to see where they live and that suits you. Mystery and distance intrigue you big-time. You often set things up so that your relationship has automatic and frequent time apart. Your seduction style is full-on swashbuckling: You like to blow in with a blast of big ideas and political ranting and then disappear—poof!—unexpectedly.

CAPRICORN

Gemini scorns convention. Capricorn covets it. So what to do when you have Sun in Gemini and Eros in Capricorn? You get over your hobby of falling in love with people who will be psychologically tormented by your very existence. Assuming that any relationship will be a soap opera, you reserve the best roles for yourself, casting your lover as gimped authoritarian figure while you stalk around looking amazing, with everyone in love with you and your crap.

Astro karma drama: This occurs when you meet someone like you.

AQUARIUS

You're sensational, the sort of person who can change someone's life just by walking into a room and then out again. You're ultra ahead of your time, free spirited, and a natural-born individualist. Your Sun in Gemini and Eros in Aquarius synergize beautifully together. There are no major contradictions between your Core Persona and Love Drives.

Celestial love glitch: You can get too caught up in personal fabulosity to actually pair-bond. Or your relationships wind up sibling-combative, sexless "friendly" affairs.

PISCES

You don't mean to mess with people's minds—you just can't help it. Your base impulse is to beguile everyone. You do this more or less innocently but with devastating efficiency. Then, once said person is utterly enchanted, you lose interest. They ring up for a date. You say you feel stalked. Admit it. You like them to be hard to get, preferably impossible. Your Sun in Gemini is contrary and Eros in Pisces cherishes the highest, over-the-top ideals of love. Normal, everyday relating gets in the way of your fantasies.

To do: Get real.

Or your Psyche is in...

ARIES

Psyche in Aries can't help but be combative in love; it takes a special person to break through your barriers. But Sun in Gemini likes to project as carefree and light-hearted, a kind of wandering minstrel of love. So picture this: the part of you that's sparkling Gem doesn't give a damn whether a certain someone calls back or not. It's like, "whatever." But your Psyche-in-Aries self sees all romantic activity as a challenge. Getting to grips with this inner drama of yours awakens soul mating potential. Anger management?

TAURUS

Only boring people get bored and nobody has ever accused you of being boring. Infuriating, yes. Amoral? Probably. Sun in Gemini craves nonstop novelty and variety. So you upset a few mediocrities in your quest for the new...it happens. But perhaps you are repressing a vital aspect of yourself? This Psyche placement is a part of you forever, Taurus! So you do require a degree of stability. Part of your life needs to run along sensible lines.
Cosmic flash: For you, gardening is spiritual.

GEMINI

With your Sun and Psyche in Gemini, you are so multifaceted. It could even be that you're more comfortable with multiple realities! You zoom straight from the gym to cocktails without batting an eyelid. You're a multitasker, determined to extract every iota of value from each moment. So, what about love? You can be perversely drawn to people who would diss you for being so flexi-minded. You need someone as multi-everythinged as you.

CANCER

You're a hard-boiled cynic who cries during nature documentaries. Why couldn't the cameraman have done something? Gemini skims merrily across the surface of the most turgid scenario. You enlighten life with quips or amoral observations. But your Cancerian Psyche is the most sensitive of all! You're empathetic, compassionate, and often too perceptive for duller-witted people.

Cosmic tasks: To get over the idea that being a feeling person undermines your mental sophistication. Mentor the shy.

LEO

Charisma Central: you're too much for many people and this makes you happy. You'd rather fly fabulously solo than dumb down for anyone. There is something showbizzy about your love performance, sorry, love life. Blessed with the gift of living fully in the moment, carpe diem is your motto.

Karma drama: When you lose yourself in your own genius, so busy putting the spin on your latest hilarious anecdote that you do not notice your lover's eyes glazing over as he/she calculates escape options. Fear? Being upstaged.

VIRGO

Guilt, for Geminis, is an unknown emotion. You guys are cheerfully amoral, refusing to judge or to be judged. But for Psyche in Virgo, guilting is a core competency! You alternate between glib self-loving and way over-the-top neuroses about personal foibles.

Astro tip: For peace of mind, channel Virgo energies into decluttering and administrivia...not into over-analysis of your alleged defects or (worse) love life. In love, you're part easygoing (Gemini) and part Virgoan perfectionist. Ideally, you express the best aspects of both signs.

Soul mating

LIBRA

Lovely and beguiling as you no doubt are (your Psyche is ruled by Venus, the Goddess of Love and Beauty), you are an enigma...perhaps even to yourself. Never listen overly to those who would have you be more fixed in character. As a Sun Sign Gemini you're symbolized by the Twins. And your Libran Psyche tips back and forward in order to find perfect balance. You are all about making constant little adjustments to create harmony.

Astro alibi: You're not fickle. You're a flexible being, responding to the zeitgeist.

SCORPIO

Geminis just want to have fun! Psyche in Scorpio wants to reunite with a soul mate from past lives, pair-bond, and work through issues together. To Psyche in Scorpio, the relationship must be far more than the sum of its parts. Or why bother? You see love as an intense transformative experience. If it doesn't hurt, you're not doing it right. The idea of a whimsical dalliance is kryptonite to your super-person. You're not casual about anything, let alone something so important as love and sex.

To do: Lighten up ASAP. A bit?

SAGITTARIUS

Sun in Gemini and Psyche in Sagittarius? Freedom fetish! Someone asking where you were all week feels like an unacceptable space invasion. You love that feeling of nobody knowing exactly where you are. You like to see yourself as an "open book" but really you're a raving enigma, even to yourself.

Celestial love lesson: You're often so fulfilled by your own company and that of the cool people you meet on your adventures, that true love can pass you by altogether! Cultivate the gorm to be as daring emotionally.

CAPRICORN

Your Gemini self is just so flip, free-minded, and modern. Your Psyche in Capricorn mitigates against this part of yourself, adding a subtone of sober self-awareness (*très* useful for someone with the Sun in Gemini, actually) and uncommon sense. You ideally use this paradigm to create a secure foundation for your Gemini Sun to shine out from.

What could go off: This Psyche sign can be prone to undue melancholy or harsh self-carping. If this is you, engage your Gemini side to shrug and smirk "Let's move on!"

AQUARIUS

You're the space cadet of love! You like nothing better than an unknown relationship frontier to explore. Familiar terrain? It irks you. Anything which vibes a little too safe, suburban, or just plain banal has you making a few flimsy excuses and oozing out that door. There is no contradiction between your Gemini Sun and Aquarian Psyche. That's challenging in that you could live way too much in your mind.

Astro karma drama: Swept off your pretty feet by an immensely thick chic physique, you are forced to become more feeling,

PISCES

You have the Sun in Gemini and Psyche in Pisces! This combo has you highly likely to find true love via following your brilliant career bliss. It's true! It also makes you a beautiful femme/homme fatale type. You smash hearts with a tinkly little laugh. You care only for the one on your mind at that moment, until the moment he/she succumbs to your wicked wiles and becomes thus "tedious." Your fave lover is a figment of your fantasy-prone mind. Remember that both Gemini and Pisces are Twin signs. Your soul mate is scarily like you.

If you are a Cancer...
june 22 - july 23

Crabs like you (and U.S. writer Hunter S. Thompson) know that "When the going gets weird, the weird turn pro." One of the most amazing things about you is how you can totally freak out over a trivial irk yet remain calm and gracious under real pressure. Ruled by the Moon, you are empathetic, seductive, and nurturing. Nobody creates an emotional comfort zone like you guys. Off-form? Okay, you are prone to power-sulking and the invisible guilt rays you emit can poison the atmosphere for months. But mood-swinger or not, if you're in that come-hithery frame of mind, few can resist you and your great big googly bedroom eyes.

and your Eros is in...

ARIES

Your Cancerian Sun makes you a highly emotional person—the astro motto for Cancer is "I feel." But Eros in Aries counteracts your hyped feeling nature by marching up and, in effect, bellowing "I'm here now! Let's get it on!" Your manner is so brash and direct: "You want it, or not?" You freak yourself out! But fret not, it's just your Inner Ramzilla out for a romp. You're a lot less slushy than the "typical" Crab. You freak out when you sense lack of respect.

Celestial love lesson: Accept that part of yourself is a full-on philandering Don Juan/ita.

TAURUS

Sun in Cancer—Eros in Taurus? Apart from the fact that you're undoubtedly highly sexed, you have a weird astro-fate thing going on. You could well wind up dating and mating within a certain social set more than once, you understand. You have fascinating frissons with apparently platonic friends and, no, the attraction is not going to dissipate with time. This combination makes you suave in love. The two signs involved are *très* compatible and you come across as deceptively calm and sane.

Astro flash: You could give it all up for security.

GEMINI

People sometimes say that Gemini is the sign of no feelings while, of course, your Cancerian Sun is *all* about feelings. Lots of feelings. Feelings expressed eloquently at the drop of a hat. Your Eros in Gemini is the trickster of love—manipulative, elusive, and game-playing. Yes, you're all that beneath your Cancerian sensitivity so is it any wonder lovers freak out? They're busy trying to revenge-manipulate the Gemini You and then you go all guilting and emotive on them. Or you suddenly morph into a cold-hearted "Do I know you?" Gemini type.

Soul mating

CANCER

Wow! How about this? Your Sun and Eros signs match, making you a scarily empathetic and sensitive lover.

Astro karma drama: You're so psychic, you could find it tricky to distinguish where you stop and another begins. Seek solo Q-space to restore personal energies on a regular basis. Seduction-wise, you know in the first five seconds whether you and Mr./Ms. Prospective are destined to spend any time together. Oddly, for someone who is so attuned to feelings, you can sometimes be what you euphemistically refer to as the "victim" of your moods.

LEO

You're interested in emotional interplay. A sentimentalist, you consider honoring the feelings of another to be the most vital aspect of any love affair. Cool, but your Eros in Leo is something else again. It's the part of you that longs to stalk into any room, dazzling all with sheer chic, full-on repartee, and general personal hotness. An integral part of you doesn't give a damn about the emotions, unless they're part of your act. What to do: Try not screaming "Cut!" if someone's "performance" irks you or appears not to be following your plot.

VIRGO

Tradition, ceremony, and family—the combination of a Cancerian Sun with Eros in Virgo makes them vital to you. You like things to be done right. You can't for a moment warm to someone whom you disapprove of. Actually, you can't get aroused with crumbs in the bed. Your ethical standards sustain you throughout what can be a tumultuous early mating history.

Astro karma drama: You can be so-o-o attracted to those "naughty" (that is, dysfunctional) people whom you feel you ought to rescue. You do this even against their will!

LIBRA

Cancerian Sun and Libran Eros? With this placement, you may not want to even know what you're feeling. Eros in Libra cares about elegance, harmony, and eloquence. You could have no qualms suppressing any ugly or messy emotions that seem to get in the way of your *dolce vita* ideal. And yet, for true happiness, you need to feel free to gush forth emotion whenever you want. Romancing relaxes you—you're the most suave of seducers, then you give adorees a hell of a fright by unleashing your true self.

To do: Create an authentic you.

SCORPIO

Cancer and Scorpio are both Water signs so you're predominantly a Water person: creative, artistic, and comfortable with depths of emotion some might consider oceanic, overwhelming. To say that you are a true romantic is to understate the situation. Vow now to never try and conduct a love affair with someone who begrudges his/her love or tries to make out like it's casual. You deserve—and are destined for—a soul mating.

Astro flash: Being so Watery, you do need to "dry out" some of the sogginess via a dose of sanguine thought.

SAGITTARIUS

Cancerian Sun and Eros in Saggo? Hmmm. These are two of the most disparate signs of all. You're a sensitive, home-loving Cancerian but your love persona is that of wanderlusty and extroverted Sagg! If smitten, you may project a personality that is completely different from the real you. You may be a bit messed up but you sure as hell are lucky in love! Being double blessed by Jupiter and the Moon exerts a protective energy in love.

Cosmic love flash: You can be both amusing as well as emotionally with-it, did you know?

Soul mating

CAPRICORN

You go on gut instincts. Eros in Capricorn weighs up shoes (expensive?), the body (worked out), the hair (kempt?), and innumerous other little factors on the patented Capricorn Suitability Index. For example, someone mentions a little tax debt to you and the rating falls. Mum's a neurosurgeon? Up it goes again. Oh, it all sounds so harsh, but it really *is*! You can skip some sensational romantic experiences by being so hung up on the material-security reality.

Astro weirding: Eros in Cap hates that your Cancerian self is so touchy-feely. You worship competence.

AQUARIUS

Does anyone have the map to your mind? It's like a labyrinth in there. As a Sun Sign Cancerian, you're emotionally complex, *très* profound, and so-o-o sentimental. Aquarius, the sign of your Eros, signifies the Higher Mind and futuristic-thought style. This is a beautiful (and unusual) combination and you are likely *très* talented and alluring. But learning to use this scenario is akin to handling an expensive sports car. Yes, you're highly strung!

Cosmic flash: Don't ever try to do just mind or heart. It's both.

PISCES

Your Eros in Pisces makes you prone to fantasy and idealized visions of romance. Combine these two traits with that sentimental Cancerian Sun and, voila! The love machine! You consider relationships to be an art, not a science and you don't listen to a word anyone (or any article) tells you about it. Yearning for your soul mate from the second you hear your first love story, you follow your heart with fascinating results. You give excellent seasoned romantic advice.

Potential ick factor: You're a mood-swinger extraordinaire.

Or your Psyche is in...

ARIES

Drama-Queenie? Technically, Cancer (your Sun Sign) and Aries (your Psyche sign) are radically different. Cancer is ruled by the Moon while Aries comes under macho Mars. Cancer is considered one of the most feminine signs of all and Aries is traditionally masculine. But, guess what they have in common? Both signs love a good scene. Your Cancerian Sun is as moody as hell—freedom to change your mind is a prerequisite for your happiness. And Psyche in Aries enjoys clearing the air—dramatically.

TAURUS

This combo signifies one of the most accomplished seducers of all. It's not that you go around pouncing on people—you are too subtle for that. It's that they spend five seconds in your company and never want to leave. You have an innate knack of making others not just at ease, but understood like never before. You're sophisticated enough to not let on all that you've gleaned. The dark side? You can vibe possessive re your partner's other friends.

GEMINI

As a Sun sign Cancerian, you're in tune with your heart, able to recognize, articulate, and process feelings. But your Psyche in Gemini doesn't want to know. No matter how sky-high your EQ (Emotional Intelligence), there is an aspect of you that just wants to be amused. This astro energy is tricky to handle.

What to do: Don't beat up an emotion when it doesn't exist. Accept you sometimes need frivolity and to feel pleasantly shallow or flip. Humor, like honey, catches more "flies."

CANCER

Your Sun and your Psyche are both Cancerian! Happily, your core persona (the Sun) is identical to your secret soul persona as symbolized by Psyche. This placement is often linked to the ability to express emotions and thoughts via art or music.

Astro karma drama: You could feel inclined to throw your beautiful self (creative/psychic gifts and all) at someone who simply does not (and will never) get you. Don't!

Cosmic challenges: Moving on from the past graciously. Dismantling the shrine to your ex-lover.

LEO

The person with the Sun in Cancer is happy to exist quietly behind the scenes. The murmured appreciation of a grateful few are enough. You value chez you and the peaceful life. Okay, so that's part of the lovely you. But then there's your Psyche in Leo! This is the aspect of you craving the limelight, who won't leave the house without perfect hair or a full face of make-up and simply must be honored en masse, sweetie.

Cosmic lesson: To learn to love your inner diva. Hair homage is always a good start.

VIRGO

You are capable of immense compassion. You'd rather go with the emotional flow than get hung up on the details. Aha! Your Psyche sign is Virgo, the details fetishist. Do you find that, no matter how immersed in the moment you may be, part of you is forever making little lists? Or objectively analyzing the situation? That's your Psyche in Virgo and, though it is the source of so much of your genius (most people are not as observant), you must not let it cramp Cancerian flow—that is, the ability to express emotion without hyperventilating.

LIBRA

Entrepreneurial and canny as it is (and are you), your Cancerian Sun is about spontaneity of feeling. Great! But your Psyche in Libra doesn't trust that sort of thing. Libra thinks everything goes much better with stage management—that is, the right lighting, a little styling, properly rehearsed lines. You understand? So part of you just wants to emote. Another aspect of you needs things to be "done right." Your Psyche in Libra goes crazy if not acknowledged. Keep her happy via scent, flowers, body lotions.

SCORPIO

Tantalizing and elusive, you are adept at managing your love life. Psyche in Scorpio lends a certain steely strength to your Cancerian Sun, while bolstering the already-present highly refined perceptions. You are the ultimate confidante and the accuracy of your advice astounds.

Potential ick factor: You can be insanely manipulative—setting would-be lovers secret little "tests," imagining far-out conspiracies, and/or flying into a flip-out at some faux slight.

What to do: Tame psycho-dramatic tendencies ASAP.

SAGITTARIUS

As a Sun Sign Cancerian, you are preoccupied with scoring security (emotional, material, whatever). Your life is all about being in the comfort zone. But Psyche in Sagittarius screeches "Don't fence me in!" Yes, a *très* important part of you is actually quite different from the core persona aka Sun-sign you! You just want to say "Stuff it" and fly off to some beautiful secluded beach. You want to rant out opinions that aren't all about shoring up security needs and the status quo.

Astro flash: Wilderness getaways and sports will heal your soul more than you imagine.

CAPRICORN

Psyche in Capricorn adds a worldly dimension to your oft-intuitive Cancerian Sun. And it is, in fact, this mature edge that saves you from classic feelings-driven acts of idiocy such as letting your compassion lure you into a relationship with some dysfunctional vampire. Capricorn can see the creature coming a block away and takes evasive action. So, don't guilt yourself the next time you have a strong self-preservation instinct even if it does seem a bit harsh and material. Like money, for instance. It's your secret Capricorn soul looking out.

AQUARIUS

Loving those blissful bonding moments, your Cancerian Sun murmurs "Hold me" to the lover. Then you get the giggles. That's your Psyche in Aquarius kicking in. It's the part of you that feels embarrassed at intimacy and hits the roof when you can't do exactly as you please. But it is also the part of you that's avant-garde and open-minded. You may not exactly want to hang out with people in general (they get on your nerves) but, then again, you sure stick up for their rights.
Astro flash: Alternative forms of healing are lucky for you.

PISCES

Your Sun (in Cancer) and your Psyche (in Pisces) are both Water signs! So you're at home in the realms of feeling and highly likely to have artistic talent. You're also prone to passive aggression, driving the more direct types who are always so drawn to you absolutely bonkers! Ideally, you learn to express angst or rage without being totally chaotic about it. Or not? Your Psyche in Pisces adds some tolerance and broad-mindedness to your Cancerian compassion. You find it truly hard to judge and, as a result, you are Mr./Ms. Popularity.

If you are a Leo...

july 24 - august 23

"I was born with sophistication and sex appeal," boasted legendary Leo Mae West, perhaps speaking for all Lion folk. Glam, inspirational, and big-hearted, you are the performance artistes of the Zodiac. The neo-Leo life is an epic production. It may have a cast of thousands, but Leo is always the producer, director, and star. To the theatrical mindset, critics don't count. Only the applause matters. Leos don't walk into a room. They make an entrance. Their bathroom is more akin to a dressing room. They are always on stage. Off-form, our Leo is vain, pompous, and a pathological attention seeker. The astro motto for Leo is "I rule."

and your Eros is in...

ARIES

There is only one star sign as egomaniacal as Leo and that's Aries. Your syrupy charm is overwritten by the direct approach of Ramzilla. Rather than the slithering, glamourous seduction of the Leo cliché, the lines are suddenly along the lines of "Well, are we going to do this or what?" The self-regarding regality of the Leo mixed with the athletic directness of the Aries is a potent force and the result is a highly successful pouncing bounder.

To do: Forget the figure for a moment. Could your bloated ego benefit from fasting?

TAURUS

Leo loves to be the best—at everything! And Eros in Taurus just *has* to be the best in bed. Combining the Big Cat's haughty fabulosity with a ruttish Eros influence, you are a totally fascinating hybrid. The Taurus Eros could easily manifest—in Leo—as a desire to dress up for your bedroom performance, or even a willingness to commit your incredibleness to film! Taurus Eros is about the unashamed enjoyment of one's body; Leo is always thinking of hair. When they reside in one person you can expect some boudoir theater.

GEMINI

Imagine a larger-than-life, theatrically alluring creature who swans into the party and transfixes all who go there. It's you! You're beloved by everyone and warm instantly to those who attract you. This is the classic Leo pose. But add the tricky and troublesome Eros in Gemini and your MO (Modus Operandi) is about going off a lover even before anything has happened. You're all gush, hype, and compliments when the show is actually on. But, in the morning, it's like "Sorry, but do I know you?" Watch this!

Astro karma drama: Someone does it back to you!

CANCER

The temperamental star? You are a fabulous and accomplished trouper with massive lashings of self-confidence and belief in your innate amazingness. Add that to your somewhat needier Eros-in-Cancer influence and run for cover! You can't help but be tempestuous and prone to dramatic scenes. The saggy waitress (unfairly) serves the table next to you first? It's all on. Doesn't she know who you are? You're the ultimate mega-maintenance diva, combining clingy emotions with high-demand ego.

To do: Give back to "your people."

LEO

The central joke of the Eros-in-Leo love style is that everything is a show and your part in it is the star turn. This falls in with the Leo personality that demands theatricality in all that they do. Potential lovers who are shy or overly modest could be quite intimidated by double Leo you. Mind you, such a person might be mistaken for the help by our regal one. You are a person who is never really off the stage.

Your seduction-pursuit style: It can be like revisiting the signature lines from a lot of very bad movies.

VIRGO

Wow! Are your suitors in for a big surprise! Sucked in by the classic Leo glitz, hype, and dazzle, they suddenly get hit with fussbudgety Eros in Virgo! Your Leo self luxuriates in the moment of love, the sensation of mutual regard, and that gaze "held just a fraction too long" kind of stuff. Eros in Virgo notes the slight stutter, misuse of a pronoun, and gulping of wine. Can you turn Eros in Virgo off for a moment? No!

Cosmic love task: To recognize that your standards are ludicrous! Don't drop someone for having split ends!

Soul mating

LIBRA

You're so in love with yourself that any interloper from the outside (aka a romantic partner) feels like a kinky threesome. You almost get guilty about betraying yourself with another. Yet the irony of beautiful You is that you pull nonstop. The queue forms wherever you are that particular day! Your Leo charisma and Eros-in-Libra charm is irresistible to all but those who've already dated someone like you. You can keep applicants dangling for decades, too dithery or self-obsessed to give them an honest answer, unwilling to narrow options.

SCORPIO

Leos know that the show must go on. Just as long as it's their show. So what happens when a luvvie Leo has Eros in Scorpio? A great deal of intensity in romantic pursuits, a lot of toxic paranoia about how much you are divulging, and a desire to mate with one other for the rest of eternity. Eros in Scorp takes love very seriously. It adds a deeper and more profound dimension to garishly glamourous Leo You, with your serial mass-seductions and air of self-importance.

Astro flash: Could family introduce you to your true love?

SAGITTARIUS

Imagine two people who are both brassy about life. While one likes to be out flitting from one experience to another, the other person prefers to limit their adventures to locations where they are the center of attention. So it goes with you! Eros in Saggo likes crowded hours and whirlwind romances in new places. But the Leo side of the equation is far more fixed about having special space where the Leonine specialness can shine.

Astro joke: Saggo tactlessness and social gaffes are sure to puncture big Leo's pomposity.

CAPRICORN

One of the best things that can ever happen to a Leo is having something in their life that balances up the fabulosity and ego enough to make them functional. And, you've also got Eros in Capricorn! You're dazzling, talented, and sophisticated. Capricorn mops up Leo excess and adds extra discriminating savvy. You lot can allow vanity to lure you into ludicrous love affairs. For example, the octogenarian matinee idol and the late-teens showgirl. But this Eros sign keeps you strictly sane.
Most likely: To be successful and so admired.

AQUARIUS

Wondering why you find it hard relating to the suave, self-assured (up themselves) Leos of legend? Your Eros is in Aquarius, which is the opposite sign to Leo! The Big Cat loves to touch—some would even say "feel up." And, while Aquarius can't stand physical intimacy in public, Leos are socially warm. Unless they feel they are in compatible company, Aquarians are renowned for their sangfroid. Ideally, you gotta learn to love your Aquarius side. It makes you (shhhh) much more aware, cool, and progressive than the typical Leo.

PISCES

A star is born. And reborn! Every day you wake up and reinvent yourself, after taking the requisite contemplation time for tuning into the Universe, of course. Artistic talent, spiritual yearnings, and desirability are your currency in love, in everything. You're a delicately calibrated blend of other-worldly concerns and real-politik ambition. Your true love must really get both these aspects, not merely one. For example, the relationship with that yoga guru won't last if they've got nerdy hair.
Astro flash: Don't resent pragmatic reality and you'll truly shine.

Or your Psyche is in...

ARIES

What happens when the schmoozy, high-touch-factor Leo is influenced by the volatile Psyche in Aries? You should know! The Leo You loves to build consensus, to seduce agreement out of people. But your secret love nature is combative and belligerent in disagreements. In the right (crappy) mood, you can escalate anything—even a compliment—into a psycho-theatrical scene.

Astro blessing: You take your authentic star quality for granted.

TAURUS

Leo's secret nerdy side? With Psyche in Taurus, you've certainly got one. Sure, you seldom reveal it to your public but you like slothing out on the couch with a pile of carbs and a steady supply of wine to watch less-than-salubrious television. As Taurus is an Earth sign, this is literally a *très* grounding influence on Leo hubris. Stressed? Getting into the garden or any form of greenery will always calm those diva nerves.

Love weirding: You're happy with someone who loves nerdy you.

GEMINI

Leo is the king/queen of the jungle. Psyche in Gemini can't stand to be told what to do. You're so bolshie and wayward! Gemini is the sign of communicators and Leo's all about self-expression. You are a natural performer, writer, poet, or chronicler of life. You may well have a startling faculty for words and should certainly pen love letters whenever you have the chance or correct inspiration.

Your muse: A man or woman who's completely changeable. You like to be kept guessing and amused.

CANCER

Ready for the highly sentimental version of the Leo? The energy of Psyche in Cancer brings a sometimes tricky aspect to your Leo love nature. Whereas Leo likes to keep things light and showy, Psyche in Cancer is far more suited to hoarding feelings, sulking, and wanting to endlessly discuss the "Us." Luckily, if this fits with Leo's psychodrama du jour, then the desire to pick apart and analyze the relationship can be filtered very much through the luvvie Leo prism.

Astro flash: You could easily skew to ancestor-worship.

LEO

The planets align! When the outward Big Cat matches the secret inner Leo love nature, what do we get? The potential to make all relationships from marriage to casual conquests a total drama trip. Leos are showy anyway, but with Psyche in Leo the urge to bring flowers, put on a show, write poems, and pledge undying love becomes an absolute necessity.

Astro flash: Don't let anyone trample on your beautiful neo-Leo dreams! You're a natural-born creative person with the talents (and temperament!) to prove it.

VIRGO

Hmm. Your Sun in Leo likes the big picture—that part of you is only too happy just glossing over stupid details. You'll wing it on the night, trusting your own glib beauty and charisma to fill in any gaps. But Psyche in Virgo is all about the minutiae of life...and love! Your Psyche in Virgo is that insistent little voice inside of you whispering on about budgetary concerns and correct form. Yes, it drives you gaga and gets in the way of your Leonine greatness but honoring it is also the way to true fabulosity. So, next time, make sure you listen.

Soul mating

LIBRA

Sun in Leo with Psyche in Libra? You're surely an official catch. Perhaps even an official beauty? You're so Sun-Venus influenced that you've probably been sought after from an early age. Weren't you the Mr./Ms. Popularity in first grade? The issue with this placement is not coasting along on your charm! If you're a little over-smarmy, ease the sleaze!

To do: Practice following through on what you say you'll do. Leos know exactly what they want—Libra can be *très* indecisive. You ideally learn to accept this about yourself.

SCORPIO

Your Psyche in Scorpio makes you heaps deeper than the classic Leo: You're more perceptive (to the extent that you are highly likely to be psychic) and interested in alternative theories about reality. Whereas the Leo part of you is only interested in one reality. That's right, *you*. Yours. Yourself. So you're a more evolved Leo, a neo-Leo. But the problem here is that both Leo and Scorpio are what we call "Fixed" signs. You need to take extra efforts not to become stuck.

To do: Practice embracing something new each day.

SAGITTARIUS

The future is here and it looks like fun! Thus thinks your ever-optimistic and youthful Psyche in Sagittarius. You're forever youthful and in motion. With this Psyche sign and Sun combo, no matter what happens you will always be able to tune into a bubbling little fountain of hope and positivity. You could also be slightly over the top, of course. You are a highly fiery, extroverted, and gregarious person (No? Then you are repressing your Psyche sign!) and can exhaust other people.

Astro hint: Be more receptive. Lots more.

CAPRICORN

Who's the most likely to succeed then? Your Psyche in Capricorn could irk you immensely as you fret over whether or not you are rich enough, thin enough, respected enough, successful enough, and so on. But, wow! Do you make it fast! The combo of being a super-glam Sun sign Leo with Psyche in Capricorn—the most ambitious sign of all—is almost unbeatable.

Weirdo astro karma drama: Despite all the social genius and brilliant career scheming, you could have a secret thing for really unsuitable types.

AQUARIUS

Wow! Complicated or what! Leo and Aquarius are opposite signs of the Zodiac. When your Sun and Psyche signs are in opposition, you get a dynamic personal tension syndrome operating within you!

To be avoided: Stalemating. Getting too stuck at either end of the opposition. You ideally learn how to both be Leonine (outgoing, showbizzy, generous, glam) and to honor your more inner Aquarian Psyche self. How to do it? By being ahead of your time, in touch with alternate realities, and emancipated.

PISCES

Both your Sun and Psyche signs (Leo and Pisces) signify the beautiful dreamer. You are a creative soul and don't let anyone tell you otherwise. Romantic and extremely seductive, you are more than adequately equipped for love.

Astro glitch: You're *so* idealistic and the more mundane aspects of everyday loving could leave you feeling lukewarm, searching for fresh thrills or to revisit the throes of new loving. You ideally learn to make even the "dull" stuff fun and pleasurable, as opposed to mindless pleasure seeking. Also, your love of manipulations and mind games may not be as much fun for your lover.

If you are a Virgo...
august 24 - september 23

You're helpful, witty, suave, and polite. But you're also prone to what you think of as "correctional motivation"—aka nagging. You agree with fellow Virgo Leo Tolstoy (FYI: An amazing proportion of well-known writers are born under the sign of Virgo) that "true life is lived when tiny changes occur." You are a work in progress, always tweaking something or other. Your astro motto is "I analyze": You do indeed have honed powers of observation and discrimination that are ideally not turned to the Virgoan off-form traits of fuss-budgetry, guilting, and nit-pickery. You benefit immensely from a little less use of those famed critical faculties and a bit more time for reverie in your life.

and your Eros is in...

ARIES

The Sun in Virgo with Eros in Aries? Do you glow in the dark? Yes, you're a sensible and suave little Virgo, able to be taken anywhere, productive and sane and always functional. But your Arian Eros is what turns you into a love monster. Eyes lock across the room...or it's just you and Mr./Ms. Spesh who seem to get the joke and you're off. Eros in Aries is all about conquest and heat. You love to feel that buzz and, frankly, this part of you could sometimes be an embarrassment to your more straitlaced and shy Virgo Sun. But so what? The famous Aries blowhardery can annihilate that innate Virgoan modesty.

TAURUS

Both Virgo and Taurus are Earth signs, which means they are pragmatic and sensual. Oddly enough, this combo is most likely to be turned on by people utterly unlike you. You are inextricably drawn to complicated, game-playing creatures of allure but little libido. They like to mess with your hard-won Earth-sign stability. Are you over this phase yet? The only real conflict between your Virgo and Taurus side is this: Virgo is easily aroused by intelligence and likes to seduce accordingly. Taurus is purely physical...you need both brains and beauty!

GEMINI

Astro destiny: To fall in love via following your brilliant career bliss. Your soul mate could even be someone with whom you form a business. An overling? Underling? Both your Virgo Sun and Gemini Eros are ruled by Mercury, trickster of the gods and the planet-ruling intellect. So communication is absolutely vital to you. No matter how divine-looking or adoring the potential lover, if there's no mental spark between you guys you find it impossible to get even remotely interested.

Soul mating

CANCER

Your Virgo side prides itself on being logical. Your Cancerian Eros does not give a damn about logic, received opinion, or anything but its own emotions at the time. And, wow! What emotions! If you've ever wondered why, as a Virgo, you are so prone to being overwhelmed with strong feelings, here is your answer.

Astro clue that you could be neglecting your Eros: You dream of water—raging flash floods, tidal waves, torrential rain. You ideally combine that Virgo uncommon sense with Cancerian intuition and emotional intelligence.

LEO

Okay, so there's you—sensible, suave Virgo—and then there's this eccentric egomaniac that seems to emerge whenever love is involved. Virgo, meet your Eros in Leo. It's like your Sun sign wants to find out more about the person (background, parents, life goals, any addictions, etc) while Eros in Leo is rushing out to purchase airline tickets for travel to romantic places, composing love poetry or turning up at dawn to serenade the object of desire. Repressing Eros is pointless.

To do: Find ways of letting your Leo out every day.

VIRGO

Sun and Eros in Virgo! At least you don't spin people out by coming on all strong in one mode and then proving to be a completely different person. No, you're *très* clear about who and what you are. You're a perfectionista, showing the rest of us just how sexy it is to be productive and sane.

The potential ick factor? You could be over-critical of both yourself and would-be lovers. You're a double Virgo! Next time you find yourself crossing someone off your cocktail party list because of (say) their poor grammar, think again.

LIBRA

As a Sun sign Virgo, you tend to demonstrate love via being practical and helpful. For example, you remember what book someone said they wanted to read and pick it up for them. You are one of the best long-term lovers of all—familiarity actually turns you on. But romantic gesturing is not you. You often think flowers et al are cheap and tacky. Okay, but your Eros in Libra really loves all that stuff. Moonlight, gorgeous gifts of scent, red roses, cute little "I love you snookums," personalized dating rituals, and love song requests. Admit it!

SCORPIO

You're so intense! The combination of Sun in Virgo with Eros in Scorpio makes you quietly charismatic, hypnotically alluring. But not to everyone. You polarize people. They are likely to have strong reactions to you either way, you understand. Dislike? They'll ring ahead to check that you're not going to be at a party before rasping. Like? They'll adore you forever and a day, refusing to hear a word against you. Your psyched-up love and romance style freaks out the conservative Virgo You, of course...

To do: Find a suave Scorp role model.

SAGITTARIUS

Finally! The explanation you have been waiting for. Yes, you are a Virgo. But your Eros in Sagittarius is all about escape. You yearn to just do it, to just go! While your Sun in Virgo slogs away, ticking off the bills as they are paid, responding dutifully to all emails, your Saggo Eros is fantasizing about blowing all the rent money on a junket to Tahiti. While your Virgoan side feels smug and self-congratulatory about all the productivity, Sagg thinks "This is my life"...

Karma drama: You attract people who awaken Saggability.

CAPRICORN

With the Sun in Virgo and Eros in Capricorn, art is oddly important to your romantic life. Your soul mate somehow shares your cultural ideas or perhaps you even meet through a some creative pursuit? You may even admire their work. Virgo and Capricorn are intensely compatible signs so it is unlikely you have any major internal conflict going on here except that you can overdo the prerequisites for seeking Mr./Ms. Right. You automatically rule out whole tribes of people whereas you are so extended and uplifted by being more open-minded.

AQUARIUS

Sun in Virgo and Eros in Aquarius? This is so often the combo of people who are good writers or photographers, eccentrics, and alternative health converts. And you? Both Virgo and Aquarius share an interest in others and their life choices; you are bound to have a vast, eclectic bunch of friends. In love you find it almost impossible to warm up for anyone who you think of as thick or a dullard. Even in love you can be cruel should you think your lover is dumbing down for any reason. You may well be the most eccentric "dark horsie" Sun-Eros combo of all.
To do: Be more comfy with intimacy.

PISCES

Here we go! Your Sun in Virgo believes in two people in a mature relationship bonding by shared beliefs and goals. Your Eros in Pisces believes in twin souls reuniting after lifetimes spent apart. Your Sun in Virgo believes in what is in front of you such as information from trusted sources. Eros in Pisces believes in unicorns and foes. Their druid song stays on your mind. Both of these two extremes are you! You will only find true romance once you own up to your Eros in Pisces. soul mating is you!

Or your Psyche is in...

ARIES

As a Sun Sign Virgo, your core competency is modesty. You're often so unaware of your better qualities. How you manage to combine this with your martyr skills is an astrological mystery. But the Virgo vibe is ameliorated by Psyche in Aries, an influence that will not let a single achievement go unsung. This is a great combo; when Virgo feels put upon, your Aries acts as cheer squad.

To do: Accept that you've got an ego happening and buff it up!

TAURUS

Virgo and Taurus are naturally compatible signs. Your Sun in Virgo finds it easy to understand your more inner Psyche in Taurus as both are Earth signs. You are blessed with a natural-born ability to heal and nurture yourself.

Astro tip: Psyche in Taurus benefits from exposure to nature and greenery. Get thee to the wilderness without letting your Virgo side guilt you into a long hike—and just be. Or take up gardening. Virgo can over-intellectualize. Your Psyche helps you detune.

GEMINI

Did you know that Virgo is a Mutable sign? That is, you're flexi-minded and able to accept change with ease. This is what will allow you to access the gifts of your Psyche in Gemini. For you to feel at ease, life ought to be evolving. Both your Virgo Sun and Psyche in Gemini like the minutiae of life, creating and re-creating routines, lifestyles, ideas du jour. In love, what you most fear is not abandonment or being alone but boredom.

To do: Start your autobiography.

CANCER

Your Sun in Virgo values logic and streamlined systems. Your Cancerian Psyche wants to put feeling first. You could flip back and forth between the two. What to do? Ideally, you let your Virgoan self balance any emotional extremes while letting Cancerian intuition enhance the Virgo thought style. Your Psyche sign is what allows you those sudden leaps of faith and instinct.

Astro destiny: Friends are fated. It feels like you've known them before and maybe you have.

Astro flash: Soul mate comes via friends?

LEO

Psyche in Leo is the prima diva. There's a part of you that wants to make an entrance, hog the limelight, and graciously acknowledge the applause. No? You may be too immersed in your Sun-in-Virgo vibe to be in touch with your Psyche sign. Yet, it is vital (for your spiritual well-being) that you tune into your Leo aspects.

Cosmic flash: Leo rules Hair and honoring your hair reality is always the quickest way to bring out any repressed Leonine aspects of yourself. More involved? Find your voice. Have you considered singing?

VIRGO

Okay, so inner you and outer you make a perfect match. Beautiful! You are likely to especially embody the classic Virgoan attributes and be smart, witty, suave, and polite. Of course, you are also thus more at risk of being an off-form Virgo—fussbudget, a guilter, and hypochondriac. Eeek? Not at all. Fitness and nutrition are a really good way to antidote any excess of Virgo. Far better to be addicted to the gym or counting every single carbohydrate than to be in constant self-guilting mode.

Astro flash: Pisceans are good for you.

LIBRA

Between your Virgoan Sun's analytical jags and Psyche in Libra's seesawing in order to find balance, you could be a *très* deep character indeed. This combo affords a light and sparkling intellect, innate charm, and—often—dazzling beauty. Even if you are not officially an utter stunner, you project as if you are.

Celestial love lesson: Subliminal messages you give off draw a lot of people to you but the attraction may be only one way. So learn the art of the tactful brush-off. Feeling blue? Beauty treatments are Zen for you.

SCORPIO

Adaptability is—or should be—your aim in life. As a Virgo, you're able to make sense of everyday complexities and, in fact, it's one of your joys in life! But Psyche in Scorpio can become rigid about change and communication. You're a deep thinker and probably prone to clairvoyant dreams, sudden little "hunches" or even full-blown paranormal experiences. But true happiness depends on being more with-it on the mundane plane.

To do: Channel your witchy Scorpionic Psyche correctly by writing a dream journal.

SAGITTARIUS

Wow! What a bundle of cute contradictions you must be. It's like you are both Bugs Bunny and Elmer Fudd! Your Sun in Virgo feels most content within clear-cut boundaries and following a routine. Your Psyche in Sagittarius is strictly free range, chafing at any kind of prescribed style of life. You find the fullest expression of happiness by not completely upsetting that Virgoan wish list but via succumbing to spontaneity, throwing over the sensible course of action from time to time.

Astro flash: Hang out with Saggos!

CAPRICORN

An altruistic Virgo, you're motivated by self-interest at heart. Eeek? Not at all. If you have Psyche in Capricorn aligned with the Sun in Virgo, as you do, it's there for a reason. You are probably over-interested in others' lives, too ready to help out and so nice that you don't declare your own boundaries strongly enough. Psyche in Capricorn is the worldly and sophisticated part of you that says "come on" to some cadger trying to take advantage of the quiet shy Virgoan You.

Astro witchery: So-called power-dressing strengthens your soul!

AQUARIUS

Everyone wants to say they love you! But you're not listening. As a mixture of Sun in Virgo and Psyche in Aquarius, you're free-spirited, super-smart, and progressive. But, yeah, you may not be mega-comfy with intimacy. Both Virgo and Aquarius are head-oriented signs and happiest in the realms of the intellect. Your Psyche in Aquarius is just brilliant for antidoting any over-judgmental tendencies of your Virgoan Sun.

To do: Activate your Psyche sign by reading up on alternative realities, politics, cuisine.

PISCES

With Sun in Virgo and Psyche in Pisces you could feel as though an aspect of you is always whirring along to undo all your good work to date. Virgo and Pisces are astrological opposites, but guess what? They need each other. A Virgo with Psyche in Pisces is blessed. Your Virgo self is prone to overwork and self-guilting. Your Piscean Psyche is the part of you that forgives, forgets, and lets you relax. It's the "Life is good—let's party" you.

How to access it: Keep a dream journal. You could be amazed at how accurate you are.

If you are a Libran...
september 24 - october 23

You're born under the sign of the beautiful person. Ruled by Love Goddess Venus, your astro motto is "I cooperate" and, you do! You are blessed with the ability to see both sides of any equation, which is probably where you get your reputation of being indecisive and dithery from. Known for your "whim of steel," social climbing skills, and occasional hypocrisy, you are also sweet, tactful, loving, and charming. You agree with Libran great actress Sarah Bernhardt that "we must live for the few who know and appreciate us, who judge and absolve us, and for whom we have the same affection and indulgence."

and your Eros is in...

Soul mating

ARIES

You're romantically sophisticated and an elegant passive-aggressive. Timing is your particular forte. The ugly, ill-thought spontaneous outburst is not for you. Another gift of your Sun in Libra is the ability to see all aspects of a scenario. You can detach from your own ego-driven viewpoint. So how do you go with Eros in Aries? Eros is the part of you which is brash, domineering, and impulsive to the point of insanity. In courtship, you can inadvertently conceal your complexity. Do you seethe beneath that cute carapace of yours?

TAURUS

In love, Libra is light-hearted and flirtatious, a master/mistress of the seductive arts. But your Sun in Libra is enhanced by Eros in Taurus, the only other sign of the Zodiac to be ruled by Venus. So? You're blessed with supernatural sex appeal as well as possibly one of the most maddening personalities in the solar system. Your Libran Sun specializes in dithering around an apparently bedazzling array of possibilities. Eros in Taurus picks a path and bulldozes through, no matter what.
Astro flash: "Cleave to the sunnier side of doubt."

GEMINI

Both Libra and Gemini are Air signs; you're most likely sanguine, breezy, and socially progressive. In fact, you are one of the most elegantly tolerant and least judgmental of all people. You have the gift of instantly enhancing the lives (and egos) of those lucky enough to be in your orbit.
Potential ick factor: Your Libran Sun is wowed by love and happiest when living life in tandem with a beloved other. Eros in Gemini can come across as a "take it or leave it," person, thus giving off the incorrect impression that you're fine flying solo.

CANCER

Sun in Libra with a Cancerian Eros? This is officially tricky. Why? Because your Sun sign bestows on you the blessing of being cool-headed and civilized in love. You are easily able to repress uncomfortable or socially inconvenient feelings. For example, if you make a scene, it will probably be when you are looking officially fabulous. Yet your Eros is in Cancer which gives you a strong desire to simply express your emotions without even straining them through the sieve of social efficacy.

Cosmic love lesson: Not alternating between cloying and avoiding.

LEO

Your astro destiny is to be sought after and adored, to never be alone and to always be in love. Yes, that's what you get with the Sun in Libra and Eros in lusty Leo. So, what's the catch? You could be adulation addicted and selfish, unable to truly give to another. Dependability may be a challenge to you. Ditto accepting a partner when he/she is in non-snazzy mode. You find it horrendously easy to beguile other people but true contentment comes once you move beyond mere ego gratification.

Cosmic serendipity: Long-time friend could become lover.

VIRGO

As a Libran with Eros in Virgo, you probably need more solo quality time than you imagine. Your Libran self appreciates more or less nonstop company. You may even think that you are afraid to be alone. But you benefit big time from taking that space to yourself. You may need it to sort out your so-irritating contradictions. Your Libran self is a beauty lover, you have aesthetic standards that must be met for you to feel anything...but Eros in Virgo likes brains.

Astro flash: You are SO hard to please! Too hard?

LIBRA

You're a double Libran! Bossy and beautiful, you take the concept of "lifestyle" seriously. Happily, there is no conflict between your core persona and the you that is aroused the moment you're romantically turned on. As you seduce is how you are. You make love your highest priority in life. You're capable of throwing over anything or anybody to follow your romantic bliss.

Potential ick factor: You could be mad for love, letting your idealized notions of Mr./Ms. Perfect take over from tedious old reality. You could profitably look into your dream lover—are you punishing the one who loves you because of unrequited love for a figment?

SCORPIO

Sun in Libra—Eros in Scorpio: This fascinating scenario can see lovely Libran You occasionally appalled by the over-the-top antics of your Eros in Scorpio. Scorp, you understand, is the sign of sex and the occult. In love, you suddenly switch on Scorp style and come across far more intensely than your Libran self can stand. The part of you that's Scorpy likes confrontational conversations that take the participants to a new level of understanding. Libra likes to amuse, flirt, and cajole.

What to do: Bedwork de-angsts in a hurry.

SAGITTARIUS

As a Sun sign Libran, you are the mistress of metaphor, the master of euphemism. You prefer your facts polished, the airbrushed look in favor of au naturel. So, what happens the moment love gets involved? You start being all gauche and candid! Why? How? Blame your Eros in Sagittarius, the sign of utter honesty. Eros in Saggo needs complete candor in all relationships, but especially love. It so irks the Libran "dim all the lights" aspect of yourself.

Astro cliché: You're not like the others. No, really!

CAPRICORN

Both Libra and Capricorn are extremely status conscious and aesthetically driven signs. So, you're especially about image as well as ambition. You're also a natural-born entrepreneur as both your Eros and Sun are in so-called Cardinal signs. Whatever you're involved in, you wind up in charge of the whole venture. Your Eros in Capricorn is that part of you that needs to impress and be impressed before your heart can become engaged. On its own, Libra can go for charm and cuteness. Eros in Capricorn holds out for the "good catch."

AQUARIUS

Libra is the socialite, the crowd-pleaser. Aquarius is the iconoclastic maverick. Your Libran Sun is so adept at love and relationships. Eros in Aquarius isn't even sure it believes in romance. What if it's just a social construct designed to ensure mass compliance? Or something? So how come you can't stand not being in a close, simpering one-on-one relationship? Yes, if you confuse yourself, how on earth do you think you come across to others?

Astro to do: Bodywork, physicality, and sensuality solve quite a lot of mental dilemmas.

PISCES

You're the sensualist, the dreamer, the Bohemian. You're so alluring that you need to take precautions against having too many people floating around. Some kind of anti-suitor spray? Your sex appeal is ethereal and inconsistent. Both your Sun sign of Libra and your Piscean Eros are utterly changeable. You like him, you hate him but, then again, maybe not. It helps if you get to grips with your essential weirding early on. You need someone quite strong to be able to cope with your surrealism.

Astro flash: Artiste?

Or your Psyche is in...

ARIES

As a Sun sign Libran you're supposed to be harmonious and peace loving. But let's get one thing straight: Your Psyche in Aries craves a good scrap. You're far more competitive and hyped than you may be letting on. Sports and martial arts are a wonderful way to express your Psyche sign. If this energy is not channeled healthily, it can turn into random spite or restless ambiguity.

Cosmic flash: It's lucky for you to be a "woman's woman." Or a man who understands them. Never reject the female side.

TAURUS

So your Sun sign (Libra) and your Psyche sign (Taurus) are both ruled by Venus. You're attractive and aesthetically gifted. No doubt chez you is a haven of beauty and tranquility. You're sweet and sought after. But, guess what? Beneath all that niceness lurks a tyrant! For this combo to bring you happiness, you need to make constant little adjustments to expectations. Relying overly on your winsome ways to score needs ultimately disappoints.

GEMINI

Astro flash: Accept right now that you're so-o-o fickle! Or, as we prefer to put it, flexible and free thinking. With Sun in Libra and Psyche in Gemini, your spirit is modern. You don't like being limited by anything or anybody. You need total liberation. You may attract people who want to dominate your mind and push their (prejudiced?) point of view but that's just your little karmic challenge. They're not meant for you. Your soul mate is someone so much like you! Perhaps they even come across like a twin.

CANCER

Libra will be ruthless about getting rid of anyone or anything she/he does not think is appropriate. For example, that dingy sofa and who cares if it's a family heirloom? Or the friend who's gone a bit "off" of late. But Psyche in Cancer represents another aspect of you: You're also a sentimentalist. You need time and space to wallow in emotion, to be maudlin about Cousin Thing or to trawl through old love letters, mooning about the one who got away.

To do: Don't freak out at this part of yourself. Go with it. Just do it in chic Libran style!

LEO

With Psyche in Leo, part of you definitely needs to perform. Your Sun in Libra may be able to turn over his/her share of the limelight to another but your Leonine aspect simply can't. You are naturally charismatic and able to bedazzle.

Astro weirding: No matter what the temptation, you must never forsake your friends for the lover. To get in touch with your Psyche sign you could try acting, painting, dancing, singing, writing children's stories, and/or just dressing up and theatrically enjoying life. Camp it up!

VIRGO

Psyche in Virgo need not be the "skeleton in the closet" of your gorgeous Libran house. But it can sure feel like it from time to time. As a Sun sign Libra you are above petty morality and stupid judgments. You're elegant, self-assured, and cosmopolitan in outlook. But your Virgoan Psyche leaps up at the oddest times to bug you with nitpicking little concerns. You suddenly wonder whether you are shallow...or decadent? It's Psyche in Virgo that gives you your discrimination and observational skills. Channel it via compulsive cleaning and beautifying.

Soul mating

LIBRA

Sun and Psyche in Libra make you a beguiling creature. You are also inclined toward harmony and must avoid those psychodramatic on-off-on-again love affairs at all costs.

Astro destiny: If other factors in your horoscope do not contradict, you are fated for one major soul mate whom you will probably meet early in life. You need peace in love. Don't let other types of people convince you otherwise. When you're feeling out of sorts, honor your Psyche sign via various forms of physical alignment, such as yoga or Pilates.

SCORPIO

Your Sun in Libra likes the light touch. You don't like being bogged down with anything too heavy or intense. But, ha ha! You've got Psyche in Scorpio creating an emotional need for full-on relating. You really want to go there in conversations and intimate encounters, brassing off your Libran self immensely.

What to do: You are probably smart enough to gradually create your social circle of friends so that it is full of people who are similar to yourself. That way you get depth but without any horrid coarseness of perception.

SAGITTARIUS

Psyche in Saggo needs space and lots of it. This part of you would cheerfully leap on a mystery destination flight, go extreme camping, or hang out on one of those solo-in-the-wilderness kind of journeys. However, your Libran Sun thinks not. That's the version of you that loves luxury and enjoys entertaining like-minded people. But, true happiness really comes from honoring your Psyche sign and so you ideally find some way to express your inner adventurer/adventuress...

Cosmic flash: Your soul mate could be wanderlusty or foreign.

CAPRICORN

My dear! This can be a tough combination! Vow now to stop being so hard on yourself. Yes, you tend to carp at yourself, applying those ludicrously high standards and feeling sad when you (and nearly everyone else) falls short. For astro reasons too complicated to go into here, any angst of yours is actually best healed via you feathering your nest. Home as a true expression of your creativity becomes a source of comfort. You are also blessed with extrasensory powers of aesthetic style and harmony.

Astro flash: Style heals.

AQUARIUS

Psyche in Aquarius is the most provocative of all. Feeling free to express your maverick leanings is a prerequisite for you feeling comfortable in the world. Yet your Sun in Libra wants only peace and concord. You officially would never say anything to offend so you are naturally confused when you come out with the oddest statement. Blame your Psyche sign and remember that you can avoid such sudden manifestations by channeling it into keeping a journal, getting involved in politics, eco issues, or taking up philosophy. Accept that you're so-o-o complicated!

PISCES

Melodramatic? You? Well, maybe just a little bit. You do, after all, have needs—and requirements. There is a little touch of the 19th century grand diva in you. Like them, you are keen on cultivating your talents and perceptions. You believe in "singing for your supper"—that is, being always amusing and giving in a social sense. You could even change clothes 10 times a day and prefer to stay up late and sleep until noon. You are a huge believer in true romance and heaven help the person who comes between you and your illusions.

If you are a Scorpio…

october 24 - november 22

"Oh Lord, give me chastity and continence but not yet," prayed the Scorpio Saint Augustine in classic Scorpy mode. Your astro motto is "I desire" and you certainly do. You're governed by Pluto, the planet of transformation. Your symbol is the Scorpion but it could just as easily be the perpetually reborn phoenix bird. You're sexy, strong, and inscrutable. You make fabulous friends but the most foul enemies of all. Yes, you can be a tad obsessive and grudge-bearing. You are most renowned for your intensity. You don't take anything casually. You agree with the Scorpio military man General George S. Patton who said, "Do your damndest in an ostentatious manner all the time."

and your Eros is in…

ARIES

Great! You like to come across as some kind of stealth bomber of love. On one hand, you're all Scorpy-smoldering sexuality and into weird—apparently never to be answered—questions and then there's your Eros in Scorpio, who is a kind of Don Quixote of love. This part of you gallops around tilting at windmills, completely freaking out the locals. You can blame your Eros in Aries for those sudden gauche announcements you make when you're in "courtship" mode. But, you know what? You also have your Aries side to thank for your childlike belief in the power of love.

TAURUS

Scorpio (your Sun) and Taurus (your Eros) are astro opposites. Not that you'd care. But it does create within you a kind of dynamic tension which adds to your charisma (good) and to your stress levels (not so good). Your Scorpio Sun gives you a need to look beneath the surface, to understand the workings of almost everything. You're a metaphysical kind of a person. But Eros in Taurus projects in a far more straightforward manner and you could attract people who are not your kind at all.

To do: Tweak your public persona.

GEMINI

Sun in Scorpio with Eros in Gemini? You must surely have chosen this set-up—in one of those karmic deals we all apparently strike—in order to teach yourself some important lesson. But what? Your Sun in Scorpio makes you a mysterious and secretive person. You like to be inscrutable. It takes years to get to know you. Eros in Gemini is out there. It's the part of you that will say anything, just for effect. Scorp is deep. Gemini is shallow. Your first romantic challenge is to better bond with yourself.

Astro flash: Love is more of a buzz when you can lighten up.

Soul mating

CANCER

Scorpio and Cancer are both of the Water element, two of the most compatible signs of all. This means, happily, that there is little conflict between your core persona and the you activated when in love, or lust. You are so adept with emotions—perceiving them, feeling them, expressing them—that you could scare off the less emotionally intelligent. You ideally learn how to gauge where another is at. That is, you become more strategic (but not manipulative) with your feelings. Astro flash: Two philosophers in love.

LEO

You transfix people! That sexy Scorpionic gaze. The regal Leo presence. Do you even have to do anything to attract people? Or do you just sit there spider-like and wait for your "prey" to meander into your web? This is a fascinating combo.

The potential ick factor: You could be overly keen to impress people and perhaps omit the bit where you ask about them? If the ego is in cruise control, you're a loyal and devoted lover.

Cosmic love flash: Image is a spiritual issue to you, not a matter of political correctness.

VIRGO

Left to your own devices, you can be a bit taciturn. Your desire to project mystery may actually manifest as someone who seems to be a bit glum. That's the Sun in Scorpio for you. So thank heavens for your Virgoan Eros, the storyteller, gossip, and info-broker of the Zodiac. This side of you prefers to seduce via mental communion. It's a useful antidote to the Scorpy silent treatment. But the "Scorpio with feeling" side of you serves to deepen the sometimes overly rational Virgo Eros. In love: You love the mutual "shrinking" style of relationship.

LIBRA

Scorpio wants intense rapport. Your idea of a fun conversation is drilling right down to the important stuff. For example, the new world order and saving the planet. Libra likes to cajole and charm. In love, you go a bit Libran and project as light-hearted, gloriously shallow, and perhaps even slightly faux. Then, as someone gets to know the "real you," they get blasted with the full force of Scorpionic passion, paranoia, and conspiracy theories.

Astro ick potential: Don't succumb to any hermit urges. Love really *is* like oxygen to you.

SCORPIO

Sun and Eros in Scorpio? You could be like something out of a silent movie, all googly eyes, Cupid-bowed lips, and yearning writhing. With this combination you probably only have two speeds in relationships. You either don't give a damn—in which case you can't be bothered even registering a person's presence on earth. The other reaction is that you are extraordinarily in love, realizing that this is one of the most significant relationships of your life, if not *the* one.

Astro resolution: Don't even bother pretending to have casual dalliances. They won't work.

SAGITTARIUS

For reasons you may not fully understand—yet—you can project a completely different persona in romance. Imagine this. Here you are, a sexy and deep-thinking Scorpio, and yet one hint of lust, love, or even like and you turn all Saggo, vibing sporty, light-hearted, and generally gung-ho. You could find yourself gabbing away at a million miles an hour, making faux pas all over the place, eagerly nodding "yes" to spontaneous away trips when normally you like to thoroughly investigate the terrain or person. It's Eros in Sagg. It's you, too!

Soul mating

CAPRICORN

So how come so many of your romance scenarios resemble daytime television drama? You're possibly a super control-freak! Chic (or suave), empowered with a brilliant career and determined never to show a single shred of weakness. Both your Sun and Eros signs are intense and obsessed with relationship real politik. Luckily, you scare off all but your true psycho peers, your twin souls who want to enjoy a spot of power-struggling with you.

Astro hint: Never get involved with someone weaker or overly needy. They'll wind up running you!

AQUARIUS

As a Sun sign Scorpio, you're very deep and obsessed with meaning and perhaps a little overly interested in conspiracy theories. And your Eros in Aquarius is surprisingly similar! Yet there is one major difference. Aquarius shies away from intimacy. Scorpio needs to sense it for the conversation to even get going. You have myriad "tests" that you run before allowing rapport to boot up. So, once you're attracted to someone, your Eros takes over and creates an impression of you that is quite different from your wildly emotive Scorp self.

PISCES

Your combination of Eros in Pisces and Sun in Scorpio reels in would-be lovers like nothing else on this planet. It's like you can zoom into someone else's mind and say what needs to be said for maximum impact. You're fabulous at creating instant intimacy. People meet you for just five minutes and already you've got your own little "us" jokes going. And, of course, you are horrendously attractive. The Eros in Pisces adds a lighter touch to your famed Scorpy intensity.

Potential ick factor: You giving off falsely flirty signals.

Or your Psyche is in...

ARIES

Your Sun in Scorpio is so subtle and cunning. Your Psyche in Aries is anything but! Remembering that we should honor our Psyche sign for psychological well-being, what are you supposed to do? Kickboxing? Basketball? Debating? Synchronized swimming? Karaoke competitions? Yes, that's right. All or any of the above will do to give your Arian Psyche a healthy outlet. If not? You seethe away, becoming competitive in inappropriate situations of intimacy.

TAURUS

Scorpio and Taurus are opposite signs of the Zodiac so going with your Psyche in Taurus will make you feel more balanced and real. It will actually enhance your Scorpionic Sun. You have an aspect of yourself that is simple where your Scorpy self is complex. You ideally learn to relax and realize that some scenarios do, in fact, have *très* obvious solutions. As Taurus is the sign of the Earth Angel, you will find any form of gardening (don't roll your eyes) to be cathartic, thought-provoking, and relaxing.

GEMINI

Your Scorpio Sun is Fixed. Psyche in Gemini is Mutable. The Sun in Scorpio likes to drill down deep into any issue. Glib Gemini gleans just as much meaning from skimming across the surface. It is as if you need to send constant memos between these disparate parts of yourself. But the effort is so worth it. Your Psyche in Gemini needs the anchoring effects of your Sun sign but your Scorpio aspects so benefit from the no-hassle insights of the Psyche.

Vow now: Have whole days when you just dabble.

Soul mating

CANCER

Your Sun and Psyche signs are so compatible. You must surely find it fairly easy to gain peace and clarity.

Astro destiny: Maybe you feel bizarrely drawn to another country? As a child, did you experience a special connection to another place or its people? You are hugely likely to be psychic and your feelings about where others are at will aid you and them. But this may certainly hinder your love life as you doubt your sensitivity—and even beauty!—and find yourself drawn to lovers who will make it go underground.

LEO

As a Scorpio, you are naturally shy and a creature of mystery. You can take years to reveal some hidden talent of yours—or that you once had your own television show or whatever. It's part of that Scorpio mystique. But with your Psyche in performance-artiste Leo, the game is up! You need to be more of a luvvie for your own psycho well-being. It's astro prescribed. Getting over your inhibitions in this regard will enhance every aspect of your life. Which talent have you been nurturing in secret? What skill have you been ignoring or refusing to talk about? It's time!

VIRGO

Believe it or not, your combination of Sun and Psyche signs finds bliss via massive household-filth purges. You're successful at whatever you set your mind to—corporate sharkery, surfing, global enterprise—but for true fulfillment, cleaning, administrivia, and general Tao of organizing activities are the go for you. What to beware of? Nitpicking and guilting. You could be far too prone to holding a grudge.

Astro destiny flash: Quite apart from romantic love, a close friend is likely to be a special soul mate of yours.

LIBRA

Your Sun in Scorpio often likes to see itself as ruggedly individualist. Deep down, you don't need anybody, let alone their stupid opinion. So it can be difficult for you to assimilate your Psyche in Libra. This is an astro energy that truly cares about what other people think and likes to be surrounded by them, well, always. And expressing your Psyche is vital for holistic fabulosity.

Think it through: Isn't it true that there's always been an aspect of you who's a person who needs people? Opening up to others can be an amazingly rewarding experience for you.

SCORPIO

With both your Sun and Psyche in Scorpio, you probably have a decent understanding of yourself and your motivations. You would also be highly tuned in to the not-so-secret (to you, anyway) thoughts of other people. From an early age you realize that you can't just switch off this flow of insights. Your big astro challenge: to learn how to separate the incoming (other people's stuff) from your own emotions and ideas.

Astro flash: Don't allow less profound types to talk you into disowning your truth.

SAGITTARIUS

As a Sun sign Scorpio, you could be slightly irked by your Psyche in Sagg. You are strategic and are able to hold back the gush of conversation in order to get what you want. However, the Psyche-in-Sagg side of you just says "whatever." Yes, there is an important part of you that needs to be able to say whatever you feel like, however you feel like it and whenever it works for you, without having to process the emotion behind it or think through whether or not it's appropriate.

Astro karma drama: Learning to love your inner "parrot."

Soul mating

CAPRICORN

You're the It Person of whatever your scene is but, boy, do you know how to burn out your brain cells with over-achievement. Scorpio is, of course, the sign of compulsive-obsessive ambition and so is Capricorn! It's great should you be trying to put in untold slog to achieve some awesome, rarely attained end—that is, beating the world record for shot-put—but tricky when it comes to relaxing and going to sleep at night. Or maybe you don't? Psyche in Cap can find staying up all night to brainstorm brilliant career schemes more relaxing.

AQUARIUS

Both Scorpio and Aquarius are so-called Fixed signs. You can find it so easy to become stuck in one attitude or persona. Yet your Aquarian Psyche finds peace and harmony via looking into ideas that challenge you. You can always heal angst by investigating a whole new tangent of thought. This is often the combo of the beautiful loner—no matter how crowded your life, part of you feels essentially alone. In love, you tend to extremes. You're either single for seemingly ever or happily married at a *très* young age. It's like there is Scorpy You—the last of the red-hot lovers, even if it is just in your lunchtime and the Ice Maiden within.

PISCES

Psyche in Pisces is the Prince/Princess position, a nice blend with your Scorpio Sun. As a double Water sign, you are powerfully intuitive and creative. Love often follows from some creative endeavor of yours or, weirder, via another lover! Psyche in Pisces requires that you take frequent little mental breaks, swimming away from the usual haunts so that you can tune in to other realities. Of all people, you are the most aware that there are weirder forces in the world than we imagine.

If you are a Sagittarius...
november 23 - december 21

Spunky, fun-loving, and incorrigibly candid, you can also be self-centered and irresponsible. You're renowned for "foot in mouth" disease, often leaving behind a wake of people gasping "Did she say that?" You are also the great escape artiste of the Zodiac, a traveler and adventurer through life. This can also have its drawbacks. Like Saggo cartoon genius Charles Schultz, you think that "no problem is so formidable that you can't walk away from it." In love you demand—and dish out in return—an exceptional combo of space and loyalty. Your ultimate Saggo advice for life comes from British playwright Noël Coward who said: "You've got to look after your legend."

and your Eros is in...

Soul mating

ARIES

Easy-peasy! Sagittarius and Aries are probably the two most similar signs of all! Both are gregarious, extroverted, and non-interested in tedium no matter what the societal rewards. Some call it tactlessness but both signs are also proud of telling it like it is. So your Eros in Aries enhances your Sun in Sagittarius, making you even more charismatic (and bombastic) than you already are. Yes, you are a double Fire sign with the sunny persona and the heat to prove it.

Astro flash: The art of listening may be your greatest achievement.

TAURUS

Astro destiny: Work and well-being somehow play an interesting role in your love life! You meet your soul mate on the day job? At the gym? Wait and see. Okay so you are a Sun sign Sagittarius, totally into freedom for yourself and everyone else. What of this Eros in Taurus? It means you could come across in love quite unlike the way you truly are. Partners get a hell of a fright when you suddenly announce—in typical Sagg style—that you've thrown in the stupid job and are heading off to South America to be a tennis coach for a year.

GEMINI

Gemini and Sagittarius are opposite signs of the Zodiac. Your Eros in Gemini makes you even more fascinating than the "typical" Saggo! You're charming and entertaining, possibly the ultimate raconteur. So why do you wind up somehow psychologically tormenting so many would-be adorees? The Gemini You is prone to telling a few little white lies. It's just for entertainment's sake, you understand. However, this is totally at odds with your core—and so candid—Sagg personality.

Cosmic flash: You are the ultimate requirer of space.

CANCER

Sun in Sagittarius and Eros in Cancer! You're an odd bird all right but nobody cares because you're so quirky and cute. The Sun in Saggo, as you know, is all about speed, cheek, and freedom. You've got a personality that's a bit like that of the Road Runner too. However, your Eros in Cancer means you get one whiff of love and, suddenly, you come over all emotional! Your feelings flow. The one thing you and your Eros have in common is that both Sagg and Cancer are honest signs...but you just can't bear how clingy you become in relationships. Accept it ASAP.

LEO

You're a glamour queen/king! Your Saggo Sun combines brilliantly with this Eros in Leo to produce a proud, gorgeous, and fun-loving monster of ego. In love, you go all out to impress, and you do! Nobody is as full on as you on your day...or night.

The potential ick factor: You may not know how to listen to another person. You could get so wound up in your performance that you don't notice the "audience" quietly snoozing off behind that dutifully attentive air.

Vow now: To work on this. Give back to your fan club.

VIRGO

Eros in Virgo is the seducer via detail. For example, "I love that tie," "I really admire what you did today in the boardroom," and so on. Nothing escapes the googly bedroom eyes of Eros in Virgo. Okay, so what happens when your Saggo self—the big picture, don't bother with the minutiae, it's the forest, not the trees—emerges? You so often have this interesting romance destiny of meeting your partners literally on the job. Eros in Virgo can even insist on employing his/her former lovers which brings with it all kinds of interesting complications.

LIBRA

Your ideal love persona is that of best friends doing everything exciting together. You have this blissful idealized-companion thing going on in your mind. Sagittarius loves the idea of a buddy for life with sex thrown in and your Eros in Libra is the most likely Eros of all to want pair-bonding. Yet you can freak out at the slightest hint of dissent. For all your talk about honesty, you can't hack authentic emotional expression. Astro flash: One person—your true lover—arrives for extended education on the issue du jour.

SCORPIO

Does your Eros in Scorpio wanna write a check that your Sun in Sagittarius can't cash? Your Eros sign adds a deeper dimension to your beautiful Saggo persona and certainly a sexier vibe. You are more sensitive and emotionally aware than the "average" Sagittarius. And yet you could inadvertently lead people on by being so intense and also, ultimately, because you are a Sagittarius, the relationship you want is less fraught, more fun, and companionable. You make Water signs (Pisces, Cancerians, Scorpios) go really gaga.

SAGITTARIUS

Okay, so you win some kind of award for honesty in love. You can't help but be authentic. With Eros and the Sun in Sagittarius, nobody is going to be in a moment's doubt about where they stand with you. Your seduction style is more of a nonstop monologue rant, complete with an built-in CV and a summary of the latest jokes. Amazingly, you can pull in the prospective partners.

Cosmic love lesson: To slow it down, take a deep breath and tune into what other people are trying to tell you.

Astro cliché: You can run and hide.

CAPRICORN

As a Sagittarius you are worry-free and liberated. You certainly don't give a crap for pompous drivel and other people's ideas of what constitutes a good life. Respectability? Whatever. You make up your own rules. But with Eros in Capricorn, part of you is seriously turned on by success and even power-mongering. You do get more interested in people if you think they've got it together in the material-security stakes and you're not totally unmoved by the idea of having piles of money. Can you be an honest enough Sagg enough to admit this aspect of your character?

AQUARIUS

Sun in Sagittarius and Eros in Aquarius? You are utterly without artifice. Your sweet authenticity disarms even the most game-playing of would-be lovers. But that's not to say that you are not complicated. You just prefer to deal with it yourself, rather than foisting it onto others. Humor is one of your many saving graces, along with a catch-me-if-you-can and hard-to-get kind of appeal. You're so naturally independent and amazing that you never have to play any idiot games. Look out for those psychic vampires who try to drain your independence.

PISCES

Welcome to the Wilding! You're untamable, completely alluring—the sexy beast of civilized romance. You are so easily bored that, if you are to find long-term love, you essentially need someone as changeable and practically feral as you. You're a surrealist and a big schemer. You are immensely candid in some areas (only when it suits you) and an amazingly good fibber in others—once again, only when it suits you. Nobody leaves behind a bigger selection of broken hearts than you but, somehow, you turn the whole thing around to you being the victim.

Or your Psyche is in...

ARIES

All you want is a room of your own. Or maybe an island of your own. It'll need lots of space for you and your ego. You believe in true romance but only with the person you consider good enough to mate with the Great You. This paragon may take time to find but that won't stop you practicing on lesser beings in the meantime.

The challenge: You find spiritual peace through ranting on about yourself but who will listen? Money, beauty, and/or being good in bed help your romantic cause immensely.

TAURUS

Psyche in Taurus blends nicely with your Sun in Sagittarius. Both signs are nature lovers though Taurus can prefer the wilderness slightly more manicured than does the Saggo side of you. You find your tranquility and heart's ease by being close to the green, and also by slowing down the Saggo speed-racer mentality and embracing the Taurean sloth ethos. You realize there is nothing wrong with a night (a week?) spent on the couch. Ditto, you enter the comfort zone via gourmet foodie experiences. So non-Sagg.

GEMINI

Your Saggo Sun likes to make big statements about everything. But the well-being of your Psyche relies on bolstering your soapbox pedestal experience with Gemini-style trivia, apparently useless facts, and gossip. Whenever you are feeling down, the gleaning and brokering of info will always feel healing. In relationships, a talk about something seemingly inconsequential often works better for you than the big official "us" chat.

CANCER

Astro destiny: It's amazing how a seemingly tedious obligation, something to do with debt or in-laws or a former lover, will bring you closer to a profound and significant life scenario. But this combination is also about owning up to deeper emotional realities beneath the Saggo bluster. Your famed candor should extend beyond tactlessness and into admitting a few feelings. With your Cancerian Psyche you find that the sharing (that's as in you and someone else relating, not just you raving on to a not-so-rapt audience) can be just so healing.

LEO

Your Sun in Sagittarius is an adventurer/adventuress. You may dislike staying in one place for too long and sometimes you even have issues about creating a permanent home base for yourself. However, Psyche in Leo demands a firm center for genius to best flourish. Yes, genius. This Psyche sign is all about the nurturing and developing of your talent. Psychic peace comes through this process, whether it be stand-up comedy, writing stories for children or photography. You can't run away from it.

VIRGO

Psyche in Virgo is that insistent little inner voice of the nagging cavalier saying, "Sagittarius You, have you taken your vitamins, today? Do you really want to take this trip instead of paying your credit card by the due date? Isn't that outfit too young for you?" Eeek! But this Psyche sign provides a valuable brake for some of your more extreme Saggo "path of excess leads to the palace of wisdom" moments. You're more discriminating, employable, and (yes!) classy than the "average" Saggo. Owning up to control-freaky tendencies makes Pysche in Virgo more appealing.

Astro flash: You're in denial about being fussbudgety in love.

LIBRA

You believe fully in free love but you want the one you love to be by your side, all the time...except for when you suddenly need space that second and your partner is expected to vacate the premises, leaving you with all his/her money, of course. Psyche in Libra can be easily evoked and pampered via aesthetic surroundings (unlike many a Sagg, who is spiritually allergic to tackiness) and the day spa reality.

Astro challenge: To learn how to afford others the same privileges you so sweetly demand for yourself.

SCORPIO

The combination of Sun in Sagittarius and Psyche in Scorpio? You're highly sexed and mega-spiritual! No way are you going to give up either aspect of yourself—for example, by becoming a celibate yoga guru—because you are also someone who crusades on the having-it-all cause. You are a fascinating blend of extroverted blunder-puss and mysterious traveler through life. Always remember that Psyche in Scorpio needs to be acknowledged. You are naturally drawn to studies in psychology, the occult, and religion.

SAGITTARIUS

Restless and ambiguous about every aspect of your life, you aim to be forever evolving. Both your Sun and Psyche in Saggo need fresh air, new horizons, and the freedom to change your mind whenever you feel like it. In love? You seek someone who will let you be you, even if you being you does involve a cast of hundreds—friends, other lovers, traveling companions, your osteopath—and, guess what? Such a person is almost impossible to find.

To avoid: Hooking up with someone who is inferior and then making their life a misery.

CAPRICORN

Your Psyche in Capricorn makes you a lot more security-conscious than the classic Sagittarius! You have a higher chance of being able to fund all your Saggo navel-gazing, sports activities, and travel. You have the enviable knack of fitting into systems and then subtly subverting the paradigm so that you get precisely what you want. Mediocrities loathe you. They watch you strutting out of the office early to go surfing or for a ski weekend. You have your work all done, the client is in love with you, and they wonder how you do it! Not even you know!

AQUARIUS

Both your Sagittarius Sun and Psyche in Aquarius can have a few issues with intimacy. It's not that you can't fake it if you need to but your base attitude is along the lines of "Why bother?" However, you tend to attract high-maintenance lovers with intense demands for reassurance and closeness.

What to do: You ideally recognize that these people (they will quite often be Water signs—Cancer, Pisces, Scorpio) are drawn to you for a spiritual reason. Yes, they're there to ensure that you actually get a life and have a heart.

PISCES

Astro challenge: Psyche in Pisces means you need to go against Saggo wanderlusty instincts and create a beautiful base camp situation for yourself. Nest-feathering will always make you happy at heart. This is an amazing blend of two individualista signs. You're utterly original and unable to be tamed. Yet, like some strange wild unicorn creature, you allow yourself to be a doting idiot for love with just a few people. Others can ask you the time and you hit the roof about commitment, encroachments upon your precious privacy, etc.

If you are a Capricorn...
december 22 - january 20

You're sophisticated, loyal and know how to commit to someone. In love—as in business—there is no fickleness in the Goat. You're a highly focused, upwardly mobile person who sees mating activity in similar terms. From the outside, you can seem rigid, suited to corporations, and government. But in your relationships, your sign often attracts someone very different to you: It is not unusual for the Goat lawyer to marry the artist or the writer. Your greatest assets? A physiognomy that defies age: You look younger as you get older. But, above all, Caps lure lovers with their get-ahead personalities. Or, as Capricorn billionaire Howard Hughes put it, "success is the best deodorant."

and your Eros is in...

ARIES

Fire and ice? When a Capricorn has Eros in Aries, it is either the bane of their life or their saving grace. Capricorn is symbolized by the Goat—tenacious, loyal, and solid as a rock. Nothing gets between them and their precious status, which can make them seem cold. This personality is turned on its head when their love nature is ruled by Eros in Aries. This is a fiery, passionate, and physically driven energy. It's impulsive and hair-triggered and can lead Capricorn into many regrettable couplings. The ideal way to handle this? Keep your loving in the bedroom and your money in the bank. In other words, allow Aries to rule your Eros but quarantine that mad-dash energy from your fiscal energy.

TAURUS

Love out of focus? For the highly driven Capricorn, having Eros in Taurus is likely to feel confusing. The Goat is about scaling the mountain—it's about endeavor, and the love nature follows this. But the Cow is a grazer of lush pastures and an enjoyer of effortless rounds of seduction, sex, and romance. Eros in Taurus means you're a natural and potential lovers feel this very strongly about the Taurean energy. For Caps it could be a fillip if they can just unbutton a little and go with it.

GEMINI

Capricorns may like to put a bit of effort into thinking how to handle their love nature. Their Sun sign is organized, trustworthy, and a person who can be relied upon to follow through on promises. But their love lives may clash with this if they have Eros in Gemini. Not to put it too daintily, the Eros in Gem energy can be heavily themed in favor of fibs, fickleness, and flirting. Gems love the sparkle and the laughter—getting them to an altar may trigger issues. Worth thinking this over.

CANCER

Capricorns with Eros in Cancer may have the perfect approach to their relationships. On an outward level, the Goat Person is reliable, ambitious, and loyal. But adding this to the Eros in Cancer energy brings a whole new dimension of nurturing and empathy into the relationship. It is a wonderful mixture that balances the Capricorn drive for success with an instinctive sense of how to love and how to parent. It means you can be hard in the boardroom and soft in the home. The only drawback? Eros in Cancer comes with a walloping great temper.

LEO

What do you get when you cross a corporate Titan-in-training with someone whose falling-in-love extravaganzas come with great flourishes of flowers and grandiose announcements? Try a Capricorn Sun sign with Eros in Leo. When Eros in Leo rules the love nature of the pragmatic and hard-headed Capricorn, two personalities have to essentially live side by side. Can the über-Caps make luvvie phone calls from an all-important meeting? With Eros in Leo, they will certainly give it a try.
Astro flash: Power-tripping in relationships.

VIRGO

A match made in seventh heaven? Capricorns with Eros in Virgo have a love nature that fits almost perfectly. Eros in Virgo is about sophistication, pickiness, and discernment. They are just like canny Capricorns. The big difference in the Virgo love nature is the comparative worldliness about sex and romance matters—subjects that many Goats have not stopped to dwell upon.
Astro karma drama: You tend to fall in love with highly strung, mega-emotional types who then proceed to cast you as the relationship's official police officer.

LIBRA

So fussy! You vibe like one of those spoiled pedigree show cats. Capricornian elegance and standards are fine when it comes to business outcomes, yet it's hard to carry these benchmarks over into your love life. No matter, as Eros in Libra is the all-time relationship guru. From a very early age, you've been studying the labyrinths of love and sex. As a result, you give the best advice in the Zodiac. You are, okay, amazingly "looksist" and manipulative. The loving space is your domain and you can't resist opportunities to swing things your way with a few passive-aggressive ploys.

Astro flash: You have a psychic sense of smell. It's true!

SCORPIO

Capricorn with Eros in Scorpio would do well to watch for any personality crisis that might threaten with the combination of these two so-powerful signs. This mix has the capacity to produce a sexually magnetic person who is focused in love and who does not tell lies. However, the result could also be rigidity, paranoia, inappropriate intensity, and a focus on the negative rather than the positive. Watch for an internal clash between the Eros-in-Scorpio's interest in the soul and your Goaty material obsession.

SAGITTARIUS

Solid as a rock...but about to fly away? So goes the dilemma when a Capricorn has Eros in Sagittarius. Capricorn, the Goat, is sure-footed but constantly upwardly mobile. You are a real rock, a reliable player of systems, and you have all the trappings of the good egg. However, give the Goat the love nature informed by Eros in Sagittarius and you have some interesting results. The solid citizen act may hide a flighty heart of passion. For example, you would be prepared to drop everything if it meant pursuing love's freedom of the heart!

Soul mating

CAPRICORN

Hint: Vow now not to write up a template document binding your potential lover to minimal hours of work at a certain level of salary. With Eros in Capricorn, the Goat could easily slide into a rigid system of relationship management where the objects of their interest are put through the money-status-sanity test every day. The Capricorn interest in the material world is understandable but constantly talking in terms of pre-nuptial agreements and rights waivers is not really a love life. Is it?

AQUARIUS

Even the straightest Capricorns, with the most stable employment histories, could find themselves heavily involved with an anarcho-communist or an experimental refugee poet thanks to Eros in Aquarius. This Aquarian influence is an explorer of people rather than the Goaty judger. The Eros-in-Aquarius love life is therefore total anathema to the Capricorn personality. Caps think that people who are too interesting may be a liability while Eros in Aqua will not touch anyone who is not interesting *enough*! When you put these factors together in a love nature, the results could be either very happy or quite disastrous.

PISCES

Canny Cap in the kaftan? Capricorns may spend all day doing banking deals or making money for people, but when they have Eros in Pisces they have love lives that are quite obviously out there. Eros in Pisces translates as highly emotional, instinctive, and in contact with universal themes such as love, sex, and power. The Eros-in-Pisces love nature is difficult, temperamental, and highly artistic. Where, exactly, it can be integrated with the Capricorn love of order is the challenge.
Astro bonus: People can't help but be intrigued.

Or your Psyche is in...

ARIES

Lacking energy? Listless? No motivation? It sounds like advertising for a new vitamin supplement but in terms of your love life it could be as simple as accessing your secret Ram. With Psyche in Aries, Capricorns are given the secret key to a love nature they may have wished they had. With this Psyche energy, a Cap with the right motives can evolve beyond their outward personality and trigger a far more dynamic and risk-taking love persona.

Astro hint: Access the energy but not the craziness.

TAURUS

You have the shares portfolio, the corner office, and the flash house. But is something missing? Some Caps get too rigid about themselves and try to run a relationship in the same way they run an investment strategy. If you have Psyche in Taurus you are in a very good position to tune in to a sensual side of yourself and lose some rigidity. The Taurean influence is at the adequate end of the love and sex spectrum. Tune in, work at it and it all falls into place.

GEMINI

An irresponsible imp just waiting to get out? You are all status and maturity on the surface...and sometimes you feel that it shows in your love nature. But when Caps have Psyche in Gemini you have a reservoir of flighty and fickle behavior itching to unleash itself. Psyche in Gemini is the energy of the love-taker and heartbreaker—without a word of malice, just a wink and a laugh. When Canny Goats learn to tap into this secret love persona, they learn how to unlock a whole new universe for themselves.

CANCER

Time to soften your image? Ready to go into the touchy-feely space where the heart overrules the head? Capricorns with Psyche in Cancer have a secret power source that is theirs to unlock when they decide to go there. Of course, most of you spend your lives avoiding losing control or appearing too vulnerable to what lies in the heart. If you want to see how the other side of life exists in love, entrust your love nature to your Psyche-in-Cancer guide. A great balancer, if nothing else.

LEO

Longing to try on the duck suit? Toying with a small costume or maybe an accent in the boudoir? With Psyche in Leo you *très* straight Caps could be hiding an instinct to camp it up and put on a show. Or, if you're solo at the moment, the Psyche-in-Leo energy is all about being more dramatic and diva-like. Psyche rules the secret You and accessing your inner Leo love nature requires some leaps of faith.

To do: Think creativity—try singing, go to the opera, or dress up in a spangled leotard and stand at the front of your group exercise class. The typical Goat looks at a luvvie Leo and is mildly appalled at the vulgarity. But, it's true—Big Cats have more fun.

VIRGO

When you're a Capricorn Sun sign with Psyche in Virgo it's a good indicator that there may be a more sensual you hiding beneath the serious, responsible Goat that you project to the world. Psyche rules your secret love nature and when it's in Virgo it's a very strong opportunity for you. Feeling a bit unworldly with sex or slightly not with it in the flirting and pouncing stakes? The sophistication and sensual confidence of Psyche in Virgo is a perfect surprise package to unlock and let into your armory.

LIBRA

Are you *really* so certain? Caps can become slightly too fond of your certainties—great when you're a fund manager or senior bureaucrat, but not so hot when you're in relationships. To take the edge off your empirical approach to life and love you could make some effort to access your Psyche-in-Libra influences. Libra in love is about weighing things up and avoiding the tags of "right" and "wrong." Pysche in Libra takes an easy question and turns it into a dilemma. However, Caps would simply call it dithering.

Astro flash: Psyche in Libra loves good looks and your soul could certainly do with some bubbly spa time.

SCORPIO

What on Earth could Psyche in Scorpio bring to Capricorn? Well, one of the biggest image perceptions that you lot may like to overturn is that image of you as the person who manages a love affair in the same way you manage your wealth planning. That is, with as little emotion as possible. Tuning into the secret love nature as set out by Psyche in Scorpio allows you to admit to greater levels of intensity and everlasting love. Whether you want this or not, it is your secret love nature, so *listen* to it.

SAGITTARIUS

There's no rule to say that Capricorns don't drink or raise hell at any time. However, you lot generally don't do it like a Sagittarius. Saggo will dance on a table, recite poems, or do handstands if it means there's a good chance of it leading to a romantic conquest. When you have Psyche in Sagittarius you have a secret side to your love nature that really wants to be extroverted and loud about the pursuit of romance. It's not like this behavior is an alien thing that is out to embarrass you. This is You.

The eeek factor: If in doubt, go out!

CAPRICORN

Regardez! The perfectly integrated Canny Cap! When you outwardly have the ambition, the organization, and the pragmatic approach to your life and you also have the secret love nature of Psyche in Capricorn, you are aligned as the cosmos may well have intended it. Your take on success and wealth-building—that it can only be done by never dealing with any tricky or mad person—is cemented when Psyche is in Capricorn. You pretend to like the duds, but Psyche brings you back to reality.

AQUARIUS

Go on, admit it! You Capricorns can't go through your lives having romances that mirror your careers. It's lucky that you have Psyche in Aquarius—your secret love nature and the ultimate key to happiness. Many Caps would repress this influence because it skews heavily toward unorthodox people and potentially dangerous ideas. If you developed such romantic tastes, who knows where it could lead? You could even find happiness with someone that the bank doesn't approve of.

PISCES

The Bourgeois-Bohemian romance? When you Capricorns have Psyche in Pisces, you have to think very carefully about where you want to take this. The Pisces energy is a bit like the *Cat in the Hat* and the nagging but sensible fish is the Capricorn. Goats are hardly cold—they are ruttish Earth signs after all. But the Capricorn in love is a person in control and not given to the highs and lows or the workplace "us" chats of other types of people. Because Pisces is highly emotional, in touch with dreams, artistic, and slightly unstable, you may decide that you'll have to repress this side of yourself. However, it is your secret love nature and you may gain more by accepting it than by totally rejecting it.

If you are an Aquarius...

january 21 - february 19

Your astro motto is "I know." And you really think you do. You know about the law of aerodynamics, how pollen works, and how to make uranium batteries. But with love matters you can vibe cold and distant, unable or unwilling to engage in silly concepts such as monogamy and mutual trust. You are a revolutionary thinker and officially hilarious. But you also need a "security blanket" lover at home while insisting on your "freedom." Not surprisingly, you have fun trying to reconcile this love nature with a serious affair. "It's really hard to maintain a one-on-one relationship if the other person is not going to allow you to see other people."—Guns N' Roses lead singer Axl Rose.

and your Eros is in...

Soul mating

ARIES

Your usual wise-cracking, unorthodox persona sits well with the hyped-up Ram energy that is also big on joking and owning up to a totally unique personality. The Eros-in-Aries outlook is also that they are the genius and others are there to support their brilliance—a system that works fine for Aquarians. Where these influences come undone is in stickability: The Aries way is to stick with their mate through everything. Aquarians, however, need a bit of help to understand the monogamy concept.

Astro flash: Think friendship, not ownership.

TAURUS

You have a life in the mind—Taurus has very much a life of the body. So when you theoretical and highly intelligent Aqua-Maddies with Eros in Taurus stray into the realm of love, you can surprise everyone with your readiness and expertise. Anyone who has Eros in Taurus should count themselves lucky. Taurus is ruled by Venus and the Cow's love energy is totally natural and sensual.

What to do when feeling blue: Access your peaceful Taurus self via nature...think garden, greenery, wilderness. Just being outdoors for you is very is healing.

GEMINI

Here comes trouble! You lot are already a bit shy of the commitment side of love and even when you do settle down you like to feel that your lover is there as a sort of support act. So go figure out how irritating it could be to have your love nature ruled by the vagaries of Eros in Gemini. An Aquarius with this Eros should watch very carefully for being a lying, glib flirter who collects hearts and breaks them. It's a good idea to tune into the best of Gemini. Mix with great communicators. This includes those who are good at writing letters.

CANCER

This is the love switcheroo: The normal insistence of most Aquarians that their lover play the at-home hearth-keeper role is reversed when Eros is in Cancer. This energy triggers your need to be the nurturer, to provide the warm place to come home to. More than any other Eros energy, this is the one that pushes Aquarians into a whole new space. It's a very female Eros indicator and it is also one that can come with a range of terrible moods.

Astro nightmare: You freaking out when your lover won't go for the special crank diet that you've just concocted.

LEO

Taking flowers home to Mr./Mrs. Aqua? Wooing the talent with romantic candlelit dinners and weekends away? Chances are you have Eros in Leo. You can be the coldest, most distant Aquarian, astral-traveling through the Cosmos of your own genius. But Eros in Leo makes you treat the pursuit of love as a big excuse to put on a grand show. All of that Aquarian insouciance seems to falls away when you start putting some real theater back into love. Eros in Leo is the influence that comes to the fore when you're out dancing the night away or wandering through a picturesque vineyard. Whether it comes out in the pursuit of love or in the consolidation phase, it's the luvvie romantic impulses that give it away. It's the rose between the teeth and the little love poems.

To do: Learn to love your Eros in Leo; it's important, as this is what gives you your warmth and charisma.

VIRGO

Having trouble connecting the romantic dots? This is not an unusual problem with Aquarians—you deal better with ideas and stories than you do with other people who may actually need something. However, when you have Eros in Virgo you are blessed with sophisticated romancing skills. Make all the jokes you want about control-freaky Virgos, but they sure know how to run relationships.

Astro flash: Noting something via your super-human powers of observation does not place you under any obligation whatsoever to voice it.

Soul mating

LIBRA

By day, you lot could easily be real know-it-alls. You're very smart people who are paid never to have a second of doubt about your expertise. But when you have Eros in Libra you may be blessed with some equivocation. Some people call it dithering, but the Eros-in-Libra vibe is also about being able to see both sides. The Aquarius You is a know-all. And Libra is conciliatory. The only drawback of this Eros? Libra is an absolute looks-snob. The beauty standard is very high for Lib and that clashes with your Aquarius "love everybody equally" ethos.

SCORPIO

Learning to live with your alter ego? The standard relationship pattern for Aquarians is to find a mate who will be happy to keep house, while the Aqua genius gets out and about. But when Eros in Scorpio is your love nature you are far more focused and intense about where your lover is and how much they love you. When your Eros is in Scorpio you break all the Aquarian rules and actually admit to jealousy. Yes, you are likely to be far more in touch with your emotions than the classic Aquarius of legend.

SAGITTARIUS

If you Aquarians are lucky enough to have Eros in Sagittarius, you may have landed the love nature most compatible with your general outlook. Eros in Sagittarius bolsters your instincts to keep the romantic intensity at "low" while pursuing lots of other interests. The Eros-Saggo vibe is also skewed toward theoretical love as opposed to the physical and emotional psychodrama that so many often demand.

Astro flash: You are a mixture of Fire and Air and, as such, you are both attractive and inspiring. But try not to outsource your emotions to your partner.

CAPRICORN

The Aquarius You is appalled by your Eros in Capricorn. You are a radically minded, aware, and socially progressive creature. Your Eros in Capricorn cares about societal structures. Cap does not want to tear them down as you would like to do to a few, but in order to be an actual pillar of it. Yes, it's your secret straight! But, your Eros in Capricorn is also a blessing. Cap is a sensual sign and so it antidotes some of your Aquarian live-in-the-mind frigidity.

Astro flash: True teamwork and deep friendship come before lust and true love.

AQUARIUS

If your experiences of love have no bearing on what you read in romance novels, then you could have Eros in Aquarius. With this energy, you don't get it...and you don't care. You have a romantic model but it has nothing to do with putting your feet up with spousie and doing a bit of canoodling. You have a meeting to go to or an obsessive hobby to put time into. Yes, and it does make you happy. You relish the idea of a romance that's like no other—but it's one that liberates and intoxicates in equal measure with no demands. It's a figment!

PISCES

What would happen if someone had all the outward signs of being a bit of a cold fish, but in the pursuit of their love life they were needy, skittish, and totally subsumed with emotion? They would probably have Eros in Pisces—the love nature that throws the Aquarian coolness on the scrap heap and delivers instead a high drama emotionalism that can't be shrugged off. You're a strange blend of detachment and overblown passion. You can switch feelings on and off for seemingly no reason.

Astro weirding: You cherish the crush.

Or your Psyche is in...

ARIES

Ever seen the movie where the main character wants to throw off their sangfroid and just openly pursue the object of their lust? This is your story, Aquarius, when you have Psyche in Aries. You may talk about your freedom and being free from the chains of love, but when your secret love nature is revealed as Aries, you have some changes to implement. Aries is all about rescuing good sorts from dragons. You thrill to the chase, the challenge, and/or the opportunity to save someone, whether they like it or not.

TAURUS

Quiz: Do you shirk your bedwork load by pretending it's not really your thing, but have a niggling desire to be The Natural? When you lot have Psyche in Taurus your secret love nature is that of the über-physical, sensually confident Cow people. The trick to the Psyche is that it has to be worked at—to be unlocked. If you stop fighting it, the Taurean gift of physical pleasure is right there, waiting. Other ways of evoking the gifts of your sensual and fulfilling Psyche sign is to grow flowers, bake cakes, have a massage.

GEMINI

Sun in Aquarius and Psyche in Gemini! You are a slippery customer! You could live in your head, refusing to condescend to the masses by not feeling anything. As long as things are kept on the intellectual plane, you are one of the most charming people on the planet. But when the tryst moves toward commitment, true love, and trust, your Psyche in Gemini balks. Aqua values honesty but Gemini will say anything to protect privacy and freedom.

CANCER

Aquarians can take your "freedom" in a relationship to absurd lengths. Your need not to be tied down lands you virtually on the Moon. However, if your secret love nature is influenced by Psyche in Cancer, there could be a very clingy theme that you are not giving voice to. There is a strong need to be closer to your mate but this is something you'll have to work on. You also have clandestine nurturing, guilting, and corrective nagging urges. Compared with the classic Aqua-Maddie you're EQ (Emotional Intelligence) is at genius level.

LEO

While you are witty, charming, and lovable, you are, perhaps, not that openly affectionate. Why? Because of your Psyche in Leo, there is a totally luvvie show pony waiting to get out of that coldish exterior of yours. The Leo influence is your secret romantic self—the person who wants to dance, sing, and generally dazzle the person you adore. Yes, you need to discover your inner vain, glorious, performance-artiste diva personality. Any form of creativity is good for you and for your soul!
Vow now: To never think you can do without love.

VIRGO

Aquarians are known for being great lovers mentally but not really following through on the hurly-burly aspects. But when you have Psyche in Virgo, you have a secret romance identity as a sexual sophisticate and a worldly sensualist with high standards. Aquarians should do what they can to trigger this Psyche aspect of their love life. Why not start by hanging out with people who are more driven physically. They will inspire you. How to deal with your Aqua moods? You could easily cure them via the Virgoan arts of administrivia and well-being jags.

Soul mating

LIBRA

Aquarius is forever looking for the cool people to hang out with and eventually to mate with. Aqua-Maddies are drawn to cool. But when you have Psyche in Libra your love secret is going to be that you are unashamedly drawn to beautiful people. It's not really snobbery—you love the symmetrical features and the balance of the face. You love the fact that these people are gorgeous no matter which angle you view them from. In spite of your own best intellectualizing of your motives, beauty gets you every time. Unfortunately, this goes against your cool act. Sort it! Psyche in Libra is also able to be spiritually enlightened by beautiful fragrance.

SCORPIO

Secretly wanting more? Keeping the part of you that cares hidden away? The standard Aquarius act of keeping a distance from the ones you love is going to feel more and more strange if you have Psyche in Scorpio. Under this influence, you are forced to admit (if only to yourself) that you would rather be pulling the intensely loyal and mildly jealous act with your loved one. Trying to incorporate this repressed part of your personality into the open part could be challenging as well as fun.

SAGITTARIUS

Consider it confirmed. Your Aquarian desire to have a trophy lover living at home while you flit off on your adventures with a bunch of cool people is basically supported by your Psyche in Sagittarius. Saggos also like to stay mobile and keep active. There's just one large difference between the two: Psyche in Saggo is the energy of someone who wants spousie along on all the adventures. A nice mix? It's divine.

Astro karma: To hook up with someone who needs your gorm and optimism. They give you emotional sustenance.

CAPRICORN

Are you a secret materialist? All of the ideological stuff you rave on with is most often about rejecting materialism. However, when you have Psyche in Capricorn you may at some point have to own up to the idea that you not only like financial security, but that you also like your mate to be part of the plan to gain it. Living one side of your life preaching on a soapbox, and the other in the arms of an avaricious lover, is your destiny. Ideally, you combine the two, working within the system to effect real change. On the negative side, you could reject a lot of potentially suitable friends because of the fiscal vibes. Learn to be reasonable.

AQUARIUS

You are totally comfortable with who and what you are in the love game. Not only do you like to flex your intellectualism and crack a few weird jokes, but your secret love nature as explained by Psyche in Aquarius wants you in that space, too. You are probably destined to find the lover who doesn't mind holding the fort while you go out and have long-winded conversations about eccentric topics. Jilt the jaded lovers who insist on trying to force you into their own so-narrow paradigm. You're an über-original.

PISCES

Secretly an emotional swamp? With Psyche in Pisces, you lot have a secret love nature that is far removed from the arid love life you like to construct for public consumption. Psyche in Pisces craves a surreal degree of fated love—for example, utter immersion and flashbacks to past lives spent ruling the city of Atlantis together. So, yes, no matter how rational and distant you like to be, you have an inner romantic teenager inside you. Don't try to be too "mature" about love or relationships. You have the gift of keeping that spark alive indefinitely.

If you are a Pisces...
february 20 - march 20

You are the genius flake, the worldly adolescent, the miracle worker who can't drive. In relationships you are plain impossible. In spite of your intellect you swing between a wise knowingness and an infuriating immaturity. You are charming and a great lover. But your over-the-top tantrums, or your taking dreams seriously, can put too-straight lovers under pressure. Your motto is "I believe," and this trait—cute at first—can drive people nuts when they realize that you don't just throw the I-Ching for effect, that you do think animals can talk. Most of all, Pisceans know about sex and power: "You can only sleep your way to the middle."—actress Sharon Stone.

and your Eros is in...

ARIES

You are Yin and the Ram is Yang. Hey, this could be fun! The mystery of how the Piscean mind works is a matrix-like adventure with no definitive answer. But, if you're looking for a slightly more straightforward love nature, you are in luck: Eros in Aries is like someone taking all of your funny games and manipulations and turning them into an "on" or "off" switch. Pisces with Eros here are still complicated and difficult people but they are far less eccentric in a relationship or in the pursuit of love—you don't have the urge to reel someone in just for the fun of it. Eros in Aries is about passion and action and it's very hard to establish your habit of lying. This combo boosts energy, spunkiness, and self-belief.

TAURUS

Getting too cerebral? Pisceans can be a bit sleazy when they are young, but as they mature they run the risk of making their love life a bit too emotional or even metaphysical. Eros in Taurus blasts you out of that by making you highly focused on the natural sensuality that Venus affords. Pisceans can blossom under this love nature because, when love is influenced by Taurus, the physical side of things is so natural that there are no freak-outs—of the type that Fishies are known for. Think Zen—the fish.

GEMINI

When a Pisces has Eros in Gemini, they have a lot of choices as to the ethical basis for their behavior. Other Eros signs may keep you on track, but Gemini? It is the one influence that will make you a lot more likely than before to lie, manipulate, and use people for your own ends. The best part of Eros in Gemini for you lot is that it creates the impetus to communicate after the first date—one of your pet hates. And, all right, it hypes your cuteness to practically criminal levels. You're charmed and dangerous.

Soul mating

CANCER

Whimsical Pisces You goes your own sweet way, whenever you feel like it. Similarly, your Cancerian Eros does whatever it wants, while always justifying it in a huge emotional acting-out orgy, of course. You're compassionate, clever, and pre-hysterical a lot of the time. You are almost certainly psychic. In love, you baffle lovers by being doting and over-nurturing or control-freaky one moment and utterly not there the next. You are kind-hearted in the morning but jaded and cynical by midday. People will either hate you or become addicted to your presence.

LEO

Reconstructing your love nature to make superficial what is already mysterious? Try tapping into your romance persona, Eros in Leo. The Leo influence lifts you out of a fairly tricky personality. It's not really that you are a liar, but you do like to avoid people trapping you emotionally or being put in a position where you have to match what you say with the "facts." The Eros in Leo takes you out of that space and more into the gauche show-off. It's not that you don't lie, it's more that you no longer have the time with the costume changes and grooming demands. Frustrated? Then act!

VIRGO

Pisceans can dwell a little too long in the adolescent space when it comes to pursuing romance. It's not intentional—it's just an easy way to stop certain persons from getting close enough to think they can crush the Fishie specialness. But Eros in Virgo is the love nature energy that could easily give you lot the confidence to be a little more adult and forthright about your relationships. Go with the Virgo feeling and allow yourself to become more of the vampish Virgoan sophisticate.
Your destiny: Ordered love without the tantrums.

LIBRA

What if you Pisceans had a chance to force along and even out some or all of those ups and downs and shrieking outbursts or sleazy stunts that you get up to when love is around? Would you take it? For those with Eros in Libra, an evening out is exactly what you get. Libra loves to balance out the extremes and find a happy middle—somewhere between the manic stirrer Fish and the neurotic phobic Pisces. In other pursuits of your life, you may not want this "Stepford" approach, hating as you do any tinkering with your subconscious. But in love? It's a good thing. Astro flash: You flirt.

SCORPIO

Pisces with Eros in Scorpio really have to work at staying on an even keel. You're already quite strange and not at all an easy proposition in the relationship stakes. But, here you are with your love nature deeply affected by Scorpio. This means increased intensity and wild paranoid imaginings of conspiracies to commit adultery. It also means intense loyalty and a commitment to stay and work things out—a trait hardly in the standard Piscean love manual. Along with all the depth? You're a seduction diva.

SAGITTARIUS

With Eros in Sagg, you could be airing out your mind with some much-needed travel. You are not a great traveler in the tourist sense—you much prefer the luxuries of home and you travel only if there's a reason for it. But with Saggo ruling your love nature, relationships go hand in hand with moving about the place. Or, they manifest as love blending with expansion of your mind! You can't for a moment fancy anyone whose principles are not right on.

Astro destiny: There's a stranger in a strange land. Your true love may be a foreigner.

Soul mating

CAPRICORN

Pisces can be their own worst enemies in the love game—too much following the instincts and reacting to impulses (and dreams) and not enough due diligence about who these people are. But with the powerful influence of Eros in Capricorn you have the outlook that if someone is not signed on to your corporate goals and your performance benchmarks, then the person is a dud. This adds an important aspect to the Piscean personality and can be used to great effect as a filter.
Astro bonus: You get physical self-discipline!

AQUARIUS

At first glance, Pisces and the Eros-in-Aquarius influence would appear to be quite similar: eccentric, intelligent, hard to pin down. But, look closer and you find that with Eros where it is, you are more likely to be able to put a lover in his/her place. The pure Piscean lover tends to attract people with something to prove whereas the Aquarian energy is about keeping their lover distant enough that they can essentially divide their life into home and life. It's a sense of total control but without the Piscean freakery.

PISCES

Is anyone up for what you have to offer? You're a Pisces with Eros in Pisces—a love combo that is really not a good idea for so many of those who put themselves forward as The One. You are mysterious, complicated, tempestuous, and in touch with worlds that most don't know exist. Your amazing intellect, creativity, and bed skills are just the beginning. To follow is your fibbing and the way that any hint of neglect is rewarded with an extramarital fling or the threat of such. The Pisces with Eros in Pisces is the archetypal high-maintenance lover, requiring almost as much understanding as forgiveness. You're demanding, but worth it.

Or your Psyche is in...

ARIES

Affairs that start promisingly, then go nowhere, may have something to do with your inability to be direct with your romantic interests. It's a pity because you're sitting on an asset, your Psyche in Aries, which, if you want to work on it, is a perfect way to get rid of some of the passive aggression in your relationships. The next time you feel a petty manipulation coming on, think about the direct and passionate energy that Aries brings.

Astro hint: Fitness pursuits help evoke it.

TAURUS

There is a skittish quality about Pisces who are chasing love. You get funny about the smallest things and start either panicking or lying. A personal challenge—and possibly an aid to you—is the existence in your internal Cosmos of the Psyche-in-Taurus energy. This combo is ruled by Venus and earths you in your body. It's not as deep as it sounds. Taureans are good lovers and totally at home in their bodies. This Psyche aspect is there for your taking. Get it on!

GEMINI

Have you had an experience where a person you were pursuing suddenly turned into a pumpkin and you've been ducking them ever since? Sounds truly Piscean, right? Well, Geminis are twice as bad at this. However, they do have the saving quality that, rather than hiding from a certain person, they bluff and charm their way out of it. With Psyche in Gemini, you have the ability to tap into this energy and work on your social skills. They do count in soul mating.

To consider: Do you live in parallel worlds?

CANCER

There is something fractured about the Piscean—when it comes to developing relationships they are only ever giving away small snippets of their overall selves. It's fine for brief liaisons, but what about building love with The One? Luckily, you have Psyche in Cancer—your secret love nature and the influence that can draw you into giving more of yourself and creating a nurturing environment along the way. Wouldn't you like to try some caring rather than always being the one who's being cared for?

LEO

Secretly wanting to put on a show? One of the theatrical things about you Pisceans is the strength of your tantrums. They are quite operatic. However, with Psyche in Leo, you may be covering up a secret desire to play-act and show off, a desire that takes you out of the swampy mysteries of your mind and into a more demonstrative space. Say what you want about Leos—that they are tantrum-throwing show-offs who think they own the limelight—but they are still able to show their feelings in a free and open manner that doesn't involve intrigues. Tap into this great gift. Go and perform! Expressing creativity is your birthright.

VIRGO

Pisceans often have slutty stages in their love lives, especially when they're younger and they love the sound of their own charm. However, when you have Psyche in Virgo, your love nature has the potential to be transformed into something more sophisticated and discerning. The Virgo energy is also very worldly in the ways of love. Pisceans are worldly in love, too, but a Psyche in Virgo can pick a person's kink before things get to sex.

Astro flash: Your "inner Virgo" ensures that you will always be able to perk yourself up via household filth purges and decluttering.

LIBRA

A secret looks-snob? You Pisceans like to think that you are attracted to people for reasons that are more than just skin deep. And often, you prove this correct. However, with Psyche in Libra your secret love nature is totally into looks as the first and most important filter. By accepting this Psyche, you lot reserve the right to limit your trawlings to the "drop-dead gorgeous" variety. It's also an energy that helps you balance emotions and aesthetically harmonize your soul so that it's almost as pretty as your face. Do you dither? Yes. Maybe no? But so what?

SCORPIO

When you're ready to settle on one mate, you'll be glad you have Psyche in Scorpio sitting there as your secret love nature. Scorpio in relationships is the energy that can be a little obsessive but is really just totally intense about the relationship. Even during your flighty and flirty episodes, this could have been a personality trying to break through and be accepted by you. If you're trying to drop the "date, mate, and hate" act from your repertoire, you're in luck with the Scorpio Psyche.
Astro weirding: You're a brilliant interpreter of dreams.

SAGITTARIUS

You Fishies can get trapped in your safe little places like your bedrooms, your minds, or your baths. When they're inside themselves there is a whole ocean for Pisces to explore, but people are so often a drag! Perhaps there's a more expansive way to run a love life? Your Psyche is in Sagittarius—the action traveler of the love-scope who gives gregariousness a good name. It's a secret side of your nature that you are probably repressing, but it could be the real you. To evoke it? Fly off to a great beach. Try an extreme sport. Get involved in politics.

CAPRICORN

Why do you have such a problem with the so-called straights? Have you ever gone out with one? Well, okay, have you ever given one a second chance? Don't scoff at this—your Psyche is in Capricorn, the Sun sign of people with good jobs, good prospects, and stable finances. It's the sign of straights and it's fundamental to your love life when you choose to accept it. That niggling sound is your Psyche telling you that a stable lover with a real job may be a good bet for a change. Or could that person be you?

AQUARIUS

The Piscean who says "Yes" to their Psyche in Aquarius is inviting themselves to step up a grade of seriousness. The Piscean motto is "I believe" while the Aquarians say "I know." What Pisceans believe is not often appropriate for public consumption, the things that an Aquarian knows have to be put out there to prove how smart they are. If you can hook into this Psyche of yours, igniting your secret love nature, you get to keep your mystery but communicate on a more accessible level. It may be that Psyche in Aquarius for the Fish is the energy that urges you out of the subjective space and into a realm where a lover has many motivations, the least of them being to irritate you.

PISCES

It's not a secret any more! With Psyche in Pisces, you really do have an excuse to lead lovers on and then dump them. Also, you are allowed to throw titanic tantrums that bring restaurants to a halt or drop a promising lover because you didn't like the way they spoke to you in a dream. With this Psyche operating in your love nature, you can behave to the utmost of your creative brilliance and still sleep as much as you want. And be loved for it.

You just need to find kindred souls and devotees!

"Many waters cannot quench love,
nor can the floods drown it."

Song of Solomon—The Bible

Ephemeris:
Eros

All dates are inclusive

1920

January 1—January 6 in Aquarius

January 7—February 15 in Pisces

February 16—March 26 in Aries

March 27—May 5 in Taurus

May 6—June 4 in Gemini

June 5—July 14 in Cancer

July 15—August 13 in Leo

August 14—September 12 in Virgo

September 13—October 22 in Libra

October 23—December 1 in Scorpio

December 2—December 31 in Sagittarius

1921

January 1—January 20 in Sagittarius

January 21—March 11 in Capricorn

March 12—May 10 in Aquarius

May 11—December 31 in Pisces

1922

January 1—January 5 in Pisces

January 6—February 14 in Aries

February 15—March 26 in Taurus

March 27—April 25 in Gemini

April 26—May 25 in Cancer

May 26—June 24 in Leo

June 25—August 3 in Virgo

August 4—September 12 in Libra

September 13—October 22 in Scorpio

October 23—December 11 in Sagittarius

December 12—December 31 in Capricorn

Soul mating

1923

January 1—January 30 in Capricorn

January 31—March 21 in Aquarius

March 22—May 10 in Pisces

May 11—June 29 in Aries

June 30—August 18 in Taurus

August 19—September 27 in Gemini

September 28—October 27 in Cancer

October 28—December 6 in Leo

December 7—December 31 in Virgo

1924

January 1—January 5 in Virgo

January 6—February 24 in Libra

February 25—April 4 in Scorpio

April 5—July 3 in Libra

July 4—September 11 in Scorpio

September 12—November 10 in Sagittarius

November 11—December 30 in Capricorn

December 31 in Aquarius

1925

January 1—February 18 in Aquarius

February 19—April 9 in Pisces

April 10—May 19 in Aries

May 20—June 28 in Taurus

June 29—July 28 in Gemini

July 29—September 6 in Cancer

September 7—October 6 in Leo

October 7—November 5 in Virgo

November 6—December 15 in Libra

December 16—December 31 in Scorpio

1926

January 1—January 24 in Scorpio
January 25—March 5 in Sagittarius
March 6—November 20 in Capricorn
November 21—December 31 in Aquarius

1927

January 1—January 9 in Aquarius
January 10—February 29 in Pisces
March 1—April 9 in Aries
April 10—May 19 in Taurus
May 20—June 18 in Gemini
June 19—July 18 in Cancer
July 19—August 27 in Leo
August 28—September 26 in Virgo
September 27—November 5 in Libra
November 6—December 15 in Scorpio
December 16—December 31 in Sagittarius

1928

January 1—January 24 in Sagittarius
January 25—March 14 in Capricorn
March 15—May 13 in Aquarius
May 14—September 20 in Pisces
September 21—November 19 in Aquarius
November 20—December 31 in Pisces

1929

January 1—January 18 in Pisces
January 19—February 27 in Aries
February 28—March 29 in Taurus

March 30—April 28 in Gemini

April 29—June 7 in Cancer

June 8—July 7 in Leo

July 8—August 16 in Virgo

August 17—September 25 in Libra

September 26—November 4 in Scorpio

November 5—December 24 in Sagittarius

December 25—December 31 in Capricorn

1930

January 1—February 12 in Capricorn

February 13—April 3 in Aquarius

April 4—May 23 in Pisces

May 24—July 12 in Aries

July 13—August 31 in Taurus

September 1—October 20 in Gemini

October 21—November 29 in Cancer

November 30—December 31 in Leo

1931

January 1—January 8 in Leo

January 9—May 28 in Virgo

May 29—July 27 in Libra

July 28—September 25 in Scorpio

September 26—November 14 in Sagittarius

November 15—December 31 in Capricorn

1932

January 1—January 3 in Capricorn

January 4—February 22 in Aquarius

February 23—April 12 in Pisces

April 13—May 22 in Aries

May 23—July 1 in Taurus

July 2—August 10 in Gemini

August 11—September 9 in Cancer

September 10—October 9 in Leo

October 10—November 18 in Virgo

November 19—December 18 in Libra

December 19—December 31 in Scorpio

1933

January 1—January 27 in Scorpio

January 28—March 18 in Sagittarius

March 19—July 16 in Capricorn

July 17—September 14 in Sagittarius

September 15—November 23 in Capricorn

November 24—December 31 in Aquarius

1934

January 1—January 22 in Aquarius

January 23—March 3 in Pisces

March 4—April 12 in Aries

April 13—May 22 in Taurus

May 23—June 21 in Gemini

June 22—July 31 in Cancer

August 1—August 30 in Leo

August 31—September 29 in Virgo

September 30—November 8 in Libra

November 9—December 18 in Scorpio

December 19—December 31 in Sagittarius

1935

January 1—January 27 in Sagittarius

January 28—March 28 in Capricorn

March 29—May 27 in Aquarius

May 28—August 15 in Pisces

August 16—December 3 in Aquarius

December 4—December 31 in Pisces

1936

January 1—January 22 in Pisces

January 23—March 2 in Aries

March 3—April 11 in Taurus

April 12—May 11 in Gemini

May 12—June 10 in Cancer

June 11—July 20 in Leo

July 21—August 19 in Virgo

August 20—September 28 in Libra

September 29—November 7 in Scorpio

November 8—December 27 in Sagittarius

December 28—December 31 in Capricorn

1937

January 1—February 15 in Capricorn

February 16—April 6 in Aquarius

April 7—May 26 in Pisces

May 27—July 25 in Aries

July 26—September 23 in Taurus

September 24—December 31 in Gemini

1938

January 1–March 2 in Gemini

March 3–April 1 in Cancer

April 2–May 11 in Leo

May 12–June 20 in Virgo

June 21–August 9 in Libra

August 10–September 28 in Scorpio

September 29–November 17 in Sagittarius

November 18–December 31 in Capricorn

1939

January 1–January 6 in Capricorn

January 7–February 25 in Aquarius

February 26–April 16 in Pisces

April 17–June 5 in Aries

June 6–July 15 in Taurus

July 16–August 14 in Gemini

August 15–September 23 in Cancer

September 24–October 23 in Leo

October 24–November 22 in Virgo

November 23–December 31 in Libra

1940

January 1 in Libra

January 2–February 10 in Scorpio

February 11–March 31 in Sagittarius

April 1–June 9 in Capricorn

June 10–October 7 in Sagittarius

October 8–December 6 in Capricorn

December 7–December 31 in Aquarius

Soul mating

1941

January 1–January 25 in Aquarius

January 26–March 16 in Pisces

March 17–April 25 in Aries

April 26–May 25 in Taurus

May 26–July 4 in Gemini

July 5–August 3 in Cancer

August 4–September 2 in Leo

September 3–October 12 in Virgo

October 13–November 11 in Libra

November 12–December 21 in Scorpio

December 22–December 31 in Sagittarius

1942

January 1–February 9 in Sagittarius

February 10–March 31 in Capricorn

April 1–December 16 in Aquarius

December 17–December 31 in Pisces

1943

January 1–February 4 in Pisces

February 5–March 16 in Aries

March 17–April 15 in Taurus

April 16–May 15 in Gemini

May 16–June 24 in Cancer

June 25–July 24 in Leo

July 25–September 2 in Virgo

September 3–October 2 in Libra

October 3–November 21 in Scorpio

November 22–December 31 in Sagittarius

1944

January 1–February 19 in Capricorn

February 20–April 9 in Aquarius

April 10–June 8 in Pisces

June 9–August 17 in Aries

August 18–November 15 in Taurus

November 16–December 31 in Aries

1945

January 1–January 4 in Aries

January 5–February 23 in Taurus

February 24–March 25 in Gemini

March 26–April 24 in Cancer

April 25–June 3 in Leo

June 4–July 3 in Virgo

July 4–August 22 in Libra

August 23–October 11 in Scorpio

October 12–November 30 in Sagittarius

December 1–December 31 in Capricorn

1946

January 1–January 19 in Capricorn

January 20–March 10 in Aquarius

March 11–April 29 in Pisces

April 30–June 8 in Aries

June 9–July 18 in Taurus

July 19–August 27 in Gemini

August 28–September 26 in Cancer

September 27–November 5 in Leo

November 6–December 5 in Virgo

December 6–December 31 in Libra

Soul mating

1947

January 1—January 4 in Libra

January 5—February 13 in Scorpio

February 14—October 11 in Sagittarius

October 12—December 10 in Capricorn

December 11—December 31 in Aquarius

1948

January 1—January 29 in Aquarius

January 30—March 19 in Pisces

March 20—April 28 in Aries

April 29—June 7 in Taurus

June 8—July 7 in Gemini

July 8—August 16 in Cancer

August 17—September 15 in Leo

September 16—October 15 in Virgo

October 16—November 24 in Libra

November 25—December 31 in Scorpio

1949

January 1—January 3 in Scorpio

January 4—February 12 in Sagittarius

February 13—April 13 in Capricorn

April 14—August 31 in Aquarius

September 1—October 10 in Capricorn

October 11—December 19 in Aquarius

December 20—December 31 in Pisces

1950

January 1—February 7 in Pisces

February 8—March 19 in Aries

March 20—April 28 in Taurus

April 29—May 28 in Gemini

May 29—June 27 in Cancer

June 28—August 6 in Leo

August 7—September 5 in Virgo

September 6—October 15 in Libra

October 16—November 24 in Scorpio

November 25—December 31 in Sagittarius

1951

January 1—January 3 in Sagittarius

January 4—February 22 in Capricorn

February 23—April 23 in Aquarius

April 24—June 22 in Pisces

June 23—November 19 in Aries

November 20—November 29 in Pisces

November 30—December 31 in Aries

1952

January 1—January 28 in Aries

January 29—March 8 in Taurus

March 9—April 7 in Gemini

April 8—May 7 in Cancer

May 8—June 16 in Leo

June 17—July 16 in Virgo

July 17—August 25 in Libra

August 26—October 14 in Scorpio

October 15—December 3 in Sagittarius

December 4—December 31 in Capricorn

1953

January 1—January 22 in Capricorn

January 23—March 13 in Aquarius

March 14—May 2 in Pisces

May 3—June 21 in Aries

June 22—July 31 in Taurus

August 1—September 9 in Gemini

September 10—October 9 in Cancer

October 10—November 8 in Leo

November 9—December 8 in Virgo

December 9—December 31 in Libra

1954

January 1—January 17 in Libra

January 18—February 26 in Scorpio

February 27—May 17 in Sagittarius

May 18—August 15 in Scorpio

August 16—October 24 in Sagittarius

October 25—December 23 in Capricorn

December 24—December 31 in Aquarius

1955

January 1—February 11 in Aquarius

February 12—March 23 in Pisces

March 24—May 2 in Aries

May 3—June 11 in Taurus

June 12—July 21 in Gemini

July 22—August 20 in Cancer

August 21—September 19 in Leo

September 20—October 29 in Virgo

October 30—November 28 in Libra

November 29—December 31 in Scorpio

1956

January 1–January 7 in Scorpio

January 8–February 26 in Sagittarius

February 27–April 16 in Capricorn

April 17–July 25 in Aquarius

July 26–November 2 in Capricorn

November 3–December 31 in Aquarius

1957

January 1 in Aquarius

January 2–February 10 in Pisces

February 11–March 22 in Aries

March 23–May 1 in Taurus

May 2–May 31 in Gemini

June 1–July 10 in Cancer

July 11–August 9 in Leo

August 10–September 8 in Virgo

September 9–October 18 in Libra

October 19–November 27 in Scorpio

November 28–December 31 in Sagittarius

1958

January 1–January 16 in Sagittarius

January 17–March 7 in Capricorn

March 8–April 26 in Aquarius

April 27–July 5 in Pisces

July 6–September 13 in Aries

September 14–December 31 in Pisces

Soul mating

1959

January 1 in Pisces

January 2—February 10 in Aries

February 11—March 12 in Taurus

March 13—April 21 in Gemini

April 22—May 21 in Cancer

May 22—June 20 in Leo

June 21—July 30 in Virgo

July 31—September 8 in Libra

September 9—October 18 in Scorpio

October 19—December 7 in Sagittarius

December 8—December 31 in Capricorn

1960

January 1—January 26 in Capricorn

January 27—March 16 in Aquarius

March 17—May 5 in Pisces

May 6—June 24 in Aries

June 25—August 13 in Taurus

August 14—September 22 in Gemini

September 23—October 22 in Cancer

October 23—November 21 in Leo

November 22—December 21 in Virgo

December 22—December 31 in Libra

1961

January 1—January 30 in Libra

January 31—September 7 in Scorpio

September 8—October 27 in Sagittarius

October 28—December 26 in Capricorn

December 27—December 31 in Aquarius

1962

January 1—February 14 in Aquarius

February 15—April 5 in Pisces

April 6—May 15 in Aries

May 16—June 24 in Taurus

June 25—July 24 in Gemini

July 25—September 2 in Cancer

September 3—October 2 in Leo

October 3—November 1 in Virgo

November 2—December 11 in Libra

December 12—December 31 in Scorpio

1963

January 1—January 10 in Scorpio

January 11—March 1 in Sagittarius

March 2—May 10 in Capricorn

May 11—June 19 in Aquarius

June 20—November 16 in Capricorn

November 17—December 31 in Aquarius

1964

January 1—January 5 in Aquarius

January 6—February 24 in Pisces

February 25—April 4 in Aries

April 5—May 14 in Taurus

May 15—June 13 in Gemini

June 14—July 13 in Cancer

July 14—August 12 in Leo

August 13—September 21 in Virgo

September 22—October 31 in Libra

November 1—December 10 in Scorpio

December 11—December 31 in Sagittarius

Soul mating

1965

January 1–January 19 in Sagittarius

January 20–March 10 in Capricorn

March 11–May 9 in Aquarius

May 10–December 31 in Pisces

1966

January 1–January 4 in Pisces

January 5–February 23 in Aries

February 24–March 25 in Taurus

March 26–April 24 in Gemini

April 25–June 3 in Cancer

June 4–July 3 in Leo

July 4–August 12 in Virgo

August 13–September 11 in Libra

September 12–October 31 in Scorpio

November 1–December 20 in Sagittarius

December 21–December 31 in Capricorn

1967

January 1–February 8 in Capricorn

February 9–March 30 in Aquarius

March 31–May 19 in Pisces

May 20–July 8 in Aries

July 9–August 27 in Taurus

August 28–October 6 in Gemini

October 7–November 5 in Cancer

November 6–December 15 in Leo

December 16–December 31 in Virgo

1968

January 1—January 24 in Virgo

January 25—July 12 in Libra

July 13—September 10 in Scorpio

September 11—November 9 in Sagittarius

November 10—December 29 in Capricorn

December 30—December 31 in Aquarius

1969

January 1—February 17 in Aquarius

February 18—April 8 in Pisces

April 9—May 18 in Aries

May 19—June 27 in Taurus

June 28—August 6 in Gemini

August 7—September 5 in Cancer

September 6—October 5 in Leo

October 6—November 14 in Virgo

November 15—December 14 in Libra

December 15—December 31 in Scorpio

1970

January 1—January 23 in Scorpio

January 24—March 14 in Sagittarius

March 15—November 19 in Capricorn

November 20—December 31 in Aquarius

1971

January 1—January 18 in Aquarius

January 19—February 27 in Pisces

February 28—April 8 in Aries

April 9—May 18 in Taurus

May 19—June 17 in Gemini

June 18—July 27 in Cancer

July 28—August 26 in Leo

August 27—September 25 in Virgo

September 26—November 4 in Libra

November 5—December 14 in Scorpio

December 15—December 31 in Sagittarius

1972

January 1—January 23 in Sagittarius

January 24—March 13 in Capricorn

March 14—May 22 in Aquarius

May 23—September 9 in Pisces

September 10—November 28 in Aquarius

November 29—December 31 in Pisces

1973

January 1—January 17 in Pisces

January 18—February 26 in Aries

February 27—April 7 in Taurus

April 8—May 7 in Gemini

May 8—June 6 in Cancer

June 7—July 6 in Leo

July 7—August 15 in Virgo

August 16—September 24 in Libra

September 25—November 3 in Scorpio

November 4—December 23 in Sagittarius

December 24—December 31 in Capricorn

1974

January 1—February 11 in Capricorn

February 12—April 2 in Aquarius

April 3—May 22 in Pisces

May 23—July 21 in Aries

July 22—September 9 in Taurus

September 10—October 29 in Gemini

October 30—December 31 in Cancer

1975

January 1—February 26 in Cancer

February 27—April 27 in Leo

April 28—June 16 in Virgo

June 17—August 5 in Libra

August 6—September 24 in Scorpio

September 25—November 13 in Sagittarius

November 14—December 31 in Capricorn

1976

January 1—January 2 in Capricorn

January 3—February 21 in Aquarius

February 22—April 11 in Pisces

April 12—May 31 in Aries

June 1—July 10 in Taurus

July 11—August 9 in Gemini

August 10—September 18 in Cancer

September 19—October 18 in Leo

October 19—November 17 in Virgo

November 18—December 27 in Libra

December 28—December 31 in Scorpio

Soul mating

1977

January 1—January 26 in Scorpio

January 27—March 17 in Sagittarius

March 18—July 5 in Capricorn

July 6—September 23 in Sagittarius

September 24—December 2 in Capricorn

December 3—December 31 in Aquarius

1978

January 1—January 21 in Aquarius

January 22—March 12 in Pisces

March 13—April 21 in Aries

April 22—May 21 in Taurus

May 22—June 30 in Gemini

July 1—July 30 in Cancer

July 31—August 29 in Leo

August 30—October 8 in Virgo

October 9—November 7 in Libra

November 8—December 17 in Scorpio

December 18—December 31 in Sagittarius

1979

January 1—February 5 in Sagittarius

February 6—March 27 in Capricorn

March 28—June 5 in Aquarius

June 6—August 4 in Pisces

August 5—December 12 in Aquarius

December 13—December 31 in Pisces

1980

January 1–January 31 in Pisces

February 1–March 11 in Aries

March 12–April 10 in Taurus

11 April–May 10 in Gemini

11 May–June 19 in Cancer

20 June–July 19 in Leo

20 July–August 18 in Virgo

19 August–September 27 in Libra

28 September–November 16 in Scorpio

17 November–December 26 in Sagittarius

27 December–31 December in Capricorn

1981

January 1–February 14 in Capricorn

February 15–April 5 in Aquarius

April 6–June 4 in Pisces

June 5–August 3 in Aries

August 4–December 31 in Taurus

1982

January 1–February 9 in Taurus

February 10–March 11 in Gemini

March 12–April 20 in Cancer

April 21–May 20 in Leo

May 21–June 29 in Virgo

June 30–August 18 in Libra

August 19–October 7 in Scorpio

October 8–November 26 in Sagittarius

November 27–December 31 in Capricorn

Soul mating

1983

January 1—January 15 in Capricorn

January 16—March 6 in Aquarius

March 7—April 25 in Pisces

April 26—June 4 in Aries

June 5—July 14 in Taurus

July 15—August 23 in Gemini

August 24—September 22 in Cancer

September 23—October 22 in Leo

October 23—December 1 in Virgo

December 2—December 31 in Libra

1984

January 1—February 9 in Scorpio

February 10—April 9 in Sagittarius

April 10—May 19 in Capricorn

May 20—October 6 in Sagittarius

October 7—December 5 in Capricorn

December 6—December 31 in Aquarius

1985

January 1—January 24 in Aquarius

January 25—March 15 in Pisces

March 16—April 24 in Aries

April 25—June 3 in Taurus

June 4—July 3 in Gemini

July 4—August 12 in Cancer

August 13—September 11 in Leo

September 12—October 11 in Virgo

October 12—November 20 in Libra

November 21—December 30 in Scorpio

December 31 in Sagittarius

1986

January 1—February 8 in Sagittarius

February 9—March 30 in Capricorn

March 31—December 15 in Aquarius

December 16—December 31 in Pisces

1987

January 1—February 3 in Pisces

February 4—March 15 in Aries

March 16—April 24 in Taurus

April 25—May 24 in Gemini

May 25—June 23 in Cancer

June 24—July 23 in Leo

July 24—September 1 in Virgo

September 2—October 11 in Libra

October 12—November 20 in Scorpio

November 21—December 30 in Sagittarius

December 31 in Capricorn

1988

January 1—February 18 in Capricorn

February 19—April 18 in Aquarius

April 19—June 17 in Pisces

June 18—September 5 in Aries

September 6—October 5 in Taurus

October 6—December 31 in Aries

1989

January 1—January 23 in Aries

January 24—February 22 in Taurus

February 23—April 3 in Gemini

Soul mating

April 4—May 3 in Cancer

May 4—June 2 in Leo

June 3—July 12 in Virgo

July 13—August 21 in Libra

August 22—October 10 in Scorpio

October 11—November 29 in Sagittarius

November 30—December 31 in Capricorn

1990

January 1—January 18 in Capricorn

January 19—March 9 in Aquarius

March 10—April 28 in Pisces

April 29—June 17 in Aries

June 18—July 27 in Taurus

July 28—August 26 in Gemini

August 27—October 5 in Cancer

October 6—November 4 in Leo

November 5—December 4 in Virgo

December 5—December 31 in Libra

1991

January 1—January 13 in Libra

January 14—February 22 in Scorpio

February 23—June 22 in Sagittarius

June 23—August 1 in Scorpio

August 2—October 20 in Sagittarius

October 21—December 19 in Capricorn

December 20—December 31 in Aquarius

1992

January 1—February 7 in Aquarius

February 8—March 18 in Pisces

March 19—April 27 in Aries

April 28—June 6 in Taurus

June 7—July 16 in Gemini

July 17—August 15 in Cancer

August 16—September 14 in Leo

September 15—October 24 in Virgo

October 25—November 23 in Libra

November 24—December 31 in Scorpio

1993

January 1—January 2 in Scorpio

January 3—February 11 in Sagittarius

February 12—April 12 in Capricorn

April 13—August 10 in Aquarius

August 11—October 19 in Capricorn

October 20—December 28 in Aquarius

December 29—December 31 in Pisces

1994

January 1—February 6 in Pisces

February 7—March 18 in Aries

March 19—April 27 in Taurus

April 28—May 27 in Gemini

May 28—July 6 in Cancer

July 7—August 5 in Leo

August 6—September 4 in Virgo

September 5—October 14 in Libra

October 15—November 23 in Scorpio

November 24—December 31 in Sagittarius

Soul mating

1995

January 1—January 12 in Sagittarius

January 13—March 3 in Capricorn

March 4—April 22 in Aquarius

April 23—July 1 in Pisces

July 2—September 19 in Aries

September 20—October 19 in Aries

October 20—December 18 in Pisces

December 19—December 31 in Aries

1996

January 1—February 6 in Aries

February 7—March 7 in Taurus

March 8—April 16 in Gemini

April 17—May 16 in Cancer

May 17—June 15 in Leo

June 16—July 25 in Virgo

July 26—September 3 in Libra

September 4—October 13 in Scorpio

October 14—December 2 in Sagittarius

December 3—December 31 in Capricorn

1997

January 1—January 21 in Capricorn

January 22—March 12 in Aquarius

March 13—May 1 in Pisces

May 2—June 20 in Aries

June 21—July 30 in Taurus

July 31—September 8 in Gemini

September 9—October 18 in Cancer

October 19—November 17 in Leo

November 18—December 17 in Virgo

December 18—December 31 in Libra

1998

January 1—January 26 in Libra

January 27—March 17 in Scorpio

March 18—April 26 in Sagittarius

April 27—August 24 in Scorpio

August 25—October 23 in Sagittarius

October 24—December 22 in Capricorn

December 23—December 31 in Aquarius

1999

January 1—February 10 in Aquarius

February 11—April 1 in Pisces

April 2—May 11 in Aries

May 12—June 20 in Taurus

June 21—July 20 in Gemini

July 21—August 29 in Cancer

August 30—September 28 in Leo

September 29—October 28 in Virgo

October 29—December 7 in Libra

December 8—December 31 in Scorpio

2000

January 1—January 6 in Scorpio

January 7—February 25 in Sagittarius

February 26—April 25 in Capricorn

April 26—July 14 in Aquarius

July 15—November 1 in Capricorn

November 2—December 31 in Aquarius

Ephemeris: Psyche

All dates are inclusive

1920

January 1—January 16 in Aquarius

January 17—March 16 in Pisces

March 17—May 25 in Aries

May 26—August 3 in Taurus

August 4—December 31 in Gemini

1921

January 1—May 10 in Gemini

May 11—July 29 in Cancer

July 30—October 27 in Leo

October 28—December 31 in Virgo

1922

January 1—April 15 in Virgo

April 16—May 5 in Leo

May 6—September 12 in Virgo

September 13—November 21 in Libra

November 22—December 1 in Libra

December 2—December 31 in Scorpio

1923

January 1—October 27 in Scorpio

October 28—December 31 in Sagittarius

1924

January 1—January 15 in Sagittarius

January 16—April 4 in Capricorn

April 5—September 11 in Aquarius

September 12—October 1 in Capricorn

October 2—December 31 in Aquarius

1925

January 1—January 9 in Aquarius

January 10—March 20 in Pisces

March 21—May 9 in Aries

May 30—August 7 in Taurus

August 8—December 1 in Gemini

1926

January 1—May 14 in Gemini

May 15—August 2 in Cancer

August 3—October 21 in Leo

October 22—December 31 in Virgo

1927

January 1—April 9 in Virgo

April 10—May 9 in Leo

May 10—September 6 in Virgo

September 7—December 5 in Libra

December 6—December 31 in Scorpio

1928

January 1—October 20 in Scorpio

October 21—December 31 in Sagittarius

1929

January 1–January 8 in Sagittarius

January 9–April 8 in Capricorn

April 9–September 5 in Aquarius

September 6–October 5 in Capricorn

October 6–December 31 in Aquarius

1930

January 1–January 13 in Aquarius

January 14–March 24 in Pisces

March 25–May 23 in Aries

May 24–August 11 in Taurus

August 12–December 31 in Gemini

1931

January 1–May 18 in Gemini

May 19–July 27 in Cancer

July 28–October 25 in Leo

October 26–December 31 in Virgo

1932

January 1–April 12 in Virgo

April 13–May 2 in Leo

May 3–September 9 in Virgo

September 10–December 8 in Libra

December 9–December 31 in Scorpio

1933

January 1–October 24 in Scorpio

October 25–December 31 in Sagittarius

Soul mating

1934

January 1–January 12 in Sagittarius
January 13–April 2 in Capricorn
April 3–August 30 in Aquarius
August 31–October 9 in Capricorn
October 10–December 31 in Aquarius

1935

January 1–January 17 in Aquarius
January 18–March 18 in Pisces
March 19–May 27 in Aries
May 28–August 5 in Taurus
August 6–December 31 in Gemini

1936

January 1–May 11 in Gemini
May 12–July 30 in Cancer
July 31–October 18 in Leo
October 19–December 31 in Virgo

1937

January 1–September 3 in Virgo
September 4–December 2 in Libra
December 3–December 31 in Scorpio

1938

January 1–October 18 in Scorpio
October 19–December 31 in Sagittarius

1939

January 1—January 6 in Sagittarius

January 7—April 6 in Capricorn

April 7—September 13 in Aquarius

September 14—September 23 in Capricorn

September 24—December 31 in Aquarius

1940

January 1—January 11 in Aquarius

January 12—March 21 in Pisces

March 22—May 20 in Aries

May 21—July 29 in Taurus

July 30—December 31 in Gemini

1941

January 1—May 15 in Gemini

May 16—July 24 in Cancer

July 25—October 22 in Leo

October 23—December 31 in Virgo

1942

January 1—September 7 in Virgo

September 8—December 6 in Libra

December 7—December 31 in Scorpio

1943

January 1—October 22 in Scorpio

October 23—December 31 in Sagittarius

Soul mating

1944

January 1—January 10 in Sagittarius

January 11—March 30 in Capricorn

March 31—December 31 in Aquarius

1945

January 1—January 14 in Aquarius

January 15—March 15 in Pisces

March 16—May 24 in Aries

May 25—August 2 in Taurus

August 3—December 31 in Gemini

1946

January 1—May 9 in Gemini

May 10—July 28 in Cancer

July 29—October 16 in Leo

October 17—December 31 in Virgo

1947

January 1—September 1 in Virgo

September 2—November 10 in Libra

November 11—November 30 in Libra

December 1—December 31 in Scorpio

1948

January 1—October 15 in Scorpio

October 16—December 31 in Sagittarius

1949

January 1–January 3 in Sagittarius

January 4–April 3 in Capricorn

April 4–December 31 in Aquarius

1950

January 1–January 8 in Aquarius

January 9–March 19 in Pisces

March 20–May 18 in Aries

May 19–July 27 in Taurus

July 28–December 31 in Gemini

1951

January 1–May 13 in Gemini

May 14–August 1 in Cancer

August 2–October 20 in Leo

October 21–December 31 in Virgo

1952

January 1–September 4 in Virgo

September 5–December 3 in Libra

December 4–December 31 in Scorpio

1953

January 1–October 19 in Scorpio

October 20–December 31 in Sagittarius

Soul mating

1954

January 1–January 7 in Sagittarius

January 8–March 28 in Capricorn

March 29–December 31 in Aquarius

1955

January 1–January 12 in Aquarius

January 13–March 13 in Pisces

March 14–May 22 in Aries

May 23–July 31 in Taurus

August 1–December 31 in Gemini

1956

January 1–May 6 in Gemini

May 7–July 25 in Cancer

July 26–October 13 in Leo

October 14–December 31 in Virgo

1957

January 1–August 29 in Virgo

August 30–November 27 in Libra

November 28–December 31 in Scorpio

1958

January 1–October 23 in Scorpio

October 24–December 31 in Sagittarius

1959

January 1—January 11 in Sagittarius

January 12—April 1 in Capricorn

April 2—December 31 in Aquarius

1960

January 1—January 6 in Aquarius

January 7—March 16 in Pisces

March 17—May 25 in Aries

May 26—August 3 in Taurus

August 4—December 31 in Gemini

1961

January 1—May 10 in Gemini

May 11—July 29 in Cancer

July 30—October 17 in Leo

October 18—December 31 in Virgo

1962

January 1—September 2 in Virgo

September 3—December 1 in Libra

December 2—December 31 in Scorpio

1963

January 1—October 17 in Scorpio

October 18—December 31 in Sagittarius

Soul mating

1964
January 1–January 5 in Sagittarius
January 6–April 4 in Capricorn
April 5–December 31 in Aquarius

1965
January 1–January 9 in Aquarius
January 10–March 20 in Pisces
March 21–May 19 in Aries
May 20–July 28 in Taurus
July 29–December 31 in Gemini

1966
January 1–May 4 in Gemini
May 5–July 23 in Cancer
July 24–October 21 in Leo
October 22–December 31 in Virgo

1967
January 1–September 6 in Virgo
September 7–November 25 in Libra
November 26–December 31 in Scorpio

1968
January 1–October 20 in Scorpio
October 21–December 31 in Sagittarius

1969

January 1—January 8 in Sagittarius

January 9—March 29 in Capricorn

March 30—December 31 in Aquarius

1970

January 1—January 13 in Aquarius

January 14—March 14 in Pisces

March 15—May 23 in Aries

May 24—August 1 in Taurus

August 2—December 31 in Gemini

1971

January 1—May 8 in Gemini

May 9—July 27 in Cancer

July 28—October 15 in Leo

October 16—December 31 in Virgo

1972

January 1—August 30 in Virgo

August 31—November 28 in Libra

November 29—December 31 in Scorpio

1973

January 1—October 14 in Scorpio

October 15—December 31 in Sagittarius

Soul mating

1974

January 1—January 2 in Sagittarius
January 3—March 23 in Capricorn
March 24—December 29 in Aquarius

1975

January 1—January 7 in Aquarius
January 8—March 18 in Pisces
March 19—May 17 in Aries
May 18—July 26 in Taurus
July 27—December 31 in Gemini

1976

January 1—May 1 in Gemini
May 2—July 20 in Cancer
July 21—October 18 in Leo
October 19—December 31 in Virgo

1977

January 1—September 3 in Virgo
September 4—November 22 in Libra
November 23—December 31 in Scorpio

1978

January 1—October 18 in Scorpio
October 19—December 31 in Sagittarius

1979

January 1—January 6 in Sagittarius

January 7—March 27 in Capricorn

March 28—December 31 in Aquarius

1980

January 1 in Aquarius

January 2—March 11 in Pisces

March 12—May 20 in Aries

May 21—July 29 in Taurus

July 30—December 31 in Gemini

1981

January 1—May 5 in Gemini

May 6—July 24 in Cancer

July 25—October 12 in Leo

October 13—December 31 in Virgo

1982

January 1—August 28 in Virgo

August 29—November 26 in Libra

November 27—December 31 in Scorpio

1983

January 1—October 12 in Scorpio

October 13—December 31 in Sagittarius

1984

January 1—March 20 in Capricorn

March 21—December 31 in Aquarius

Soul mating

1985
January 1—January 4 in Aquarius
January 5—March 15 in Pisces
March 16—May 14 in Aries
May 15—July 23 in Taurus
July 24—December 31 in Gemini

1986
January 1—May 9 in Gemini
May 10—July 28 in Cancer
July 29—October 16 in Leo
October 17—December 31 in Virgo

1987
January 1—September 1 in Virgo
September 2—November 30 in Libra
December 1—December 31 in Scorpio

1988
January 1—October 15 in Scorpio
October 16—December 31 in Sagittarius

1989
January 1—January 3 in Sagittarius
January 4—March 24 in Capricorn
March 25—December 31 in Aquarius

1990

January 1—January 8 in Aquarius

January 9—March 9 in Pisces

March 10—May 18 in Aries

May 19—July 27 in Taurus

July 28—December 31 in Gemini

1991

January 1—May 3 in Gemini

May 4—July 22 in Cancer

July 23—October 10 in Leo

October 11—December 31 in Virgo

1992

January 1—August 25 in Virgo

August 26—November 23 in Libra

November 24—December 31 in Scorpio

1993

January 1—October 9 in Scorpio

October 10—December 31 in Sagittarius

1994

January 1—January 7 in Sagittarius

January 8—March 28 in Capricorn

March 29—December 31 in Aquarius

Soul mating

1995

January 1–January 2 in Aquarius
January 3–March 13 in Pisces
March 14–May 22 in Aries
May 23–July 31 in Taurus
August 1–December 31 in Gemini

1996

January 1–May 6 in Gemini
May 7–July 25 in Cancer
July 26–October 13 in Leo
October 14–December 31 in Virgo

1997

January 1–August 29 in Virgo
August 30–November 27 in Libra
November 28–December 31 in Scorpio

1998

January 1–October 13 in Scorpio
October 14–December 31 in Sagittarius

1999

January 1 in Sagittarius
January 2–March 22 in Capricorn
March 23–December 31 in Aquarius

2000

January 1–January 6 in Aquarius

January 7–March 16 in Pisces

March 17–May 15 in Aries

March 16–July 24 in Taurus

July 25–December 31 in Gemini

your Sun sign notes

your Sun sign notes

your soul mate notes

your soul mate notes

your soul mate notes

your soul mate notes

With love for Ramzilla, the multi-Leo Heart-Throb, and gorge baby Gemini

THUNDER BAY
P · R · E · S · S

Thunder Bay Press
An imprint of the Advantage Publishers Group
5880 Oberlin Drive, San Diego, CA 92121-4794
www.thunderbaybooks.com

All notations of errors or omissions should be addressed to Thunder Bay Press, Editorial Department, at the above address. All other correspondence (author inquiries and permissions) concerning the content of this book should be addressed to Murdoch Books Pty Limited Australia, GPO Box 4115, Sydney NSW 2001, Australia.

Library of Congress Cataloging-in-Publication Data
Mystic Medusa.
    Mystic Medusa's sun signs & soul-mating: what your friends won't tell you, your sun sign will.
    p. cm.
ISBN 1-59223-346-5
1. Astrology. 2. Soul mates. I. Title: Sun signs & soul-mating. II. Title: Sun signs and soul-mating. III. Title.

BF1729.L6M97 2004
133.5--dc22

        2004058013

Printed in China by Sun Fung Offset Binding Company Ltd in 2004
1 2 3 4 5 09 08 07 06 05

Creative Director and Design Concept: Marylouise Brammer
Designer: Tracy Loughlin, Redback Graphix
Illustrations: Tracy Loughlin, Redback Graphix
Editor: Carla Holt
Production Manager: Megan Alsop

DISCLAIMER: The author and the publisher of this work intend the contents of the work to be used for entertainment purposes only and the work must not be used as a professional or counseling resource.